THE EMPERORS AND THE JEWS

ARI LIEBERMAN

Copyright © 2019 by Mosaica Press

ISBN-10: 1-946351-74-1
ISBN-13: 978-1-946351-74-6

All rights reserved. No part of this book may be used or reproduced or transmitted in any form or by any means, electronic or mechanical, including photocopying, recording, or by any information storage and retrieval system, without written permission from the publisher.

Published by Mosaica Press, Inc.
www.mosaicapress.com
info@mosaicapress.com

THE EMPERORS AND THE JEWS

לעילוי נשמת
אבי מורי
ר' יעקב ליברמן
בן הרב אהרן מרדכי הי"ד

שרד את חורבן אירופה

עד נאמן לעבר מפואר

שלאורו חינך דורות

נעים הליכות ומאיר פנים

בעל, אב, סב וחבר מסור ואהוב

נפטר בשב"ק י"ב ניסן תשע"ג

לעילוי נשמת
אמי מורתי
רחל שושנה ליברמן
בת ר' שמחה בונים הלוי ונעמי

אשת חיל יראת ה'

זכתה להקים דור ישרים מבורך

בצניעות, בעדינות ובאמונה

דרכיה דרכי נעם

רעיה, אם וסבתא מסורה ואהובה

נפטרה ה' שבט תשע"ט

תנצב"ה

RABBI BEREL WEIN

The Emperors and the Jews is a most fascinating and informative read. It covers much of the Jewish story of Second Temple times and is a necessary adjunct to understanding the world of the Mishnah and Talmud. It belongs in the home of every Jew interested in our tradition and history.

All blessings,

Berel Wein
www.jewishdestiny.com

יחיאל מיכל טווערסקי

באאמו"ר הרה"צ כמוהר"ר יעקב ישראל זצללה"ה מהארנאסטייפאל

Rabbi Michel Twerski

בעזהשי"ת
כ' טבת תשע"ט

לאחינו בני ישראל בכל מקום שהם הי"ו

I have perused sections of Rabbi Ari Lieberman's highly intriguing treatise, <u>The Emporors and the Jews</u>, exploring the relationships between the Sages of the Talmudic era and the rulers of the Diaspora. I was delighted to find it both extremely informative and captivating. Rabbi Lieberman provides a singular service to B'nai Torah who will appreciate discovering the context for the many Aggados Ha'Shas and Medrashim involving these important protagonists. I am confident that this work will be welcomed by the Olam Ha'Torah with great interest and enthusiasm. I offer my humble blessings to Rabbi Lieberman that he have great naches from this important contribution, and that his massive effort and research to bring this material to fruition will be rewarded with ברכה and הצלחה.

בברכת כל טוב סלה

יחיאל מיכל באאמו"ר הרה"צ כמוהר"ר יעקב ישראל זצללה"ה
מהארנאסטייפאל

Rabbi Zev Leff

Rabbi of Moshav Matityahu
Rosh HaYeshiva—Yeshiva Gedola Matityahu

בס"ד

הרב זאב לף

מרא דאתרא מושב מתתיהו
ראש הישיבה—ישיבה גדולה מתתיהו

D.N. Modiin 71917   Tel: 08-976-1138 טל'   Fax: 08-976-5326 פקס'   ד.נ. מודיעין 71917

Dear Friends,

I have read portions of "The Emperor and the Jews" by Rabbi Ari Lieberrman. The author presents a study of the relatioship between various emperors and their Jewish counterparts, from "Alexander the Great and Shimon HaTzaddik to Marcus Aurelius and Rabbi Yehuda HaNassi".

The book offers historical information culled from Torah and secular sources as well as fine commentary from a true Torah perspective as to the lessons one can derive from this historical information.

I commend the author on a quality presentation and recommend this book to all those who want to understand these historical periods and the interaction of Gedolay Yisroel with secular leaders and to be inspired, by comparison, of the greatness of our Torah leaders.

I pray that Hashem Yisborach bless Rabbi Lieberman and his family with life, health, and the wherewithal to continue to merit the community with further works.

Sincerely,
With Torah blessings

Rabbi Zev Leff

RABBI YITZCHAK BREITOWITZ

Rabbi Ari Lieberman has written a truly fascinating book on a largely unstudied topic—the interaction of our great Torah Sages with the powerful emperors of the ancient world. He skillfully collects and analyzes many passages in the Talmud and Midrash, provides many insights from the commentaries, and most importantly, shows how these long-ago encounters furnish valuable spiritual lessons for the politics of today. As the proverbial lamb among the seventy wolves, Klal Yisrael can certainly benefit from Rabbi Lieberman's wisdom.

With much *berachah*,

Yitzchak Breitowitz
Rav of Kehillas Ohr Somayach

RABBI DR. SHOLOM GOLD

The Emperors and the Jews by Ari Lieberman is a fascinating and vital contribution that helps us understand pivotal periods in Jewish history.

It grips the interest of the reader as it enriches our grasp of those crucial times that are so distant but impact upon us until this very day.

It is a book that should be on everyone's reading list.

Rabbi Dr. Sholom Gold

RABBI MOSHE TURK

The Emperors and the Jews by Ari Lieberman is a deep yet riveting exposition of both Torah literature and world history. Welding together extensive research of both Chazal and secular sources, the author has succeeded in providing an insightful and exciting look at five crucial relationships in the history of Am Yisrael. With great scholarship and through arduous study, the author has succeeded in producing a most unique and remarkable contribution to *Torah She'baal Peh* and the critical need today to be *binu shnos dor v'dor*.

With great admiration,

Rabbi Moshe Turk
Jewish Heritage Center
Queens, New York

TABLE OF CONTENTS

Acknowledgments XV
Introduction 1

SECTION I: ALEXANDER THE GREAT 5
1. Biography 7
2. The Battles 17
3. Alexander and Shimon HaTzaddik 38
4. The Ten Questions 50
5. Africa, Gan Eden. 75
6. The Accusations 82

SECTION II: KING PTOLEMY 93
1. Ptolemy Soter 95
2. Ptolemy Philadelphus 105
3. The Targum Shivim 111
4. The Result 126
5. The Letter of Aristeas 133

SECTION III: VESPASIAN. 137
1. Vespasian. 141
2. Titus. 145
3. Rabban Yochanan ben Zakkai 151
4. Yavneh 154

SECTION IV: HADRIAN 165
1. Trajan 167
2. Hadrian 173
3. Rabbi Yehoshua ben Chananya 178
4. In the Emperor's Home 184

SECTION V: EMPEROR ANTONINUS 199
1. Antoninus Pius 205
2. Marcus Aurelius 208
3. Rabbi Yehudah HaNasi 212
4. The Encounters: Prince and Emperor 224

Summary 249
Conclusion 253
Appendix A 258
Appendix B 280
Endnotes 298
Sources 343
Index 351

ACKNOWLEDGMENTS

Thank you to the Ribbono Shel Olam for giving me the motivation and strength to undertake and complete this book.

It has been a privilege to be associated with Mosaica Press since its inception. Thank you to the entire hard-working, exceptionally professional Mosaica team including Sherie Gross, Rabbi Reuven Butler, Rayzel Broyde, Shanie Cooper, Brocha Mirel Strizower, Binyamin Lieb, and Esti Halberg.

My relationship with Rabbi Yaacov Haber and Rabbi Doron Kornbluth, founders of Mosaica Press, has been the impetus behind *The Emperors and the Jews*: Rabbi Haber, Rav of Kehillas Shivtei Yeshurun, Ramat Beit Shemesh, is a dynamic, inspirational teacher of Torah to thousands and thousands worldwide. Rabbi Doron Kornbluth, a dear friend, neighbor, and mentor, is recognized internationally as an accomplished author, sought-after speaker, and top-rate tour guide. Thank you!

Thank you to Binyomin Prenzlau, an outstanding *talmid chacham*, who professionally reviewed all the Hebrew endnotes.

Thank you to Rabbis Breitowitz, Gold, Leff, Turk, Twerski, and Wein for taking of their valuable time to review the manuscript and offer kind words of *haskamah*.

Thank you to Beis Medrash Ahavas Shalom and Beis Tefillah Yonah Avraham, of Ramat Beit Shemesh, for the use of their valuable *sefarim*.

Heartfelt thanks to my mentors and friends Allen and Barbara Rothenberg, Esqs., founding partners of the Rothenberg Law Firm.

Thank you to my brother-in-law and sister-in-law, Dan and Irene Lawson, and their families.

Thank you to my brother-in-law and sister, Elazar and Esther Darshevitz, and their families.

Thank you to my brother and sister-in-law, David and Debbie Lieberman, and their families.

My very special in-laws, Jacob and Tamar Lawson, have constantly showered our family with their love and support. Thank you!

My mother, Shoshana Lieberman, of blessed memory, was always my biggest fan and supporter. We miss her very much!

My father, Yaakov Lieberman, of blessed memory, taught Torah to and impacted the lives of thousands of children and adults. He was a true *yodei'a sefer*, whose cherished fatherly love, wisdom, warmth, and advice is missed daily.

Thank you to my wonderful children: Tuvia, Chana, and our recent addition, Rachel Shoshana "Shani" Frankel, Shmuel, Binyamin, Tzvi, Baruch, and Yehuda.

To my dear wife and life partner, Lilly (Yocheved Zissel). Shlomo HaMelech sums it all up: "Enjoy life with the wife you love."[1] Thank you for all of the joy! And the Talmud declares: "Blessing is found in a person's home only due to his wife."[2] Thank you for all of the *berachot*!

Ari Lieberman
Ramat Beit Shemesh
Adar II 5779

---

[1] *Kohelet* 9:9.
[2] *Bava Metzia* 59a.

INTRODUCTION

Throughout the ages, historians have extensively chronicled the exploits of such larger-than-life historical figures as Alexander the Great, Ptolemy II, Vespasian, Hadrian, and Marcus Aurelius.

- Modern armies and strategists worldwide still study the epic military triumphs and unparalleled leadership skills of Alexander.[1]
- Ptolemy's Septuagint, the translation of the Bible into Greek, remains an authoritative source of the translated Bible.
- Every year, millions of people visit the Roman Colosseum built by Vespasian, founder of the Flavian dynasty, who besieged Jerusalem prior to the destruction of the Second Temple by his son Titus.
- The notorious emperor Hadrian, architect of Rome's second-century foreign policy of retreat, built monumental architectural projects, including the celebrated seventy-three-mile Hadrian's Wall, that continue to attract widespread interest and study.
- People of influence, politicians, as well as movers and shakers from all walks of life count Marcus Aurelius' Stoic philosophical diary, *Meditations*, as their favorite reading.[2]

---

1 "At West Point we studied his lessons tactically—all the principles of war we studied date back to Alexander." General Wesley K. Clark (ret.), introduction to *Alexander the Great* by Bill Yenne.

2 "*Meditations* has been a Clinton favorite since at least 1994." Carolyn Kellogg, "An American Reader: Bill Clinton," *LA Times*, July 4, 2009.

These five world leaders controlled large populations and dominated extensive territory. As such, they came into contact with the Jewish people and its leaders. Alexander, Ptolemy, Vespasian, Hadrian, and Marcus Aurelius are not only major figures of world history; they are also an integral part of Jewish history and the story of the Jewish people.

There is much to learn from the encounters between these non-Jewish emperors and the Jewish leaders of their times. This work, *The Emperors and the Jews*, does the following:

- Explores the fascinating and celebrated encounters of Alexander the Great, Ptolemy II, Vespasian, Hadrian, and Marcus Aurelius with leading Jewish personalities and representatives
- Studies the dramatic rendezvous between Alexander the Great and Shimon HaTzaddik as well as the ten questions posed by Alexander to the Jewish Elders of the South
- Investigates the reasons why Chazal, the Sages, vehemently opposed Ptolemy's translation of the Bible into Greek and even designated its completion as a tragic day within the fast day of the Tenth of Tevet
- Covers the pivotal meeting between Vespasian, on the cusp of his destroying the Second Temple, and Rabban Yochanan ben Zakkai, looking to secure the continuation and viability of the Jewish people
- Analyzes the back-and-forth discussions between the infamous Hadrian and the eminent debater Rabbi Yehoshua ben Chananya
- Probes the personal, private, and enigmatic relationship between Rabbi Yehudah HaNasi, Judah the Prince, and the Roman Emperor Antoninus
- Examines the ancient sources and background of the Four Kingdoms: Babylon, Persia, Greece, and Rome

The historical journeys of Alexander, Ptolemy, Vespasian, Hadrian, and Antoninus, and their encounters with the Jewish world are riveting and capture the imagination.

Still, questions remain:

- How do these encounters resonate today as the Jewish people continue to interact with a dominating non-Jewish world?
- Are these encounters prototypes of how the Jewish people and its leadership associate and cooperate with non-Jewish leaders?
- Do they help determine who exactly is qualified to be at the forefront of Jewish leadership representing the Jewish people to the outside world?

The answer to these questions begins with a passage in the Gemara *Berachot*.

"Rav Sheshet teaches, '…the temporal earthly kingdom is like the Heavenly Kingdom…'"

The great kingships and empires throughout world history project power, might, royalty, dominion, and control. They can be viewed as a reflection of the Divine all-powerful Kingship, *Malchut*, of God. Earthly kingdoms represent a kind of mini-*malchut*, a truncated likeness, yet a resemblance nonetheless.

That being the case, if the earthly kingdoms are somewhat, somehow, like the Heavenly Kingdom, if they are conduits and reflections of Kingship:

- What does that mean for the Jewish people as a whole?
- What does that mean for us as individuals?
- How do the Jewish people, when encountering the world at large, reveal God's beneficent Kingship, in the world, to the world?

Historians and moralists speak of the Arc of History,[3] a pantheistic trajectory that "history" perforce travels. It presumes that history is the story of mankind's inevitable ongoing progress, a movement towards

---

3   "I do not pretend to understand the moral universe; the arc is a long one, my eye reaches but little ways; I cannot calculate the curve and complete the figure by the experience of sight; I can divine it by conscience. And from what I see I am sure it bends towards justice." Theodore Parker, https://en.wikiquote.org/wiki/Theodore_Parker.

greater human rights, justice, civil liberties, and the certain ultimate triumph of good over evil.

Torah Judaism posits that world history and Jewish history are inexorably linked; both are part and parcel of God's ultimate purpose in the totality of His Creation.[4] The Jewish people stand at the center of God's creation, manifested by the Torah that He has revealed to the Jewish nation, and all that it includes, as the Will of The Almighty.

History, in the Jewish view, has a guiding Hand. It has meaning and purpose, rhyme and reason, mercy and justice; it has beginning, end, and everything in between.

The great kingdoms of world history, the famous emperors of history, and the Jewish people who are meant to serve as God's ambassadors to the world at large are the actors and actresses on the Divine stage of history.

The Emperors and the Jews presents their story. It's the ongoing narrative of how the Jewish people interact with illustrious historical personalities, and how through those encounters, the Jewish nation fulfills its unique redemptive, historic mission.

---

4   At the revelation on Mount Sinai, God introduces himself not as the Creator of the World but rather as the God of History: "I am the Lord, your God, Who took you out of the Land of Egypt, out of the house of bondage" (*Shemot* 20:2).

SECTION I

ALEXANDER THE GREAT

1. BIOGRAPHY

Four years before the Purim miracle (355 BCE), centered in Susa, Persia,[1] and 220 years prior to the Maccabee Chanukah victory (139 BCE)[2] against the mighty Greeks in the Land of Israel, King Philip II (382–336 BCE) began his rule of Macedonia.

Philip II, Alexander the Great's father, placed Macedonia on the global map through political insight, cunning, determination, and strategic vision. As a result of Philip's efforts, "backwards" Macedonia, situated just north of the "advanced" Greek city-states, overtook Greece itself. Philip accomplished all this by first consolidating his power base in Macedonia and then moving on to control the Hellenic Greek city-states. He was able to succeed as a result of his ability to raise and train an army utilizing innovative strategies and techniques.[3]

MONUMENT OF KING PHILIP II

---

1 Susa (or Shushan) was an ancient capital city of Persia. It is referenced numerous times in the Book of Esther and is mentioned in the books of Nechemiah and Daniel. Both Daniel and Nechemiah lived in Susa during the Babylonian captivity, and a tomb traditionally accepted to be that of Daniel, known as *Shush-Daniel*, is located in the area.

2 The issue of reconciling traditional Jewish dates of history with secular records is a complicated subject beyond the scope of this work. For an overview of the topic, see http://www.daat.co.il/daat/kitveyet/shmaatin/horaat-2.htm. See also Rabbi Alexander Hool, *The Challenge of Jewish History* (Mosaica Press, 2014).

3 "It was Philip who first gave shape to the army, transforming what was a mere manhood duty of service, or obligatory militia system, into a standing army, which rose under him to

He appointed professional officers and promoted the best of the best to be his generals and future military leaders.

Philip advanced his interests and ambitions to the point that, as he stood poised to deliver his decisive blow against the Greek city-state Athens, the famous Athenian orator Demosthenes warned:

> *Have you been paying attention to Philip's progress? Have you seen how he has risen from weakness to strength? First he takes Amphipolis, then Pydna, not to mention Potidaea. After that comes Methone and Thessaly. Then he invades Thrace, removing the chieftains and replacing them with his own men.*[4]

It was a prescient warning, but for Athens it was far too little and much too late.

With the most powerful army in the area, Philip became the regional superpower.

But only the regional one.

For Philip, the ultimate goal was the global superpower of the time, Persia.[5] Everything done in the Hellenic Mediterranean was in order to get to the point where he could challenge Persia for world domination.

---

number forty-thousand men. This was the first instance in which a free people subordinated itself to a military autocracy whose head was king. It was this which made Macedonia the superior of Greece." Theodore Ayrault Dodge, *Alexander* (New York: Barnes & Noble Inc., 2005 ed.), pp. 109–110.

4 Philip Freeman, *Alexander the Great* (New York: Simon & Schuster, 2011), p. 21.

5 Persia is the second of the four kingdoms supplanting the superpower Babylon. The new Persian world empire covered vast territory, far-reaching countries, and extensive, diverse populations unlike any empire beforehand. The great Persian Empire created a far-flung global administrative marvel. Satraps—local governors—were given enough leeway and authority to effectively govern but were kept under control via a mechanism of checks and balances. The empire's huge size necessitated an advanced communications and transportation network. An organized system of relay riders and a sophisticated grid of highways—including the 1,677-mile-long Kings Highway—helped advance the empire's rule.

BIRTH

Alexander was born in the Macedonian capital, Pella,[6] on July 20th or 21st, 356 BCE.

By this time, Pella had become a celebrated royal capital visited by emissaries and dignitaries from around the world. Alexander's father was king, and his mother, the exotic Queen Olympias, claimed ancestry from the gods.

This godly ancestry, this divine *yichus*, so to speak, would play a major role in Alexander's life and shape the view of his destiny.

RUINS OF ANCIENT PELLA

Alexander's birth was later to be recorded as a phenomenon with elements that were "otherworldly."

The Jewish historian Tzemach David writes:

> *Alexander the Macedonian was born in the year (3)423, and at his birth an awesome star was seen in the sky, the earth shook, and the foundations of the world quaked. There was lightning, thunder, and severe coldness in Macedonia that people had never experienced before.*[1]

The mythological "son of the gods" birth narrative was widespread to the point that even the Jewish historian Josephus provides a detailed version offering an alternative birth story for Alexander, questioning Philip as the natural father.[7]

---

6   Pella was the ancient capital of the kingdom of Macedon(ia), and the birthplace of both Philip II and Alexander the Great.
7   *Sefer Yuchsin*, for example, references the imaginative Josephus narrative, which includes subterfuge, sorcery, and an account that ascribes fatherhood to a pretender who bamboozled Alexander's mother, Olympias.

YOUTH

The young Alexander was raised with his father's passion for battle and world domination. In his mind, all roads led from Pella, Macedonia, straight to Babylon and Susa, Persia. It might be said that conquest of Persia flowed in Alexander's blood; it was the milk he drank from infancy.

As a child, Alexander exhibited unusual talents, quickness of mind and body, an expansive curiosity, and an innate sense of courage.

ALEXANDER & BUCEPHALUS

> The taming of the wild horse Bucephalus remains a classic Alexander story from his youth. According to the historian Plutarch,[8] Alexander's father, King Philip II, was offered a massive horse named Bucephalus, but was ready to pass on it when he saw how untamed the horse appeared.
>
> The thirteen-year-old Alexander took up the challenge, spoke soothingly to the horse, and turned it towards the sun so that it could no longer see its own shadow, which had been the cause of its distress. Alexander rode triumphantly on the horse, and Bucephalus became the horse he fought on for (nearly) all his future battles.
>
> Plutarch says that the incident so impressed Philip that he exclaimed, "O my son, look thee out a kingdom equal to and worthy of thyself, for Macedonia is too little for thee."[9] Plutarch

---

8   Plutarch (born 46 CE—died after 119 CE) was a biographer and author who wrote approximately 227 works. His most important ones are considered to be the *Bioi paralleloi* (*Parallel Lives*), in which he recounts the noble deeds and characters of Greek and Roman soldiers, legislators, orators, and statesmen, and the *Moralia*, or *Ethica*, a series of more than sixty essays on ethical, religious, physical, political, and literary topics. https://www.britannica.com/biography/Plutarch.

9   http://penelope.uchicago.edu/Thayer/E/Roman/Texts/Plutarch/Lives/Alexander*/3.html—The Life of Alexander 6:1.

> records Bucephalus' end, which speaks volumes about Alexander the person:
> After the battle with Porus [India], too, Bucephalus died—not at once, but some time afterwards—as most writers say, from wounds for which he was under treatment, but according to Onesicritus, from old age, having become quite worn out; for he was thirty years old when he died. His death grieved Alexander mightily, who felt that he had lost nothing less than a comrade and a friend; he also built a city in his memory on the banks of the Hydaspes and called it Bucephalia.[10]

Even as a young child, Alexander would probe visiting Persian diplomats to get a detailed picture of their country. Those snapshots of Persia remained with him and were utilized years later when he embarked on his conquests.[11]

For Alexander, everything was truly going his way. He was uniquely trained in political leadership, statesmanship, and aristocracy.

ARISTOTLE

King Philip, undoubtedly sensing the extraordinary potential of his son, sent Alexander away for a concentrated three-year period of studies.

The campus setting was not just your normal Ivy League type of university, but rather it was Harvard, Cambridge, MIT, Oxford, West Point, and much more—all wrapped in one.

---

10 http://penelope.uchicago.edu/Thayer/E/Roman/Texts/Plutarch/Lives/Alexander*/8.html—The Life of Alexander 5:61.

11 "They had stories to tell him about the famous hanging gardens, which were artificially constructed in the most magnificent manner...They found, however, to their surprise, that Alexander was not interested in hearing about any of these things. He would always turn the conversation from them to inquire about the geographical position of the different Persian countries, the various routes leading into the interior, the organization of the Asiatic armies, their system of military tactics, and, especially, the character and habits of Artaxerxes, the Persian king." Jacob Abbott, *Alexander the Great*, http://www.gutenberg.org/files/30624/30624-h/30624-h.htm.

Alexander was dispatched from his familiar royal capital home of Pella at the tender age of thirteen to study under and learn from the master, Aristotle—one of the greatest thinkers and philosophers of all time.[12] Aristotle taught Alexander and his companion friends[13] for three intense years. While historians don't have records of the exact curriculum covered, Aristotle certainly created a broad, challenging, and eclectic syllabus that would be the absolute envy of any top-rated university.

ARISTOTLE

> *Aristotle was an inspired teacher…Aristotle studied and wrote about everything…He practically invented logic; Aristotle was the first great experimental scientist, with physics, astronomy, biology, embryology, meteorology and much more in his realm of expertise*[14]*…He pioneered the study of ethics…*[15]

Seder Hadorot writes that:

> *Aristotle the philosopher and leading wise man was Alexander's teacher and a student of Socrates and Plato. He was born in Macedonia. He lived twenty years after the death of Alexander his student. He wrote that he spoke with Shimon HaTzaddik*[16] *regarding Godly wisdom, and was very startled from Shimon's high level of wisdom.*[II]

---

12   King Philip and Aristotle grew up together, as Aristotle's father was the court physician for Philip's father, Amyntas. When he was seventeen, Aristotle left Macedonia and spent twenty years studying under Plato at the academy.

13   Present at Mieza with Alexander were Ptolemy, future king of Egypt; Antipater, another companion who became a king after Alexander's death; Marsysa, later a biographer of Alexander; and Hephaestion, Alexander's closest lifetime friend.

14   The curriculum also included medicine. "After the battle at the Granicus, Alexander visited his wounded and examined their injuries himself, offering advice to the camp doctors based on his studies with Aristotle." Freeman, p. 82.

15   Freeman, p. 25.

16   This would be the same Shimon HaTzaddik whom Alexander met while in the Land of Israel. See Chapter 3.

In a sense, Aristotle trained Alexander to be Alexander the Great.[17]

Rav Tzadok emphasizes the historical impact of Aristotle through his student Alexander and its far-reaching (negative) ramifications for the Jewish people:

> *Aristotle was the head of the wise men of Greece during the time of Shimon HaTzaddik, who was from the last of the Men of the Great Assembly, and he was in the time of Alexander the Macedonian, the head of the Greek monarchy, and from him Greek wisdom spread and subsequently, the decrees that darkened the eyes of Israel.*[III]

The *Meam Loez* and *Shalshelet Hakabbalah* cite a fascinating document, a purported letter from Aristotle to his student Alexander. In the letter, considered by historians to be a fake, Aristotle retracts his previous philosophical teachings in favor of the truth of the Torah.

The idea that Aristotle pulled back from his beliefs is touched upon by the sixteenth-century Talmudic commentator and kabbalist Menachem Azanria da Fano:

> *Aristotle was the spark from Avtalyon who taught unworthy students who became Sadducees. And Aristotle was one of them and in the end he repented and was reincarnated in Antoninus,[18] who learned from Rabbi Yehudah Hakadosh.*[IV]

TRAINING

Upon his return from the private university of Aristotle, Alexander picked up the mantle of future leadership. At the robust age of eighteen he gained his first military experience. Under his father's command, he led the Macedonian troops in battle with vigor, courage, sense of duty, and honor. It was a key victory against the vaunted, feared, and elite Sacred Band of Thebes.

---

17   During his conquests, Alexander maintained a steady correspondence with Aristotle. He would also send animal and plant specimens he thought would be of interest to Aristotle.

18   See Section V—Antoninus.

> ...On a hot day in early August of 338 BCE, the Athenians and their allies, including the Sacred Band of Thebes, arrived at Philip's camp in a narrow valley in central Greece...Philip placed his now eighteen-year-old son, Alexander, at the crucial point on the end of the Macedonian line opposite the Sacred Band...[19]

That first highly successful battle of his military career would portend that which would later follow.

At the same time, Alexander diplomatically represented Macedonia and experienced Athens firsthand,[20] absorbing much from its culture and incorporating its ideals into his worldview.

PARTHENON ON THE ACROPOLIS, ATHENS, GREECE

> Philip was gracious in his victory...he sent an embassy, led by Alexander, to the Athenian assembly seeking peace...For Alexander, the embassy to Athens must have been a grand occasion, the only time he would visit the most famous city in Greece. There he saw the Acropolis soaring above the town, topped by the Parthenon...All of Athens stretched before him that glorious summer, the heart of Greek history and culture whose image he would cherish the rest of his life.[21]

Additionally, during his father's absence from Macedonia conducting military campaigns, Alexander was left in Pella serving as the regent in charge of running the country, thereby gaining critical administrative experience. If Alexander had earned a B.A. and M.A. under Aristotle, he now gained his Ph.D. in politics, statesmanship, and court intrigue.

---

19 Freeman, p. 29.
20 Ancient Athens was civilization's center for the arts, learning, and philosophy. It was the home of Plato's Akademia and Aristotle's Lyceum.
21 Freeman, pp. 29–31.

EXILE

Alexander's ambitions were unlimited. However, a family dispute involving an insult to Alexander's lineage (and presumed position as heir apparent) led to exile. Olympias, Alexander's mother, fled the royal court and she was soon joined by Alexander himself and his close companions.

Exile—this time not to study, but to wait, and wait some more.

The *Maharal* teaches that there is a natural order to life. When a person is not at home it is unnatural, and therefore exile is the most abnormal state of condition.[V] This is especially so when one has a mission to fulfill.

Perhaps this short exile gave Alexander time to reflect and ponder; perhaps it even better prepared him for his ultimate unparalleled role and place in history. In any event, it solidified relationships that would play important roles in the future military campaigns and in the running of the empire, as a number of his close companions joined him in exile.

ALEXANDER THE GREAT

KING AT TWENTY

Intense mediation and ultimate reconciliation with his father brought Alexander home, and his mission was now squarely back on track. That path was accelerated when King Philip was assassinated by a heretofore loyal bodyguard. Conspiracy theories have earned their place in the history books. Many involve Philip's estranged wife Olympias, and some point to Alexander himself. But regardless of who was behind the murder, the time was now ripe for the prophecies of the Third Kingdom detailed in the Book of Daniel to begin.[22]

The *Malbim* comments on Daniel's interpretation of Nevuchadnetzar's prophetic dream:

> But another kingdom will arise after you, inferior to yours; then yet a third kingdom, of copper, which will rule over the whole earth.[VI]

---

22   See, for example, Daniel 2:39, 7:6, 8:5–8, 11:3–5.

> And the Third Kingdom afterwards is of copper, which will rule over the entire world. The third part is the belly and thighs which is of copper. And this alludes to the Third Kingdom, Greece, which is a completely different kingdom from the others just as copper is different from the gold and silver. Copper shows us the power and strength of this kingdom. Just as the belly includes the entire body...so too the kingdom of Alexander will fill the entire world.[VII]

History, destiny, and the man now met, and the world would never be the same.

Plutarch writes: "Thus at the age of twenty Alexander inherited the Kingdom of Macedonia, beset as it was by great jealousy, bitter hatred, and dangers on every side."[23] Alexander acted quickly, resolutely, and forcibly to secure his position, eliminating those deemed threats while aligning himself with those who could be co-opted to play a contributory role under his control and according to his terms. Even then, at the earliest stage of his rule, his moves were daring and surprising.

Daring, bold, and surprising illustrate Alexander to a tee. He was the leopard portrayed in the detailed prophesy of Daniel; in the words of the *Maharal*:

> Daniel's vision of the leopard included the wings of a bird, for they were bold in going to conquer the entire world. Because someone who is not daring is weighed down by nature, looks for quiet, and doesn't want action! But the bold, daring ones are like fire that never rests. Therefore, this kingdom was all over the world. Therefore, Alexander, who was the primary one of this kingdom, went to capture the entire world, something that wasn't attempted until then...[VIII]

---

23   Freeman, p. 39.

2. THE BATTLES

Alexander's twelve years of kingship were twelve years of conquest, one battle after another, non-stop, covering thousands and thousands of miles over the most difficult and challenging of terrains.

These military campaigns, which define Alexander's rule, can be divided into six stages:

- A. The Hellenic City-States
- B. Barbarians in the West and North
- C. Asia Minor—Granicus, Issus (present-day Turkey)
- D. Phoenicia and Egypt (including Eretz Yisrael)
- E. Persia—Gaugamela, Babylon, Susa
- F. Hindu Kush (Pakistan, Afghanistan) and India

A. THE HELLENIC CITY-STATES—336 BCE

The ancient kingdom of Macedonia[1] was situated north of Greece, and in that period, Greece was comprised of famous city-states such as Athens, Sparta, and Thebes. After Philip's death, the Greek city-states saw themselves as being free and no longer under Macedonian rule and influence. Athens focused on strengthening its naval fleet, and Thebes

---

1   Macedonia is currently an independent country resulting from the late twentieth-century break-up of Yugoslavia. It includes only part of the ancient Macedonia, with the rest now part of modern-day Greece.

tried to evict Macedonian soldiers stationed on its land. The threats to the new king were real and could easily have marked the end of Macedonian regional leadership and the dream of a global Macedonian-led empire. In light of the situation, even Alexander's advisors pressed the new king to sue for peace instead of starting his regime on the wrong footing, with perhaps a costly, lengthy, and unnecessary war.

Alexander, however, realized that as the untested heir to his strong, battle-proven father, he needed to set a firm example early on. Otherwise, he would end up spending his time and resources constantly having to deal with the Greek city-states, perhaps never getting his chance at the coveted Persian prize. He began with Thessaly, situated just south of Macedon. He chose, as would later become one of his military trademarks, the much more difficult and unexpected path and terrain to traverse and conquer, thereby ultimately gaining the critical element of surprise.

He defeated the Thessalians but wisely persuaded them to go over to his side, which in turn brought other tribes and city-states to the Macedonian corner. He convened a Hellenic assembly to buttress his control of the city-states and those humbled states declared him Captain-General of Greece. Leading city-states Thebes and Athens—initially no-shows at the assembly—quickly came on board when Alexander threatened military action.

Through the combination of the (very) big stick and a bit of carrot, the new king, until now decidedly underestimated by his rivals, ruled the day. "The danger from east and south had been overcome, at least for the moment. Alexander returned before winter to Pella."[2]

B. BARBARIANS IN THE WEST AND NORTH

The southern and eastern borders of Macedonia were now under control. But Alexander realized that it still wasn't time to begin the great campaign. There was yet more that needed to get done in the region, and therefore, the crusade against Persian domination would have to wait.

---

2   Dodge, p. 150.

The barbarian tribes of the west and north, while not coming from established cities with the rewards of great wealth, glory, and honor, were nonetheless more than just a nuisance. As Freeman writes:

> *The Greeks to the south were subdued for the moment, but the tribes to the north of his homeland threatened to destroy his kingdom as well as his dreams of a Persian invasion.*[3]

While his father Philip fought numerous clashes against the tribes of the north, Alexander decided to undertake a full-throttle invasion of the territory north of Macedonia, the Balkans. He wanted to secure all of the borders before moving on to Persia. He also realized that these battles would be great training for the upcoming war in Persia.[4] With creative daring, he defeated the fierce Triballi tribe despite their strategically holding the high ground in battle.

Next, he set his sights on territory on the banks of the Danube, including Getae on the northern bank. Alexander and his men successfully crossed the Danube and surprised the enemy in Getae. The word had now quickly spread, and while there were other battles to be fought, including another Greek attempt to outmaneuver the young king, it was clear to all that Alexander held sway, and that it was in everyone's best interest to join him or suffer the grim military consequences.

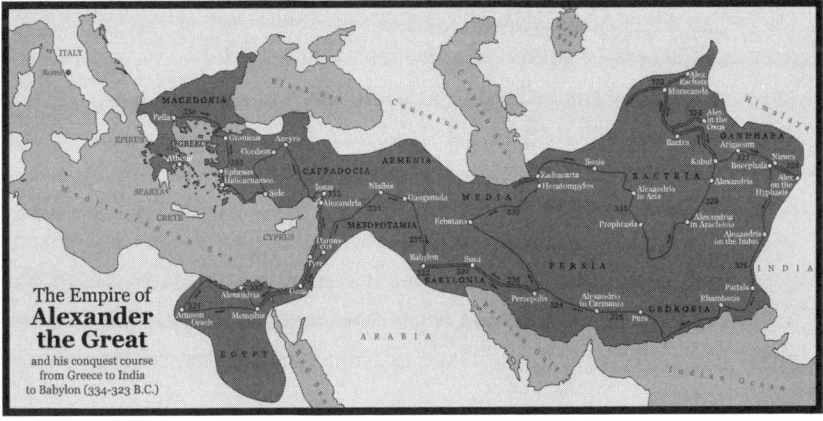

THE EMPIRE OF ALEXANDER THE GREAT

---

3   Freeman, p. 49.
4   Ibid., p. 50.

C. ASIA MINOR—GRANICUS AND ISSUS

In the spring of 334 BCE, Alexander was ready to begin his life's goal: war against the vaunted Persian Empire, a vast kingdom stretching over two thousand miles.

The crossing point separating Europe from Asia was the water of Hellespont, which connects the Aegean Sea in the southwest to the Sea of Marmora and Black Sea in the northeast. Running about sixty-five kilometers long today, the Hellespont is now known as the Dardanelles in the area of modern Turkey.[5]

After sacrificing a bull to the sea-god Poseidon, Alexander guided his ship, leapt ashore, threw a spear into this Asian territory, and shouted that he accepted Asia as his "spear-won" territory.[6]

At first, Alexander's army moved eastwards towards the Granicus River.[7] As he came closer to the Granicus, he was initially unaware that the Persians were camped only twenty miles on the other side of the river, as their governors and generals were debating the next move. General Memnon, originally from the Greek island of Rhodes, was considered to be the most capable of the Persian generals, and he advocated a creative military tactic. Having been previously in exile at the court of King Philip in Pella, he recognized the unique strength of the Macedonian infantry and the disadvantage of a face-to-face battle at the current location. He therefore proposed to destroy the surrounding lands (thus cutting off Alexander's access to food and supplies), while at the same time advocated taking the offensive by pursuing an immediate end run around the enemy forces to directly attack Macedonia. While sound advice, to the Persian King Darius and his other generals, this sensible military strategy was considered to be a cowardly approach—and it was ignored.[8]

---

5   "Europe and Asia were, in those days, as now, marked and distinguished by two vast masses of social and civilized life, widely dissimilar from each other. The Asiatic side was occupied by the Persians, the Medes, and the Assyrians. The European side by the Greeks and Romans. They were separated from each other by the waters of the Hellespont, the Ægean Sea, and the Mediterranean..." Abbott, *Alexander the Great*.
6   Freeman, p. 74.
7   Modern Kocabes River, located in northwest Turkey.
8   Memnon was also a foreigner. "But although Memnon had married a Persian wife, he was a

In a fierce and bloody battle at the Granicus, Alexander earned his first head-to-head victory against the Persians.

The prophecy of the ram and goat in the Book of Daniel is described in detail by the *Malbim*:

> *The two-horned he-goat is Alexander the Macedonian, who was a mighty warrior, and the horn was between his eyes,[9] for the eyes represent understanding and knowledge, for all of his actions were done wisely and with understanding.*
>
> *He came to the capital of the king. Darius didn't move from his place to go out to meet him [Alexander] for Alexander was like nothing in his eyes…And he [Darius] sent his commander and ordered him to bring Alexander in chains…And he [Alexander] defeated the general of the army and went towards Darius himself.[1]*

Alexander's army moved southwards down the Aegean coast and eastwards, gaining more and more territory: "The second year of Alexander's campaign against Persia began with a march through the highlands of central Asia Minor."[10] Both Alexander and King Darius were preparing their forces for the next battle, and this time Darius participated. The armies met at Issus situated at the coastal border between modern-day Turkey and Syria. Highly outnumbered and facing fierce hand-to-hand combat, Alexander's troops valiantly broke through the Persian lines, and a defeated King Darius ignobly retreated into the Persian interior, leaving behind his wife, mother, two daughters, and a son, now prisoners of Alexander.[11]

    Greek advising Persians how to fight Greeks, and there were deep objections to his policy." Freeman, p. 118.

9   The depiction of Alexander with horns is found in a number of cultures.

10   Freeman, p. 108.

11   Alexander treated Darius' family graciously, as he thought befitted royalty. Years later, in fact, he took one of Darius' daughters as a wife. When Alexander died, "Sisygambis, mother of Darius, fasted to death after only five days, mourning the man whose chivalry she had respected ever since her capture at Issus." Robin Lane Fox, *Alexander the Great* (New York: Penguin Books, 1986), p. 474.

D. PHOENICIA AND EGYPT

While the Phoenician cities on the Mediterranean coast welcomed Alexander and his juggernaut army, one city, Tyre,[12] resisted. The new city of Tyre was built on an island, a seemingly impregnable fortress city. Alexander decided to capture Tyre, and the lengthy siege of Tyre revealed Alexander's very make-up: his thinking, ambition, methodology, and his cruelty.

Years earlier, the mighty Babylonian King Nevuchadnetzar, destroyer of the First Temple in Jerusalem, lay siege for thirteen years against Tyre without breaking the city's defenses.[13] But Alexander was not one to be deterred.

According to John Clare, the seven-month siege and capture can be divided into the following steps:[14]

- First, Alexander tried building a causeway, which the Tyrians destroyed.
- Second, he gathered a navy to protect the building of the causeway.
- Third, he blockaded the harbors to try to starve them into surrender.
- Fourth, he set siege engines to batter down the walls.
- Fifth, he tried a direct assault (which failed) on a small breach in the wall.
- Sixth, he widened the breach and tried a multiple assault on the breach and both harbors.

And only then did Tyre fall.

---

12 Tyre is the subject of the Prophet *Yechezkel* (26:3–4, 17): "Therefore, so said the Lord God: Behold I am against you, Tyre, and I will bring upon you many nations, as the sea brings up its waves. And they will destroy the walls of Tyre and demolish her towers, and I shall remove her earth from her and make her a smooth rock…" See the commentary of *Abarbanel*, who makes a connection between the island city of Tyre and Venice. Also see *Yeshayahu*, chap. 23, for prophecies regarding Tyre.
13 https://www.ancient.eu/Tyre/.
14 http://www.johndclare.net/AncientHistory/Alexander_Sources5.html.

Alexander slaughtered the inhabitants, which the historian Arrian[15] justifies by inventing a story that the Tyrians had previously murdered some Greek ambassadors.[16]

After the conclusion of the infamous siege of Tyre and the difficult capture of Gaza,[17] the leading spice market of the times, Alexander the Great marched into Egypt and took over.

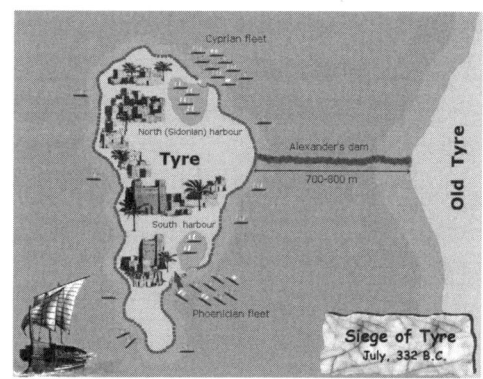

SIEGE OF TYRE

On reaching Memphis,[18] his [Alexander's] first care was to prove to the Egyptians that he was come to re-establish their ancient monarchy. He went in state to the temple of Apis and sacrificed the sacred bull, as their native kings had done at their coronations; and gained the good will of the crowd by games and music which were performed by skillful Greeks for their amusement.[19]

Alexander adroitly demonstrated his art of statesmanship and took advantage of the deep Egyptian resentment towards their Persian

---

15 Arrian, in full Latin, Lucius Flavius Arrianus (86–160), was a Greek historian and philosopher who was one of the most distinguished authors of the second-century Roman Empire. He was the author of a work describing the campaigns of Alexander the Great, titled *Anabasis*...It describes Alexander's military exploits; www.britannica.com/biography/Arrian.
16 https://en.wikisource.org/wiki/The_Anabasis_of_Alexander/Book_II/Chapter_XXIV.
17 Batis, the commander of Gaza, was confident that Alexander could not capture his city, as it stood on a high mound overlooking a plain. Alexander built a parallel mound, stormed the city, totally subdued it, and subjected Batis to a cruel death by dragging him alive around Gaza while tied to a chariot.
18 Memphis had been the seat of power for the pharaohs of over eight dynasties. Ever since the earliest days of the Old Kingdom, the city had also been the most important religious center in Lower Egypt. It was captured by Persian King Cambysis in 525 BCE in the Battle of Pelusium.
19 Samuel Sharpe, *The History of Egypt Under the Ptolemies* (London: Leopold Classic Library, Edward Moxon, 1838), p. 21.

overlords. Contrary to the Persian approach of rejecting Egyptian religion, Alexander co-opted local practice and culture, allowing the honored Egyptian priests to play a prominent role in Egyptian life.

After this visit to Memphis, then the ancient capital of Egypt and home of the priests and most revered temples, Alexander moved on.

ALEXANDRIA

The next steps are described by Dodge:

> *From Memphis he sent his army down the Nile to the coast...He sailed around Lake Mareotis, and foreseeing that a city might become very prosperous at this location...he chose the site of Alexandria and founded this famous mart...The harbor is one of the best, and Alexander's calculations as to the future value of this, his first Alexandria since crossing the Hellespont, were not disappointed.*[20]

Alexandria the city, planned and ordered built from scratch by Alexander, is a key to understanding the role of Greece and Hellenism across its captured empire. It was to be a city unlike any other city ever conceived.[21] That was Alexander's dream.

The *Tzemach David* connects Alexander, Alexandria, and the Jewish people:

> *Alexander the King built Alexandria in Egypt. He was knowledgeable in the seven wisdoms,*[22] *loved wise men, honored them,*

---

20 Dodge, p. 278.
21 Strabo writes, "The building of the city of Alexandria, which was begun before the death of Alexander, was carried out briskly by Ptolemy, though many of the public works were only finished in the reign of his son."
   "Though the rest of Egypt was governed by Egyptian laws and judges, the city of Alexandria was under Macedonian law, in that city no Egyptian could live without feeling himself of a conquered race; he was not admitted, except by especial favor, to the privilege of Macedonian citizenship; while they were granted to every Greek, and soon to Jew, who would settle there." Sharpe, pp. 37–38, 47.
22 *Berachot* 58a states: "Our Rabbis taught: On seeing the Sages of Israel one should say: 'Blessed be He who has imparted of His wisdom to them that fear Him.' On seeing the sages of other nations, one says, 'Blessed be He who has imparted of His wisdom to His creatures.' "On seeing kings of Israel, one says: 'Blessed be He who has imparted of His glory to them

and supported them; merciful on his people, loved justice, and was a friend of Israel.[II]

E. PERSIA—GAUGAMELA, BABYLON, AND SUSA

Alexander was now ready for the next stage in his global conquest, which would take him into the heart of the Persian Empire.

The shortest path from Tyre to Babylon was fewer than five hundred miles, a straight line east from the Mediterranean coast. However, only a madman[23] *would have led his army on this route across the desert wastes of Arabia. Alexander instead followed patriarchs and kings throughout history by taking an arching route along the Fertile Crescent, north beneath the mountains of Lebanon, then east across the highlands of Assyria, and finally south along the Tigris*[24] *and Euphrates to Babylon.*[25]

Upon reaching the great rivers that define Mesopotamia,[26] *Alexander moved on. But by now Darius should have learned that Alexander delighted in doing the unexpected…instead of turning south, Alexander marched his men northeast beneath*

---

that fear Him.' On seeing non-Jewish kings, one says: 'Blessed be He who has imparted of His glory to His creatures.'

"Rabbi Yochanan said: "A man should always exert himself and run to meet a king of Israel; and not only a king of Israel but also a king of any other nation, so that if he is deemed worthy, he will be able to distinguish between the kings of Israel and the kings of other nations.'"

The *Shulchan Aruch* (*Orach Chaim* 224:7–8) codifies the above, and the *Kaf HaChaim* (*Orach Chaim* 224:27) qualifies the blessing said when seeing a non-Jewish scholar: Upon seeing an outstanding non-Jewish scholar who is proficient in the "seven wisdoms," one should recite a special *berachah*. The *Piskei Teshuvah* 224:5 opines that such scholars do not exist today.

23 Alexander was daring, creative, innovative, an out-of-the-box thinker, and a risk-taker, but certainly not a military madman.

24 The four primordial rivers mentioned in *Bereishit*, 2:10–14, Pishon, Gihon, Tigris, and Euphrates, correspond to the Four Kingdoms of history: Babylon, Persia, Greece, and Rome. The Tigris is associated with Greece (*Bereishit Rabbah* 16:4); see Appendix B.

25 Freeman, p. 167.

26 Mesopotamia means the land between two rivers, i.e., the Fertile Crescent.

the mountains of Armenia toward the Tigris and the old Assyrian capital of Nineveh.²⁷

The face-to-face decisive battle occurred on a plain at a place called Guagamela.²⁸ Outnumbered roughly two-to-one, Alexander faked a night attack, came up with a last-hour innovative battle plan, then slept so deeply that he needed to be awoken in the morning by his officers before the military engagement. The fierce combat resulted in victory for Alexander and another disastrously disgraceful escape by Darius.

ALEXANDER THE GREAT VERSUS KING DARIUS

*Even more than a military triumph, Alexander's greatest prize was glory. He had risked everything and won, defeating in open battle the largest Persian army ever assembled.*²⁹

The victory marked a shift in events. Even though Darius still remained alive, Alexander was now clearly the new ruler of Persia. He was in a position to build his groundbreaking empire and realized that he needed to utilize current Persian satraps, governors, as long as they pledged total allegiance

RUINS OF ANCIENT BABYLON

---

27 Freeman, p. 169.
28 Guagamela is located near Mosul in northern Iraq.
29 Freeman, p. 180.

to him. This enabled Alexander to expedite hegemony of the empire and prevent unnecessary fighting, as, for example, he was able to avoid a battle for control of the city of Babylon,[30] where instead of resistance and bloodshed, he was warmly received.

After a march of twenty days from Babylon, the Macedonian army arrived at Susa.

The royal palace spread out there on three steep hills was the setting of the biblical tale of Esther, while just below the citadel lay the tomb of the prophet Daniel. Chief among the features of the Great King's palace was the open audience hall with dozens of pillars more than sixty feet high...[31]

CUNEIFORM INSCRIPTIONS—SUSA CASTLE

PERSEPOLIS

The next major prized city after Susa was the other capital, Persepolis,[32] whose vast

---

30 "But it was the city itself, with its beauty and antiquity, that commanded the attention not only of the king, but of all the Macedonians. And with justification. The Euphrates passes through the city, its flow confined by great embankments..." http://www.livius.org/sources/content/curtius-rufus/alexander-the-great-enters-babylon/.
31 Freeman, p. 193.
32 [17.70] "As for Persepolis, the capital of the Persian kingdom, Alexander described it to the Macedonians as their worst enemy among the cities of Asia, and he gave it over to the soldiers to plunder, with the exception of the royal palace. It was the wealthiest city under the sun and the private houses had been filled for a long time with riches of every kind.[17.71] Alexander went up to the citadel and took possession of the treasures stored there. They were full of gold and silver, with the accumulation of revenue from Cyrus, the first king of the Persians, down to that time. Reckoning gold in terms of silver, 2,500 tons were found there."
http://www.livius.org/sources/content/diodorus/alexander-sacks-persepolis/.

royal treasury surpassed even the riches of Susa. After taking control of Persepolis, Alexander attempted to chase down and capture Darius. He was preempted when Darius was killed by one of his own, an occurrence that reportedly brought Alexander to tears—having preferred an outright capture with Darius recognizing Alexander as the new king.

Though Alexander had by now successfully dethroned the Persian Empire and controlled vast lands, he did not stop.

F. HINDU KUSH AND INDIA

Over 2,300 years before the Soviet invasion of Afghanistan in 1979 and the USA's 2001 Afghan war offensive in the aftermath of the 9/11 attacks, Alexander the Great swept across the Hindu Kush.[33]

HINDU KUSH

The next phase of the campaign took the Greeks to the Caspian Sea, into Afghanistan and over the Hindu Kush into Central Asia. Outlying forces seem to have penetrated as far as Bukhara and Merv; the main army journeyed past Smarkand to the Syr-Darya River and through Mogul Tau Mountains. There, after two years of sapping warfare against local guerrillas, he negotiated a peace and marked the northern limit of his empire...[34]

The subsequent and final major foray was India. The campaign to conquer India began in the spring of 327 BCE. For western nations at that

---

33   The Hindu Kush is an 800-kilometer (500-mile) long mountain range that stretches near the Afghan-Pakistan border, from central Afghanistan to northern Pakistan.
34   Gergel, Tania, ed. *Alexander the Great: Selected Texts from Arrian, Curtius and Plutarch*. New York: Penguin, 2004, p. xi.

time, India had always been considered a fairy-tale land. The stories heard and scattered reports received were certainly enough to excite Alexander in his ambitious drive to reach and subdue all lands until what was thought to be the end of the world.

> The battle-hardened Greek army crossed the Kyber Pass and, after heavy fighting in the north-western frontier and the valley of the Swat, bridged the Indus and occupied the Indian city of Taxila. Moving further into the subcontinent, Alexander defeated the Raja of the Punjab, Porus,[35] in a savage battle close to the modern town of Jalapuur on the river Jhelum. Alexander's march continued eastwards as far as the Beas River in the present-day Indian Punjab in sight of the Himalayan foothills.[36]

KYBER PASS—
VINTAGE ENGRAVING

Rav Samson Raphael Hirsch clarifies the impact of Alexander on the Far East:

> The Macedonian hero carried his victorious arms as far as the Ganges River, bringing to the Asiatic world Greek art and manners, Greek philosophy, wisdom, and education…Ever since the Persian armies retreated before the Greeks, the nations had come to believe that the European spirit would be able to overcome the power of the Orient. They felt it to be the mission of European civilization to subdue and Europeanize the peoples of the Orient. Driven by this

---

35 "Porus, fourth-century BCE, was an Indian prince who ruled the region between the Hydaspes (Jhelum) and Acesines (Chenab) rivers at the time of Alexander the Great's invasion (327–326 BCE) of the Punjab. Unlike his neighbor, Ambhi, the king of Taxila (Takshashila), Porus resisted Alexander. But with his elephants and slow-moving infantry bunched, he was outmatched by Alexander's mobile cavalry and mounted archers in the battle of the Hydaspes. Impressed by his techniques and spirit, Alexander allowed him to retain his kingdom and perhaps even ceded some conquered areas to him." https://www.britannica.com/biography/Porus.

36 Gergel, *Alexander the Great*, pp. xi–xii.

conviction, the hero of Macedonia (Alexander the Great) drew his sword and, by conquering all the nations in his path as far as to the east as the River Indus, turned his ideas into reality that not even his premature death could reverse entirely...[37]

THE END

As prophesied in the Book of Daniel, the life of Alexander was cut short at an early age—though, when measured by experience and success, no longer a "tender" age. In his prime, flushed with victory after victory, Alexander's advances were stopped by his own loyal troops who had enough and simply wanted to return home to finally enjoy the fruits of those victories. On the way back from India, presumably on his eventual anticipated return to Pella, Alexander stopped off at Susa, evaluated the status of his new empire, and enforced critical administrative changes that had been ignored during the years of warfare. Concurrently, he attempted to implement his ambitious policy of uniting the various cultures now under his control, including staging a mass wedding between his Macedonian officers and local Persian women. This demonstrative ceremony was poorly received on the Macedonian side. Alexander's last stop was Babylon, where he fell ill and died far from his native home. He was only thirty-two.

Seder Hadorot calculates the exact Hebrew date and concludes that Alexander was born and died on the same date:

> *Alexander's birth was on Iyar four in the morning and on Iyar four during sunset he died. And he lived thirty-two years and ruled for twelve years for he became king at age twenty.*[III]

The stage was now set for the next episode of Daniel's prophecy, which predicted that the one ruler—Alexander—would be succeeded by four separate kingdoms.[38]

---

37 Rav Samson Raphael Hirsch, *The Collected Writings*, vol. 2. (Phillip Feldheim Inc., 1988, p. 227.
38 *Daniel* 11:4: "And when he arises, his kingdom will be broken, and it will be divided to the four directions of the heavens, but not to his posterity, and not like the dominion that he ruled, for his kingdom will be uprooted and to others besides those."

For at the end,

> ...When he was barely conscious, an officer leaned over him and asked to whom he would leave the empire. "To the best," Alexander reportedly whispered. And that evening he died, ending a reign of twelve years and eight months.[39]

As events evolved, it became clear that quite a few of Alexander's key generals believed that they were "the best" and deserving of the Empire.

Similar to his father's assassination, Alexander's death is shrouded in speculation, rumor, and multiple conspiracy theories.

What caused his death? "Even before the body of Alexander had grown cold, rumors began to circulate that the king had been murdered."[40]

Some of the options include:

- General Antipater, through his sons Cassander and Iolaus, the royal cupbearer, poisoned the wine.
- Aristotle had a hand from afar in killing his student.[41]

And if by natural causes, some options include:

- Malaria
- Dysentery
- A punctured lung suffered in the India battles.
- Twelve years of war under the most severe conditions.[42]
- Typhoid.

And the favorite of many:

- Liver failure as a result of regular very, very, heavy Macedonian-style drinking celebrations, which escalated in the last year of the military campaign.

---

39 Charles Mercer, *Alexander the Great*. New Word City, Inc., 2016, p. 156.
40 Freeman, p. 319.
41 Actually, the death of Alexander triggered anti-Macedonian incidents in Athens, which forced Aristotle to flee the city.
42 "He had cheated death a dozen times since with wounds and illnesses that would have killed most men." Freeman, p. 320.

SUMMARY

In only eleven short years, beginning with the sacking of the Greek city-state of Thebes and followed by his crossing of the Hellespont to invade Asia, Alexander conquered the superpower of his era, the Persian Empire. It was his military conquest coupled to an unusual sensitivity to the cultures and values of his defeated enemies that provided the catalyst and the vehicle for the spread of Hellenism, and with it the values of Greek civilization, through the Near East and Central Asia. By embracing local cultures and blending them with that of classical Greece, Alexander established a multicultural empire whose values and edifices, such as the city of Alexandria, continued to thrive and prosper long after his death.[43]

It seems safe to say that without the Macedonian king and his conquests, the philosophy, art, and literature of ancient Greece that have so influenced our lives for more than two thousand years would instead have been only one of many voices in a chorus of ancient civilization.[44]

Pirkei D'Rebbi Eliezer describes Alexander the Conqueror:

> The eighth king [ten kings are listed] is Alexander the Macedonian who ruled from one end of the world to the other, as it states in Daniel [8:5]: "Behold, a he-goat came from the West over the face of the whole world." It is written over the entire world; in order to know what is at the ends of the world. And more so he wanted to go up to the heavens in order

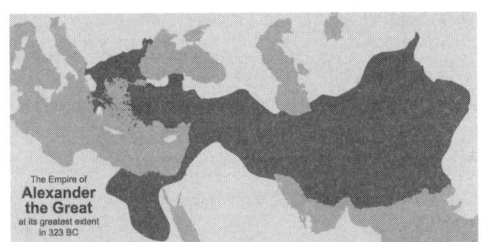

THE EMPIRE OF ALEXANDER THE GREAT 323 BCE

---

43 Dodge, introduction, p.32.
44 Freeman, p. 323.

to know what is up in the skies, and to go down to the depths in order to know what is there. And his kingdom was divided into the four directions of the heavens, as it says [Daniel 11:4]: "And when he shall stand up, his kingdom shall be broken, and shall be divided toward the four winds of heaven."[IV]

HISTORIANS ON ALEXANDER

The historical view of Alexander is diverse. The classical scholar William Tarn developed the thesis that Alexander's strategic vision was *homonoia*—the unity of mankind. According to Tarn, Alexander "tried to create a sense of oneness."

The ancient historian Plutarch wrote:

> ...Believing that he had come as a god-sent governor and mediator of the whole world, he overcame by arms those he could not bring over by persuasion and brought men together from all over the world, mixing together, as it were, in a loving-cup, their lives, customs, marriages and ways of living...[45]

In describing the "friendly" conquest of Egypt, Sharpe declares:

> This is perhaps the earliest instance that history has recorded of a conqueror governing a province according to its own laws, and upholding the religion of the conquered as the established religion of the state; and the length of time that the Greco-Egyptian monarchy lasted, and the splendor with which it shone, prove the wisdom and humanity of the founder...[46]

More recent historians have attempted to refute the visionary position. By the 1970s, writers such as historian A.B. Bosworth were attacking this view. Bosworth seeks to show that Alexander had not really attempted to "fuse" the two peoples; but that what he was doing actually was playing one off against the other.

---

45 http://www.johndclare.net/AncientHistory/Alexander_Themes5.htm.
46 Sharpe, p. 25.

Historians debate Alexander's place in history. Was he a "good guy," an enlightened ruler, a visionary who accomplished positive things, the one who spread Greek culture to an uncultured barbaric world, or was he a cruel, vindictive, superstitious, and paranoid tyrant on par with the evil and destructive modern twentieth-century dictators who murdered millions upon millions of innocent people?

Regardless of which side one takes in typecasting Alexander, it is almost unanimously agreed that Alexander possessed a rare "once in history" combination of the following qualities:

- upbringing
- training
- innovation
- ambition
- childlike curiosity
- innate intellect
- ability to think quicker on his feet than others
- top-notch education in a broad range of subjects
- military acumen
- acute skill of improvising
- physical strength and agility
- tremendous courage
- good looks
- ability to speak to the common soldier
- facility to take advantage of propitious timing
- ability to motivate

all wrapped up in a charismatic personality that shone on and off the battlefield. He was the worthy fulfillment of Daniel's prophecy predicting the outstanding global power of the first king of the Third Kingdom who, in twelve "short" years, shook up the world and history. When Alexander left Macedonia to embark on his incredibly ambitious journey to conquer the entire world, it was the last time he would see his home. From that day on, the entire "civilized" world would become his new home.

Interestingly, the Talmud, Chazal, and traditional Jewish sources consistently refer to Alexander as "Alexander the Macedonian" and not Alexander the Great.

Perhaps we can explain this usage in the following way:

- They wanted to be historically accurate as to Alexander's origin.
- They did not want to give Alexander the title "Great." This is reserved for righteous people.
- They were highlighting the irony that even though Alexander was the king of the Third Kngdom, Greece, he was not from Greece. The writing of Homer, the Greek literary icon, could be found in his back pocket. Greek glory was his life mission. Aristotle, the proponent of Greek philosophy, was his teacher. But Alexander, the one who spread Greek culture worldwide, was not Greek. He was from Macedonia, considered to be that "backwards little country"[47] bordering to the north of Greece.

ALEXANDER THE GREAT'S TIMELINE

All dates are BCE (Before the Common Era)

359	Philip becomes king
356	Birth of Alexander
343	Alexander begins studying with Aristotle
340	Alexander is left as regent in Macedonia while Philip leaves on campaigns
338	Battle of Chaeronea (Philip) Alexander visits Athens Alexander sent into exile
336	Alexander recalled to Pella Murder of Philip and ascension of Alexander Hellenic League at Corinth
335	Campaigns on the Danube: Thrace, Illyria, and Thebes

---

47   Charles Mercer, p. 7.

334	Campaign in Asia Minor Battle of Granicus
333	Knot of Gordium Battle of Issus
332	Siege of Tyre, Gaza captured Alexander invades Egypt Eretz Yisrael
331	Alexander visits Oracle of Ammon at Siwah, Egypt Foundation of Alexandria in Egypt The Conquest of the Persian Empire: Battle of Gaugamela Alexander in Babylon
330	Capital Persepolis captured Darius found murdered near Hacatompylus
329	Campaign in the Hindu Kush and Bactria Alexander sends veterans home
327	Marriage to Roxanne Invasion of India
326	Battle of the Hydaspes against King Porus Death of Bucephalus Mutiny at the River Hyphasis (Beas)
325	The return home The Gedrosian (Makran) Desert
324	Alexander returns to Persia; mass marriages at Susa Death of Hephaestion
323	Alexander returns to Babylon Death of Alexander

The Talmud reports a number of episodes involving Alexander, including:

- Alexander's meeting with Shimon HaTzaddik,
- the ten questions Alexander addressed to the Elders of the South,
- advice Alexander sought regarding the journey to beyond the Mountains of Darkness.

- Alexander versus the women rulers in Africa.
- Alexander's attempt to enter the Garden of Eden/Gan Eden.
- Alexander adjudicating the claims of the Africans, Egyptians, and Yishmaelites against the Jewish people who were represented by Geviha ben Pesisa.

3. ALEXANDER AND SHIMON HATZADDIK

Who was Shimon HaTzaddik?

In order to strengthen the Jewish people as a result of the destruction of the First Temple, Ezra the Scribe gathered the leading Sages of his time and created what became known as the Great Assembly—the *Knesset HaGedolah*.[1]

Serving the Jewish people during the early years of the Second Temple, the Assembly's members included the prophets Haggai, Zechariah, and Malachi, as well as Mordechai, Yehoshua the High Priest, and Nechemiah, who played the leading role in the rebuilding of the Second Temple. The *Rambam*, Maimonides, in his introduction to the *Mishneh Torah*, clearly spells out that Shimon HaTzaddik was from the last of the Great Assembly members and was one of its one hundred twenty members.[I]

The Mishnah in *Pirkei Avot* 1:1–2 teaches:

> *Moshe received the Torah from Sinai and conveyed to Yehoshua, Yehoshua to the Elders, the Elders to the Prophets, and the Prophets to the Men of the Great Assembly...Shimon HaTzaddik was one of the remnants of the Great Assembly. He used to say, "The world stands on three things: on the Torah; on the service of God, and upon acts of loving-kindness."*[II]

---

1   "The establishment and success of the Great Assembly was a result of it receiving the authority directly from the Persian King." Rav Avigdor Miller, *Torah Nation*, p. 52.

Rarely throughout the long history of the Jewish people has the title *tzaddik*—righteous one—been attached to any individual, and use of such an honorific title speaks volumes.[III] Shimon HaTzaddik served as a pivotal generational link during the early years of the Second Temple and subsequently earned the title of *tzaddik*.[2]

Ben Sira[3] portrays Shimon as a virtual angel, the lofty leader of Israel who preserved the sanctity of the Holy Temple and propelled the Jewish nation forward.[IV]

Historically, Shimon HaTzaddik led the Jewish people during what has been described by *Dorot Harishonim* as the "middle period." This is the period between The Great Assembly and the advent of the Tanna'im, which began with Hillel and Shammai and their schools. The Great Assembly sealed and canonized the Books of the Bible, established the principles of the Mishnah, set down the guidelines and principles for interpretation of the Torah, and standardized the prayers. All this occurred during the beginning of the Second Temple, with a main part of Jewry in the Diaspora, and at the advent of the Greek period, that is, the Third Kingdom.[V]

Rav Avigdor Miller links the Great Assembly to the continuation of the Greek (and subsequent Roman) empire:

> ...Now after the Great Assembly had completed its work and the members of that body had passed away, the miraculously benevolent and tranquil era of Persian rule was ended. Henceforth the Jews in the Land of Israel would be under very

---

2   *Dorot Harishonim* contends that modern historians who attempted to capture Shimon HaTzaddik's life totally misread the situation. This was a result of their not understanding the exemplary nature of the Jewish people, which impacted both on their misguided overall take on Jewish history, as well as their mistakes in the details. He discusses, for example, the reason why Shimon became known as "the Tzaddik," and offers a compelling historical analysis.

3   "Sirach, *The Book of Ecclesiasticus*. Deserving a category of its own [among the books of the Apocrypha] is the book of Sirach (Ben Sira), which the Talmud itself quotes a number of times. Also called the 'Wisdom of Sirach,' it would seem that of all the books of the Apocrypha, this work was the closest to being included in the Canon. It appears that the Sages considered at least some of the teachings to have value—if understood properly." https://www.chabad.org/library/article_cdo/aid/3671027/jewish/What-Is-the-Jewish-Approach-to-the-Apocrypha.htm.

different regimes: the Ptolemies of Egypt, the Syrian Greeks, and the Romans.[4]

Shimon HaTzaddik not only served as the High Priest, the *Kohen Gadol*, but was also the leading sage in Israel as the head of the Sanhedrin.

The Talmud in *Yoma* 39a describes Shimon's historic legacy as it relates to the observances in the Temple.[VI] Each example demonstrates his unique spiritual influence on extraordinary occurrences that ended when his tenure was over.

For example:

- Our Sages taught: Throughout the forty years that Shimon the Righteous served as *Kohen Gadol*, the lot ["For Hashem"] written on Yom Kippur would always come up in the right hand; from that time on, it would sometimes come up in the right hand and sometimes in the left.
- And [during the same time, also on Yom Kippur] the crimson-colored strap would become white. From that time on it would at times become white, at others not.
- Also: Throughout those forty years, the westernmost light of the Menorah continuously burned; from that time on, it sometimes burned and sometimes became extinguished.

ALEXANDER IN ERETZ YISRAEL

After consolidating control of the Hellenic city-states and the bordering barbarians, Alexander swiftly crossed into Asia, captured "Greek" cities under Persian rule, swept down the Phoenician Mediterranean coast, and took over Egypt.

According to Josephus, Alexander requested assistance from the Jewish community via the High Priest in his efforts to successfully manage the siege of Tyre.

---

4   Miller, *Torah Nation*, pp. 90–91.

> *Alexander the Great had required of the High Priest of the Jews, when he was at the Siege of Tyre, Auxiliaries, and Provisions, the same tribute which he had aforetime paid to the Persians. The High Priest returned answer that having taken an oath to Darius not to bear arms against him, he never would do it while Darius lived. Upon which Alexander was very angry and threatened that after he had taken Tyre, he would lead his army against the High Priest; and by his punishment, teach all men to whom they were to keep their oaths.*[5]

The Jewish people in Eretz Yisrael were loyal contributing residents of the Persian Empire.[6]

After the Purim miracle, Mordechai served as the king's right-hand man, and it was the Persian king who gave permission for the Jewish nation to rebuild the Holy Temple in Jerusalem.

In the words of the Abarbanel:

> *And the face of a person (in the prophecy of Yechezkel 1:10) hints to the kings of Persia/Media, as they did not do evil to Israel in their rule. Compared to the other nations who were like cruel animals of prey, Persia/Media were compassionate, like people. We see that they returned Israel to its land, provided them with great help, and permitted Israel to build God's House. They returned the holy vessels that Nevuchadnetzar took, and likewise, Josephus wrote that the servitude of Israel for Persia/Media was a sweet one.*[VII]

At some point in this leg of his long journey, Alexander came face-to-face with the Jewish people. What he knew of them is not known.

What we do know about Alexander is that he always acted quickly and with resolve. He assessed a situation, determined how his interest

---

5 http://penelope.uchicago.edu/josephus/whiston_alexander_Jerusalem.xhtml.
6 "And when the Babylonian Empire was replaced by the mild regime of Persia, which took pride in uniting so many different peoples and tongues beneath its scepter, and which most graciously invited the exiles of Judea to bask in the sunshine of its imperial court, the sons of Judea were unable to resist these blandishments…" Hirsch, *Collected Writings*, vol. 2, p. 428.

would be best served, made his decision, and immediately proceeded to implement that choice. He adjudicated between factions in local populations, leaving civil control in indigenous hands while ensuring that military control would be firmly held by his loyal Macedonian officers. As in other situations, he sought the cooperation and assistance of the local population, assuming, usually correctly, that, as the victor, he would sway the native residents to his side.

According to the Talmud in *Yoma* 69a, Alexander first met the Cutheans, sworn enemies of the Jewish people.[7] This meeting posed a threat to the welfare of the Jewish nation and to the very existence of the Second Temple, then in its early years.

The situation appeared dire. If the Cutheans had Alexander's receptive ear and could demonstrate to him that the Jewish people and its leaders still remained loyal to the Persian king, while they, the Cutheans, were on Alexander's side, the results would be catastrophic.

The Talmud relates:[VIII]

> *The twenty-fifth of [Tevet] is the day known as the Day of Mount Grizim,[8] on which one is not permitted to eulogize. It is the day on which the Cutheans requested of Alexander the Macedonian permission regarding the House of our God, to destroy it, and he granted it to them.*

---

[7] "When the Assyrians exiled the Ten Tribes hundreds of years earlier, the conquerors brought in a foreign people from Crete called Cutheans to populate the vacated territory. These people were idol-worshippers, and God sent lions to decimate them. Out of fear of the lions, the Cutheans converted to Judaism, but the rabbis of the Talmud debated whether their conversion was valid or not. The Cutheans' Torah observance was spotty—extremely strong in some areas, but very weak or nonexistent in others. Settling in the Samaria region of Eretz Yisrael, over time the Cutheans became known as Samaritans. Fearing that the Jews returning from Babylonian exile would reclaim their ancestral lands, the Cutheans became bitter enemies of the Jewish people, even going so far as to attempting to sabotage the construction of the Second Temple." https://www.chabad.org/library/article_cdo/aid/2836152/jewish/The-Samaritans-Cutheans.htm.

[8] "A mountain south of the valley in which Shechem was situated. After their separation from the Jews, the Samaritans built a temple on it, which was destroyed by John Hyrcanus. But the mountain continued to be, as it is today, the holy place of the Samaritans." http://www.jewishencyclopedia.com/articles/6601-gerizim-mount.

Messengers came and informed Shimon HaTzaddik.

What did he do?

He donned priestly vestments and wrapped his head in priestly vestments, and set out to meet Alexander accompanied by some of the most prominent people in Israel. And there were lit torches in their hands. All night long this group [Shimon HaTzaddik and his entourage] were approaching from this side and that group [Alexander and his army] were approaching from that side until the light of dawn rose.

Once the light of dawn rose, he [Alexander] asked the Cutheans, "Who are those people?"

They answered, "It is the Jews who have rebelled against you."

As he reached Antipatres,[9] the sun shone forth and they met up with one another.

As soon as Alexander saw Shimon HaTzaddik, he alighted from his chariot and bowed down before him.[10] The members of his entourage said to Alexander, "Shall a great king like yourself bow down before this Jew?"

He replied to them, "An image in the likeness of this man gains victory before me on all my battlefields."

He then turned to the Jews and said to them, "Why have you come?"

They replied, "Is it possible that you would destroy the very House in which we pray for you and for your empire because the idolaters mislead you to destroy it?"

---

9   "Built on the ruins of the Biblical city Aphek, site of a great battle between Israel and the Philistines recorded in the Book of Samuel, Antiparis is mentioned in the Talmudic description of the proliferation of Torah study during the reign of King Chizkiyahu." https://ohr.edu/2895.

10 Ironically, Alexander would attempt to implement a national policy of *proskyesis*, the Greek term for the Persian custom of showing homage before a king. "To Greeks and Macedonians, such degrading behavior before any king was inconceivable. Free Greeks did not bow down before kings…" Freeman, pp. 262–65.

> He said to them, "Who are these people?!"
>
> They said to him, "It is the very Cutheans who stand before you."
>
> He said to the Jews, "Behold they are given into your hand…"

This episode is also related by secular historians. The Greek scholar and early Christian theologian Origen [b. 184–d. 253]:

> The Jewish nation was so preserved by the divine Power, that they did not undergo any Affliction, even under Alexander, the Macedonian, nor by him; altho' they would not take up Arms against Darius, on Account of certain Leagues and Oaths, [by which they were bound to him.] Then it was, they say, that the High Priest of the Jews, as he was clothed with his priestly [sacerdotal] Garment, was ador'd by Alexander: Who said, that a Person was seen by him in that very Habit, who promised, in a Dream, to subdue Asia to him.[11]

Similarly Eusebius of Caesarea (260/265–339/340), a historian of Christianity, writes in the *Chronicon* (as recorded by his translator Jerom):

> Alexander, when he had taken Tyre, invaded Judea; where when he was favourably received, he offered Sacrifices to God, and paid great Honours to the High Priest of the Temple: Leaving Andromachus as Governor of those Parts, who was afterward slain by the Samaritans. Upon which Alexander, when he returned out of Egypt, inflicted great Punishments upon them and their City [Samaria], and gave it to Macedonians to inhabit.[12]

Josephus contends that Yedua the High Priest met with Alexander, but *Dorot Harishonim* explains that Josephus erred when he wrote that the High Priest at the time, Yedua, was the one who confronted Alexander. Rather it is clear, argues the *Dorot Harishonim*,[IX] based on the Talmud and other authentic sources, that Yedua sent his grandson,

---

11   http://penelope.uchicago.edu/josephus/whiston_alexander_Jerusalem.xhtml.
12   Ibid.

the future High Priest Shimon, to meet Alexander. Shimon (not yet known as HaTzaddik) came as the representative of the office of the High Priest. He was sent with the support of the Kohanim and, most importantly, with the backing of the people. His reputation had already been cemented as the leading sage and as an impressive lofty individual whose very countenance spoke of deep wisdom and righteousness.

Following *Dorot Harishonim*, Rav Avigdor Miller concurs with the contention that Shimon HaTzaddik at this time was not yet the High Priest but was rather the grandson of the *Kohen Gadol* Yedua. When Alexander sent a message requesting help from the local Jewish community in Israel, the *Kohen Gadol*, as the official representative of the Jewish people, responded: "He had given his oath to Darius (the Persian) not to bear arms against him, and he would not transgress this oath while Darius was still alive."[13]

As Alexander headed to the area, Yedua realized he needed to act quickly. So he sent his grandson, Shimon, to represent his office and the community.

Rav Miller writes:

> *When Alexander alighted from his steed and bowed low to Shimon, it was too great an honor for Josephus to ascribe to this great leader of the Pharisees (the Torah Sages) to whom Josephus was hostile; he therefore credited this honor to Yedua the Kohen Gadol. The unanimous traditions of the nation declare this a falsehood although agreeing with Josephus in all other details.*[14]

Toldot Tanna'im v'Amora'im attempts to reconcile the versions of the Talmud and Josephus. As the Talmud states, it was Shimon HaTzaddik who came out to meet Alexander, and at that time indeed, his grandfather Yedua was the High Priest. But, at the same time, Shimon could be called a high priest since he then held the title of the "serving High Priest," a position that did not entail supervision of the Temple rituals.[x]

---

13   Josephus, *Antiquities* XI:8:3.
14   Miller, *Torah Nation*, p. 89.

Rav Miller further sources Josephus and determines:

> *The Book of Daniel was brought and shown to Alexander wherein Daniel foretold that the Greeks would destroy the Persian Empire. Now that Darius had fallen, the Jews were free of their oath. Alexander granted the people the right to keep the Torah and extended this to the Jews in Babylon and Media.*[15]

Toldot Tanna'im v'Amora'im (also sourcing Josephus) writes that Alexander came to Jerusalem and was met by Yedua, the High Priest.

Additionally, according to Rav Miller, "Alexander invited the Jews to join him and his army, and there were those who indeed joined."[16]

If the reading of Daniel's prophecy was read in front of Alexander and the interpretation that the king of the mighty Third Kingdom was Alexander himself, such an event would certainly resonate well with Alexander. He constantly consulted with the oracles and always sought signs to confirm his godly lineage and historic destiny.[17] The prophecy in Daniel would be another religious stamp of approval and would affirm in Alexander's mind the fateful role ordained for him from Above.

Ben Yehoyada describes the majestic side of this encounter:

> *He clothed himself in the priestly garments. The priestly garments which the High Priest wore in the Holy Temple had a shine of light that any person who saw them would feel the illumination which was present only in the Holy Temple.*
>
> *But now Shimon the Righteous saw that it was necessary that this light shine on the clothes outside of the Temple. Therefore, through his intentions, the light continued to shine even when he went out of the Temple. And that's why the Talmud says he*

---

15 Ibid.
16 Ibid., p. 90. "Long before Zionism, Jews throughout the world spoke of their fighting brethren as the 'new Maccabees,' cultivating every story of Jewish heroism in foreign service from Alexander the Great (!) until their own day." Avi Wolf, Feb 25, 2014 review of Derek Penslar, *Jews and the Military: A History*, Princeton University.
17 "After the initial battles with the Greek city-states, Alexander visited the oracle at Delphi to hear the local priestess declare: 'You are invincible.'" Freeman, p. 49.

wore the main priestly garments and wrapped himself in the priestly clothes with the luster that illuminated on the clothes.

And that which they carried torches of fire, it seems to me that this was a reminder of the merit of the Torah they possessed. The light of Torah would protect them.

And the torches were held with the intention to hint at the holy Name of God of Adir Ron, sourced from the verse, "Your right is adorned with power" (Shemot 15:6).

And this word has the letters of אור (aleph, vav, resh), light, and יד (yud, dalet) for hand, and נר for candle. Therefore, they held torches of fire in their hand—fire, hand, and light—alluding to the Name of Adir Ron for their protection.

And that which they walked all night, their intention was to travel during the second half of the night, which is a propitious time. And the sun rose and the meeting of the two sides which took place then was Divine providence and a good sign, for at sunrise there would be a miraculous deliverance.[XI]

SENDER

As a result of this dynamic encounter between Alexander and Shimon HaTzaddik, the name Alexander joined the list of common Jewish names.[18]

The *Sefer Yuchsin*, in line with the account rendered by Josephus, writes: "And he [Alexander] requested that any sons born that year be called Alexander after him. And that they should count from that year."[XII] *Tiv Gittin*, the acclaimed legal/halachic work on divorce law and the names used in the Jewish divorce document, the *get*, opines:

---

18 "Variations of the name include Aleksender, Aliksender, Sender, Sander, Sando and Sendush, very often coupled with Ziskind. First used in Jewish circles in gratitude to Alexander the Great for his kindness to the Jewish nation during his battles to conquer the world. This form was so close to the non-Jewish family name that many Jews whose father's and grandfather's name was Sander, simply adopted the surnames Sanders or Saunders after migrating to English-speaking countries. Alexander also became a family name." https://www.chabad.org/library/article_cdo/aid/3825225/jewish/Popular-Jewish-Hebrew-Boy-Names.htm.

> Many children were called Alexander and it has become commonplace to name after Alexander the Macedonian, as we found in Josephus that the Kohen Gadol promised Alexander to make for him a remembrance in the Sanctuary in that every Kohen who was born that year would be named Alexander, and he was pleased by this.[XIII]

Rav Moshe Feinstein, addressing a question regarding the name Alexander, substantiates the words of the *Tiv Gittin*:

> And that which is written that the name Alexander was through pressure that they needed to compensate Alexander because they wouldn't let him put his picture in the Sanctuary; this is a false claim contrary to our Talmud. Shimon the Tzaddik was very important in Alexander's eyes, as we learned in Yoma 69a for when he [Alexander] saw, he went down from his chariot and bowed down saying that he saw a likeness of Shimon leading the battle in front of him in war. This was rather an honor for Alexander, done out of gratitude. And that which I saw in Tiv Gittin, who brings Josephus that the Kohen Gadol promised Alexander that all Kohanim born that year would be named after him. And this reason is also correct, since the issue [of naming Jewish babies with a Greek name] isn't something that is prohibited but merely a question of a measure of inappropriateness, it is something that may be done to demonstrate gratitude. Indeed, they did so happily, and the name Alexander entered the lexicon of Jewish names…[XIV]

While the encounter between Alexander and Shimon HaTzaddik included a miraculous Divine intervention, it still offers a number of insights into the interaction between the Jewish people and non-Jewish leaders:

- Facing an imminent threat, the office of the High Priest and Shimon HaTzaddik assessed the full import of the situation and responded swiftly and emphatically.

- The main spokesperson of the Jewish people was an acknowledged Torah scholar, community leader, and representative of the office of the High Priest.
- Shimon HaTzaddik clearly understood the nature of the other side and determined that in this case a dramatic, public, theatrical presentation was necessary.
- Based on the *Ben Yehoyada*, Shimon and his assembly prepared and came with the merit of the Torah, which they understood was the ultimate protector of the people.
- The attribute of *hakarat hatov*—gratitude—a hallmark of the Jewish people throughout history, includes far-reaching gratitude towards non-Jewish leaders.
- The request of the Jewish leadership to Alexander was for one thing only: the right to keep the Torah and mitzvot and to preserve the Holy Temple.
- According to the account that Alexander was shown the prophesy of his kingship in Daniel, Jewish leaders should never hesitate to proudly present authentic Torah sources to non-Jewish leaders who in turn might very well respond positively.
- Throughout history the Jewish people have prayed for the welfare of non-Jewish kings, rulers, and governments. The nation demonstrated time and time again that its people were consistently loyal citizens wherever they resided.
- The Jewish nation and its leaders recognize the profound spiritual concept that earthly kingdoms below resemble the Divine Kingdom above. This recognition directed the overall approach taken vis-à-vis emperors and kings. As such, they related to Alexander with respect, honor, and awe. Since the four kingdoms were part of God's blueprint of history and since Alexander's kingship (prophesied in detail) was a reflection of Divine Kingship, they realized that interacting with emperors was an opportunity to "touch" kingship. It was an opportunity as messengers of God to the world to reveal Divine Kingship by revealing earthly kingship.

4. THE TEN QUESTIONS

Alexander interacted with many nations and their leaders, usually from his advantaged position of conqueror to the conquered. Being in absolute military control, he could exhibit a full range of emotions, responses, and behaviors. Alexander might be magnanimous, inquisitive, humiliating, indifferent, destructive, kind, or revengeful.

The Talmud in *Tamid* 31b records ten questions that Alexander posed to the Elders of the South.[1] These questions can be viewed on different levels, from the literal to the metaphorical; from the scientific/astronomical to the philosophical and theological.

Rav Eliyahu HaItamari provides the backdrop for this encounter and the questions asked:

> And since Alexander the Macedonian was the wisest of the wise and a philosopher who explored the hidden matters in order to know the truth of matters, he wanted to explore the knowledge of God in order to reach the truth…His heart was filled with the desire to see every place and go up to the heavens and go down to the depths in order to see if there was any other

---

1   "Plutarch records the following from Alexander's journey in India: He captured ten of the Gymnosophists who had done most to get Sabbas to revolt, and had made the most trouble for the Macedonians. These philosophers were reputed to be clever and concise in answering questions, and Alexander therefore put difficult questions to them…" http://penelope.uchicago.edu/Thayer/E/Roman/Texts/Plutarch/Lives/Alexander*/9.html.

god, God forbid. And he wanted to reach the truth for this is the purpose of why man was created.[I]

THE ELDERS OF THE SOUTH

We know who Alexander was, but who were the Elders of the South?

The expression "Elders of the South" is unique in Talmudic sources and appears only here in this discussion in Tractate *Tamid*. However, we often find in Jewish sources that the idea of "the South" is one that corresponds to wisdom.

Already by Avraham Avinu, "the south" is highlighted and interpreted spiritually. Commenting on the Torah's description of Avraham's travels, "Avraham traveled back and forth in the south" (*Bereishit* 12:9), Rabbeinu Bachya states: "These travels were undertaken to reach the high prophetic level of '*Kel Shakai*,' the Holy Name of God. The numerical value/gematria of *hanegba*, "the south," equals the gematria of God's name, א, ד, נ, י (65)."[II]

The Talmud in *Bava Batra* 25b further discusses "the south":

> Rav Yitzchak says: One who wants to become wise should go south and one who wants to become wealthy should go north; and the sign for this is the Table [in the Sanctuary] in the north and the Menorah in the south. Rav Yehoshua ben Levi said: Always go south, for when you become wise you will become wealthy, as it says, "Length of days is in her right hand; in her left hand are riches and honor"(Mishlei 3:16).[III]

A more direct reference is found in *Eruvin* 53b:

> They said to Rabbi Elai: Show us where Rabbi Abbahu is hiding, as we do not know where he is. He said to them: He has taken counsel with the one who crowns, i.e., the Nasi, who appoints the Sages, and has gone south [hingiv] to Mephibosheth, i.e., he has headed to the Sages of the south, referred to here as Mephibosheth, who was King Saul's grandson and a great sage of his time.[IV]

And, *Rashi*, in his commentary in *Eruvin*, makes direct mention of the Elders of the South: "'Elders of the South' who were very wise, as Mephibosheth was a great man, and therefore they were called that name—South."

An additional reference to Rabbis of the South (though not Elders) is found in *Yevamot* 62b:

> *And the world was desolate of Torah until Rabbi Akiva came to our Rabbis in the South and taught his Torah to them. This second group of disciples consisted of Rabbi Meir, Rabbi Yehudah, Rabbi Yosi, Rabbi Shimon, and Rabbi Elazar ben Shamua. And these are the very ones who upheld the study of Torah at that time. Although Rabbi Akiva's earlier students did not survive, his later disciples were able to transmit the Torah to future generations.*[V]

It appears that the Elders of the South responded to Alexander knowing full well who he was and what he had already accomplished. It could very well be that the elders were also aware that Alexander was the subject of the prophecies in Daniel, the conqueror-king of the Third Kingdom. At this point, we can assume that Alexander had captured Persian territory in Turkey, Lebanon, Syria, Eretz Yisrael (and perhaps Egypt), but did not yet have his overwhelming victory against Darius and the Persian army in the heartland of Babylon and Persia.

The interaction between the two sides was subtle—the two protagonists sparring with each other and trying to get their respective world views across. The Elders, as seen in other classical Jewish–Gentile interactions in history, were circumspect and careful to some degree, and yet bold and courageous in other ways.

It is clear from the conclusion of the exchange—though not mentioned explicitly at the start—that Alexander had assured the Elders that they could speak freely without any repercussions.

And so they did; they clearly faced the difficult challenge of going head-to-head with Alexander. This was Alexander the trained philosopher and accomplished student of natural knowledge. And this was Alexander the military leader, now in the midst of a grand roll in his conquests, garnering more and more power. It certainly was not a game for the mild or meek.

Alexander of Macedon inquired of the Elders of the South regarding ten matters:

1. Heaven to earth/east to west
2. What's first?
3. Light or darkness
4. Who is wise?
5. Who is a mighty man?
6. Who is a rich man?
7. Living life
8. Dead man
9. How to make friends
10. By land or by sea?

QUESTION 1—HEAVEN TO EARTH/EAST TO WEST

Q. He said to them: "Is the distance greater from heaven to earth, or from east to west?"

A. They told him that from east to west is greater, for when the sun is in the west, near sunset, everyone can look at it as well, but when the sun is in the middle of the sky, no one can look at it.

The Talmud comments:

> But the Sages say this distance and that distance are exactly the same, for it says (Tehillim 103:11–12): "For as high as Heaven is above the earth…as far as east from west." Now, if one of those were more than the other, then both overwhelming kindness and our distanced transgressions should be written as comparable to the one that is more…[VI]

Rashi explains:

> Which is the greater distance?
> "From east to west is farther than from earth to the heavens. For when the sun is in the east everyone can look at it; when

> the sun is in the sky you cannot look at it." And why? Because when the sun is in the east or west, it is far, and since it is far you can look at it, for the brightness of the sun does not damage the eyes; but when it is in the middle of the sky, it is closer and the sunlight is so bright one cannot look at it.
>
> "And the Sages say that the distances are equal—this is proven by the verse; one verse says, "As the height of heaven above the earth..." For as the height of the heavens over the earth, so great is His kindness toward those who fear Him; "And the other verse reads as the distance of east to west"—As the distance of east from west, He distanced our transgressions from us.
>
> And if their distances wouldn't be equal, but rather east to west is greater, why did the verse mention the lesser one in distance? It should have said the greater one, so certainly the two distances are the same; therefore, it mentioned both.
>
> What is the reason that all cannot look at the sun when it is in the middle of the sky, as they can look when it is in the east or west?
>
> Because it is open and not covered; therefore its light is brighter and it damages those who look at it.[VII]

What is behind this first question of Alexander? Why did the Elders of the South answer Alexander differently than the opinion of the Sages?

On the one hand, the question can be viewed simply as a scientific one, befitting Alexander who studied science and astronomy with Aristotle. Perhaps it was a first stab on his part to gauge the level of wisdom of the Elders of the South.

The *Chatam Sofer* established that on the simple level, the question revolves around the issue of whether the world is round or egg-shaped, which the *Chatam Sofer* says is an argument among the wise men.[VIII] The *Chatam Sofer* understands that "east to west" does not refer to the distance from the eastern horizon to the western horizon (that would be double the distance than from earth to the sky). Rather, it refers to the distance from where a person stands to the eastern horizon when the sun rises, or the distance from where a person stands to the western horizon as the sun sets.

On the other hand, the question and answer touch upon the difference between earthly matters and those of a higher dimension. It centers on divergent worldviews. The west-to-east continuum represents the movement and accomplishments of people and armies in this world. The earth-to-heaven dimension represents that which is above man, the dreams, the visions, and the understanding of that which is beyond the actual world.

The Elders chose to answer Alexander with the first opinion of the Talmud and not according to the Sages. They were attuned to the spiritual dimension of the earth-to-heaven axis and answered that the distance from the earth to heaven is smaller than the distance from east to west. Man is spiritual, and closeness to heaven is found within each person and soul. Heaven and earth touch. Perhaps they specifically wanted to emphasize this point to the very earthly Alexander. [IX]

The Elders did not quote the opinion of the Sages who argued that east to west and earth to heaven are equal based on the verses, "For, as the height of the heavens over the earth, so great is His kindness toward those who fear Him," and "As the distance of east from west, He distanced our transgressions from us." (*Tehillim* 103:11–12.)

These verses are discussing spiritual distances comparing God's great kindness and forgiveness to the concepts of human heights and distances. The relationship between people—east to west—requires one to tap into a higher dimension of heaven to earth. God's kindness not only brings mankind closer to God but also brings man closer to man.[X] The distances are equal, say the Sages, and man needs to learn to adroitly balance equals, the earthly with the heavenly. Again, this concept might not have resonated with Alexander, so the Elders kept it simple: take the heavenly over the earthly.

The *Ranan L'boker* suggests that the question concerned Divine providence—*hashgachah*, versus human effort—*hishtadlut*. The earth-to-heaven represents Divine providence, while east-to-west represents human effort.[XI] Which is closer (or farther) to bringing results in this world?

> *As it is stated: "So said Hashem: The heavens are My seat, and the earth My footstool" (Yeshayahu 66:1).*
>
> *But the Rabbis say: Both this and that were created as one, for it is stated: "Indeed, My hand has laid the foundation of the earth, and My right hand has spread out the heavens; when I call to them, they stand up together" (ibid. 48:13), implying that they were created as one.*
>
> *The Gemara asks: And the others, Beit Shammai and Beit Hillel, what, in their opinion, is the meaning of "together"? The Gemara responds: It means that they do not separate from each other. In other words, the term "together" is referring not to the moment of their creation but to the manner of their positioning.*
>
> *The Gemara comments: In any case, the verses contradict each other, as heaven is sometimes mentioned first, while on other occasions earth is listed beforehand. Reish Lakish said: When they were created, He first created the heavens and afterward created the earth, but when He spread them out and fixed them in their places, He spread out the earth and afterward He spread out the heavens.*[XIII]

The *Tzlach* explains that there is a connection between this dispute and Alexander's question:

> *The argument between Beit Shammai and Beit Hillel whether the heavens came first or the earth came first is the argument of the philosophers. Beit Shammai is of the opinion that the heavenly elements do not have any life and their movement was imbedded in nature, just as fire always moves up and as a stone always drops down. They have no life and will; therefore, they are unimportant and one would not make a mistake that they are godly and so heavens were created first (no one would err). Beit Hillel holds that they do have life, will, intellect, which is the Rambam's opinion, and therefore the earth was created first because it is inferior (and one could err regarding the heavens).*[XIV]

Alexander, as the student of Aristotle, was an accomplished master student of philosophy, and as the Tzlach wrote, the question of the precedence of heaven or earth was an ongoing argument between the philosophers.

On the other hand, Alexander, as student of Aristotle, believed that the world was eternal without necessarily a prime Creator. Alexander's question was based on the worldview of his protagonists. *Rashi* understands that he was asking: Were the heavens alone created first, or were the heavens and earth created together? In their answer, the Elders emphasized to Alexander that the spiritual, i.e., the heavens, is primary.

The question of the chronological order of what was created first is a question involving the pull and tug between the spiritual and the physical. What is man? Spiritual or material? Soul or body? What dominates? How does one live a spiritual life in a material body and world?

The Elders of the South, contrary to the Rabbis and Beit Hillel, placed heaven first. Perhaps this choice was specifically aimed at Alexander in an attempt to emphasize to the world's new ruler that there is a Cause beyond the earthly here and now. Philosophy in and of itself, the focus on how to live a truthful life, does not offer the complete solution. The ultimate truth only comes from the Divine and Godly truth.

The *Afikei Yam* argues that Alexander was troubled by the contradiction of the Torah verses, whereby in the first verse of the Torah it mentioned the heavens first, while later on in the Creation narrative it mentioned the earth before the heavens. The resolution follows the Sages who explain that the heavens were created first and the earth was placed first. He explains this concept as follows: "The heavens" means the seven heavenly upper spheres, and "the heavens" mentioned on the second day of creation are the two lower spheres including the curtain between the upper and lower. The upper spheres were created before the earth for they are very spiritual, beyond real comprehension; initially the Elders thought Alexander's question was a random one of what came first. So they answered by bringing the first verse of the Torah and did not discuss the hidden nature of the heavens, a topic they wished to avoid.[xv]

The *Chatam Sofer* sources the opinion (*Rashi*) that the question asked was: Were heaven and earth created together first or was heaven alone created first?

The *Chatam Sofer* questions this approach: Why can't we say that the question was simply, "Was heaven or earth created first?" as it appears in the Beit Shammai/Beit Hillel dispute?

Also, what exactly is the proof from the first verse of the Torah that heavens were created first? Perhaps both were created at the same time and the verse mentions one first, since you can't say both first simultaneously!

The *Chatam Sofer* concludes that (according to *Rashi*'s approach), we must say that Alexander did not reach the level of God's secrets as understood by Shammai and Hillel. Their argument deals with the deepest secrets and mysteries of creation. Alexander's question, on the other hand, was based on Greek wisdom, which he learned from Aristotle.[XVI]

Common sense would dictate the heavens should be first, as this is the natural progression: from the fine to the coarse. The followers of Aristotle believed that God was the Creator but "randomly," without a beginning to creation. The Elders emphatically answered: Heavens were created first. God created the world ex nihilo.

QUESTION 3—LIGHT OR DARKNESS

Q. Alexander said to them: "Was light created first, or darkness?"
A. They said to him: "This matter has no resolution."

> *But let them tell him that darkness was created first, for it is written first, "And the earth was astonishingly empty with darkness upon the surface of the deep," and only afterwards, "And God said let there be light and there was light" (Bereishit 1:1–2).[XVII]*

> *They considered it dangerous to give him the true answer in case Alexander would come to ask, "What is above, and what is below, what is before, and what is after [the limits of the universe]." If so, then they should not have told Alexander that the heavens were created first either. Initially they thought that he was simply asking about the plain meaning*

> of the verses, but once they saw that he asked again about the sublime subject, they thought we should not tell him the real answer in case he might come to ask what is above, and what is below, what is before, and what is after.

The Elders of the South appear extremely wary of this third question. They took the previous question at face value, but this question now alerted them that perhaps Alexander was seeking to delve into deep uncharted waters.

The Mishnah in *Chagigah* 2:1 would later set the parameters for the quest into the metaphysical mysteries of creation:

> One does not delve into and study the act of creation with just two people, and not the Maaseh Merkavah with one person, unless he is wise and understands. Anyone who looks at four things, it is appropriate as if he was not born: what is above; what is below; what is within; and what is after.[XVIII]

It is clear that once the Elders determined the real intent of the questions, they responded accordingly, avoiding what they considered would turn into a dangerous metaphysical discussion.

Rav Yigal Ariel finds the question perplexing, as it assumes that darkness is an actual entity and not just the absence of light.

He suggests a number of ways to understand "darkness":

- Physical entity, such as the "black hole."
- The constriction of the primordial light of creation—a vacuum of darkness.
- Light represents Torah and wisdom, and darkness connotes the very opposite.
- Light and darkness symbolize good and evil.[XIX]

Alexander was now in Persian territory, where Zoroastrianism, with its dualistic good and evil worldview, was practiced. The Elders, as seen above, simply did not want to engage Alexander on these weighty theological issues. By answering as they did, they hinted that their deepest wisdom would remain hidden from him.

While the first three questions deal with deep veiled matters involving the secrets of the creation of the universe, the next three questions leave the enigmatic realms and relate to the human condition: how to live life and attain the keys to wisdom, strength, and wealth.

QUESTION 4—WHO IS WISE?

Q. Alexander said to them: "Who is called a wise man?"

A. They said to him: "Who is a wise man? He who sees a future development."[XX]

We see the same idea expressed by King Solomon in *Kohelet* 2:14: "The wise man has eyes in its beginning, but the fool goes in the darkness, and I too know that one event happens to them all."[XXI][2]

QUESTION 5—WHO IS A MIGHTY MAN?

Q. He said to them: "Who is called a mighty man?"

A. They said to him: "Who is a mighty man? He who overcomes his evil inclination."[XXII]

And again King Solomon teaches, this time in *Mishlei* 16:32: "One who is slow to anger is better than a mighty man, and one who rules over his spirit [is better] than one who conquers a city."[XXIII]

QUESTION 6—WHO IS A RICH MAN?

Q. He said to them: "Who is called a wealthy man?"

A. They said to him: "Who is called a wealthy man? He who is happy with his portion."[XXIV]

These three questions posed by Alexander mirror the saying of Ben Zoma in *Pirkei Avot*. They are also similar to the account in *Kiddushin* 49b of one who proposes to a woman to be his wife with conditions such as: "If I was a wise man"; "If I was a strong man"; "If I was a wealthy man."

---

2 The *Midrash Kohelet* learns that this verse refers to two pairs: Moshe (wise) and Bilaam (foolish), as well as King David (wise) and Nevuchadnetzar (foolish).

Kiddushin 49b	Alexander and The Elders of the South	פרקי אבות Ethics of the Fathers Ben Zoma
If a man says to a woman, "Be betrothed to me on the condition that I am a scholar," one does not say that he must be like the scholars of Yavneh, like Rabbi Akiva and his colleagues. Rather, it is referring to anyone who, when he is asked about a matter of wisdom on any topic related to the Torah, responds appropriately and can say what he has learned.[XXV]	Q. Who is called a wise man? A. He who sees a future development.	Who is the wise one? He who learns from all men, as it says, "I have acquired understanding from all my teachers" (*Tehillim* 119:99).
If a man says to a woman, "Be betrothed to me on the condition that I am strong," one does not say that he must be as strong as Avner ben Ner, King Saul's cousin and general, or as strong as Yoav ben Zeruiah, King David's nephew and general. Rather, it means anyone of whom others are afraid due to his strength.[XXVI]	Q. Who is called a mighty man? A. He who overcomes his evil inclination.	Who is the mighty one? He who conquers his impulse, as it says, "Slowness to anger is better than a mighty person, and the ruler of his spirit than the conqueror of a city" (*Mishlei* 16:32).
If a man says to a woman, "Be betrothed to me on the condition that I am wealthy," one does not say he must be as wealthy as Rabbi Elazar ben Charsom or as wealthy as Rabbi Elazar ben Azariah, but rather it can refer to anyone who is honored by the members of his town due to his wealth.[XXVII]	Q. Who is called a wealthy man? A. He who is happy with his portion.	Who is the rich one? He who is happy with his lot, as it says, "When you eat [from] the work of your hands, you will be happy, and it will be well with you" (*Tehillim* 128:2). "You will be happy" in this world, and "It will be well with you" in the World to Come.

The *Maharsha* writes that Alexander's intention in asking some of these questions was that the Elders should be forced to praise him. Naturally, Alexander considered himself to be wise, as he was an accomplished philosopher, a student of Aristotle. Of course he was mighty, a great warrior who had already conquered many nations. And finally, through his victories, Alexander had accumulated vast amounts of riches.[XXVIII]

In a stunning rebuke, the Elders explained that he did not truly possess any of the three! Their approach regarding these three attributes was based on the words of the prophet Yirmiyahu (*Yirmiyahu* 9:22–23): "A wise man shall not pride himself in his wisdom, and a strong man shall not pride himself in his strength; a rich man shall not pride himself with his wealth. Rather one should pride himself with this: contemplate and know Me."[XXIX]

Yirmiyahu teaches us that a wise man prides himself using his *sechel*—intelligence. He needs to enhance his knowledge of God. Through such knowledge, one achieves true happiness and fulfills the purpose of his life. When Alexander wanted to be praised for his intellectual ability, the Elders told him that the true wise man is one who can see the *"nolad."* According to the *Maharsha,* this means that a person understands and appreciates the ultimate purpose for which he was born—seeing the *nolad*. Knowing Hashem.

When Alexander wanted to be praised for his might, the Elders replied that his conquests and power do not prove that he is a man of might. Real might is demonstrated only by one who is able to overcome his evil inclination. Real might is validated when one controls his impulsive emotions that lead to anger or rage.

Alexander the philosopher could display penetrating intelligence, extreme patience, rigorous control of emotions, and calm moderation. On the other hand, he could exhibit incredible bursts of anger that led to revengeful murderous acts, some even towards his loyal companions, that he would later come to gravely regret. He also participated in wild Macedonian-style drinking with complete abandon of control and *sechel*.

Similarly, regarding wealth, the Elders told him that real wealth is not measured by the amount of riches that one has earned. Rather, a truly wealthy man is one who is happy with his lot and enjoys the labor of his own hands.

The *Chatam Sofer* says that perhaps in asking the question of "Who is wise?" Alexander was mocking, making fun of the Elders of the South, for we know that Alexander was an accomplished philosopher. He did not have any doubts regarding all of the questions he asked because he had delved into these matters with the greatest of philosophers, including, of course, Aristotle. He was just testing the Sages with these questions to determine the wisdom of the Jewish people. And when they previously answered regarding light and darkness that this matter has no resolution, he asked the question regarding wisdom. The question was, "How can you call yourself wise men if you can't answer a matter that the philosophers can answer?" And the Elders in their (deeper) wisdom answered, "Who is wise? One who sees the future," thus hinting to him that they know the truth of this matter but they saw the future, i.e., that is to say, if they gave him the true answer, he would begin to ask, "What is above, What is below..."—and this they wanted to prevent.[xxx]

Akeidat Yitzchak (*shaar* 65) analyzes the questions and answers as follows:

> *One who learns from all people is wise, because he knows what is missing from his knowledge and knows he needs to learn. And therefore he learns from all people. And according to the Elders of the South, it is one who sees the future developments, because one who is lazy with gaining wisdom is immersed in the present and can't see the future. But a wise person is not immersed only with the present.*
>
> *And he says that one who controls his inclination is strong/mighty, because a mighty person controls himself and his body first, and later others. And a rich person is one who believes what he has is enough and understands that if Hashem created him with what he has, that is what is necessary and not more. Therefore, this is learned from the verse, "From the sweat of your effort you shall eat bread" (Bereishit 3:19). That is to say, Hashem gave you your brow/sweat and not gold, because that is enough.*[xxxi]

QUESTION 7—LIVING LIFE

Q. He said to them: "What should a man do to live?"
A. They said to him: "He should kill himself."[XXXII]

QUESTION 8—DEAD MAN

Q. He asked them: "What should a man do to die?"
A. They said to him: "He should enliven himself."[XXXIII]

Rashi explains that this matter refers to haughtiness and self-abnegation. The *Aruch* also explains the matter this way. If one wants to live, one needs to be modest (kill himself). And, on the contrary, if one wants to die, one should be boastful (enliven himself).[XXXIV]

A modest life ensures that one is not subject to the *ayin hara*, evil eye, and following *Rashi*'s explanation, one can connect the Elder's answer to that concept.

Rabbeinu Yonah, commenting on *Pirkei Avot* 2:15, learns:

> *Rabbi Yehoshua says it's the "evil eye," meaning one who is not happy with his portion and looks contemptuously at his wealthy friend saying, "When will I get rich like him…" Such a person causes harm to himself and to his friend. As the ones wise in human nature said, "One who desires something of his friend, air arises from his thoughts and burns the things he views contemptuously with his 'evil eye.' And his insides also burn up since he sees these things that he cannot achieve. And these thoughts destroy his body, shorten his life, and take him out of this world."*[XXXV]

The *Michtav M'Eliyahu* explains the matter this way: The working of the "evil eye" is rooted in the fact that the souls of all people are spiritually connected. If one is jealous of his friend, then the very existence of his friend bothers him and he wishes bad things for him. Since his friend's life depends also on him, it is possible that one can diminish another's happiness, making the other more susceptible to getting hurt. The *Maharal* learns that if one simply does not care about the needs of another, this too can be considered an "evil eye." One who sees the needs of another and can help but doesn't do so is saying that he does not care about the other's existence.^{XXXVI}

The *Maharsha* disagrees with such an explanation:

> But it appears to me more that "What should a person do to live, he should kill himself" means: In this world a person should distance himself from the pleasures of this world so that he will live in the World to Come, as it says, "This is the Torah: A person when he dies in the tent." And what should a person do to die? He should live with the pleasures of this world and die in the World to Come. ^{XXXVII}

> The Elders employ the theme that true life requires one to "kill himself," echoing the idea found in Berachot 63b: For Reish Lakish said: Where do we learn that words of Torah are firmly held by one who kills himself for it? Because it says, "This is the Torah, if a man dies in a tent" (Bamidbar 19:14).

Attaching oneself to the sublime and holy guarantees living life, faithfully and completely.

QUESTION 9—HOW TO MAKE FRIENDS

Q. He said to them: "What should a man do to be received well by other people?"

A. They said: "He should maintain an aversion to royalty and governance."

Alexander said to them: "My approach is better than yours. He should make himself familiar with royalty and governance, and thereby do favors for people."

In this case, unlike the other questions and answers, Alexander responded to the Elders' response, offering his own opinion.^{XXXVIII}

Was Alexander just asking a self-help question, albeit an important one in his eyes? Was he trying to see if the Elders understood what he perceived to be the key to succeeding in life when dealing with other people?

The Elders' response mirrors Shemaya's teaching in *Pirkei Avot* that his students should "not make themselves known to the government" (*Avot* 1:10).[XXXIX]

However, in *Avot* 2:3, there is room for dealing with authorities albeit tempered with caution: "Be careful with the authorities because they only become close to a person for their own benefit. They befriend when it helps them but do not stand up for you when things are difficult."[XL]

Tosafot Yom Tov explicitly states that the two Mishnayot do not contradict each other:

> *Shemaya never denied the great service that court Jews such as Mordechai and Rabbi Yehudah HaNasi offered to Am Yisrael. The former's work with Achashveirosh helped save the Jewish people, and the latter cultivated an important friendship with a Roman emperor. Shemaya would not think them mistaken; he would applaud their efforts.*[XLI]

It would appear that Chazal convey a deep disdain for "politics" and advise us to stay away from the machinations and manipulation that government/politics brings. On the other hand, how do you get things done? How do you accomplish for the community without relationships, connections, and protektzia?

Perhaps the message from Chazal is that as a whole, most people should stay away from these matters, as the potential negative impact and risks are too great. But there are select individuals who need to take responsibility and involve themselves in such matters. We clearly see this during Jewish history. There have been many great people involved on behalf of the community, dealing with authority and government, even if it impacted them negatively on a personal level.[3]

An important theme emerges. Difficult and potentially dangerous endeavors can be necessary. Numerous sermons regarding the evils

---

3   See *Abarbanel, Pirkei Avot* 1:9. "The *Abarbanel*, who served as treasurer in the royal courts of Spain and Portugal, chillingly shows how people in positions of authority are liable to contravene every single one of the Ten Commandments." http:\\blog.webyeshiva.org\\insights-in-pirkei-avot-avoiding-or-interacting-with-the-authorities.

of politics do not change the fact that one can make a positive difference in the houses of power. We proceed with caution, but proceed nonetheless.[4]

Alexander was strictly goal-oriented. His approach was: How do you get things done? It was very utilitarian. Did he see people as individuals? Or did he view them just as a means to an end? He certainly had close friends,[5] his trusted companions who learned with him and fought together with him, but who at the same time, in a fit of Alexandrian anger, could be in danger of being killed by him.

Shemaya is telling us that unless absolutely required, one should stay away from close contact with government. These interactions inevitably involve manipulation and duplicity; they are fake and not real. We need to be real. So too, in our everyday relationships with others, we must look at people humanely, caringly, as people and not as objects. The Jewish way is to never view people only as a means to an end.

This advice contains deep wisdom and is a penetrating insight on how one must conduct themselves in day-to-day relationships.

Rabbi Chill, in his commentary on *Pirkei Avot*, writes:

> *In a parenthetical addition, Abarbanel cites an incident related in the Talmud—Tamid 31b—regarding Alexander the Great and his conversation with the Sages of the Negev. He asked them a number of questions among which was: "Who is a wise man?" They replied, "He who can see into the future." Abarbanel asks why those Sages did not give Ben Zoma's definition. Alexander asked further: "Who is acceptable to society?" The answer was, he who resents the power of government. Here, too, the reply was not similar to Ben Zoma in our Mishnah. Abarbanel explains that Alexander the Great was under the impression that power, strength, riches, and a profound knowledge of military*

---

4 Ibid.
5 For example, Ptolemy, Nearchus, Harpalus, and Erigyius who were banished by his father, Philip, to exile. Freeman, p. 36.

tactics were all that he needed to conquer the world. *The rabbis, on the other hand, taught him that if he could not look into the future, his crown was in jeopardy. Furthermore, when his fortunes will begin to change, no amount of wealth nor power will help. Finally, as for respect and honor, he must understand that anyone in the public eye is subject to resentment and animosity. Thus the answers which the Sages of the Negev gave were specifically directed to Alexander and his mistaken beliefs, whereas Ben Zoma was giving the abstract definitions which he knew to be true.*[6]

The *Ranan L'boker* learns that the Elders of the South advocated a path of how one could be received well by other people with love. On the other hand, Alexander's path would lead to a relationship based on fear,[7] an approach the Elders felt was inferior to their recommendation. Love is simply better than fear. When you cannot deliver the goods for other people, then the relationship will end if based on fear. And as per the *Maharsha*, one cannot do well for all people all the time. Also, the more time devoted to a relationship with government, the less precious moments one ends up spending on acquiring wisdom. For this he points to Mordechai, whose heroic efforts on behalf of the Jewish nation and his position as viceroy to the king actually led to a "demotion" in his role as leader in Torah matters.[XLII]

---

6   Rabbi Abraham Chill, *Abrabanel on Pirke Avot*, pp. 228–29.
7   This analysis finds expression in the teaching of the renowned fifteenth-century political philosopher Machiavelli: "And here comes in the question whether it is better to be loved rather than feared, or feared rather than loved. It might perhaps be answered that we should wish to be both; but since love and fear can hardly exist together, if we must choose between them, it is far safer to be feared than loved."
    http://www.bartleby.com/36/1/17.html.
    On a more sublime level: "In our religious lives, we are not able to choose only the aspect of love, or only the aspect of fear. A person who chooses only love can end up heading into paganism, while a person who chooses only fear will lose the ability to experience an encounter with God and to serve God with passionate emotion. The dialectic between love and fear is vital to our existence as mortals living in God's shadow, and as servants of God in particular." HaRav Aharon Lichtenstein, "Moshe Hid His Face, For He was Afraid to Look at God", http://etzion.org.il/en/moshe-hid-his-face-he-was-afraid-look-god.

QUESTION 10—BY LAND OR BY SEA?

Q. Alexander said to them: "Is it better to dwell upon the sea or is it better to dwell upon dry land?"

A. They said to him: "It is better to dwell upon dry land because all the seafarers' minds are not settled until they disembark upon dry land."[XLIII][8]

What is the intent of his tenth question? Who lives on the waters?

The Vilna Gaon, in his commentary on *Sefer Yonah*, explains that this world is compared to the sea, and the next world to dry land:

> Therefore, he says, that in the Talmud, Alexander Macedon asked ten things of the Elders of the South: Is it better to live at sea or on the dry land?
>
> The Elders replied: It is better to live on the dry land as seafarers' minds are not clear until they come to land."
>
> The explanation is that he, Alexander, had all the lusts of this world available to him, and was king over the entire world.[XLIV]

The Elders are telling Alexander that one needs to work his way through the choppy waters in this world in order to get to the dry land. The goal is living a life that gets one to the dry land of the World to Come.

There is a mystical approach that says that the concepts of sea and dry land express two conditions of reality. The *Zohar* calls the sea the "hidden world" and the dry land is called the "revealed world." The dry land is the reality above the surface, that which is seen by the eye, whereupon life stands. In contradistinction, the sea is the reality that covers events. The water is the great mystery where things don't occur on it, but within it.[XLV]

Alexander is once again told that one needs to stay within the revealed reality, the dry land.

Dry land is more clearly defined than the sea. It has borders, as opposed to the sea, which has depth and is more fluid. Alexander, who

---

8   Ranan L'boker quotes *Shulchan Aruch, Orach Chaim* 248:1, "One should not embark on a sea journey less than three days before the Sabbath."

did not recognize any boundaries, however, focused on the conquest of the dry land. His strategy, especially on the Phoenician coasts, was to capture the coastal cities in order to thwart the naval advantage held by his Persian enemy. He negated the Persians' naval power not by building his own strong navy, but through land conquests cutting off his enemies' access to land.

Rav Ariel suggests that the Elders were telling Alexander that while it's good to dream, to think big and to reach beyond one's potential, one always needs to stay grounded in order to achieve peace of mind. With all of his achievements, it's clear that Alexander did not reach equanimity; he wanted to continue his conquests but was ("unjustly," in his eyes) stopped by his own men who had had enough.[XLVI]

The description of Alexander in *Bamidbar Rabbah* 13:14 renders the picture of Alexander the ultimate conqueror, but with significant limits. The earthly kingdoms might resemble the Divine Kingdom, but the differences are still as vast as heaven to earth.

> *Rav Yonah said: When Alexander the Macedonian wanted to fly upwards to the heavens, he tied himself to a famished eagle and placed an animal carcass on a pole in front of the eagle. With the carcass in front of him, the eagle flew. From above Alexander saw the whole world, from India in the east to Spain in the west. He saw the world as a ball and the oceans as a saucer. And that is why Alexander is painted with a ball in his hand and a saucer in his hand.*
>
> *But he did not rule over the waters. Hashem rules over the land and the sea; He saves us in the water and on the dry land.[9] Therefore, the princes of the tribes, when inaugurating the Mishkan, brought with their sacrifices a saucer corresponding to the seas, and a mizrak/cup representing the dry land.*[XLVII, 10]

---

9 See Section III regarding Titus and God's power over the seas.
10 See *Bamidbar*, chap. 7.

After receiving answers to his ten questions, Alexander went on the offensive against the Elders.

> Alexander said to them: "Which one of you is the wisest?"[11]
>
> They said to him: "We are exactly the same, for whatever issue you have asked us, we have all given you the same answer."

The *Maharsha* explains:

> He resented what they said, for they mocked and insulted his wisdom, strength, wealth, and empire. And therefore he asked: "Who among you is the wisest, for according to that person all of you answered?" And they said: "As you've seen, we all answered the same and we are equal; if you want to blame someone, then blame all of us." Commenting on Alexander's complaint of, "Why do you mock my position, wisdom, wealth, strength, and kingdom?" Rashi explains that it was because Alexander wanted them to accept his faith and gods. And this is difficult to understand, for there is no mention that this is the reason they spoke against him and that he requested they change their faith.[XLVIII]

Alexander was convinced that one of the Elders must be the leader of the group. Given his highly competitive nature, his winner-versus-loser outlook, he was convinced that the answers must have been determined by one of the Elders with the others following in tandem. But the Elders show Alexander the attributes of unity and modesty.[12]

The Talmud continues:

> "What is this that you reject me?"
>
> They said to him, "The adversary has enjoyed a temporary victory."
>
> "Why, I could kill you all through my orders to my royal subordinates."

---

[11] Some commentators consider this to be the tenth question and combine #7 and #8 as one.

[12] https://rgl.org.il/?section=22.

This short exchange reveals the potential dark side of an angry Alexander. He obviously felt that the Elders' answers demonstrated their lack of total acceptance of his rule and legitimacy. While he could recognize that in many ways the Jewish people would be loyal citizens of his empire, he understood that they would never fully integrate into the new global society he envisioned. For Alexander, this was rejection.

They said to him, "Certainly the power is in the hand of the king."

The Elders' comeback acknowledged Alexander's power, but pointed out that by killing them Alexander would dishonor himself and his reputation.

Immediately Alexander garbed them in robes of purple and cast gold adornments upon their necks…[XLIX]

We may learn a number of principles from this extraordinary encounter.

- The Elders of the South were appropriate protagonists to deal with Alexander, as they possessed Torah wisdom as well as knowledge of the natural sciences.
- The Elders' responses demonstrate that they were aware of Alexander, his background, his knowledge of philosophy, and his position as the new ruler of the world. The Elders were prepared; they knew their "opponent."
- Discussions regarding science and creation, the spiritual and material, need to be dealt with on multiple levels—from the literal to metaphysical.
- At the same time, there is a clear attempt to avoid any discussions that touch upon the deeper wisdom of the Torah.
- The Elders were direct and honest.
- They were not fearful and, while careful in their answers, they were not apprehensive to contest Alexander and his worldview. Even when they appeared to go "too far" in their perceived "rejection" of Alexander, they were actually pointing out to Alexander the transience of earthly rule. The Jewish people

would remain loyal citizens of the new empire, but that did not mean abandoning eternal covenantal principles.
- Loyalty to Torah and tradition earns the respect of intelligent non-Jewish leaders.
- Unity of purpose, coming as a unified group, is an effective and preferred method when dealing with the non-Jewish challenger.

5. AFRICA, GAN EDEN

The conversation between Alexander and the Elders of the South continued with an unusual request by Alexander.

He said to them, "I wish to go to the African region." They said to him, "You will not be able to go, for the Mountains of Darkness block your way." He said to them, "It is unacceptable for me not to go. That is why I am asking you what can I do." They said to him, "Bring Libyan donkeys which travel amid darkness. Bring spools of flax cord and tie one end to something on this side of the Mountains of Darkness so that when you come back you will be able to take the cord in hand and return to your point of departure."[1]

It's hard to imagine that the advice given by the Elders was topographical military reconnaissance instruction! Certainly Alexander didn't need that from the Elders.

What can be said is that besides for telling Alexander how to get to the Mountains of Darkness, the Elders imparted another message to him as well—to plan the way back. Alexander, they understood, in his unconstrained ambition, is focused on the goal ahead. Only once he reaches his destination, would he begin to concentrate on the return trip. The Elders were telling him that one needs to plan the trip forward and the trip back. Alexander's years of conquest were primarily uni-directional. His return trip was cut short, and he never had the chance to fully deal with the critical issues of consolidating his far-flung empire.

The *Aruch Hashalem* understands that the episode is referring to Northern Africa.

> *Alexander wanted to go to Lower Egypt to the people that live in Katzia. And, in Vayikra Rabbah we find that Alexander went to the King of Katzia in Carthage.[1] So that which the Talmud called Africa is known as Carthage [modern-day Tunisia].*[II]

Allegorically, the Mountains of Darkness represent a non-physical zone, the lack of existence.[III] Going beyond the Mountains of Darkness implies a quest to probe beyond the physical reality of existence. This is the realm the Elders of the South were trying to avoid discussing with Alexander. The Elders were telling Alexander that you need the tools that allow you to see in the realm of darkness. And you must to be rooted in this world so you can successfully return, whole and complete, from the metaphysical inquiries that go beyond the material world.

The story continues:

> *Alexander did this and went to the African region. He reached a certain city that was comprised entirely of women. He wanted to do battle with them. They said to him: "If you succeed in killing us, people will say, 'All he did was kill women.' If we kill you people will say, 'He was the king who was killed by women.'"*
>
> *Alexander said, "Bring me bread." They brought him a loaf of bread made out of gold upon a golden table. He said to them, "Do people eat bread made out of gold?" They said to him, "But if it is regular bread you want, do you not have bread to eat in your place that you picked yourself up and came here?" When Alexander was in the process of departing, he inscribed upon*

---

1 "Alexander never fought against Carthage. Towards the end of his life upon his return to Babylon, he was brimming with plans for future conquest…he has nursed a grudge against Carthage for aiding Tyre ever since his siege of that doomed city. He also knew that the next logical step of expansion west into the Mediterranean beyond Cyrene would bring him into conflict with this powerful mercantile kingdom of North Africa. He decided that it was both expedient and necessary to crush Carthage and seize control of the whole African coast…" Freeman, pp. 303–4.

the gate of the city, "I am Alexander of Macedon. I was a fool before I came to the country of Africa belonging to women, and learned sound thinking from the women."[IV]

The episode above highlights a world opposite of the normal.

The African city is a city ruled by women, and Alexander the mighty warrior now faces women who contest his apparent intent to fight.[2] Additionally, the bread they serve Alexander is inedible, made out of gold.

This is another example of Alexander's unlimited ambition and worldview being challenged. Was the reasoning of the women of Africa so compelling for Alexander? Did it make an impact influencing Alexander's future action? Or was Alexander simply playing the gracious, magnanimous gentlemen as he often displayed?

The Talmud continues and reports:

> As he was journeying, he sat by a well and began to eat. He had some salted fish with him, and as they were being washed, they gave off a sweet odor.[3]
>
> He said: "This shows that this well comes from the Garden of Eden." Some say that he took some of the water and washed his face with it; others say that he went alongside it until he came to the entrance of the Garden of Eden.
>
> He cried out, "Open the door for me."
>
> They replied, "This is the gate of the Lord [the righteous shall enter into it]."
>
> He replied, "I too am a king; I am also of some account, give me something."
>
> They gave him an eyeball. He went and weighed all his silver and gold against it, and it was not equal to it.

---

[2] Rav Ariel explains that this land was not the land of the Amazon Women. The Amazon Women imitate and fight like men. These women were wise and did not look for a fight. https://rgl.org.il/?section=22

[3] "Plutarch records that Alexander was sensitive to smell and always had a very pleasant odor about him." Freeman, p. 27.

The Elders answered that east to west is farther—that it is harder to achieve results, since human effort is open and revealed. This is compared to looking at the sun from earth, so when everyone looks at the open, revealed sun, success is lost. But Divine providence is closer to getting results, as it is "hidden," that is, concealed and protected—as per *Tehillim* 31:21, "You shall hide them in the secrecy of Your countenance, from bands of men; protect them in a shelter from the strife of tongues."

QUESTION 2—WHAT'S FIRST?

Q. He said to them: "Were the heavens created first, or the earth?"

A. They said: "The heavens were created first, as it says: 'In the beginning, God created the heavens and the earth.'"[XII]

On the surface, this appears to be a straightforward question, which the Elders simply answered with the support of the first verse of the Torah.

However, this was the subject of debate between Beit Shammai and Beit Hillel in *Chagigah* 12a:

> *Beit Shammai and Beit Hillel dispute the order of creation, as the Sages taught: Beit Shammai say: The heavens were created first and afterward the earth was created, as it is stated: "In the beginning God created the heaven and the earth" (Bereishit 1:1), which indicates that heaven came first.*
>
> *And Beit Hillel say: The earth was created first, and heaven after it, as it is stated: "On the day that the Hashem/God made earth and heaven" (ibid. 2:4).*
>
> *Beit Hillel said to Beit Shammai: According to your words, does a person build a second floor and build the first floor of the house afterward? As it is stated: "It is He Who builds His upper chambers in the heaven, and has founded His vault upon the earth" (Amos 9:6), indicating that the upper floor, heaven, was built above the earth.*
>
> *Beit Shammai said to Beit Hillel: According to your words, does a person make a stool for his feet, and make a seat afterward?*

> He said to the Sages, "How is this?"
>
> They replied, "It is the eyeball of a human being, which is never satisfied."
>
> He said to them, "How can you prove that this is so?"
>
> They took a little dust and covered it, and immediately it was weighed down; and so it is written, "The grave and Gehinnom are never satiated [so the eyes of man are never satiated]."[v]

The *Maharal* in *Netivot Olam* analyzes how ambition and ego detach a person from this world.

> A person who is always running after riches will never be satisfied. As it says in Kohelet, "His eyes will not be satisfied with his wealth." And it linked this to the eye, because the eye sees from east to west and takes it all in. And when this deficiency is attached to him, one is not complete at all. One always wants to get and is not satisfied.
>
> And therefore it says in Tamid 32b: "Regarding Alexander the Macedonian that he went to capture the entire world until he got to the end of the world and arrived at Gan Eden. And they didn't open the gates of Gan Eden, saying to him that only the righteous can enter, and they gave him the eyeball..."
>
> The explanation is: Alexander went and captured the entire world and he wasn't satisfied with just his kingdom which he already captured; until he wanted to even enter the Garden of Eden! And this wasn't appropriate for him. Alexander believed that the fact he captured everything made him important...Therefore, he claimed: "I am a king; I should be able to enter!" Certainly if his kingship was desired by Hashem, there wouldn't be any deficiency and he would have been satisfied and wouldn't go to capture that which was off-limits. But since his rule was one that was not complete, he was not satisfied.

So they gave him an eyeball, meaning to say: "That which you are going to capture so much, it's all not appropriate for you. That which you have the attribute of an eye that is never satisfied is because you are flesh and blood, a physical body. That which is missing for you will not satisfy you. Therefore it does not outweigh all of the gold and silver for, because of its lacking, it is not full at all. And he did not believe that the eyeball is never satisfied, and as soon as he put the dust on it, it was satisfied, as the dust is appropriate as a cover.

And they hinted to him from Gan Eden that as your eye is never satisfied, you can't satisfy it except though the dust; that is that the eye should be covered with dust through death; as he deserves this as he is always lacking and never satisfied…And thus it happened to Alexander that he died before half of his years as the commentators wrote on Daniel: "And his horn broke." And he did all this because he was never satisfied and there was always something missing. And one should always be careful regarding this trait.[VI]

Rav Shmuel Brazil further elaborates:

Chazal say his eye deceived and misled him. Tamid 32b relates the story of Alexander the Great who followed a stream until he reached the gates of Gan Eden, through which they did not allow him to enter. The Maharal in his Chidushei Aggados explains this enigmatic Gemara as follows: that Alexander had an insatiable eye to conquer the entire world. The nature of the eye and earth has two differing characteristics. The eye reveals while the earth covers. The more the eye reveals, the more the earth, which symbolizes death, has the possibility to cover one up by premature death. For the greater the desire for physical objects and pleasures occupies one's life, the more he wants. And consequently, the greater is the degree of severity and pain experienced by never ever fulfilling his cravings. For Chazal teach us that if a person has a hundred he wants two hundred…This is meant by the words of Chazal that a little earth stops the desire for materialistic acquisitions. This was hinted to Alexander who died at a young age.[4]

Rav Poalim examines the story on different levels:

Alexander came to the entrance of Gan Eden and it did not open up for him, for this is the gate of God and only the righteous may enter. If we understand this on a simple level: that he arrived at Gan Eden and knocked on the entrance and they answered him.

And as to Alexander's question as he knocked on the entrance of Gan Eden, if it is to be understood literally: Know that Gan Eden has a yard around it. And, the main entrance to Gan Eden is within that yard. However, that yard also has an entrance, and within the yard are the Cherubim and flaming sword to guard the path to the Tree of Life.

And when Alexander knocked on the entrance, he knocked on the entrance to the yard and not on the main entrance of Gan Eden which is within the yard. And that which was answered to him was from the Cherubim in the yard. And they gave him the item that was like an eyeball, as they were commanded by Heaven.[VII]

Why did Alexander now "smell" the garden?

It's a wonder: Alexander returned from Africa exactly in the way he went there, for he tied the rope in order to know how to return as per the advice of the Elders of the South. If so, how is it that he didn't smell the smell of Gan Eden when he went and only when he returned? And in my youth I heard a nice explanation for this. When Alexander was going to this country [Africa] he was filled with his desire to conquer and with the feeling that through his strength he went with confidence.

---

4 https://matzav.com/rav-brazil-on-parshas-korach/.

> *And such a person is not worthy to smell the odor of Gan Eden. But when he returned from there after he learned the lessons from the women of Africa and returned humbled, then he could smell Gan Eden!*[VIII]

In the Gan Eden episode, Chazal were acknowledging Alexander's position as one of the prominent historical figures of all time. Otherwise, why was he even allowed to get near to the elusive Gan Eden? At the same time, Chazal hammered home the point that ultimately, it was a futile attempt. Alexander's unbridled ambition was ultimately devoid of a Gan Eden pathway leading to truth, mercy, justice, and righteousness.

6. THE ACCUSATIONS

A. AFRICANS

The Sages taught in a *Beraisa* (*Sanhedrin* 91a):

> On the twenty-fourth of Nissan, the challengers (foreign governors) were removed from Judea and from Jerusalem when the Africans came to contend with the Jews before Alexander the Macedonian.
>
> The Africans said to him, "The Land of Canaan is rightfully ours, for it is written in the Torah of the Jews that they were to take the Land of Canaan as an inheritance, and Canaan was the ancestor of these very people standing before you."
>
> Geviha ben Pesisa said to the Sages: Give me permission and I will go to debate them before Alexander the Macedonian. If they defeat me, say to them, "You have defeated an ordinary one among us."
>
> And if I defeat them, say to them, "The Torah of Moshe has defeated you." The Sages gave him permission and he went and debated the Africans.

Who was Geviha ben Pesisa?

He was not one of the Sages or leaders of the Jewish people at that time. Both *Toldot Tanna'im v'Amora'im* and *Margaliot Hayam* cite *Megilat Taanit* and provide some background: He was a wise man from the priests who was a watchman at the Temple. And he was called Geviha as he was a hunchback, and the word *geviha* in Aramaic denotes hunchback. In order to emphasize that condition, he was called "the son of Pesisa," as *pesisa* means tall.[1]

> *He said to them, "From where do you bring proof?" They said to him, "From the Torah." He said to them, "I too will bring you proof only from the Torah, for it is stated in Bereishit 9:25: 'And Noach said, "Cursed is Canaan: A slave of slaves shall he be to his brothers."' If a slave acquires property, to whom belongs the slave and to whom the property? And not only that, but it is many years that you have not served us."*
>
> *Alexander the King said to them: "Respond to him." They said: "Give us three days' time." He gave them the time. They searched but did not find an answer. They immediately fled, abandoning their fields sowed as they were and their vineyards planted as they were, and that year was shevi'it, the sabbatical year in which all agriculture is forbidden.*[II]

A few questions require explanation:

- Who exactly were these Africans who claimed the land?
- Was Geviha ben Pesisa's argument so compelling?
- Didn't the Africans know that his apparently obvious answer would destroy their claims?

Regarding the first question, the Africans made a claim to the Land of Canaan as inheritors of the land. According to the *Aruch Hashalem*, these were the Girgashites who fled Eretz Yisrael at the time of Yehoshua.[1]

Regarding the second and third questions, the *Ben Yehoyada* explains what went on behind the scenes and how Geviha's answer was subtle yet effectively compelling:

---

1   See *Yerushalmi, Shivi'it* 6:1; *Aruch Hashalem, Aleph*, pp. 243–44.

> "I too will bring you proof only from the Torah."—This is difficult for they knew what was written in the Torah! And they brought a claim from the verse: "Take as an inheritance the Land of Canaan." How did they not know that it is written in the Torah: "A slave of slaves shall he be to his brothers?" And it appears to me that they thought that he [Geviha ben Pesisa] would not use that answer because that verse would incur the wrath of Alexander, who was from Yefet [Greece].
>
> Alexander could say to Geviha, "How did you take all of it for yourselves, since the verse says, "A slave of slaves shall he be to his brothers Shem and Yefet.'" If so, then half should belong to the descendants of Yefet. But Geviha felt the possibility of this claim from the king and addressed this in his answer. He said, "To whom belongs the slave and to whom the property?" and also "But it is many years that you have not served us." His intention in phrasing his answer this way was to provide an opening for Alexander to claim the portion of Yefet. Geviha was saying: We took our portion in land. And you should take your portion now from the money they earned from all those years they did not serve both of us. Also their new land in Africa is precious, it should be yours...[III]

Next came the Egyptians with their historical claim against the Jewish nation.

The Gemara relates:

> On another occasion, the people of Egypt came to judgment with the Jewish people before Alexander of Macedon. The Egyptian people said to Alexander: "It says in the Torah: 'And the Lord gave the people favor in the eyes of Egypt, and they lent them, etc.' (Shemot 12:36). Give us the silver and gold that you took from us; you claimed that you were borrowing it and you never returned it!"
>
> Geviha ben Pesisa said to the Sages: "Give me permission and I will go and deliberate with them before Alexander of Macedon.

> *If they will defeat me, say to them: "You have defeated an ordinary person from among us, and until you overcome our Sages, it is no victory." And if I will defeat them, say to them: "The Torah of Moshe, our teacher, defeated you, and attribute no significance to me." The Sages gave him permission, and he went and deliberated with them.*
>
> *Geviha ben Pesisa said to them: "From where are you citing proof that you are entitled to the silver and gold?" They said to him: "From the Torah." Geviha ben Pesisa said to them: "I too will cite proof to you only from the Torah, as it is stated: 'And the sojourning of the Children of Israel, who dwelt in Egypt, was four hundred and thirty years,' (Shemot 12:40) during which they were enslaved to Egypt, engaged in hard manual labor. Give us the wages for the work performed by the 600,000 men above the age of twenty (see Shemot 12:37) whom you enslaved in Egypt for four hundred and thirty years."*
>
> *Alexander of Macedon said to the people of Egypt: "Provide Geviha ben Pesisa with a response to his claims." They said to him: "Give us time; give us three days to consider the matter." The emperor gave them the requested time, and they examined the matter and did not find a response to the claims. Immediately, they abandoned their fields when they were sown and their vineyards when they were planted, and fled. The Gemara adds: And that year was a Sabbatical Year.*[IV]

Couldn't the Egyptians make the argument that it was Pharaoh who enslaved the Jewish people and therefore they had no right to take any compensation from the Egyptian people themselves?

The *Meshech Chochmah* anticipates this question and explains that many years before the enslavement of the nation, the Torah recounted the episode whereby Yosef sold the people's land to Pharaoh (*Bereishit* 47:15–24). Why tell us this story? Because the Torah later writes that Bnei Yisrael asked their neighbors for gold, silver, and garments when they left Egypt. And the Egyptians argued before Alexander that Israel should give back the gold, silver, and garments that they borrowed from us. And Geviha said to them to give Bnei Yisrael the wages for the work they performed for 210 years. But the Midrash tells us that Israel slaved for Pharaoh, "They built storage houses for Pharaoh," so how did they take the silver and gold from the people? "But since Pharaoh acquired the people in the times of Yosef, all that belonged to them actually belonged to Pharaoh. So it is now clear why they took from the people their wages for the work performed."[v]

Geviha made the claim that 600,000 Jews worked for 430 years. How could he make that claim? We know that 430 years is calculated from the Covenant of the Pieces when Avraham was seventy years old (and 400 years from the birth of Yitzchak). The Jews were in Egypt for only 210 years. And according to tradition they were slaves for only eighty-six years!

The Midrash teaches that during the Plague of Darkness, four-fifths of the people of Israel died. That means that there were actually five times the number of Jews as indicated. Eighty-six years plus another four times is 430 (86 + (86 x 4) = 430)! There was indeed equivalent to 430 years of slavery performed by 600,000 people!

The *Torah Temimah*[VI] teaches that the verse in *Tehillim* 105:37 actually references this specific episode with Alexander: "And He brought them forth with silver and gold; and there was none that stumbled among His tribes." The Targum reads that it refers to a judgment the Jewish people had with the Egyptians regarding the silver and gold taken from Egypt. Even though Bnei Yisrael went out with the silver and gold they did not stumble; they did not fail in the case with the Egyptians and won the case in front of Alexander.[2]

---

[2] "The loud chortling sound you may have heard last week (2003) was the collective mirth of countless Talmud-conversant Jews as they read about a lawsuit being prepared by a group of Egyptian expatriates in Switzerland...Dr. Hilmi's lawsuit is ostensibly being filed against 'all the Jews of the world' for recovery of property allegedly stolen during the exodus of the Jewish people from Egypt approximately 3,300 years ago. Citing the Torah, Dr. Hilmi is demanding, presumably on Egypt's behalf, the return of 'gold, jewelry, cooking utensils, silver ornaments, clothing and more,' not to mention interest thereon, taken by the ancestors of today's Jews 'in the middle of the night'—a 'clear theft of a host country's resources and treasure, something that fits the morals and character of the Jews.' According to Dr. Hilmi's mathematical computations, which include an annual doubling in value of the material in

Ben Yehoyada notes that the language of the text hints that the Egyptians specifically followed the Africans. Initially, the Egyptians thought that they would have encountered the following arguments: "Did our forefathers take land from you?" "No, they only took movable objects and those are lost!" "And why are we responsible for what they did over a thousand years ago? Everyone should only be liable for what he or she did themselves!" But when they saw that the Africans came and were answered even though their claim was old, they made their claim.

After the Africans and the Egyptians approached with their lawsuit, the descendants of Yishmael, Avraham's first son, then presented their claim.

The Gemara relates:

> And on another occasion, the descendants of Yishmael and Keturah came to debate with the Jewish people before Alexander of Macedon.
>
> They said to the Jewish people: "The land of Canaan is both ours and yours, as it is written: 'And these are the generations of Yishmael, son of Avraham, whom Hagar the Egyptian, Sarah's maidservant, gave birth with Avraham' (Bereishit 25:12), and it is written: 'And these are the generations of Yitzchak, son of Avraham' (Ibid., 25:19).
>
> Therefore, the land should be divided between Avraham's heirs."
>
> Geviha ben Pesisa said to the Sages: "Give me permission and I will go and debate with them before Alexander. If they will defeat me, say to them: 'You have defeated an ordinary person from us, and until you defeat our Sages, it is not a victory.' And if I will defeat them, say to them: 'The Torah of Moshe, our

---

question, 1,125 trillion tons of gold are owed by the Jews for each of the 300 tons he estimates was taken. And that doesn't include interest, which he claims, without explanation, should be calculated for 5,758 years.

"The merriment that greeted the report was born of the fact that the Talmud tells of precisely such a claim lodged over 2,000 years ago in a world court of sorts presided over by none other than Alexander the Great." Rabbi Avi Shafran, *A Truly Historic Lawsuit*, http://www.aish.com/jw/s/48891502.html.

> teacher, defeated you, and do not attribute it to me.'" The Sages gave him permission, and he went and debated with them.
>
> Geviha ben Pesisa said to them: "From where are you bringing proof that the Land of Canaan belongs to both you and the Jewish people?" They answered: "From the Torah." Geviha ben Pesisa said: "I too will cite proof to you only from the Torah, as it states: 'And Avraham gave all that he had to Yitzchak. But to the sons of his concubines, Avraham gave gifts, and sent them away from his son, while he yet lived, to the east country' (Ibid., 25:5–6).
>
> In the case of a father who gave a document of inheritance to his sons during his lifetime and sent one of the sons away from the other, does the one who was sent away have any claim against the other?
>
> The father himself divided his property."^VII

In this case as well, the *Ben Yehoyada* argues that the *Yishmaelim* only came with their claim after they saw that the Egyptians made a claim. Initially they thought that since the Jewish people were the ones that fulfilled and paid off the debt of slavery given to Avraham, then only the Jews had a claim to the Land of Israel. But then they saw that Geviha answered the Egyptian claim by showing that Israel earned their reward for the years of slavery, the *Yishmaelim* could now say that the Jews did not pay off the debt of Avraham with slavery, for now they were paid for that work.

In all of these episodes, Alexander sits as judge, jury, and executioner. Indeed, throughout his long journeys, between battles Alexander would adjudicate matters brought before him.[3] He constantly needed to delicately solve conflicting claims from a variety of adversarial tribes and nations.

In the case of the Africans and the *Yishmaelim*, the discussion revolves around the rights to the Land of Israel. The two parties contested the

---

3   "...He would sit down to breakfast. If the army was not breaking camp, he would spend the day organizing military affairs, answering correspondence, administering justice, or, if there was time, hunting with his friends." Freeman, p. 83.

exclusive rights of the Jewish people to Israel. The court hearing ironically takes place before Alexander, the king who captured this land. The answer of whose land it was could very well have been answered by Alexander—that it was his land! Alexander, however, was appreciative of the issue of the historic rights of people to their land, culture, and heritage, even those he conquered. He did not destroy cultures, but instead attempted to co-opt them.

Noted American jurist Nat Lewin summarizes the amazing courtroom victory:[4]

> *The Talmud in Sanhedrin 91a relates the wonderful story of the first Jewish advocate on behalf of the Jews in a foreign court, and with minor differences the account appears also in Megilat Taanit. When Alexander the Great swept into Jerusalem sometime between 325 and 320 BCE, the Africans, Egyptians, and Ishmaelites separately petitioned his court for title to the Land of Canaan and for return of the gold and silver carried away at the time of the Exodus. A modest hunchback priest named, according to the Talmudic text, Geviha ben Pesisa, volunteered to defend against these claims in the court of Alexander. His advocacy resulted not only in rejection of the claims made against the Jews, but in successful counterclaims that compelled the petitioners to flee the jurisdiction and forfeit their own property to the Jewish people."*

From the episode involving Geviha ben Pesisa, the Lubavitcher Rebbe extrapolates: When a Jew speaks to the non-Jewish world simply, honestly citing the verses from the Torah (Bible), even if those words are said by a very "simple" Jew, and even if that Jew is a hunchback, nonetheless, since the words are words of Torah, they achieve the desired intent.[5]

---

4 Nat Lewin, "Protecting Jewish Observance in Secular Courts," *Tradition* 38:1, 2004.
5 *Likutei Sichot, Parashat Shelach*, 5742.

The *Toldot Tanna'im v'Amora'im* sources a Midrash whereby Alexander requested to visit the Temple in Jerusalem and was to be accompanied by Geviha ben Pesisa, the champion of Jewish rights. Geviha heard that the Cutheans told Alexander that the Jews would not let him go all the way into the Temple because he was uncircumcised. Geviha prepared special gold shoes with precious stones for Alexander and put them on Alexander when they arrived at the Temple Mount. When they reached the Holy of Holies, Geviha told Alexander that he could not proceed any further.[VIII]

These court proceedings raise a number of points:

- In all three episodes, the Jewish people are represented by just one person.
- That person, Geviha, was not an acknowledged sage. Furthermore, he was not handsome or charismatic, but rather hunchbacked and short.
- He had a fallback position in the event he lost. He would try to claim that he wasn't an authorized, legitimate representative of the Jewish people.
- He took the mission upon himself only after receiving permission of the Sages.
- He bested his opponents by staying true to the Torah sources, anticipating potential counterarguments and claims. In the end, he proved to be a very worthy proponent of the nation's cause.

JUSTICE AND MERCY

The *Talmud Yerushalmi* and midrash bring down the following story:

> Alexander of Macedon visited King Katzia beyond the Mountains of Darkness.
>
> The king approached Alexander offering him golden bread on a golden tray.
>
> Alexander demanded: "Do I then need your gold?"
>
> King Katzia said: "Have you nothing to eat in your own country that you have to come here?"

Alexander retorted: "I came only because I wished to see how you dispense justice."

A man came to the king with a complaint against his neighbor.

The buyer said, "This man sold me a heap of dung and I found a treasure in it. But I only bought the heap not the treasure."

The seller maintained, "I sold the heap and all that it contained including the treasure."

King Katzia said to one of them, "Do you have a son?" "Yes," he replied.

And he asked the other, "Do you have a daughter?" "Yes," was the answer.

"Then marry them off to each other and let the treasure belong to both of them."

King Katzia noticed Alexander sitting astonished, and asked him, "Have I then not judged well?"

"Yes," Alexander replied.

King Katzia asked, "Had this case happened by you, how would you have judged?"

Alexander said, "I would have killed both and kept the treasure for myself."

King Katzia asked, "Does it rain in your country?"

Alexander replied, "Yes."

King Katzia: "Does the sun shine?"

Alexander: "Yes."

King Katzia: "Have you small cattle [sheep and goats]?"

"Yes," Alexander replied.

"By Heaven!" Katzia exclaimed. "It is not for your sake that the rain falls but for the sake of the cattle, as it is written, "You save both man and beast…Man for the sake of beast."[IX]

While this episode does not involve the Jewish people, it echoes the cry of the prophet Yirmiyahu (*Yirmiyahu* 9:23): "But let him that boasts exult in this, that he understands and knows me, for I am the Lord Who practices kindness, justice, and righteousness on the earth; for in these things I delight, says the Lord."

Kindness. Justice. Righteousness.

> *Rabbeinu Yerucham teaches that when one looks at all of the laws of the Torah, it is clear that its basis is a world established with lovingkindness/chessed.*
>
> *And from the pillar of chessed all of the laws of the Torah are derived. Man and Torah are only chessed. The beginning of Creation is chessed as God wanted only to give good with His creations…The image and behavior of Man is rooted in chessed…*[x]

Rav Moshe Stav contrasts the Alexandrian worldview with the Jewish one (based on *chessed*) as reflected in the King Katzia episode:

> *Alexander the Great operated on the premise that the purpose of life and its true content are expressed in the development of human wisdom and technology and scientific and cultural advancement, which make the world into a more comfortable and pleasant place to live in. The way to achieve this is through competition and the glorification of aspiration, which sanctifies the human desire to attain more and more, even if this necessitates trampling others in the process, as this is what makes the world progress.*
>
> *In Alexander's view, satisfaction with one's lot, as well as any perspective that does not aspire to consume but rather to give, is dangerous for the world and should therefore be punishable by death. The truth is, however, that the world is actually driven by the will to give, "Olam chessed yibaneh." This is reflected in the rain, which falls in the merit of the animals, which fulfill their roles without deviation.*[6]

---

6   Rav Moshe Stav, *The World View of Alexander the Great*, www.kby.org/english/torat-yavneh/view.asp?id=7431).

SECTION II
KING PTOLEMY

1. PTOLEMY SOTER

PTOLEMY I SOTER

Alexander the Great trained, nurtured, and maintained an impressive array of commanders and high-ranking military officers. These included those battle-tested generals he inherited from his father, King Philip, as well as those he handpicked from his devoted and loyal companions.

Ptolemy the son of Lagos belonged to the latter group.

Ptolemy I (366–283 BCE) was born in the upper Macedonian region of Eordaia. As a member of the Macedonian aristocracy, Ptolemy grew up in the invigorating and stimulating imperial court at Pella.

As part of the inner circle in the royal court, Ptolemy joined Alexander at Mieza where, together with Alexander and the future king's companions, he studied for three years with the one and only Aristotle.[1]

Ptolemy served as an older colleague, friend, advisor, and confidant of the future king. When the explosive dispute took place between Alexander and his father, King Philip, Ptolemy sided with his friend Alexander. King Philip took a very dim view of Ptolemy as a result of his advice to, and efforts on behalf of, Alexander. Ptolemy was forced

---

[1] "...As a place where master and pupil could labour and study, he assigned them the precinct of the nymphs near Mieza, where to this day the visitor is shown the stone seats and shady walks of Aristotle." http://penelope.uchicago.edu/Thayer/E/Roman/Texts/Plutarch/Lives/Alexander*/3.html.

to join Alexander in exile, and the relationship between the two was further cemented.

In 336 BCE, before he had a chance to begin his dream of replacing the Persian empire, King Philip was assassinated. Now it was Alexander's shot at the throne. But it was not a forgone conclusion that Alexander would be the one to replace his father's place on the Macedonian throne. As always in the royal courts of yesterday (and today) the intrigue immediately began, and matters needed to be taken care of quickly and efficiently. Ptolemy played his role by returning to the court and supporting Alexander's claim to take over Philip's successful rule. When Alexander swiftly consolidated his position, he appointed Ptolemy to various positions, such as companion and *seneschal*, the officer in charge of the household and servants.

Arrian writes:

> *In the time of Alexander, the title of somatophylax was given to those generals on whose wisdom the king chiefly lent, and by whose advice he was usually guided. Among these, and foremost in Alexander's love and esteem, was Ptolemy the son of Lagos.*[2]

Ptolemy accompanied Alexander on his initial military campaigns to regions in the Danube in 336 BCE, and in the battles to crush the rebellion in Corinth and to destroy Thebes in 335 BCE.

He participated and successfully contributed in the major battles later won by Alexander in Asia, Persia, and India, though it's unclear as to the full extent of Ptolemy's involvement and role.

Pausanias[3] portrays an extremely positive picture:

> *He had earned the good opinion of Alexander by his military successes in Asia, and had gained his gratitude by saving his life when he was in danger among the Oxydracae, near the*

---

2   Sharpe, p. 27.
3   Pausanias (110–180 CE) was a Greek traveler and geographer who lived in the time of Roman emperors Hadrian, Antoninus Pius, and Marcus Aurelius. He is famous for his *Description of Greece*, a lengthy work that describes ancient Greece from his first-hand observations.

> river Indus; moreover Alexander looked up to him as the historian whose literary powers and knowledge of military tactics were to hand down the wonder of future ages those conquests of which he was eye-witness.[4]

With the death of Alexander and breakup of the empire into four smaller kingdoms (as prophesied in Daniel), Ptolemy wisely focused on his desired prize, Egypt. By then, Ptolemy was acknowledged as a formidable general, popular with the troops:

> ...And Ptolemy's high character for wisdom, generosity, and warlike skill had gained many friends for him among the officers; they saw that the wealth of Egypt would put it in his power to reward those whose services were valuable to him; and hence crowds flocked to his standard.[5]

> ...but Ptolemy, on the contrary, was generous and fair and granted to all the commanders the right to speak frankly. What is more, he had secured all the most important points in Egypt with garrisons of considerable size, which had been well equipped with every kind of missile as well as with everything else. This explains why he had, as a rule, the advantage in his undertakings, since he had many persons who were well disposed to him and ready to undergo danger gladly for his sake.[6]

Ptolemy perhaps (correctly) understood that only an Alexander could conquer the entire world; that perhaps only an Alexander could have maintained that world empire and forged a new global culture which included Greek, Persian, Asian, and Indian traditions.

For Ptolemy, there was plenty to be done with Egypt and the surrounding region. At the same time, Ptolemy made sure to maneuver events so that he was seen as the natural continuation of Alexander's

---

4   Sharpe, p. 28.
5   Ibid., p. 32.
6   http://penelope.uchicago.edu/Thayer/E/Roman/Texts/Diodorus_Siculus/18B*.html.

great legacy. He forcibly kidnapped Alexander's body[7] when it was on route for burial in Macedonia, and ceremoniously interned him in Egypt. It could be argued that this "body grab" was as important and significant as the land grabs attempted by the various other successors to Alexander.

According to Diodorus Siculus, "The wise and mild plans which were laid down by Alexander for the government of Egypt, when a province, were easily followed by Ptolemy when it became his own kingdom."[8]

Ptolemy's role as a bearer of Alexander's legacy was, without doubt, assisted by the fact that Ptolemy himself had written a military biography on Alexander. That work is currently not extant, but the second-century historian Arrian's work, which focused on the military campaigns of Alexander, is based on Ptolemy's writings together with the work of Aristobulus (also not in existence). Ptolemy's accounting of events, and his participation in them, whether totally accurate or not, was preserved and highlighted throughout history via Arrian and subsequent historians.[9]

---

[7] "The original plan had been to return Alexander's body to Macedonia where it would be received by his mother and his wife and children. The method of transportation chosen was to take the body overland, travelling in state in a massive mobile tomb known as a *cataflaque*. Descriptions of this travelling edifice are quite astonishing; it was said to have taken the form of a mini ionic temple, 20 x 13 feet and fully decorated in marble and gold. One can only imagine what it must have looked like, the hot sun glinting off the incredible moving tomb as it slowly chugged its way across the desert into Syria.
Things came to an end in Syria, however, as Ptolemy was waiting with a large detachment of his men. They moved on the tomb party and forced them to turn south. Over the next few weeks the kidnapped corpse travelled south through Syria and into Egypt to the city of Memphis—at the time Alexandria was only seven years into construction and hadn't yet replaced Memphis as the administrative capital of Egypt. Once he had arrived there Ptolemy dispensed with the incumbent satrap (whom Alexander had appointed) and declared himself the ruler of Egypt. He became known as Ptolemy I *Soter* (the saviour) and the first of a new dynasty of Greek rulers of Egypt, taking the title of King in 305 BCE." https://sbhistorygeek.wordpress.com/2013/01/12/the-man-who-stole-a-god/.

[8] http://penelope.uchicago.edu/Thayer/E/Roman/Texts/Diodorus_Siculus/home.html.

[9] "But in my opinion the narratives of Ptolemy and Aristobulus are more worthy of credit than the rest…and Ptolemy, not only because he accompanied Alexander in his expedition, but also because he was himself a king afterwards, and falsification of facts would have been more disgraceful to him than to any other man."
https://en.wikisource.org/wiki/The_Anabasis_of_Alexander.

Once in power in Egypt, Ptolemy I Soter[10] engaged in numerous military campaigns to preserve his Egyptian "empire" and at times fought to extend his reach and secure his regional claims.

Some of these battles were for control of Eretz Yisrael against the Seleucid rule, with Ptolemy controlling areas of Israel during his reign.

Toldot Yisrael explains that during the reign of Ptolemy I, the prophecy of *Daniel* 8:8 was completely fulfilled: "And the he-goat [Alexander] magnified himself exceedingly; and when he was strong, the great horn was broken; and instead of it there came up the appearance of four horns toward the four winds of Heaven."

- Macedonia and Greece in Europe, which was one kingdom.
- Persia, Aram, and Babylon, which formed one kingdom in Asia.
- The kingdom of Asia Minor.
- Egypt, including Eretz Yisrael and parts of Africa.[I]

It would only be years later that the Seleucid Empire would wrest complete control of Eretz Yisrael from the Ptolemies, leading to the severe oppression of the Jewish people resulting in the Maccabian war, Chanukah miracle, and rise of an independent Chashmonian Jewish state.

Back home in Egypt, Ptolemy I focused his efforts on building his Egyptian empire. He originated numerous new innovative projects, of which a number stand out.

It was Ptolemy who actualized Alexander's dream of creating a new port city that would be the center

PHAROS LIGHTHOUSE

of Mediterranean trade and commerce. From its start, the Ptolemic dynasty was based in Alexandria, where it developed a new type of

---

10   Ptolemy "liberated" the island of Rhodes and for that the Rhodians called him Soter, or savior, a title which stuck to him.

bustling, vigorous port city encompassing Greeks, Jews, foreigners, and Egyptians.

In 290 BCE, he began to build the magnificent Pharos Lighthouse—one of the seven wonders of the ancient world—in Alexandria, which was later completed by his son, Ptolemy Philadelphus.

Ptolemy I created the famous Library of Alexandria and within it the Mouseion, Alexandria's famous ancient university. This scholarly center of collected wisdom would play a role in the eventual translation of the Torah into Greek. It was Ptolemy's son who enlarged the library and invited leading scholars from all fields to teach and study at the university. Ptolemy I himself had been a student of Aristotle together with Alexander. He was a thinker and a scholar known for his biography of Alexander, which is still used as a source of Alexander's life, and which remains the subject of heated debates among modern Greek historians.

Perhaps more significantly, Ptolemy I set in motion the foundations of a dynasty. Ptolemy is credited, therefore, for being the founding father of what was to be known as the Ptolemaic dynasty of Egypt, a family of fifteen kings and queens, including the Cleopatras, who reigned over Egypt for more than three hundred years. It was a dynasty of Greece in Egypt. Indeed, it has been claimed that only the last ruler of this dynasty—the renowned Cleopatra of "Anthony and Cleopatra" fame—spoke Egyptian!

Clearly, Ptolemy was following in the footsteps of Alexander. Like Alexander before him, Ptolemy was a Macedonian embracing Greek culture, philosophy, and wisdom. He initiated and built an Egyptian dynasty that was a Greek one.

E.R. Bevan, author of *The House of Ptolemy*, summarizes Ptolemy I Soter as follows:

> So far as we can see Ptolemy's personality through the mists of time, he was a robust, full-blooded Macedonian, with the sound common sense which often characterizes the leaders of a people of country farmers, the shrewd caution which looks a long way ahead, and likes to play a safe game and secure solid advantages…a man rather of vigorous bodily and mental

constitution than of fine fibre. Yet he was not without interest in Greek letters; young Macedonians of the upper class had learnt for a generation or two to talk Greek and read Greek; and Ptolemy was not only eager to get Greek men of letters and philosophers and artists to his court, but himself made, as an author, a very creditable addition to Greek historical literature—a narrative of the campaigns of Alexander distinguished by its plain adherence to fact and its freedom from rhetorical claptrap.[11]

The Jewish view of Ptolemy I highlights his negative actions vis-à-vis the Jewish people tempered together with his recognition of the value of the Jewish people to his empire.

Josephus describes how Ptolemy captured Jerusalem:

He also seized upon Jerusalem, and for that end made use of deceit and treachery; for as he came into the city on a Sabbath day, as if he would offer sacrifices he, without any trouble, gained the city, while the Jews did not oppose him, for they did not suspect him to be their enemy; and he gained it thus, because they were free from suspicion of him, and because on that day they were at rest and quietness; and when he had gained it, he ruled over it in a cruel manner...But when Ptolemy had taken a great many captives, both from the mountainous parts of Judaea, and from the places about Jerusalem and Samaria, and the places near Mount Gerizim, he led them all into Egypt, and settled them there. And as he knew that the people of Jerusalem were most faithful in the observation of oaths and covenants; and this from the answer they made to Alexander, when he sent an embassage to them, after he had beaten Darius in battle; so he distributed many of them into garrisons, and at Alexandria gave them equal privileges of citizens with

---

11 Edwyn R. Bevan, *The House of Ptolemy: A History of Hellenistic Egypt under the Ptolemaic Dynasty*, http://penelope.uchicago.edu/Thayer/E/Gazetteer/Places/Africa/Egypt/_Texts/BEVHOP/2*.html.

the Macedonians themselves; and required of them to take their oaths, that they would keep their fidelity to the posterity of those who committed these places to their care.[12]

The Letter of Aristeas provides some additional details:

> ...The number of those whom he transported from the country of the Jews to Egypt amounted to no less than a hundred thousand. Of these he armed thirty thousand picked men and settled them in garrisons in the country districts. As I have already said, Ptolemy picked out the best of these, the men who were in the prime of life and distinguished for their courage, and armed them, but the great mass of the others, those who were too old or too young for this purpose, and the women too, he reduced to slavery, not that he wished to do this of his own free will, but he was compelled by his soldiers who claimed them as a reward for the services which they had rendered in war.[13]

The *Tzemach David* concurs:

> Ptolemy was the first king in Egypt after Alexander in 3454 and he is called by the Sages Talmi the son of Lagos, and all of the kings of his dynasty are called for his name. And he commanded to begin to translate the Torah but was unsuccessful. He was an oppressive king towards the Jewish people and exiled more than 100,000 Jews to Egypt. He ruled for thirty years until 3484.[II]

Dorot Harishonim references the ploy used by Ptolemy on the Shabbat to conquer Jerusalem from an innocent, unsuspecting populace. He also concurs that the number of people exiled by Ptolemy from Jerusalem to Egypt was 100,000. But he also states that Ptolemy quickly came to realize that the Jewish people were always loyal citizens of their countries

---

12   http://penelope.uchicago.edu/josephus/ant-12.html.
13   http://www.ccel.org/c/charles/otpseudepig/aristeas.htm.

(as they were under Darius and Persia, and then under Alexander) and that they could be counted on to be so to him as well.[III]

Rav Avigdor Miller follows the traditional Jewish historians (and Josephus) in describing Ptolemy I Lagos as an oppressor of the Jewish community in Israel. At the same time, he recognized that the Jewish people were a loyal one as per Josephus' writings.

> *Despite their sufferings because of him, the Jews were loyal subjects of Ptolemy Soter. He entrusted the fortresses of Egypt in their hands, knowing that they would keep them loyally and courageously for him; and when he desired to secure the rule over Cyrene and other cities of Libya for himself, he sent a number of Jews to inhabit them.*[14]

This concurs with *Toldot Yisrael* who puts the number of Jewish soldiers at 30,000 [sourcing the Letter of Aristeas], thereby comprising a critical military force on behalf of Ptolemy. At the same time, he granted the Jews of Alexandria rights as citizens and put them in charge of the naval business activities, which were so critical to Alexandria's growth as a center of commerce and trade and to the overall financial stability of the Egyptian empire.[IV]

In the words of *Toldot Yisrael*:

> *And this Greek dictator realized that Israel was the sole loyal nation in those days who were true even to those who harmed them. He saw that the Jewish people kept their spirit with purity with their eyes focused on their work in harmony with the prophetic words of Tzefaniah 3:13: "The remnant of Israel shall not do iniquity, nor speak lies, neither shall a deceitful tongue be found in their mouth."*[V]

Ptolemy's actions are somewhat reminiscent of Nevuchadnetzar's approach. After Nevuchadnetzar destroyed the First Temple and exiled the Jewish masses to his own country, he trained the elite of the Jewish

---

14   Rav Avigdor Miller, *Torah Nation*, pp. 90–91; Josephus, *Contra Apion* II:4.

youth—Daniel being the most prominent of them[15]—to serve as his most trusted and reliable advisors. So too, Ptolemy was not an instinctive anti-Semite, but rather a practical ruler with his own agenda. He recognized the value and potential contribution of a strong Jewish presence and community not only in Alexandrian Egypt but also in other cities and garrisons under his control.

Rav Hirsch goes as far to say:

> *Not only Alexander but all the generals who succeeded him and who divided the conquered lands among themselves—the Ptolomites in Egypt, and especially the Seleicudes in Syria, and the immediate predecessors of Antiochus Epipanes—all without exception rendered respect to the Divine Law of the Jews who they had subjugated. Their decrees assuring freedom, protection, and support to those who demonstrated faith in the Law and their Temple, and the right to fulfill all their obligations under the law, have been preserved for our times.*[16]

---

15   The Book of Daniel focuses on two fundamental themes: the sanctification of God's Name and the historic structure of the Four Kingdoms. Chazal taught that the Four Kingdoms were designed as punishments for Israel. But at the same time, the Four Kingdoms enable the Jewish people to sanctify God's Name across the globe. The structure of the Four Kingdoms is the conduit, the framework, in which Israel in exile, as a people and as individuals, are tested over and over again. It is a heavy burden but at the same time a responsibility as well as an enormous opportunity. See Rav Yigal Ariel, in *Mor v'Hadas*.

16   Hirsch, *Collected Writings*, vol. 2, p. 228.

2. PTOLEMY PHILADELPHUS

After thirty-eight years of ruling Egypt, Ptolemy I decided that it was time to hand over the reigns of the kingdom to his son. According to Justinus (second-century CE):

Feeling the weight of years press heavily upon him—that he was less able than formerly to bear the duties of his office, and wishing to see his son firmly seated on the throne—he laid aside his diadem and his title, proclaimed Ptolemy, his son by Bernice, king…This is perhaps the most successful instance known of a king, who had been used to be obeyed by armies and by nations, willingly giving up his power when he found his bodily strength no longer equal to it.[1]

PTOLEMY PHILADELPHUS

Perhaps Ptolemy took to heart the intense, tension-filled relationship between Alexander and his father Philip II and appreciated the need to handle matters differently. Perhaps he saw the chaotic chasm left behind upon Alexander's sudden untimely death and the violent breakup of the hard-won empire and decided to proceed differently.

The succession to his son would therefore be seamless, steady, and smooth.

---

1   Sharpe, p. 62.

So, at the age of twenty-five, Ptolemy the Second (known in history as Ptolemy Philadelphus) became the sole ruler of Egypt.

It has been remarked:

> *Few princes ever mounted a throne with such fair prospects before them as the second Ptolemy. He had been brought up with great care, and being a younger son was not spoilt by that flattery which in all courts is so freely offered to the heir…and as he grew up he was surrounded by the philosophers and writers with whom his father mixed…*[2]

He began his reign with tremendous pomp and ceremony exhibiting the great wealth of Egypt. It was the inauguration party of all inaugurations, meant to impress and astound with its grandeur, signaling the continuation of his father's hard work in creating a future dynasty in Egypt. According to the historian Athenaeus (early third century) just a small part of his investiture included the following:

- twenty-four chariots drawn by elephants
- sixty chariots drawn by goats
- twelve chariots drawn by lions
- seven chariots drawn by rhinoceroses
- four chariots drawn by wild asses
- fifteen chariots drawn by buffaloes
- eight chariots drawn by ostriches
- seven chariots drawn by stags

Then came chariots loaded with the tributes of the conquered nations:

- men of Ethiopia carrying six hundred elephants' teeth
- sixty huntsmen leading two thousand four hundred dogs
- one hundred fifty men carrying trees, in the branches of which were tied parrots and other beautiful birds

---

2   Ibid., p. 65.

Next walked the foreign animals:

- Ethiopian and Arabian sheep
- Brahmin bulls
- a white bear
- leopards
- panthers
- bears
- a giraffe
- a rhinoceros[3]

Bevan describes in detail Ptolemy Philadelphus in contrast to his father:

Ptolemy the son was of a very different character from Ptolemy the father. The softening of fiber which became more pronounced in several of the later kings already showed itself in the son of the tough old Macedonian marshal…His education had been directed by Strato, one of the chief representatives of the school of Aristotle, and Ptolemy II's eager interest in geography and zoology was, no doubt, quickened by the attention devoted to scientific studies by Aristotle and his disciples. Yet probably the climate of Egypt had not yet changed the robust Macedonian stock in the second Ptolemy as far as it had done in later kings. He was of fair complexion, an obvious European, probably of a ruddy corpulence; there was plainly in the kings of this house an inherited tendency to grow fat in later life. Some constitutional weakness, or, it may be, too tender care for his own health, made him averse from bodily exertions.[4]

Ptolemy Philadelphus came to power with the help of his father and commenced his rule under the long shadow of his father's legacy. Historians credited him with being up to the task:

---

3   Ibid., pp. 66–68.
4   http://penelope.uchicago.edu/Thayer/E/Gazetteer/Places/Africa/Egypt/_Texts/BEVHOP/3*.html.

> *But Philadelphus…had more of wisdom than is usually the lot of kings; and though we cannot but see that he was only watering the plants and gathering the fruit where his father had planted…yet we must acknowledge that Philadelphus was a successor worthy of Ptolemy Soter.*[5]

Ptolemy Philadelphus completed the great lighthouse on the island of Pharos which helped thousands of ships navigate in and out of the harbor of Alexandria, now an international center of commerce. He also finished the royal burial site in the city and moved Alexander the Great's remains from Memphis to Alexandria.

The intellectual, cultural, and academic cornerstone of Ptolemy's Egypt was the Museum of Alexandria (university and library) which "held at this time the highest rank among the Greek schools whether for poetry, mathematics, astronomy, or medicine, the four branches into which it was divided."[6]

ANCIENT LIBRARY ALEXANDRIA

The staff of the Museum included the leading scholars, the "who's who" of the era. For example, heading the school of mathematics was Euclid, known today as the "Father of Geometry." Euclid's famous work entitled *Elements*[7] was studied as the main textbook for mathematics from the time of its publication until the early twentieth century. The work consists of thirteen books and it has been said that they were "the most studied books apart from the Bible."

---

5   Sharpe, pp. 65–66.
6   Josephus, *Antiquities* XII:2; Sharpe, p. 75.
7   The Greek philosopher Proclus who wrote about Euclid states: "Ptolemy once asked Euclid if there was not a shorter road to geometry than through the *Elements*, and Euclid replied that there was no royal road to geometry."

Regarding the Jewish nation, Josephus portrays a positive picture of Ptolemy II, in contrast to the negative one he painted of Ptolemy I:

> *When Alexander had reigned twelve years, and after him Ptolemy Soter forty years, Philadelphus then took the kingdom of Egypt, and held it forty years within one. He procured the law to be interpreted, and set free those that were come from Jerusalem into Egypt, and were in slavery there, who were a hundred and twenty thousand.*[8]

EUCLID

Furthermore, "The Jews who lived in Lower Egypt, in the full enjoyment of civil and religious liberty, looked upon that country as their home."[9]

The *Tzemach David*, sourcing a number of Jewish authorities, once again concurs with Josephus:

> *Ptolemy II, who was called Philadelphus the son of Ptolemy I, ruled over Egypt in 3484. He excelled in all of the wisdom, loved wise men, honored and supported them. He had a center for the wise men in Alexandria. He built the Pharos Tower [lighthouse] in the port of Alexandria as is written in Josephus. And Sefer Yuchsin wrote that he had 300,000 books of knowledge. And in Meor Einayim and in Julio it says he had more than 700,000 books from all of the wisdoms and languages from all four corners of the world. And all of these books were burnt by the army in wars of Julius Cesar and Pompey.*[1]

Toldot Yisrael describes how Ptolemy Philadelphus loved all knowledge and scholarship, thereby positioning Alexandria as the hub of the leading thinkers, mathematicians, and scientists of the time. Furthermore, even though he was naturally drawn to his own Greek cultural treasures,

---

8   http://penelope.uchicago.edu/josephus/ant-12.html; *Antiquities* XII.
9   Josephus, *Antiquities* XII:2; Sharpe, p. 87.

he welcomed the works of other peoples and supported the intellectual and cultural efforts of other nations.[II]

Ptolemy sought the good graces of the Jewish people in part because the capital Alexandria did not contain a majority of Macedonians and Greeks, and therefore the Jewish community was viewed as a welcome bulwark against the indigenous population and the numerous enemies within Ptolemy's own people. He also recognized that his rival Seleucid rulers in the north could favor the Jewish nation and leverage that relationship against Ptolemy's regional interests. This all led to a release of the Jewish captives and to the appointments of Jews at the highest echelons of the Greek-Egyptian regime. It also helped create a positive, friendly policy towards the Jews in the Land of Israel as well as towards the Temple in Jerusalem.

3. THE TARGUM SHIVIM

TRANSLATING AND TEACHING TORAH

The translation of the Hebrew Bible into Greek (what became known as the Septuagint) during the Ptolemaic rule has been called one of the major events in the history of the world.[1] Several questions stand out:

- How did that translation come about?
- Was it seen by Chazal as a positive event?
- Were there any precedents to translating the Torah into other languages in Jewish history?
- If so, how was this different?

PTOLEMY'S TRANSLATION AND MOTIVE

There are several Talmudic versions describing Ptolemy's request of the Sages to translate the Torah into Greek.

The Gemara in *Megillah* 9a states:

> *Rabbi Yehudah said: Even when our Rabbis permitted the use of Greek, they permitted it only for a Torah scroll because of the incident with King Ptolemy, as it was taught in a Beraisa: there was an incident with King Ptolemy that he gathered*

---

1   Nina L. Collins, *The Library in Alexandria and the Bible in Greek*.

seventy-two elders and placed them in seventy-two rooms and he did not reveal to them at first for what purpose he had gathered them. He then visited each one of them, and told them, "Write for me a Greek translation of the Torah of Moshe your teacher." The Holy One, blessed is He, placed counsel in each of their hearts and all of them independently arrived at a common decision about how to translate various words of the Torah.[I]

In Tractate *Sofrim*, two translation incidents are recorded. *Sofrim* 1:7:

> There were once five wise Jews who wrote the Torah in Greek for King Ptolemy and that day was difficult for Israel like the day the Golden Calf was made, for the Torah could not be properly translated.[II]

And in *Sofrim* 1:8:

> And again there was another incident with Ptolemy the King, who gathered seventy-two elders and sat them in seventy-two rooms and did not reveal to them why he gathered them. He went into each one and told each one to translate the Torah of Moshe your teacher. Hashem gave insight into the hearts of each and every one and they wrote the identical translations. And they made thirteen changes…[III]

The *Siftei Chachamim* commentary to *Megillah* connects the versions:

> There were two incidents with Ptolemy the King, and twice the Torah was translated into Greek. The first time five elders translated the Torah into Greek and they did not succeed in translating it properly. Therefore, he thought to bring a gathering of seventy-two elders to translate the Torah properly. The end of Megilat Taanit states that on the eighth day of Tevet the Torah was written in Greek in the days of Ptolemy, and darkness came to the world for three days…[IV]

Rav Avigdor Miller aligns Josephus' detailed reporting with the teaching of the Talmud:

> ...Ptolemy Philadelphus obtained a Greek translation of the Torah for his library in Alexandria. In return, he sent rich gifts for the Sanctuary at Jerusalem; and he also ransomed from his soldiery the many Jews who had been carried off as slaves in his father's time. The methods employed in obtaining this translation were not as princely as described by Josephus but as the Talmud related. Josephus, the flatterer of monarchs, represents Ptolemy as petitioning the High Priest to send Sages to Egypt for this purpose. The Talmud, however, reveals that the translators had no previous knowledge of their task; and Ptolemy commanded them to be confined in separate chambers to prevent collaboration in concealing anything in the Torah from him.[2]

Many—perhaps most—of the classical commentators express skepticism as to Ptolemy's real motive in commissioning the translation:

- Was it an authentic intellectual endeavor, an honest attempt to learn from the wisdom of the Jewish people?
- Was it actually a premeditated scheme to try to find errors, inaccuracies, contradictions, and inconsistencies in the Torah?
- Was it, perhaps, a subtle combination of motives and intentions?

The *Siftei Chachamim* commentary to *Megillah* views Ptolemy's goals in a negative light. He points out linguistically that the fact that Ptolemy specifically asked the elders to translate "Moshe your teacher's Torah" indicates that he was trying to prove that Torah was not God-given. That is was the handwork of man, of Moshe the man. The miraculous seventy-two-fold consistent translated result turns out to be the ultimate proof that the Torah was God-given![V]

---

2   Miller, *Torah Nation*, p. 97.

The *Ben Yehoyada* goes even further in his highly negative view of Ptolemy's intentions:

> It appears to me that Ptolemy wanted to malign the Jewish people and Torah. Ptolemy's name is the numerical equivalent (gematria) of Lilith, the symbol of the evil inclination, the other side. But Hashem did not abandon us, for the study of Torah protects us. For Talmud is the gematria of Ptolemy and if you break the letter yud in Talmi into two letters you will get the vav and daled, Talmud! And that which he gathered seventy-two elders was a sign from God for good for His kindness won over. The gematria of חסד (kindness) equals seventy-two, and the chessed was the miracle that all of the elders came to the same translation, and Israel emerged victorious![VI]

The Book of Our Heritage concurs:

> If Ptolemy wanted an accurate translation he could have from the start told the elders his intention and revealed to them the place and time for them to sit together; and they could go back and forth regarding any questions in the translation until they reached a similar conclusion…[VII]

The *Torah Temimah* (Bereishit 1:15) introduces his in-depth analysis of each of the changes made by the seventy-two elders:

> And that which specifically seventy-two were gathered is obvious that he [Ptolemy] intended that it be the number of the Sanhedrin and it's possible that the intention was to be sure of the authenticity of the translation. And even though the Sanhedrin is seventy-one men, as it states in the Mishnah (Sanhedrin 2a), in addition to the seventy-one there was one more person on top of them, and he was called "the excellent one of the Sanhedrin" and the total was seventy-two.[3][VIII]

---

3   The translation is called the *Targum Shivim*, "the translation of the seventy," even though the sources say there were seventy-two translators. This could be simply a case of rounding off

The *Torah Temimah* continues:

> *The purpose and goal of Ptolemy in this translation was possibly (as it appears from the changes that were done) to find fault in the Torah of Moshe. Therefore, he gathered them in seventy-two rooms and did not tell them in advance the reason for the gathering so that they wouldn't come up with identical versions. And it was Divine providence that even though they needed to make changes in the translation in order that he wouldn't have any complaints, nevertheless the translations of all seventy-two were the same!*[IX]

There is a discussion in Jewish sources as to whether the Greek translation of the Bible was the first of its kind.

MOSHE'S TRANSLATION

In the twilight of his life, as his nation was finally getting close to its elusive, ultimate, promised destination, Moshe Rabbeinu taught and reviewed the Torah for Bnei Yisrael.

It states in *Devarim* 1:5: "On that side of the Jordan, in the land of Moav, Moshe commenced [and] explained this Torah, saying…"[X]

It's clear that this review by Moshe of the law, of the Torah, was done **orally**.

And in his final review of the Torah to his people, on the last day of his life, Moshe commands them (ibid., 27:1–3, 8):

> *And Moshe and the elders of Israel commanded the people, saying: "Keep all the commandment which I command you this day. And it shall be on the day when you cross the Jordan to the land which Hashem your God is giving you, that you shall set up for yourself huge stones, and plaster them with lime.*
>
> *When you cross, you shall write upon them all the words of*

---

the number from seventy-two to seventy. It also calls to attention the concept that there are seventy facets to Torah. It is also a reminder that there are seventy nations in the world with seventy languages.

the Torah, in order that you may come to the land, which Hashem your God, is giving you; a land flowing with milk and honey, as the Hashem, God of your fathers, has promised you.

You shall write upon the stones all the words of this Torah, very clearly."[XI]

This command was one to **write** the Torah on the great stone.

That instruction was fulfilled by Yehoshua when Israel entered the Land, as mentioned in *Yehoshua* 8:32, "And he wrote there upon the stones a copy of the law of Moshe, which he wrote before the Children of Israel."[XII]

The commentators discuss and differ as to

- how many great stones were involved,
- where these great stones were set up,
- where they were transported to,
- when they were moved,
- what exactly was written on them.

Rashi, based on *Sotah* 32a, immediately comments on the **verbal** teachings of Moshe: "In seventy languages Moshe explained the Torah to them."[XIII]

The *Siftei Chachamim*, a "super commentary" on *Rashi*, explains:

We learn "seventy languages," since here it is written "expound," and in Chapter 27 "expound well." And the word היטב is the numerical value of seventy, when utilizing the "combined gematria" formula:

- ה is 5
- הי is 15
- היט is 24
- היטב is 26

The sum of these equals seventy.[XIV]

King Ptolemy

According to *Rashi*, we have a precedent for translating the Torah, and in this explanation it's an oral translation for the Jewish people.

Many of the commentators are troubled with *Rashi*'s explanation that during the oral teaching in *Devarim*, chap. 1, Moshe taught the Torah to Israel in seventy languages:

Why would the Jewish people need anything explained in seventy languages?

The *Ha'emek Davar* therefore qualifies *Rashi*'s interpretation:

> *This doesn't mean the languages of the other nations. It's clear that this is not the meaning of the verses but it means it was done for the nations of the world and not for the Jewish people.*[XV]

The *Oznaim L'Torah* makes a similar strong argument regarding *Rashi*:

> *"In seventy languages he explained to them." This statement is difficult to understand. For what purpose would Moshe explain the Torah in languages they don't know and never heard of? It makes sense when we are talking about explaining the Torah very plainly in seventy languages in order for the nations of the world to come and copy in their language and alphabet, but to explain the Torah orally to Israel in strange languages has no benefit. And I saw commentators who say it's seventy aspects to Torah. And it is correct.*[XVI]

Taam v'Daat is also troubled: "And this is the meaning of *Rashi*, that the Torah was explained very clearly: until matters were understood from within without any difficulties, as if it was translated into seventy languages."[XVII]

These commentators explain that *Rashi* cannot be understood literally. Still, on the other hand, *Rashi* specifically uses the term "seventy languages," which in other contexts refers to actual languages—the different languages spoken by the seventy nations originating from Noah.

The *Levush Ha'orah* "defends" the literal meaning of *Rashi* with a fascinating explanation as to why the oral teaching in *Devarim* was in seventy languages: Moshe wanted to make sure that everyone completely understood his review of the Torah and was concerned that some people did not fully understand Hebrew—Lashon Hakodesh! Moshe covered all of the bases in seventy languages in case there were some people present who would better understand in a different language![XVIII]

Perhaps the *Levush* is alluding to the non-Jewish "mixed multitudes" (*erev rav*) that went out of Egypt with Bnei Yisrael. Those people could have included Egyptians as well as non-Egyptians from different nations speaking multiple languages who were included in receiving the Torah.[4]

Imrei Shefer offers a different unique reason. Moshe saw that the Jewish people would ultimately be dispersed throughout the world and one day they would need to access the Torah in the language of their exile locale![XIX]

We do not know if the Torah taught and translated into seventy languages during the time of Moshe was preserved in any form until the period of that dispersion. The *Imrei Shefer* doesn't need to come to that conclusion; rather the intent of Moshe was to open a pathway for the Torah to be accessible in the other languages for Bnei Yisrael in anticipation of the future exiles.

The Talmud in *Sotah* (32a; 35b) elaborates on the writing commanded in *Devarim* (chap. 27) and fulfilled in *Yehoshua* (chap. 8):

> *Afterwards they brought the stones, built the altar, coated it with plaster and inscribed upon it all the words of the Torah in seventy languages as it stated: "Well clarified."*[XX]

The Rabbis taught in a *Beraisa* (*Sotah* 35b):

> *How did Israel inscribe the Torah? Rabbi Yehudah says they inscribed it directly on the stones as it is stated, "And you shall inscribe on the stones all the words of this Torah. And*

---

4   The *Zohar*, however, states that they were all Egyptians: "Who were the 'mixed multitude'? Were they Lydians, Ethiopians, or Cyprians? Were they not all Egyptians, and did they not all come from Egypt?" *Zohar, Shemot* 2:191.

> *afterwards they coated [the stones] with plaster."* Rabbi Shimon said to him, *"According to your words, how did the nations of the time learn Torah?"* Rabbi Yehudah replied, *"The Holy One, blessed is He, endowed [the nations] with an extra measure of insight and they sent their scribes who peeled off the plaster and carried away [a copy of the inscription]."*[XXI]

Clearly, we are talking here about a written translation of Torah for the nations of the world. As the *Tosafot* learn, the nations came to Gilgal, the entry point to Eretz Yisrael, every day to copy the Torah written on the great stones!

> *In the Tosefta, Rav Yehudah said it was written on the altar, but in the Yerushalmi he learned it was written on the stones of the encampment, and Rav Yosi says on the altar. The one who says it was written on the stones on the encampment holds that every day the nations of the world sent their scribes and they delved into the Torah, which was written in seventy languages.*[XXII]

One can only imagine the scene: the representatives of various nations making the trip to Israel's sizeable camp of millions, meeting and interacting with Bnei Yisrael; locating the plastered stones; peeling plaster, copying the text, and perhaps studying the holy words right then and there, with or without Bnei Yisrael. And all this as Israel is poised to attack and conquer the Holy Land.

The *Iyun Yaakov* spells out the extent of the exposure of the Torah to the local nations:

> *There were three types of stones, and the reason why there were three is so that the nations of the world would learn the Torah. And there are three parts of Eretz Yisrael: Judea, the Eastern side of the Jordan, and the Galil; it was therefore written on three stones in different places so if nations would come from each of the three lands they would be able to learn Torah. And this is according to the Tosafot who says that it occurred*

> before the war of conquest and the nations could have said that they wanted to convert and repent, to accept the Torah and commandments; and since they needed to be able to learn the Torah it was written in seventy languages.[XXIII]

The *Iyun Yaakov*'s approach contends that there was a real, sustained effort to expose the nations of the world to the Torah to show them the beauty of Hashem's message, thus allowing them the opportunity to become closer to Him.

The position that the Torah was open to the nations of the world in order to learn its contents is met with fierce opposition.

Oznaim L'Torah finds it difficult to understand why even the writing of the Torah, let alone any oral teaching, commanded by Moshe and fulfilled by Yehoshua, would be necessary in seventy languages.

Was there any hope that the nations of the world would accept the Torah?[XXIV]

Rather, the purpose of the writing in seventy languages, according to *Oznaim L'Torah*, was not for the nations to learn the Torah but rather for them to unambiguously understand and internalize that Eretz Yisrael was given by God to the Jewish people, and that the Jewish people have the singular (God-given) right to settle the Land. This explanation echoes the first *Rashi* of the Torah,[XXV] which states that since Hashem is the Creator of the world, He can apportion it to whom He deems fit. The message to the nations of the world in their own languages was a clear one: Stay away, the Land of Israel is off limits.

There are numerous opinions regarding what exactly Yehoshua wrote on the stones:[5]

- The Book of *Devarim*
- The Ten Commandments
- The Blessings and Curses
- A summary of the mitzvot
- The entire Torah

---

5   See *Yalkut Meam Loez, Yehoshua* 8:32.

Each opinion reflects a different approach as to what was revealed to the nations of the world. These disparities perhaps reflect divergent attitudes as to what is Israel's communal historic responsibility to convey to the nations of the world, from the basics of the faith to the entire corpus of the Torah.

According to Rav Yehudah, the text was written on the stones and then plastered. And as we learned above, God endowed the nations with an extra measure of insight, and they sent their scribes who peeled off the plaster and carried away a copy of the inscription.[XXVI] That being the case:

- Why cover the writing?
- Why make it harder for the nations?
- Why then give them extra insight?

The *Ben Yehoyada* suggests:

> *Since the stones were plastered, how did the nations know there was writing under the plaster? God therefore gave them insight to understand why the stones were plastered; for surely there was something covered by the plaster. And they sent their scribes, who were specialists in writing and wise in their deeds, and they peeled the plaster smartly so that the writing, even one letter, wouldn't get ruined. And they were able to copy the entire writing without anything missing. But in any case they did not learn it, even though they had it all copied!*[XXVII]

Some commentators hold that the plastering was done in order that the Torah not be taught directly from the Children of Israel to the nations, from Jew to gentile. This is in line with the prohibition not to teach Torah to non-Jews.

Oznaim L'Torah confirms this thought: "And if Bnei Yisrael would write the Torah on the stones in order for the nations of the world to copy it, then it would have been as if Israel was teaching the Torah to the nations [which isn't allowed]."[XXVIII]

This prohibition is not an absolute one, and the commentators throughout the ages differ as to what exactly is covered by the proscription of teaching Torah to non-Jews. Some would differentiate between teaching the seven Noachide laws which would be permitted versus the rest of the Torah. Others point out that if one intends to convert, then the prohibition to teach Torah to them does not apply.

Some would reference Moshe and Yehoshua to differentiate between the Written Law and the Oral Law.

This line of thought is entertained by Rav Moshe Feinstein:

> *There is reason to differentiate between the Written Torah and the Oral Torah. Perhaps it is not forbidden [to translate] the Written Torah, as we see Bnei Yisrael was commanded to write the Torah on stones in seventy languages when they entered Israel. This was done in order that all of the nations could copy the Torah and learn it [as is stated in Sotah 35b]. And if it is forbidden to teach [non-Jews] the Written Torah, then the incident would have been forbidden and we would have to say that it was only a one-time instruction in order that the nations not be able to claim that they had no way of learning Torah. And we only say that something [that Hashem commanded be done] was a one-time instruction [and not be seen as a pattern from which halachah can be applied] when we are forced to say so. And we can say that it's not forbidden to translate the Written Torah.*[6, XXIX]

Rav Hirsch sees the writing of the Torah in seventy languages as another meaningful expression of the universalistic approach of Judaism:

> *However, our Sages (Sotah 32a) interpret* באר *in accordance with that which is stated above (1:5).* באר היטב*, then, means that the words of the Torah are to be expounded, so that they may be understood. From this our Sages derive that this copy of the Torah included a translation, so that all the other nations would be able to understand it also. Far from the exclusiveness ascribed to it by outsiders, Israel was to understand from the*

---

6   Rav Moshe Feinstein, *Igrot Moshe, Yoreh Deah* 3:90.

> very outset that its mission was to help bring about the spiritual and moral salvation of all mankind.[7]

The Jewish people need not teach the nations of the world the entire Torah, the intricacies and the depth of Torah; in fact, they are prohibited from doing so. They, however, do need, says Rav Hirsch, to present to the outside world the values, morality, spirit, principles, and ideals of Torah. That, in fact, Rav Hirsch might argue, is the real Jewish earthly mission. Certainly Rav Hirsch would argue that this involves a total unmitigated allegiance to Torah, halachah, and tradition. Through a life led by consummate example, the committed Jew might best fulfill that mission. But that does not negate the mission "to help bring about the spiritual and moral salvation of all mankind."

Rav Kook takes a slightly different approach by clarifying that we cannot learn that it is permitted to teach non-Jews Torah from the instance of writing the Torah in seventy languages by Moshe.[8] We cannot use this one-time instruction to establish the halachah for generations. Rav Kook explains that at the time of the Exodus from Egypt and the giving of the Torah at Har Sinai, there was a special revelation that permeated the entire world with Divine providence that also touched the nations of the world. It was a unique event which helped the non-Jewish peoples recognize God, and access to the Torah was part of that achievement, but it did not continue. The eternal message is that the light of the world and the light for the world penetrate humanity through the light of Israel. Teaching the specific laws of the Torah to the nations can be counterproductive. The mission of the Jewish nation as the moral compass of humanity, however, remains an integral part of Israel's raison d'être.

The translation by Moshe/Yehoshua can be viewed as unique:

- First of all, the translation of the Torah at the time of Moshe and Yehoshua, according to those commentators who opine that there indeed was a translation into seventy languages, was commanded by God.

---

7   Hirsch, *Devarim* 27:8.
8   *Igrot Harei'ah*, Letters of Rav Kook, vol. 1, p. 103.

- Second, there is an argument as to exactly what was translated. Perhaps only parts of the Torah were translated.
- Third, it could very well be, following the opinion of Rav Kook, that this translation was a special one-off event necessary for its time.

The translation commissioned by Ptolemy contained changes from the original text.

In total there were fourteen changes,[9] as alluded to in the words from the *Mussaf* prayer: "מפני היד שנשתלחה בבית מקדשך—Because of the 'hand' that was sent against Your Holy Temple." The Hebrew word for hand is יד/*yad* which numerically equals fourteen (*yud* = 10; *dalet* = 4). The hand sent against the Temple caused that a hand needed to be sent to these fourteen (*yad*) verses in fear of the enemy, for if there hadn't been a destruction of the Temple and exile, the translators would not have been "handed" over to Ptolemy.[XXXI]

From the various accounts and commentators on Ptolemy's endeavor utilizing the seventy-two translators, we see the following:

- The translators received Divine assistance.
- The translators understood that while Ptolemy was truly interested in scholarship and collected manuscripts from all over the world for the Alexandrian university, one of Ptolemy's motives in having the Torah translated into Greek was to critically review it and possibly find fault with the Torah.
- They were extremely sensitive to how Ptolemy might interpret the actual verses, and therefore, changes were made in phrases and words to prevent any misunderstanding whatsoever. The changes also enabled the seventy-two Sages to avoid engaging Ptolemy in lengthy discussions regarding the deeper wisdom of the Torah.
- At the same time, any changes made were as close to the original as possible to avoid any outright untruths. The translation was

---

9   See Appendix A, "*Targum Shivim*—The Changes," for a detailed breakdown and commentary on the changes.

completed with the utmost intellectual honesty, and changes were made only when by not doing so it would negatively impact on sacred Jewish principles.
- It was paramount to ensure that the reading of the verses maintained the basic Jewish tenet that God is One, indivisible. The translation needed to secure the complete and total rejection of multiple divinities.
- It was similarly critical to guarantee that the reading of the Torah clearly stated that God was the Creator of the World, outside of the world and outside of time. There was no room for any view that smacked of deism or pantheism.
- The translation needed to preserve the completeness and unity of the Torah; nothing could be seen as missing or incomplete.
- The sanctity of the Shabbat was preserved.
- The translation required showing the "fairness" of Hashem to both men and women.
- Preserving the honor of the tribes and Moshe was critical.
- The translators understood that the perceived accuracy of the recounting of history in the Torah was necessary.
- The importance of maintaining the prohibition of idolatry by non-Jews needed to be emphasized.

Any reading of the Torah that involved concepts that the translators determined would be difficult for Ptolemy to accept, were avoided. These included:

- God "consulting" with the angels before acting,
- understanding the idea of "modesty" by God,
- the idea of an initial thought attributed to God followed by a different subsequent action,
- that the entire Torah is the Names of God,
- the inherent value of young people.

4. THE RESULT

Philo (20 BCE–50 CE), the Jewish Hellenistic philosopher and writer from Alexandria, elaborates on the miraculous nature of the translation:

Therefore, being settled in a secret place, and nothing even being present with them except the elements of nature...they, like men inspired, prophesied, not one saying one thing and another, but every one of them employed the self-same nouns and verbs, as if some unseen prompter had suggested all their language to them. And yet who is there who does not know that every language, and the Greek language above all others, is rich in a variety of words, and that it is possible to vary a sentence and to paraphrase the same idea, so as to set it forth in a great variety of manners, adapting many different forms of expression to it at different times. But this, they say, did not happen at all in the case of this translation of the law, but that, in every case, exactly corresponding Greek words were employed to translate literally the appropriate Chaldaic words, being adapted with exceeding propriety to the matters which were to be explained.[1]

---

[1] https://sites.google.com/site/greek4093spring2012/philo-judaeus-on-septuagint-creation VII 37.

The *Siftei Chachamim* concurs that the translation was miraculous:

> When the Rabbis permitted translations into Greek, they only permitted by the Torah [not Nevi'im and Ketuvim], and only because of the incident by Ptolemy. And I asked many scholars: "Because of this incident they allowed translations? Why?" And some of them explained because a miracle occurred from Heaven it showed that above it was agreed to write the Torah in Greek. And we see from the Rambam that through the incident with Ptolemy, even the Jewish people knew the Torah in Greek and therefore the Rabbis permitted the Torah to be translated.[I]

Remarkably, there were only fourteen changes in the entire translation. This, out of a total of 79,847 words in the Torah! At the same time, the seventy-two Sages made exactly the same changes—clearly as a result of Divine inspiration!

It is surprising, therefore, that the *Shulchan Aruch* (*Orach Chaim* 480:2) in recording the reasons for the fast day of Asarah b'Tevet says: "On the eighth of Tevet, the Torah was translated into Greek in the time of King Ptolemy, and the world was dark for three days."

The negative commemoration as part of the fast of the Tenth of Tevet is specifically referenced in the special *Selichot* prayers of that day.[II]

Furthermore, the translation is compared to one of the most ignoble events in Jewish history. Tractate *Sofrim* (1:7, brought above) states, "The day that Ptolemy first had the Torah translated into Greek was as harsh to the Jewish people as the day the Golden Calf was made."

Wasn't the translation clearly a miraculous event?

If so, what did the Sages see that caused them to view the translation so differently than the extraordinary occurrence of a Divine miracle?

Rav Tzadok strongly argues that the translation was actually the initial step leading to the ultimate persecution of the Jewish nation:

> The genesis of the Greek persecution/Shmad was a result of the translation of the Torah into Greek; the translation was done as the nations/Ptolemy felt the hod/majesty of the Jewish people. The request to translate the Torah was because

> they recognized the greatness of the Torah and Ptolemy honored the translators greatly; therefore the translation was done by the Kohanim; but the Sages perceived that it was the opposite of hod/majesty; it was destructive and they decreed it to be a fast day.[III]

The *Minchat Yitzchak* acknowledges the wondrous nature of the translation but explains why, despite this miracle, the translation was not beneficial to the Jewish nation.

> Others before have cried out before that which is written in Taanit and in the Tur that on the eighth day of Tevet the Torah was translated for King Ptolemy and there were three days of darkness in the world…but is it not written in Josephus and in the Meor Einaim that there was light and joy for the Jews, and they received great honors, and the nations recognized the importance of the Torah? [However] the Chatam Sofer explains at length that by translating the Torah into Greek, or into any language, the Jewish people began to taste the literal meaning of the Scripture and from this the skeptics and non-believers sprouted and did not listen to the words of the Sages of blessed memory and their commentaries.[IV]

> In fact, the Chatam Sofer writes that "when the Torah was translated to Greek the Jewish people were greatly honored and there were three days of darkness, just as there were three days of separation by the giving of the Torah and three days of fasting by Esther when the nation received the Torah with love and there was light for the Jewish people. This was turned into darkness as a result of the nation's sins, as people now learned Greek and adopted heretical views."[V]

Rav Tzadok, *Chatam Sofer*, and the *Minchat Yitzchak* all explain, therefore, that the translation had a far-reaching, undesirable impact on all of Jewish history.

Rabbi Moshe Spetter in *Translating the Torah Into Another Language*[2] proposes that there are two possible reasons why Chazal viewed the translation so negatively:

- Every translation necessarily involves interpretation, and the multi-layered meaning of each word of the Torah would inevitably result in a change in how the Torah's original intent is understood.
- The Ptolemy translation involved changes by the Sages in order to avoid Ptolemy finding fault in the Torah.

Dr. Aryeh Reich frames the question this way: If the Jewish people are to be a light unto the nations, and if the translation of Ptolemy was indeed miraculous with Divine intervention, why was it designated as a negative day?[3]

The answer, suggests Dr. Reich, is found in the wording of Tractate *Sofrim*: "The Torah could not be translated properly." Verses can be interpreted in a number of ways, and there is not just one explanation for any verse. Just as a hammer creates many sparks, so one verse has many explanations.

The Torah was given in the Holy Language, and only in the original language does it preserve all of its many meanings. The Sages throughout the generations have interpreted the verses, letters, and even the crowns (the decorations on the letters of a Torah scroll) for many laws and ideas. Anyone who translates the Torah can never preserve all of the meanings but needs to pick one meaning—usually the most literal—and set aside the others. This inevitably leads to a Torah that is static without the unique depth of the original text. This is apparently the meaning in *Megilat Taanit* that with the translation of the Torah darkness came to the world for three days.[VI]

Rav Moshe Adler explains it like this:

> The holy Torah is very complex to translate. There are seventy facets to the Torah. Every sentence has many interpretations.

---

2 https://torahmitzion.org/learn/translating-torah-another-language/.
3 https://www.biu.ac.il/JH/Parasha/eng/vayigash/rei.html.

The translations by Moshe, Yehoshua, and Aquila (student of Rabbi Akiva) were not a substitute for learning the holy Torah, but were rather meant as an aide for those who have difficulties, for the non-Jews, and for all who want to come close to Torah. It was clear that one who wants to probe more needs to learn the original. In those cases, there wasn't an attempt to translate the Torah precisely, rather the opposite; the purpose was to ensure that readers of the translation would know that this wasn't a substitution. But in the time of Ptolemy, the isolation of the seventy-two elders shows that Ptolemy wanted to ensure that the translation was true to the original; that it would be a substitution to the Holy Torah; that one could learn the translation in place of the Torah. This is the reason for the mourning and fast and explanation of the words that "The Torah could not be translated properly."[VII]

In *The Book of Our Heritage*, Rav Eliyahu KiTov concurs with the above arguments:

> Anyone who translates the Torah into another language will find that no language compares to the Holy Language in letters…
>
> What did Ptolemy do? He placed all of the treasures—the derash, the remez, the sod—in a box and only kept the literal interpretation. One who translates the Torah to another language is as if he presents it as an empty box.
>
> What is this compared to? To a lion that was hunted and caged. Before he was caged everyone was terrified and ran away; now everyone comes to look at him, and they say: "Where is his strength?"
>
> So too is the Torah, as long as it was in Israel's hand and interpreted by the Sages in the language, the Holy Language, everyone is fearful of it.
>
> And therefore the Sages compared this day to the day that the Golden Calf was made. For just as the Golden Calf was actually

nothing but its worshippers considered it to be real, so the translation of the Torah does not have the essence of Torah, however, all of the nations that see it believe in their heart that they already know the Torah, and they say about the Torah, "This is the Torah and we already understand it!"[VIII]

Rav Miller further argues that with the translation, the Torah was now positioned to be usurped from the Jewish people:

> The translation…was to result in great damage to the honor of the Torah. This was the beginning of the invasion of the Scriptures by the gentiles, who used the Scriptures to distort them into proofs for doctrines abhorred by the Torah. The sacred words which Israel had handled like precious gems were taken by the nations and debased in every way…[4]

It seems clear that for the Jews of the time, for the Alexandrian, Greek-speaking Jews, the translation and reception of it by the king, was a momentous, celebratory event.

Toldot Yisrael, who follows the Sages in their negative view, writes that at the time the Targum was:

> A beloved treasure in the eyes of the Jewish community in Egypt and it was given prominence in their synagogues as they bit by bit forgot the Hebrew language in favor of Greek. The day of its completion, the Jewish community went out to the quiet Pharos Island [adjacent to Alexandria] where Ptolemy had housed the translators, and there they ate and drank in celebration all day until the night.[IX]

The Sages' take on the event was different. They were able to discern the possible and eventual negative consequences and recognized that any celebration was to be short-lived.

They saw the big historical picture, wisely anticipating consequences that were not apparent at the time.

---

4   Miller, *Torah Nation*, p. 97.

The commentators emphasize that any tampering with *kedushah*—holiness, has potentially severe repercussions. The holier the object, the greater the potential for defilement. The more precious the relationship, the greater is the chance that just one wrong word can cause a breach. In the case of the Torah, God's revelation from above to man below, one is dealing with the holy of holies. When referencing the language of the Torah, we are dealing with the holiest of languages, and all holiness needs to be Fort-Knox guarded.

5. THE LETTER OF ARISTEAS

A detailed account of the translation of the Torah into Greek by seventy-two Sages is found in a historical document called the Letter of Aristeas (also named the Letter to Philocrates).

The letter is first mentioned by Josephus, who paraphrases around forty percent of the letter. Interestingly, this document is the first text that mentioned the famous Library of Alexandria.

The Letter of Aristeas is subject to intensive historical dispute.

Was it real? Or was it a forgery?

The document is a letter purportedly written by a non-Jew, Aristeas, to his brother Philocrates, and it deals with the reason behind the translation of the Torah into Greek. Aristeas writes as a courier at the royal court of Ptolemy II Philadelphus (reigned 281–246 BCE).

In addition to Josephus, Philo, the Jewish philosopher of Alexandria, discusses the letter in his work, *Life of Moses*.

In summary, the letter describes how Demetrios, the chief Alexandrian librarian, convinces Ptolemy to include the wisdom of the Jewish people in his wide-ranging library collection. According to the letter, Ptolemy agrees, frees Jews who had been in captivity, and then sends envoys with extravagant gifts to the High Priest in Jerusalem. The *Kohen Gadol* picks six sages from each of the twelve tribes, for a total of seventy-two translators. The king welcomes them joyously, discusses philosophical matters with them, has them translate the Torah, rewards them handsomely, and sends them back to Jerusalem.

The first Hebrew edition of the Letter was released by Azariah dei Rossi, an Italian scholar and physician in the sixteenth century.

The letter can be divided into six parts:

- Introduction (verses 1–8): Aristeas explains to his brother the background of how the Torah was translated from Hebrew to Greek.
- Part 1 (v. 9–82): Details how Ptolemy is convinced by his chief librarian to enrich the library with a translation of the Hebrew Torah. As a gesture of goodwill to the Jewish people, Ptolemy orders the freedom of 100,000 Jewish captives. Aristeas is sent with gifts to Elazar the High Priest in Jerusalem and asks for his assistance. Elazar responds favorably and prepares a list of seventy-two Elders, six from each tribe, to undertake the translation.
- Part 2 (v. 83–171): Aristeas describes Jerusalem, the Temple, as well as Elazar and the seventy-two Elders. Elazar provides Aristeas and Andrianes with an allegorical explanation of the kashrut laws.
- Part 3 (v. 172–300): This section includes a description of the Elders arriving in Alexandria and the warm reception by Ptolemy. The king holds seven days of feasts for the Elders and engages them in a range of subjects.
- Part 4 (v. 301–21): The actual translation and the return of the Elders to Jerusalem with great rewards. After seventy-two days (!) the Elders complete the translation and the work is read to the Jews of Alexandria, who praise the translation. The translation is read to the king, who is impressed with the wisdom of the Torah and is amazed that the words of the Torah are not mentioned in Greek literature.
- Conclusion: Aristeas tells his brother that he will write him again.

The Letter of Aristeas provides a wealth of detailed information on the translation. At the same time, its authenticity is questioned by most historians. However, it is possible to take the position that even if the letter is not completely authentic,

- as to its author—written as if by a non-Jew, though many say it was a Jewish author;
- as to the date of writing—written as contemporaneous to the translation, though many say it was written many years after the event,

it can still be used as a valuable source describing the translation.

SECTION III
VESPASIAN

The successors to Alexander the Great, including Ptolemy Soter and his son Ptolemy Philadelphus of Egypt, were the next generation of leaders of the powerful Greek Empire that now extended beyond the borders of the Hellenic city-states. Chazal place Greece as the third of the four historic world kingdoms, coming after Babylon and Persia, and preceding Rome.[1]

Control of the Land of Israel eventually shifted from the Greek Ptolemies in Egypt to the Greek Seleucids in Syria. The harsh anti-Torah decrees of the Seleucids under Antiochus led to the Maccabean revolt, and rise of the independent Chashmonian Jewish state.

EMPEROR VESPASIAN
(B. 9 CE–D. 79 CE;
REIGN 69–79 CE)

The appearance of the fourth kingdom, Rome,[2] however, changed everything. Pompey conquered Jerusalem,[3] ended Jewish indepen-

---

1   See Appendix B.
2   "The haughty Persian empire had vanished, and the Greek hero (Alexander) who vanquished it bowed before the priestly greatness of the dispersed (Simon the Righteous). But the Roman sword drove the sons of the Jewish Kingdom into further exile. They were thrown to the wild animals to provide amusement for the wanton Romans and sold like cattle on the slave markets. Thus, the momentous struggle with the Roman sword actually continues to this day." Hirsch, *Collected Writings*, vol. 2, pp. 392–93.
3   Josephus records Pompey's capture of the Temple: "Of the Jews there fell twelve thousand, but of the Romans very few and no small enormities were committed about the Temple

dence and incorporated Judea into the Roman Republic's empire. The harsh Roman rule ultimately led to the destruction of the Second Temple, massive loss of life, and the advent of a long, oppressive, and choking exile.

---

itself, which, in former ages, had been inaccessible, and seen by none; for there were in that Temple the golden table, the holy candlestick, and the pouring vessels, and a great quantity of spices; and besides these there were among the treasures two thousand talents of sacred money: yet did Pompey touch nothing of all this, on account of his regard to religion; and in this point also he acted in a manner that was worthy of his virtue. The next day he gave order to those that had the charge of the Temple to cleanse it, and to bring what offerings the law required to God." Josephus, *Antiquities* XIV:4.

1. VESPASIAN

Titus Flavius Vespasianus, known as Vespasian, was born in 9 CE in Reate (Rieti), northwest of Rome. He had a successful military career, commanding the Second Legion in the invasion of Britain in 43 CE and conquering the southwest of England. He later rose in the Senate to become consul in 51 CE, and governor of Africa a decade later. He became a trusted aide of the emperor Nero,[1] and was put in charge of the suppression of the Jewish Revolt (66–70 CE). His efforts succeeded and by 68 CE, most of Judea was recovered by Rome, although Jerusalem remained to be taken. Upon Nero's death, Rome experienced a year of turmoil as three emperors were killed in the span of one year, until Vespasian prevailed in 69 CE. His reign lasted for ten years until his death.

The claim is raised that Vespasian's moves in Eretz Yisrael were influenced not only by military objectives but also from a calculation, aimed at increasing his chances to become emperor.

> *It is claimed that Nero underestimated Vespasian, whose next moves indicate that he already had his eyes set on something bigger than the Judean campaign. In the winter of 67–68 CE, Jerusalem was immersed in a civil war between rebel factions that weakened the defense of the city. This would have been*

---

1   According to the Talmud in *Gittin* (56a), Nero eventually converted to Judaism and Rabbi Meir was descended from him.

the best time for an assault, but Vespasian refrained from an action that would have ended his position as leader of the Roman army in the east too quickly. Instead, Vespasian used this opportunity to restore his public name, win influence, and acquire financial support for political and military moves which he planned in Rome. Vespasian was biding his time and awaiting the right moment.

Such a moment arrived in the years 68–69 CE, during the Roman civil war, which is known (in modern historiography) as the "Year of the Four Emperors." Emperor Nero committed suicide and Rome sank into turmoil. During a single year, three different generals rose to power in Rome and were put down by bloody military coups, until the fourth, Vespasian, prevailed. Vespasian was declared Emperor by the Roman legions stationed in the East after he secured the support of the Roman governors of Syria and Egypt. This support resulted from Vespasian's machinations during his time in Judaea.[2]

The reign of Nero and the Year of the Four Emperors was characterized by its extreme instability.

Therefore, it is claimed that Vespasian's major objectives during his reign were to restore Rome's finances after Nero's wasteful reign, to restore discipline in the army

COLOSSEUM, ROME

after the civil wars, and to ensure the succession of his son Titus. He was successful in all three. The immunity from taxation that Nero had given to the Greeks was revoked, and construction of the Colosseum was begun in Rome with spoils from the conquest of Jerusalem.[3]

---

2   https://thetorah.com/why-did-vespasian-and-titus-destroy-jerusalem/.
3   Regarding the Colosseum and the Jews, upon the destruction of the Beit Hamikdash,

Roman historian Gaius Suetonius Tranquillus (69–122) sets the scene of Rome during the reign of Vespasian:

> *The empire, which for a long time had been unsettled and, as it were, drifting, through the usurpation and violent death of three emperors, was at last taken in hand and given stability by the Flavian family. This house was, it is true, obscure and without family portraits, yet it was one of which our country had no reason whatever to be ashamed...*
>
> *In other matters he was unassuming and lenient from the very beginning of his reign until its end, never trying to conceal his former lowly condition, but often even parading it.*
>
> *There had spread over all the Orient an old and established belief, that it was fated at that time for men coming from Judaea to rule the world. This prediction, referring to the emperor of Rome, as afterwards appeared from the event, the people of Judaea took to themselves; accordingly, they revolted and after killing their governor, they routed the consular ruler of Syria as well, when he came to the rescue, and took one of his eagles. Since to put down this rebellion required a considerable army with a leader of no little enterprise, yet one to whom so great power could be entrusted without risk, Vespasian was chosen for the task, both as a man of tried energy and as one who was not [in no wise] to be feared because of the obscurity of his family and name. Therefore, there were added to the forces in Judaea two legions with eight divisions of cavalry and ten cohorts...*

---

the evil Titus brought 20,000 Jewish slaves to Rome who were used to build the Roman Colosseum. Prof. Geza Alfoldy of Heidelberg University deciphered the original inscription on the Colosseum which reads: "Imp. T. Caes. Vespasianus Aug. Amphitheatrum Novum Ex Manubis Fieri Iussit." The translation is: "The Emperor Caesar Vespasian Augustus had this new amphitheatre erected with the spoils of war." According to Cinzia Conti, the director of surface restoration at the Colosseum, "There is no doubt what war this was—the sack of Jerusalem." It is estimated that over the years more than 400,000 people were killed in the Colosseum "games," and well over 1,000,000 animals killed.

> When he consulted the oracle of the god of Carmel in Judaea, the lots were highly encouraging, promising that whatever he planned or wished however great it might be, would come to pass; and one of his high-born prisoners, Josephus by name, as he was being put in chains, declared most confidently that he would soon be released by the same man, who would then, however, be emperor.[4]

---

4   http://penelope.uchicago.edu/Thayer/E/Roman/Texts/Suetonius/12Caesars/Vespasian*.html.

2. TITUS

Under his father Vespasian's tutelage, Titus was raised in the Roman military. After army duty in Britain and Germany, Titus commanded a legion serving his father in Judea (67). Following the emperor Nero's death in June 68, Titus was energetic in promoting his father's candidacy for the imperial crown. Licinius Mucianus, legate of Syria, whom he reconciled with Vespasian, considered that one of Vespasian's greatest assets was to have so promising a son and heir. Immediately on being proclaimed emperor in 69, Vespasian gave Titus charge of the Jewish war, and a large-scale campaign in 70 culminated in the capture and destruction of Jerusalem in September.[1]

Emperor Titus (B. 39–D. 81; reign 79–81)

After leaving for Rome to assume his position, Vespasian did not hesitate to entrust the conduct of the war on Jerusalem to his (inexperienced) son, Titus. This is because the Judeans posed no real threat, and the rebellion was considered to be a minor incident in the background of political intrigues in Rome.[2]

> Titus, of the same surname as his father, was the delight and darling of the human race; such surpassing ability had he, by

---

1 https://www.britannica.com/biography/Titus.
2 https://thetorah.com/why-did-vespasian-and-titus-destroy-jerusalem.

nature, art, or good fortune, to win the affections of all men, and that, too, which is no easy task, while he was emperor; for as a private citizen, and even during his father's rule, he did not escape hatred, much less public criticism.

Even in boyhood his bodily and mental gifts were conspicuous and they became more and more so as he advanced in years. He had a handsome person, in which there was no less dignity than grace, and was uncommonly strong, although he was not tall of stature and had a rather protruding belly. His memory was extraordinary and he had an aptitude for almost all the arts, both of war and of peace. Skilful in arms and horsemanship, he made speeches and wrote verses in Latin and Greek with ease and readiness, and even off-hand...Soon realizing his hope and left behind to complete the conquest of Judaea, in the final attack on Jerusalem he slew twelve of the defenders with as many arrows; and he took the city on his daughter's birthday, so delighting the soldiers and winning their devotion that they hailed him as Imperator and detained him from time to time, when he would leave the province, urging him with prayers and even with threats either to stay or to take them all with him.

Besides cruelty, he was also suspected of riotous living, since he protracted his revels until the middle of the night with the most prodigal of his friends...He was suspected of greed as well; for it was well known that in cases which came before his father he put a price on his influence and accepted bribes. In short, people not only thought, but openly declared, that he would be a second Nero. But this reputation turned out to his advantage and gave place to the highest praise, when no fault was discovered in him, but on the contrary the highest virtues.[3]

---

3   http://penelope.uchicago.edu/Thayer/e/roman/texts/suetonius/12caesars/titus*.html.

The divergent views of Titus found among (some) Roman historians, compared to those recorded in Jewish history, highlight the vast irreconcilable differences between Rome and Israel.

The Titus of the "highest virtues," extolled by certain Roman historians (as exemplified in the aforementioned quote) is as day is to night when contrasted to the methodically cruel, barbaric, and blasphemous Titus known and documented in Jewish history.

The so-called minor incident of the Jewish rebellion in Judea described by some Roman historians was a serious event for the empire, which needed to expend great resources and manpower to squash the Jewish nation.

The Talmud in *Gittin* 56b describes in astonishing details the role of Titus in the destruction of the Second Temple, leaving the reader with a picture of a bloodthirsty commander abandoning all and any of the "highest virtues."

> *Vespasian sent [his son] Titus who said, "Where is their God, the rock in whom they trusted?"*
>
> *This was the wicked Titus who blasphemed and insulted Heaven.*
>
> *What did he do? He took a harlot by the hand, entered the Holy of Holies and spread out a scroll of the Law and committed a sin on it.*
>
> *He then took a sword and slashed the curtain. Miraculously blood spurted out, and he thought that he had slain himself [euphemism for god], as it says, "Your adversaries roared in the midst of Your assembly, they set up their signs for signs" (Tehillim 74:4).*
>
> *Abba Hanan said: "Who is a mighty one like unto You O Jah? Who is like You, mighty in self-restraint, that You heard the blaspheming and insults of that wicked man and keep silent?"*
>
> *In the school of Rabbi Yishmael it was taught: "Who is like You among the gods [elim]? Who is like You among the dumb ones [illemim]."*
>
> *Titus further took the curtain and shaped it like a basket. He took all the vessels of the Sanctuary and put them in*

it, and then placed them on board the ship to show them in triumph in his city. As it says, "And I saw the wicked buried, and they came, and from the place of the Holy One they go away, and they will be forgotten in the city that they did so" (Kohelet 8:10).

A gale sprang up at sea which threatened to wreck him.

Titus said: "Apparently the power of the God of these people is only over water. When Pharaoh came He drowned him in water, and when Sisera came He drowned him in water. He is also trying to drown me in water. If he is really mighty, let him come up on the dry land and fight with me."[4]

A voice went forth from Heaven saying: "Sinner, son of sinner, descendant of Esau the sinner, I have a tiny creature in my world called a gnat. Go up on the dry land and make war with it."

When Titus landed, the gnat came and entered his nose, and it knocked against his brain for seven years.

One day as he was passing a blacksmith's, it heard the noise of the hammer and stopped knocking.

He said, "I see there is a remedy." Every day they brought a blacksmith who hammered before him. If he was a non-Jew they gave him four coins, but if he was a Jew they said, "It is enough that you see the suffering of your enemy."

This went on for thirty days, but then the creature got used to it.

It has been taught: Rabbi Phineas ben Aruba said; "I was in company with the notables of Rome, and when Titus died they split open his skull and found inside something like a sparrow two sela in weight.

---

4   Titus understood that Israel is compared to the moon, and as such, he reasoned that since the moon has power only over the seas, therefore God has power only over the water and not land.

> *A Tanna taught: It was like a young dove two pounds in weight.*⁵
>
> *Abaye said: We have it on record that its beak was of copper and its claws of iron.*
>
> *When Titus was dying, he said, "Burn me and scatter my ashes over the seven seas so that the God of the Jews should not find me and bring me to trial."*ᴵ

In Jewish history, Titus comes to symbolize the essence of the evil Fourth Kingdom, Rome. According to the "religion of Titus," the fight against the Jewish people was nothing more and nothing other than an eternal battle against the God of Israel.

The *Maharal* explains that Titus was the one who destroyed and burnt our holy Temple, and there was no other person in history like him in the fight against God Himself.ᴵᴵ

The *Shiurei Daat* states that Titus' profane acts perpetrated in the Holy of Holies were not random ones, but were rather an attempt to raise the power of impurity and have it rule the world. He realized that through his contemptible earthly blasphemy down below, he could somehow impact the force of impurity in the upper worlds.ᴵᴵᴵ

His deep understanding of the historical meaning of the Rome-versus-Israel narrative is captured in the incident regarding the famous proselyte Onkelos, his very own nephew.

> *Onkelos son of Kolonikos was the son of Titus's sister. He decided to convert to Judaism. He went and raised Titus from the dead by magical arts, and asked him; "Who is most in repute in the [other] world?"*
>
> *Titus replied, "Israel."*
>
> *Onkelos, "What about joining them?"*

---

5   "All in all, then, while certainty is obviously not attainable, I would argue that the Talmudic suggestion that Titus died of a brain tumour fits the facts, known and deducible, of the last fourteen months of his life better than any other hypothesis." The death of Titus: a reconsideration di Charles Leslie Murison, *The Ancient History Bulletin*, 9/3–4 (1995), pp. 135–42. http://www.geocities.ws/paginedistoria/murisondue.html.

Titus replied, "Their observances are burdensome and you will not be able to carry them out. Go and attack them in that world and you will be at the top as it is written, 'Her adversaries have become the head, her enemies are at ease' (Eichah 1:5); Whoever harasses Israel becomes the head."[IV]

ARCH OF TITUS

Even though Titus recognized the "truth" he could not overcome his evil nature, He was driven by a hatred of the Jewish people and attempted to battle God Himself.

3. RABBAN YOCHANAN BEN ZAKKAI

Rabban Yochanan ben Zakkai (b. 30 BCE–d. 90 CE) lived a full, productive, lengthy, and historic life. He was one of the greatest scholars, rabbis, and role models of piety and kindness in history.

In *Rosh Hashanah* 31b, it says: "Has it not been taught: 'Rabban Yochanan ben Zakkai lived altogether a hundred and twenty years. For forty years he was in business, forty years he studied, and forty years he taught.'"[1] Rabban Yochanan ben Zakkai was the prominent sage of his time and the venerated leader of his generation. His piety and devotion are described in *Sukkah* 28a:

> *They said concerning Rabban Yochanan ben Zakkai that during his whole life,*
>
> - *he never uttered mundane words,*
> - *he never walked four steps without [studying the] Torah or without tefillin,*
> - *never was any man earlier than he in the house of study,*
> - *never did he sleep or doze in the house of study, nor did he meditate while in filthy alleyways,*
> - *no one was left in the house of study when he went out,*

- never did anyone ever find him sitting in silence—only sitting and learning,
- no one but himself ever opened the door to his disciples,
- he never said anything which he had not heard from his teacher,
- he never said, "It is time to stop our studies at the house of study," except on the eves of Passover and Yom Kippur.[II]

It is brought down in *Berachot* 17a that no man ever gave him a greeting first, not even a heathen in the street.[III]

This attribute highlights a refinement of character. "If someone is quick to greet any person in the street, that shows that he really and truly respects every person as he is, regardless of his deeds, ethnic origin, or religion. It makes sense that Rabbi Yochanan ben Zakkai should be the one to find a way to respect even a thief."[1]

Rabban Yochanan ben Zakkai has been depicted as follows:

> Rabban Yochanan ben Zakkai was a mysterious figure and we don't know much about his family. Zakkai was an appellation and not the name of his father. His brother-in-law was the head of the zealots in Jerusalem, and Rabban Yochanan became head of the Pharisees when the traditional family of leaders (the descendants of Rabban Gamliel, Hillel, and King David) were forced into hiding. When Rabban Gamliel was allowed to emerge from hiding, Rabban Yochanan ben Zakkai worked to put Rabban Gamliel back into a leadership position, and made himself scarce so as not to infringe on Rabban Gamliel's position.[2]

The Talmud in *Berachot* 28b describes the sobering, chilling visit of his disciples during their teacher's final days:

---

1   Said in the name of Rabbi Menachem Mendel Schneerson, the Lubavitcher Rebbe. http://www.chabadbasel.com/templates/blog/post.asp?AID=2570355andpostid=58920andp=1.
2   http://www.torahlab.org/outoftheloop/devarim_nechmadim_on_avos_chapter_two/.

When Rabban Yochanan ben Zakkai fell ill, his disciples went in to visit him.

When he saw them, he began to weep.

His disciples said: "Lamp of Israel, pillar of the right hand, mighty hammer! Why are you weeping?"

He replied: "If I were being taken today before a human king who is here today and gone tomorrow, whose anger with me does not last forever, who if he imprisons me does not imprison me forever; who if he puts me to death does not put me to everlasting death, and whom I can persuade with words and bribe with money, even so I would weep.

"Now that I am being taken before the supreme King of Kings, the Holy One, blessed is He, Who lives and endures for ever and ever, Whose anger is an everlasting anger, Who if He imprisons me imprisons me forever; Who if He puts me to death puts me to death forever, and Whom I cannot persuade with words or bribe with money—say no more.

"When there are two ways before me, one leading to Paradise and the other to Gehinnom, and I do not know by which I shall be taken, shall I not weep?"

They said to him: "Master, bless us."

He said to them: "May it be God's will that the fear of Heaven shall be upon you like the fear of flesh and blood."

His disciples said: "Is that all?"

He said to them: "If only you can attain this! You can see how important this is, because when a man wants to commit a transgression, he says to himself, 'I hope no man will see me.'"[IV]

Rabban Yochanan epitomized Torah wisdom, as the Talmud in *Sotah* 49b declares:

"When Rabban Yochanan ben Zakkai died, wisdom ceased."[V]

4. YAVNEH

As Vespasian advanced on his stranglehold siege of Jerusalem and prepared his next moves against the Jewish community, the situation bordered on the catastrophic. The state of affairs during this period was dissimilar to that which tragically occurred subsequent to the destruction of the First Temple. During the former time, the actions of the Babylonian opponent against Israel were geopolitical; they were not fighting the Jewish people and the Torah per se. Furthermore, after that immense destruction and exile, the Jewish people found relief by the rivers of Babylon. They reached the centers of Babylon, built new homes, became valued members of the royal court, and created a new lasting polity as per the instructive messages of the prophet Yirmiyahu (*Yirmiyahu* 29:5–7).[1]

The Romans were very different. A built-up animosity towards the Jewish people, its Torah, its uniqueness, and its claim to a "manifest destiny" exploded in frightening proportions.[1] This viral hatred found expression in massacres in other parts of the empire, such as Egypt,

---

1   "In the times of the Second Temple the Jewish people faced two enemies, initially the Greeks and then the Romans. The two of them had different methods of war. The Romans plundered, robbed, murdered, and destroyed everything that stood in their way, until the Temple was totally destroyed without any hope for restoration. The Greek approach was strange. They did not plunder or destroy, did not rob or murder, for they did not want to destroy and annihilate but rather they aimed to defile and make impure. Rav Tzvi Schechter, *Nefesh HaRav*, p. 144.

Syria, and elsewhere. The situation could quickly have turned even worse, whereby the destruction of the land could have led to the destruction of the entire nation and its consecrated mission.

Torah leaders, led by Rabban Yochanan ben Zakkai, were faced with a staggering dilemma and almost unearthly choices. Rav Joseph B. Soloveitchik explains that Rabban Yochanan faced an impossible choice. Should he ask for Jerusalem and the Temple but risk losing everything, or should he ask for the Sages of Yavneh, enabling Jewish survival but relinquishing the Temple? Rabban Yochanan had to make the decision immediately without consultation with his colleagues. Neither could he find the answer in any book of Jewish law; he had to rely on his intuitive judgment alone.[2]

Dorot Harishonim remarks:

> *Their eyes and heart were focused on how to extricate the nation from this upheaval. On how to uplift the nation, now faced with the destruction, through a new location earmarked to be the heart of the people. A new center which even during the war could rehabilitate the Jewish nation. They needed to create a fresh focal point from which to send out a bright light of hope to the people. A place on which the people could lean upon and garner emotional, physical and spiritual support.*[II]

This endeavor was to be done inside the Holy Land, not outside. It was to be done under Roman rule and with the permission of Rome. Faced between the relentlessly destructive Roman legions and the extreme Jewish factions fighting to the death under a scorched-earth policy, they realized that, most likely, the physical Jerusalem was destined to be destroyed. The spiritual spark needed to be preserved, albeit outside of Jerusalem.

---

2 http://blog.webyeshiva.org/aggada-insight-the-death-bed-scene-of-r-yohanan-ben-zakkai/. According to Rav Soloveitchik, only zealots think that easy answers exist to such questions. Those aware of the complexity of questions of national significance which demand balancing competing ideals understand our lack of confidence in making such decisions. In fact, even years after the event, we remain unsure what the right decision was. For the remainder of his life, Rabban Yochanan ben Zakkai lived with the nagging question that perhaps he should have asked to save the city.

The dramatic events unfolded as recorded in *Gittin* 56a.

> *Abba Sikra the head of the zealots (Biryonim) in Jerusalem was the son of the sister of Rabban Yochanan ben Zakkai.*
>
> *Rabban Yochanan sent a message to him: "Come to visit me privately."*
>
> *When Abba Sikra came, Rabban Yochanan said, "How long are you going to carry on in this way and kill all the people with starvation?"*
>
> *He replied, "What can I do? If I say a word to the others, they will kill me."*
>
> *He said, "Devise some plan for me to escape. Perhaps I shall be able to save a little."*
>
> *Abba Sikra said, "Pretend to be ill and let everyone come to inquire about you. Bring something with a stench and put it by you so that they will say you are dead. Let your disciples, but no others, go under your bed, so that they do not notice that you are still light (since they know that a living being is lighter than a corpse)."*
>
> *He did so, and Rabbi Eliezer went under the bier from one side and Rabbi Yehoshua from the other. When they reached the door, some men wanted to lance the bier.*
>
> *Abba Sikra said to them, "Shall the Romans say, 'They have pierced their Master?'"*
>
> *They wanted to give it a push. He said to them, "Shall they say that they pushed their Master?"*
>
> *They opened a town gate and he got out. When Rabban Yochanan ben Zakkai reached the Romans he said, "Peace to you, O king, peace to you, O king."*
>
> *Vespasian said, "Your life is forfeit on two counts: one, because I am not a king and you call me king; and second, if I am a king, why did you not come to me before now?"*

He replied, "As for your saying that you are not a king, in truth you are a king, since if you were not a king, Jerusalem would not be delivered into your hand, as it is written, 'And Lebanon shall fall by a mighty one' (Yeshayahu 10:34). 'Mighty one' is an epithet applied only to a king, as it is written, 'And their mighty one shall be of them…' (Yirmiyahu 30:21); and 'Lebanon' refers to the Sanctuary, as it says, 'This goodly mountain and Lebanon' (Devarim 3:25).

"As for your question, why if you are a king, did I not come to you till now? The answer is that the zealots did not let me go."

Vespasian said to him, "If there is a jar of honey with a serpent wound around it, would they not break the jar to get rid of the serpent?"

He could give no answer.

Rabbi Yosef, or as some say, Rabbi Akiva, applied to him the verse, "He turns the wise backwards and makes their knowledge foolish" (Yeshayahu 44:25).

He should have said to him, "We take a pair of tongs and grip the snake and kill it, and leave the jar intact."

At this point a messenger came to Vespasian from Rome saying: "The emperor is dead, and the notables of Rome have decided to make you emperor."

He had just finished putting on one boot and when he tried to put on the other he could not. He tried to take off the first but it would not come off. He said, "What is the meaning of this?"

Rabbi Yochanan ben Zakkai said to him, "Do not worry; the good news has done it, as it says, 'Good news fattens the bone' (Mishlei 15:30).

"What is the remedy? Let someone whom you dislike come and pass before you, as it is written, "A broken spirit dries the bones (ibid., 17:22)."

He did so, and the boot went on.

> He said, "Seeing that you are so wise, why did you not come to me till now?"
>
> He said, "Have I not told you?"
>
> He retorted, "I too have told you. I am now going, and will send someone to take my place. You can, however, make a request of me and I will grant it."
>
> Rabban Yochanan ben Zakkai said, "Give me Yavneh and its wise men, and the dynasty of Rabban Gamliel, and physicians to heal Rabbi Tzadok."
>
> Rabbi Yosef, or some say Rabbi Akiva, applied to him the verse, "He turns the wise backwards and makes their knowledge foolish" (Yeshayahu 44:25).
>
> He ought to have said to him: "Let the Jews off this time!"
>
> He, however, thought that Vespasian would not grant so much if he asked for everything, and therefore even a little would not be saved.[III]

The same episode is brought down in *Avot d'Rabi Natan* as follows:

> Vespasian said to him, "You are Rabban Yochanan ben Zakkai, ask what you want me to give you."
>
> He replied, "I only want to request Yavneh. I will go there to teach my students, establish the prayers, and fulfill all of the commandments of the Torah."
>
> Vespasian said to him, "Go, and all that you want to do, go do it."
>
> Rabban Yochanan ben Zakkai said, "Do you want me to say one thing to you?"
>
> Vespasian said, "Speak."
>
> He said, "You will be emperor."
>
> Vespasian replied, "How do you know?"
>
> Rabban Yochanan told him, "It is our tradition that the Holy Temple cannot fall to a commoner but rather it will fall only to a king."

> *Shortly thereafter a messenger came with the news that the Caesar died and that Vespasian was chosen as the next emperor.*[IV]

Rabban Yochanan ben Zakkai chose to secure what he termed a *hatzalah purta*—a small saving. Given the dire situation and the potentially even worse results, the "small saving" turned out to be a great one. It was an act that helped later unify the people and, as noted, was accomplished with the permission of the Romans.

Rabban Yochanan tried to unify the nation without the Romans recognizing the full impact of his actions. Yavneh was to be that unifying force for the entire nation. From the text in *Avot d'Rabi Natan*, Rabban Yochanan openly declared his intent to teach his students, i.e., to raise a new generation of scholars and leaders to guide the Jewish people.

At the time, however, Rabban Yochanan's fateful decision came under heavy fire from his colleagues, including Rabbi Akiva.

The *Maharal* explains the deeply spiritual significance behind the three separate requests. He contends that Rabban Yochanan's intent was that the three requests mirror three key Divine attributes of God:

- First, the Almighty relates to the world and all of his creations with *chessed*, acts of kindness. The Sages are attached to the attribute of *chessed*, therefore he requested Yavneh and its Sages.
- Second, He acts with justice. Rav Tzadok had been fasting for forty years, an act of strict "*din*," and saving him would tap into the attribute of *din*/justice.
- Third, God's attribute of mercy permeates throughout all His creations. He asked to preserve the family of Rabban Gamliel as God had mercy on them due to their lineage.[V]

By attaching the requests to these three attributes of God, the *Maharal* learns, Rabban Yochanan ben Zakkai could help ensure the continuity of Torah for the Jewish people.

HaRav Aharon Lichtenstein contends that the requests made by Rabban Yochanan ben Zakkai can also be viewed as encompassing three fundamental levels of lifesaving caring and empathy:

- Individual—The concern for Rabbi Tzadok testifies to the importance of the individual in the eyes of Rabban Yochanan; he does not minimize or dismiss the suffering of the individual within an entire city that is under siege.
- Part of community—The second request is somewhere between concern for the individual and concern for the community; Rabban Yochanan asks for protection for the dynasty of the *Nesi'im*, the nation's aristocracy and oligarchy, a symbol of the Israelite monarchy which is no more.
- Entire nation—The third request represents concern for all of Am Yisrael; Rabban Yochanan ben Zakkai chooses Yavneh and its Sages.[3]

At the same time, the Talmud relates how Rabban Yochanan's colleagues were critical of his request: Why not ask for Jerusalem? Why settle for less?

Rav Lichtenstein proposes two possible answers:

- While Rabban Yochanan himself was able to predict the criticism that would later be directed at him for this decision, he felt that Jerusalem would not be given to him.
- The other possibility is that he perceived Yavneh and its Sages as being in some way preferable to Jerusalem. Yavneh was a town on the periphery which, at that time, was witnessing a boom in Torah scholarship. Jerusalem was a divided, warring city in which even the Torah was subject to disputes and was tainted with causeless hatred.

---

3   "Why Did Rabban Yochanan ben Zakkai Weep?" based on a *sichah* of HaRav Aharon Lichtenstein. http://etzion.org.il/en/why-did-rabban-yochanan-ben-zakkai-weep.

> Rabban Yochanan ben Zakkai elects to make a smaller request in order to be certain that his request will be approved. His calculation is realistic, pragmatic, practical, and based on facts. He makes his calculation out of uncertainty as to what exactly the Romans will be prepared to allow. This leader of Israel adopts a self-consciously cautious approach; the spiritual future of the Jewish nation is not to be gambled with, and we do not ignore realistic, practical considerations. Sometime we are even prepared to suffice with "saving a little," so long as it is the more certain option.[4]

Rabban Yochanan ben Zakkai could very well have had a tradition that it was time for a new pathway in Jewish history. It was the moment, regretfully and tragically, to pivot to a post-Temple stage of Jewish history and an eventually long exile outside of Jerusalem and perhaps later, also outside the Land of Israel. This insight might have been buttressed by his assessment, not necessarily of the geopolitical, military situation (which indeed looked desperate and which he clearly understood), but rather based on his take of the internal state of a divided, divisive Jewish people torn apart by baseless hatred/*sinat chinam*.[5]

The competing line of attack argued that Rabban Yochanan's request was an enormous missed opportunity. Perhaps a similar approach found expression sixty odd years later when Rabbi Akiva supported the Bar Kochva revolt, based on his tradition that the post-Temple period could be a short one leading to the Third Temple.

In the *Talmud Yerushalmi*, Demai 3:4, Rabbi Yehoshua ben Kabsoy comments on the verse in *Bamidbar* 19:19, "The pure person shall sprinkle upon the impure person." He says:

---

4 Ibid.
5 Ultimately, Rabban Yochanan ben Zakkai was the great "preserver" of the Torah and halachah, not a "liberal" bent on reinventing Judaism. See Rav Hirsch's detailed analysis on Graetz's "subjective" examination regarding the actions, motives, and personality of Rabban Yochanan ben Zakkai in *Collected Writings*, vol. 5, chap. 2, "Rabbi Yochanan ben Zakkai: Preserver of the Law During the Destruction of the Second Temple."

> *I always understood this pasuk to mean that one pure person may sprinkle [the ashes of the parah adumah] on one impure person, until I learned from the "treasure house of Yavneh" that one person may sprinkle on many impure people!"*[VI]

Rabbi Meir Shapiro of Lublin explained the "treasure house of Yavneh" as referring to Rabban Yochanan ben Zakkai's request of Emperor Vespasian to grant him the city of Yavneh and its Sages. Rabbi Yehoshua was inspired by Rabban Yochanan ben Zakkai's words, which teach us the power of the individual to spread abundant purity. This single achievement of Rabban Yochanan ben Zakkai enabled the entire nation to continue learning and teaching Torah.[6]

The episode between Rabban Yochanan and Vespasian appears miraculous, as Rabban Yochanan is able to predict at that exact moment that Vespasian will become the next emperor.

Aside from his keen understanding of the Roman political scene (including Vespasian's esteemed stature in the legions), Rabban Yochanan understood that in the epic historical struggle between Rome and Israel, only royalty could gain dominion over Jerusalem.

While the tradition teaches that Jerusalem will only fall to a king, the Alter of Novardok still asked the question: "But how could he take the chance and put his life in danger? We see that when Rabban Yochanan ben Zakkai approached Vespasian, he already saw a king. For him, there was no reality besides the Torah!"

In other words, this teaches that one must always place upon his or her heart and know absolutely that there is no real existence except that which is written in the Torah.

The Biala Rebbe applied this Gemara to the following story: When the Baal HaTanya was imprisoned, he was interrogated on numerous occasions. One day, the Czar of Russia decided to disguise himself and meet this rabbi, to decide for himself if the charges against him were true or false. Despite the fact that he was incognito, the Baal HaTanya

---

[6] https://www.dafdigest.org/Gittin/Gittin%20056.pdf; Rav Elazar Menachem Mann Shach, *Merosh Amanah*.

greeted him as one greets a monarch. "But I am not the Czar, so why are you giving me this honor?"

"But of course your majesty is the Czar," the Baal HaTanya respectfully parried. "Earthly kingship is likened to heavenly dominion. Just as the heavenly beings are filled with fear and awe, I was filled with awe the moment your majesty entered the cell. Although I was interrogated by a number of noblemen and officers, I never felt such intense fear inspired by any mortal before!"[7]

---

7 https://www.dafdigest.org/Gittin/Gittin%20056.pdf.

SECTION IV
HADRIAN

1. TRAJAN

Following the destruction of the Second Temple in Jerusalem in 70 CE, Rome was led by a number of historic personalities. Historians of the Roman Empire have dubbed five successive Roman emperors from 96–180 as the Five Good Emperors.

- Nerva (96–98)
- Trajan (98–117)
- Hadrian (117–138)
- Antoninus Pius (138–161)
- Marcus Aurelius (161–180)

Towards the end of his reign, the childless Emperor Nerva[1] officially adopted Ulpius Traianus, otherwise known as Trajan, then the recently-named governor of Upper Germany. Upon Nerva's death in 98, Trajan was declared emperor by the Roman Senate.

EMPEROR TRAJAN

---

[1] "In 81 CE, after a two-year reign, Titus died and was succeeded by his brother Domitian, a vicious anti-Semite. Troubled by the Jewish success at Yavneh, the new emperor's constant harassment forced the assembly to disband. Also plotting to exterminate the Jews throughout the empire, Domitian's decree was forestalled due to the intervention of a sympathetic Roman senator who gave his life to annul the edict. In 96 CE, after Domitian's assassination, Nerva, an emperor more favorable to the Jews, ascended to the throne. Relaxing many of the discriminatory decrees against the Jews, Nerva also repealed the annual tax that Jews had to pay to the temple of Jupiter." https://www.chabad.org/library/article_cdo/aid/2713657/jewish/Roman-Rulers.htm.

During his twenty-year reign, Trajan adopted a national policy of Roman expansionism and conquest. He fought two Dacian Wars (101–102, 105–106) in the area that today approximates Romania. In addition to its potential wealth, this area served as a strategic buffer between Rome and barbarians from both the east and the west.

When the King of Nabataea died, Trajan took over his land. What is roughly modern-day Sinai, the Negev, and Jordan all became incorporated into the Arabia province of the Roman Empire.

While Trajan's Roman Empire included territory that even Alexander the Great had not captured, it was still faced with an adversarial major power in Parthia, whose land covered modern-day Iraq and Iran. The only western regime to capture these territories was Alexander's army, four hundred years earlier. Rome and Parthia were particularly at odds over Armenia, which was considered a strategic asset for both of these competing empires.

ROMAN EMPIRE 117 CE

Gibbon, in his epic work on Rome, contends that Trajan attempted to be the Alexander of his time and actually gained many significant military victories, expanding the reach and scope of the empire.

> Trajan was ambitious of fame...The praises of Alexander, transmitted by a succession of poets and historians, had kindled a dangerous emulation in the mind of Trajan. Like him, the Roman emperor undertook an expedition against the nations of the east, but he lamented with a sigh, that his advanced age scarcely left him any hopes of equaling the renown of the son of Philip...He descended the river Tigris in triumph, from the mountains of Armenia to the Persian Gulf. He enjoyed the honor of being the first, as he was the last, of

the Roman generals, whoever navigated that remote sea. His fleets ravaged the coasts of Arabia; and Trajan vainly flattered himself that he was approaching towards the confines of India. Every day the astonished Senate received the intelligence of new names and new nations, that acknowledged his sway.[2]

Historians record that at this time, revolts broke out within the empire, including a number of Jewish revolts in different locations. Livius reports:

> The diasporic Jews of Egypt, Cyrenaica (eastern Libya), and Cyprus were among the rebels, but the newly conquered region of Mesopotamia was unquiet too. Their revolt started in Cyrene, where one Lukuas—sometimes called Andreas—ordered the Jews to destroy the pagan temples of Apollo, Artemis, Hecate, Demeter, Isis and Pluto, and to assail the worshippers. The latter fled to Alexandria, where they captured and killed many Jews. (With a population of some 150,000 Jews, Alexandria was Judaism's largest city.) In 116, the Jews organized themselves and had their revenge. The temples of gods like Nemesis, Hecate and Apollo were destroyed; the same fate befell the tomb of Pompey, the Roman general who had captured Jerusalem almost two centuries before.
>
> Meanwhile, the Cyrenaican Jews plundered the Egyptian countryside, reaching Thebes, six hundred kilometers upstream. The future historian Appian of Alexandria[3] records that he made a providential escape from a party of Jews pursuing him in the Nile marshes. There was nothing the Roman governor Marcus Rutilius Lupus could do, although he sent a legion (III Cyrenaica or XXII Deiotariana) to protect the inhabitants of Memphis.

---

2   http://oll.libertyfund.org/titles/gibbon-the-history-of-the-decline-and-fall-of-the-roman-empire-vol-1.
3   Appian of Alexandria (95–165 CE) was a Greek historian with Roman citizenship who flourished during the reigns of Trajan, Hadrian, and Antoninus Pius. Josephus' work *Against Apion* presents a cogent counterpoint to the vitriolic anti-Jewish writings of Appian.

> ...He [Trajan] ordered the commander of his Mauritanian auxiliaries, Lusius Quietus, to clean the suspects out of these regions. Quietus organized a force and killed many Cypriote, Mesopotamian, and Syrian Jews, in effect wiping them out; as a reward, he was appointed governor of Judaea. He was responsible for a forced policy of Hellenization.[4]

These events, placed in their historical context, point to an ongoing effort spearheaded by the Roman Empire to stamp out Jewish observance and tradition, especially in the post-Churban period. What is described as revolts were more like acts of self-defense, preservation of life, and resistance to attacks on the core principles of Jewish faith.

The traditional Jewish view is summarized as follows:

> *The emperor Trajan, who succeeded Nerva from 98–117 CE, was a vicious anti-Semite, and the Jews suffered terribly through his long reign. Dreaming of extending the Roman Empire beyond the countries Alexander the Great had conquered, even to fabled India, Trajan knew that Babylon, heavily populated by Jews, lay in his path. The Babylonian Jews found themselves in a terrible dilemma: Should they resist the Romans, thereby endangering all the Jews in the Roman Empire, or should they not fight alongside their Babylonian countrymen to repulse Trajan, and thereby being accused of treason? Alarmed at the prospect of all the world's Jews falling under Roman domination, the Jews of Babylon chose the former. As such, the Romans conquered Babylon, but held it only a short time.*
>
> *Infuriated by the Jewish role in Trajan's defeat, the anti-Semitic Greeks of Alexandria, Egypt, assisted by Roman troops, instigated pogroms against the Alexandrian Jews, the largest Jewish population of any city in the Roman Empire. Many*

---

4   http://www.livius.org/articles/concept/roman-jewish-wars/roman-jewish-wars-7/.

Jews had assembled for prayer at the Great Synagogue,⁵ which was so vast that sextons standing with flags indicated the time to respond Amen to the blessings. At prayer, the Jews were massacred to the last person.⁶

When the Jews of Cyprus and Libya discovered what had happened to the empire's largest and wealthiest Jewish community, they readied themselves to resist the inevitable attacks. Taking their preparations as a sign of incipient revolt, Trajan sent Roman legions to assist the Greeks in wiping out the Jews. To this day, Church historians, full of malice toward Jews, have distorted these events, stating that the Jews both attempted a general uprising against Rome and engaged in wholesale massacres of Greeks and Romans. However, papyrus writings of that period indicate that the Greeks were the instigators.⁷

Before being able to quell the revolts and resume his expansionist military campaigns in the east, Trajan died.⁸ With him, the current quest of a greater Roman Empire also expired.

---

5   The Talmud in *Sukkah* (51b) describes the Great Synagogue as follows: Rabbi Yehudah stated, "One who has not seen the double colonnade of Alexandria in Egypt has never seen the glory of Israel. It was said that it was like a huge basilica, one colonnade within the other, and it sometimes held twice the number of people that left Egypt during the Exodus. There were in it seventy-one cathedras of gold, corresponding to the seventy-one members of the Great Sanhedrin, not one of them containing less than twenty-one pieces of gold. There was a wooden platform in the middle on which the attendant of the synagogue stood with a scarf in his hand."

6   *Sukkah* 51b: Abaye stated, "Alexander of Macedon [this should read Trajan; see Vilna Gaon] slew them all. Why were they punished? Because they transgressed this verse: 'You shall not return that way [back to Egypt] any more' (*Devarim* 17:16), and they did return. When he came and found them reading from the Torah, 'The Lord will bring upon you a nation afar' (ibid., 28:49), he remarked, 'I should have brought my ships in a ten days' journey, but as a strong wind arose the ships arrived in five days'! He, therefore, fell upon them and slew them."
According to the Vilna Gaon and the *Yerushalmi*, the emperor was Trajan. Rav Yaakov Emden and the *Abarbanel* claim it was the Roman leader Alexander Latirus. And a third opinion would be Hadrian, as indicated in *Gittin* 57b. But it seems clear that the text of Alexander (the Great) is incorrect, as he lived much earlier than this incident.

7   https://www.chabad.org/library/article_cdo/aid/2713657/jewish/Roman-Rulers.htm.

8   http://biography.yourdictionary.com/trajan.

But the death of Trajan soon clouded the splendid prospect; and it was justly to be dreaded that so many distant nations would throw off the unaccustomed yoke, when they were no longer restrained by the powerful hand which had imposed it.[9]

---

[9] http://oll.libertyfund.org/titles/gibbon-the-history-of-the-decline-and-fall-of-the-roman-empire-vol-1.

2. HADRIAN

HADRIAN

Trajan died without leaving a clear acknowledged heir. Through a series of manipulations attributed to Trajan's surviving wife, Empress Plotina, Hadrian was recognized as the adopted son of Trajan and declared Emperor of Rome.[1]

The contrasts in policy between Trajan and his adopted heir to the throne, Hadrian, were glaring. *Dorot Harishonim* points out:

> *Hadrian was the very opposite from Trajan, for Trajan was a man of war and lived by his sword. Whereas Trajan enraged all of the nations with his wars, Hadrian attempted to make peace with all of the nations, and even in Babylon where Trajan prepared his soldiers for war a second time, Hadrian pulled Rome out of the fray.[1]*

---

1 "Hadrian had not been adopted by Trajan; he was merely a compatriot and former ward of his, was of near kin to him and had married his niece, yet he had received no distinguishing mark of favour from Trajan, such as being one of the first to be appointed consul. He became Caesar and emperor owing to the fact that when Trajan died childless, Attianus, a compatriot and former guardian of his, together with Plotina, who was in love with him, secured him the appointment."
http://penelope.uchicago.edu/Thayer/E/Roman/Texts/Cassius_Dio/69*.html.

Hadrian's role as a pursuer of global peace is described as follows:

> Hadrian abandoned all these eastern conquests and announced that he intended to consolidate the empire on an "as is" basis; there would be no more forward policies, no more expansionism. It is common criticism of Hadrian that he failed to grasp that the Roman Empire was always a dominion of conquest and, like the shark, needed to keep swimming continually.²

HADRIAN'S WALL

At the same time Hadrian was not viewed as a man without ambition. The salient personality traits of Hadrian are described by Cassius Dio as follows:

> Hadrian was a pleasant man to meet and he possessed a certain charm. By nature, he was fond of literary study in both the Greek and Latin languages, and has left behind a variety of prose writings as well as compositions in verse. For his ambition was insatiable, and hence he practiced all conceivable pursuits, even the most trivial; for example, he modeled and painted, and declared that there was nothing pertaining to peace or war, to imperial or private life, of which he was not cognizant. All this, of course, did people no harm; but his jealousy of all who excelled in any respect was most terrible and caused the downfall of many, besides utterly destroying several. For, inasmuch as he wished to surpass everybody in everything, he hated those who attained eminence in any direction.³

---

2   Frank McLynn, *Marcus Aurelius* (Cambridge, MA: Da Capo Press, 2009), pp. 25–26.
3   http://penelope.uchicago.edu/Thayer/E/Roman/Texts/Cassius_Dio/69*.html.

At the beginning of his twenty-year rule, Hadrian exhibited the quality of peacemaker, not only to the world at large but also towards the Jewish people. "The early years of Hadrian's reign appeared like a ray of light for the Jewish people. Quickly that ray of light disappeared and the sky began to darken until it became a thick cloud and darkness covered the land."[II]

Dorot Harishonim explains that the Sages saw this initial glimmer of light and moved quickly to reconvene the Sanhedrin, the great assembly of learning which ruled and guided the Jewish people, this time in Usha in the Galilee. The absence of a central assembly for learning and decision-making harmed the Jewish people. It was from the assembly that the nation received its light and truth and helped advance communal life. In just the few years that the Sages were allowed to openly meet, they were able to take significant action benefitting the people.[III]

Dorot Harishonim continues:

> In the forty-seventh year from the Churban, Hadrian commanded to rebuild Jerusalem. This is consistent to what occurred years earlier after Trajan's rule, when Hadrian ordered that the destroyed Jewish homes in Alexandria be restored. When Hadrian became emperor, the Jewish people brought their cases in front of him and he found the Greeks responsible in the claims.

Quickly, however, the tables were turned. Cassius Dio writes:

> At Jerusalem he founded a city in place of the one which had been razed to the ground, naming it Aelia Capitolina, and on the site of the temple of the god he raised a new temple to Jupiter. This brought on a war of no slight importance nor of brief duration, for the Jews deemed it intolerable that foreign races should be settled in their city and foreign religious rites planted there. So long, indeed, as Hadrian was close by in Egypt and again in Syria, they remained quiet, save in so far as they purposely made of poor quality such weapons as they were called upon to furnish, in order that the Romans might reject

> them and they themselves might thus have the use of them; but when he went farther away, they openly revolted.[4]

The cause and effect of the "Jewish revolt" is debated by historians. But the Jewish people throughout history always had their red lines that were not to be crossed. Those lines were fealty to God, His Torah and commandments, while loyally observing the secular laws of the land.

> The fact is that what provoked the war and gave it its motive force had nothing to do with the messianic pretensions of Bar Kochva. The rebellion probably arose either because Hadrian had reneged on a promise to rebuild the Temple and instead proclaimed his intention to build a temple to Jupiter where the Holy of Holies had once stood; or because of the decree against the mutilation of the body, which implied a prohibition against circumcision. Whatever the reason, it touched the very heart of Judaism and endangered the future of the Jewish people.[5]

Rav Hirsch declares:

> The indomitable will to freedom shown by the Jews only made the Romans hate them all the more. In order to break the spirit of the Jews once and for all, the Romans raged with Antiochus-like violence against any observance of Jewish religious law and particularly against the dissemination of the Law and Tradition. Hadrian and his satraps and their underlings decreed torment and torture, death and destruction for any Jew who observed the Law and especially for any scholar of the Law who taught the Law and passed on the Tradition.[6]

That glimmer of a ray of hope present at the start of Hadrian's rule transformed itself into the darkest of clouds that led to sweeping gloom

---

4   http://penelope.uchicago.edu/Thayer/E/Roman/Texts/Cassius_Dio/69*.html.
5   Rabbi Bernard Rosensweig, "If Only My Rabbis," *Tradition* 23(3), Spring 1988.
6   Rav Hirsch, *Collected Writings*, vol. 5, chap. 12, The Decree of Lydda, p. 190.

and destructive doom. The *shmad*/destruction of Hadrian against the Jewish nation epitomizes the archetype of the worse of oppressions in the long history of the people of Israel. The pejorative appellation assigned when mentioning Hadrian's name as recorded in traditional sources remains to this day: "Hadrian, may his bones rot."[7]

---

7   See *Bereishit Rabbah* 10:3 and 13:9; *Eichah Rabbah* 3:8; *Pesikta*, chap. 21; *Midrash Shochar Tov*, Psalm 12; *Kohelet Rabbah* 2:20.

3. RABBI YEHOSHUA BEN CHANANYA

Rabbi Yehoshua ben Chananya was a leading Torah Sage during the tumultuous period before and after the destruction of the Second Temple. He lived through the regimes of thirteen Roman emperors: Tiberius, Caligula, Claudius, Nero, Galba, Otho, Viteelus, Vespasian, Titus, Domitan, Nerva, Trajan, and Hadrian.

He was a student of the great Rabban Yochanan ben Zakkai,[1] together with his colleagues Rabbi Shimon ben Netanel, Rabbi Elazar ben Arach, Rabbi Eliezer ben Hurkonus, and Rabbi Yossi the Kohen. He studied and mastered not only the entire revealed Torah but also the hidden wisdom of Torah, including the *Maaseh Merkavah*.[2]

Rabbi Yehoshua was a Levi who served in the Beit Hamikdash, as seen from *Arachin* 11b:

> *Rabbi Yehoshua ben Chananya went to assist Rabbi Yochanan ben Gudgeda in fastening the Temple doors, whereupon Rabbi Yochanan said to him: "Turn back, my son, for you are of a member of the choir and not one of the door-keepers."*[1]

---

1   Rabbi Yehoshua is mentioned as one of the two students who accompanied the casket of his teacher Rabban Yochanan ben Zakkai when it was surreptitiously taken out of Jerusalem.
2   The "Divine Chariot" vision of Ezekiel, where the *Keruvim* (Cherubim) surround the Divine Celestial Throne.

It is written in *Pirkei Avot*:

> *Rabban Yochanan ben Zakkai said about Rabbi Yehoshua ben Chananya: "Happy is she who bore him."*[II]

The *Talmud Yerushalmi*[III] supports Rabban Yochanan ben Zakkai's statement and records that Rabbi Yehoshua ben Chananya's pious mother would bring him as an infant to the assembly of the Sages so that he would hear the sounds of Torah learning. From infancy, Torah was part and parcel of his being, and he grew up immersed in all aspects of it.[3]

Sanhedrin 17b attests to his worldly knowledge:

> *Rabbi Yehudah said in Rav's name: A Sanhedrin must not be established in a city that does not contain at least two who can speak and understand all seventy languages. In the city of Beitar there were three such people and in Yavneh there were four: 1. Rabbi Eliezer; 2. Rabbi Yehoshua ben Chananya; 3. Rabbi Akiva; and 4. Simeon the Temanite.*[IV]

Already during the rule of Titus, while serving as the *av beit din*, head of the court, Rabbi Yehoshua ben Chananya participated in a delegation including Rabbi Eliezer ben Horkenos and Rabban Gamliel, to Rome.

> *When they came to Rome, these magnificent men created a profound impression, and they succeeded in gaining loyal friends and admirers among the highest of the nobility of the imperial city. Under the radiance of their remarkable personalities, the emperor's nephew Onkelos became inspired toward Judaism: and despite the low state of the conquered and bleeding people, he became a Jew and a humble disciple of the Sages. He later*

---

3   The Lubavitcher Rebbe often mentioned that mothers used to rock their little ones to sleep with rhyming lullabies of Yiddishe content, such as *"Torah iz di beste sechorah"* (Torah is the best merchandise). The Rebbe said, "Some people think that it makes no difference what one sings to a young child, since anyway he does not understand. The truth is that everything that enters a child's ears affects his *neshamah* in the years ahead." Sichot 5739 sec. 1, p. 661; Sichot 5737, sec. 1, p. 112.

composed a translation of the Torah into Aramaic under the supervision of Rabbi Eliezer and Rabbi Yehoshua.[4]

A further incident that occurred in Rome testifying to Rabbi Yehoshua's great righteousness is brought in *Gittin* 58a:

> Our Rabbis have taught: Rabbi Yehoshua ben Chananya once visited the great city of Rome. He was told there that there was a child with beautiful eyes and face and curly locks in the prison.
>
> He went and stood at the doorway of the prison saying: "Who subjected Yaakov to plunder and Israel to the robbers?" (Yeshayahu 42:24)
>
> The child answered: "Was it not the Lord, He against Whom we have sinned and they did not want to go in His way and did not listen to His Torah?" (Ibid.)
>
> He said: "I feel sure that this one will be a teacher in Israel. I swear that I will not budge from here before I ransom him, whatever price may be demanded."
>
> It is reported that he did not leave the spot before he had ransomed the child at a high figure, nor did many days pass before he became a teacher in Israel. Who was he? He was Rabbi Yishmael ben Elisha.[V]

Rabbi Yehoshua was especially known as a master debater, and he recorded his own ability and prowess, and lack thereof (somewhat tongue-in-cheek) in *Eruvin* 53b:

> Rabbi Yehoshua ben Chananya remarked: No one has ever had the better of me, except a woman, a little boy, and a little girl.
>
> What was the incident with the woman?
>
> I was once staying at an inn where the hostess served me a plate with beans. On the first day, I ate all of them, leaving

---

4   Rav Avigdor Miller, *Exalted People*, p. 85.

nothing. On the second day, too, I left nothing. On the third day, she over-seasoned them with salt, and, as soon as I tasted them, I withdrew my hand.

"My Master," she said to me, "why do you not eat?"

"I have already eaten," I replied, "earlier in the day."

"You should then," she said, "have withdrawn your hand from the bread."

"My Master," she continued, "is it possible that you left the dish today as compensation for the former meals, for have not the Sages established: 'Nothing is to be left in the pot but something must be left in the plate?'"

What was the incident with the little girl?

I was once on a journey and, observing a path across a field, I made my way through it, when a little girl called out to me, "Master! Is not this part of the field?"

"No," I replied, "this is a trampled path."

"Robbers like yourself," she retorted, "have trampled it down."

What was the incident with the little boy?

I was once on a journey when I noticed a little boy sitting at a crossroad. "By what road," I asked him, "do we go to the town?"

"This one," he replied, "is short but long, and that one is long but short."

I proceeded along the short-but-long road.

When I approached the town, I discovered that it was hedged in by gardens and orchards.

Turning back, I said to him, "My son, did you not tell me that this road was short?"

He replied, "Did I not also tell you: but long?"

I kissed him upon his head and said to him, "Happy are you, Yisrael, all of you are wise, both young and old."[VI]

Bereishit Rabbah records the following incident:

> During the times of Rabbi Yehoshua ben Chananya, the Roman Empire decreed that the Temple be rebuilt. Papus and Lulinus set up booths from Acco to Antioch and provided those coming from the Diaspora with all their needs including gold and silver. The Cutheans attempted to block the endeavor, claiming that the Jews would now openly revolt. The emperor countered that his hands were tied, as he had already promised to rebuild the Temple. The Cutheans advised him to make a slight change in the location of the Temple or to slightly add to the dimensions of the Temple, knowing that these conditions would be unacceptable to the Jewish people. The Jews gathered in Beit Rimon and clamored to revolt. The leaders looked for a wise man to calm the people down and Rabbi Yehoshua was suggested to be the one. Rabbi Yehoshua told the people a parable: A lion preyed on his victim and a bone got stuck in his throat. He said that whoever is able to remove the bone would be rewarded. One stepped up, removed the bone and asked for his reward. The lion said: "Go and tell others that you were in the mouth of the lion and survived."
>
> So too here, said Rabbi Yehoshua,
>
> - we entered this nation in peace—the Romans currently do not want to seriously physically harm us or prohibit all observance;
> - now go out in peace—there is no cogent reason to rebel as that would lead to the furious and full wrath of Rome.[VII]

This episode highlights Rabbi Yehoshua's stature as a leading sage with a keen understanding of Roman politics and an innate awareness of the DNA of the Jewish people at that time in history. He was clearly the go-to person in handling immensely difficult situations that required articulating compelling arguments to an anxious people.

Rabbi Yehoshua utilized his Torah wisdom, faculty of speech, and clarity of thought not only in front of his Jewish brethren but also as the premier debater on behalf of the Jewish nation. *Sotah* 49b teaches: "When Rabbi Yehoshua died, counsel and thought ceased," to which *Rashi* comments: "He was careful in his discourses, an expert in the law and in responding to non-believers, understanding their signals..."[5][VIII]

Chagigah 5b develops this theme:

> *When the soul of Rabbi Yehoshua ben Chananya was about to go to its rest, the Rabbis said to him: "What will become of us at the hands of the unbelievers?"*
>
> *He answered them: "Counsel is perished from the children, their wisdom is vanished" (Yirmiyahu 49:7).*
>
> *But as soon as counsel is perished from the children, the wisdom of the peoples of the world is also vanished.*[IX]

Rabbi Yehoshua ben Chananya's uniqueness is summarized: "He distinguished himself in Torah, logic, leadership, and statesmanship, and was renowned for his prowess in disputations with all opponents of the Jewish people; and he became known as *Hakima D'Yehudai*, wise man of the Jews."[6]

---

5   In the royal court, the knowledge of sign language/signals was necessary in order to be an accomplished debater. Rabbi Yehoshua possessed this skill.
6   Miller, *Exalted People*, p. 69.

4. IN THE EMPEROR'S HOME

Numerous Talmudic episodes highlight Rabbi Yehoshua's role as the leading representative of the people in dealing with the Roman emperor. They portray a bold, fearless leader of the Jewish people, apparently a welcomed guest in the highly dangerous royal court of the emperor. The sources subscribe to the opinion that the emperor in question was Hadrian, as brought down for example by the *Siftei Chachamim*: "In many places in the Talmud and Midrash we find that the Caesar spoke with Rabbi Yehoshua ben Chananya, and from here it appears that 'Caesar' is Hadrian."[I]

The *Dorot Harishonim* opines that these episodes occurred during Hadrian's pre-emperor days when he was the regional governor. Even though some of the interactions appear to have happened in the palace of the emperor, *Dorot Harishonim* contends that "emperor" can also mean "governor."[II]

These interactions include:

- Gestures (*Chagigah* 5b)
- Ugly Vessel (*Taanit* 7a)
- Snowy Mountain (*Shabbat* 152a)
- Nightmare (*Berachot* 56a)
- Special Spice (*Shabbat* 119a)
- Lion of Be-Ilai'i (*Chullin* 59b)
- Facing the Sun (ibid.)

- Banquet for God (ibid.)
- The Spool (ibid.)
- The *Luz* Bone (*Vayikra Rabbah* 18:1)
- Resurrection (*Sanhedrin* 90b)
- Better than Moshe (*Kohelet Rabbah* 9:3)

GESTURES (CHAGIGAH 5B)

The diplomatic language in the royal court included communication via gestures and hand movements.

> *Rabbi Yehoshua ben Chananya was at the court of Caesar.*
>
> *A certain heretic showed him by gestures: "The Jewish people are a people whose God has turned His face from them."*
>
> *He showed him in reply: "His hand is stretched over us."*
>
> *Caesar said to Rabbi Yehoshua ben Chananya: "What did he gesture to you?"*
>
> *Rabbi Yehoshua ben Chananya answered: "'A people whose Lord has turned His face from them.' And I showed him: 'His hand is stretched over us.'"*
>
> *Caesar's aides said to the heretic: "What did you show him?" [He replied:] "A people whose Lord has turned His face from them."*
>
> *[Asked the aides:] "And what did he show you?" [He replied:] "I do not know."*
>
> *They said: "A man who does not understand what he is being shown by gestures should hold converse in signs before the king!" They took him away and killed him.*[III]

The *Maharsha* teaches that Rabbi Yehoshua ben Chananya was recognized as a famous debater especially against the heretics. That skill included the art of communicating via gestures when in front of the emperor. In this case, the fact that the heretic did not understand the gestures was proof enough to the emperor that his arguments were spurious.

A successful advocate needs to know not just the language of the royal court but even more so the nuances of the contemporary political language and jargon. At the court of Hadrian, the language of gestures was one form of diplomatic language in which Rabbi Yehoshua was proficient.

The claim of the heretic was the prototype of an ongoing claim that has been repeated over and over again in Jewish history. That allegation sought to demonstrate that the dire plight of the Jewish people was proof that God had abandoned His people. The counter-argument revealed just the opposite; punishment followed by repentance and redemption substantiated the intimate eternal covenant between God and His chosen people.

UGLY VESSEL (TAANIT 7A)

The following encounter took place between Rabbi Yehoshua and the emperor's daughter, indicating the special position Rabbi Yehoshua held with the entire royal family.

> *Torah only endures with one who is modest.*
>
> *This is illustrated by the story of the daughter of the Roman emperor who addressed Rabbi Yehoshua ben Chananya, "You are glorious wisdom in an ugly vessel."*
>
> *He replied, "Does not your father keep wine in an earthenware vessel?"*
>
> *She asked, "Where else should he keep it?"*
>
> *He said to her, "You who are nobles should keep it in vessels of gold and silver."*
>
> *She went and told this to her father, and he had the wine put into vessels of gold and silver and it became sour.*
>
> *When he was informed of this, he asked his daughter, "Who gave you this advice?"*
>
> *She replied, "Rabbi Yehoshua ben Chananya."*
>
> *The emperor had him summoned and asked him, "Why did you give her such advice?"*

> He replied, "I answered her according to the way that she spoke to me."
>
> [She then asked:] "But are there not good-looking people who are wise?
>
> [Rabbi Yehoshua replied:] "If these very people were ugly, they would be still more learned."^IV

Why would Rabbi Yehoshua give such advice, asks the *Ben Yehoyada*? What honor is there if the wine is stored in gold barrels? Who will even see it? And why would the emperor listen to his daughter's advice?

The *Ben Yehoyada* says that it appears that the wine in question was not wine designated for drinking, rather wine used in pouring for daily idol worship. And Rabbi Yehoshua told the emperor's daughter that it wasn't proper to keep that wine in earthenware vessels like the other wine stocked. The emperor thought this was sound advice. When he was told by his daughter that Rabbi Yehoshua gave this advice, he suspected that Rabbi Yehoshua's intent was to spoil the idol-worship wine as a protest against idol worship. Rabbi Yehoshua answered that he was not the one who engaged the emperor's daughter in conversation, but rather she approached him and denigrated Rabbi Yehoshua's physical appearance. Rabbi Yehoshua told the emperor that his intent was not to give advice but to teach and show how God can place very learned and wise people in "ugly vessels."^V

SNOWY MOUNTAIN (SHABBAT 152A)

> The emperor asked Rabbi Yehoshua ben Chananya, "Why did you not attend the Be Abedan, the arena for debates?"
>
> Rabbi Yehoshua ben Chananya answered cryptically:
>
> "The mountain is snowy,
>
> It is surrounded by ice,
>
> The dog does not bark,
>
> And the grinders do not grind."^VI

The emperor clearly expected Rabbi Yehoshua, the premier Jewish advocate, to be involved in the debates that took place at the Be Abedan, a meeting place where Jewish representatives debated with the heretical *Tzedukim*.

In his allegorical style of speech, Rabbi Yehoshua informed the emperor that he was simply too old to continue public debates:

> My hair is white.
>
> My mustache and beard have also turned white.
>
> My voice is becoming inaudible.
>
> My teeth don't work.

NIGHTMARE (BERACHOT 56A)

> The emperor [of Rome] said to Rabbi Yehoshua ben Chananya: "You Jews profess to be very clever. Tell me what I shall see in my dream."
>
> He said to him: "You will see the Persians [Parthians] making you do forced labor, despoiling you, and making you feed unclean animals [pigs] with a golden stick."
>
> The emperor thought about this all day, and in the night he saw it in his dream.[VII]

On the surface, it would seem absurd to test one's cleverness or wisdom, such as the emperor challenged Rabbi Yehoshua ben Chananya via a request to predict a dream.

The *Siftei Chachamim* in *Berachot* suggests that possibly the Caesar was referring to the verse in *Devarim* 4:6, "And you shall keep [them] and do [them], for that is your wisdom and your understanding in the eyes of the peoples, who will hear all these statutes and say, 'Only this great nation is a wise and understanding people.'" It is derived from the verse that a wise man is preferable to a prophet, and Caesar told Rabbi Yehoshua, "You, a wise man are better than a prophet, so you should know the future."[VIII]

The Vilna Gaon explains that it requires great wisdom to understand the true nature of a person and penetrating perception to know how to leave a strong lasting impression on another person. Only with deep insight can one figure out how the "four elements" influence another person and what needs to be said during the day so that the person dreams about a specific topic. The combination of the five points Rabbi Yehoshua mentioned to the Caesar—Persians, forced labor, despoiling, feeding unclean animals, and golden stick—created such a compelling effect to the point that Rabbi Yehoshua could accurately predict the Caesar's dream.[IX]

Ben Yehoyada writes that Rabbi Yehoshua told the Caesar alarming matters relating to war. It was customary in those days that a defeat in war did not mean the end of the vanquisher's empire, but rather the result was servitude with taxes to the victor. The pigs represent Rome who would pay taxes in gold [golden stick].[X]

For Trajan, who initiated an expansionist foreign policy against Parthia, this dream would be a nightmare scenario. For Hadrian, who withdrew from the theater of war, such a dream might appear to be less relevant. On the other hand, the thought of a Parthian victory over Rome as a result of his passive peace plan might have haunted Hadrian.

SPECIAL SPICE (SHABBAT 119A)

> *The emperor said to Rabbi Yehoshua ben Chananya, "Why does the Shabbat dish have such a fragrant odor?"*
>
> *He replied: "We have a certain seasoning, called the Shabbat, which we put into it, and that gives it a fragrant odor."*
>
> *The emperor: "Give us some of it."*
>
> *Rabbi Yehoshua ben Chananya answered: "To he who keeps the Shabbat, it is efficacious; but to he who does not keep the Shabbat, it is of no use."*[XI]

Ben Yehoyada anticipates the question of how Rabbi Yehoshua could say that the Jewish people have a spice that is called the Shabbat.

The spice is the emanation of the holiness of the Shabbat that permeates the food. The Hebrew word *tavlin*—"spice," is hinted in the letters of the word Shabbat via their numerical value.[1] And in order to "make" the Shabbat, i.e., make the special spice of the Shabbat food, one has to "observe" the Shabbat day, as it says, "Thus shall the Children of Israel *observe* the Shabbat, to *make* the Shabbat throughout their generations as an everlasting covenant" (*Shemot* 31:16). The cooked food, תבשיל/ *tavshil* is comprised of the Hebrew letters שבת לי/*li Shabbat*—my Shabbat. The reason why the special spice of the Shabbat is revealed via the sense of smell is because the Shabbat is like the World to Come, and it's known that in Gan Eden there is no eating and drinking, but one rather is sustained through the pleasant odor.[XII]

The emperor Hadrian could somehow access the smell of the Shabbat but no more. Similarly, Alexander the Great could smell the Garden of Eden but could not advance in his attempt to enter it.

LION OF BE-ILAI'I (CHULLIN 59B)

The Gemara in Tractate *Chullin* reports a series of challenges put forward by the emperor to Rabbi Yehoshua ben Chananya regarding the attributes of God:

> *The emperor once said to Rabbi Yehoshua ben Chananya, "Your God is likened to a lion, for it is written: 'A lion has roared, who will not fear? The Lord God hath spoken, who will not prophesy?' (Amos 3:8) But what is the greatness of this? A horseman can kill the lion!"*
>
> *Rabbi Yehoshua ben Chananya replied: "He has not been likened to an ordinary lion, but to the lion of Be-Ilai'i!"*
>
> *Emperor: "I'd like you to show it to me."*
>
> *He replied: "You cannot see it."*
>
> *"Indeed," said the emperor, "I will see it."*

---

[1] Shin, beit, tav ש,ב,ת. These three letters spelled out are שין, בית, תיו. Now take the letters of these three words without the first letters and you get ין,ית,יו. These equal 486; add 6 for these six letters = 492. The gematria of *Tavlin*/תבלין also equals 492.

Rabbi Yehoshua ben Chananya prayed and the lion set out from its place.

When it was four hundred parasangs away, it roared once, and all pregnant women miscarried and the walls of Rome fell.

When it was three hundred parasangs away, it roared again and all the molars and incisors of man fell out; even the emperor himself fell from his throne to the ground.

"I beg of you," he implored, "pray that it returns to its place."

He prayed and it returned to its place.[XIII]

The *Maharsha* explains that the emperor denied the capability of God and contended that there was another power greater than God.[XIV] Rabbi Yehoshua ben Chananya demonstrated the power of God through the stark fear and terror experienced by the emperor when facing the Be-Ilai'i lion.

Certainly, the emperor understood that the verse comparing God to a lion was just a parable. He argued that if this is the comparison, then it shows that God is not all-powerful for even a horseman can kill a lion. Rabbi Yehoshua countered that the analogy proves God's omnipotence because the comparison is with a special lion, the lion of Be-Ilai'i.

The *Maharal* also explains that the emperor was frightened and trembled and was told that such fear is the result of wanting to fully comprehend the might of God.[XV]

Despite the above, the emperor thought that man could literally "see" God and did not comprehend that God stands diametrically apart from man. The emperor therefore requested to "see" God.

FACING THE SUN (CHULLIN 60A)

Another time, the emperor said to Rabbi Yehoshua ben Chananya, "I wish to see your God."

He replied: "You cannot see Him."

"Indeed," said the emperor, "I will see Him."

He went and placed the emperor facing the sun during the summer solstice and said to him, "Look up at it."

He replied: "I cannot."

Said Rabbi Yehoshua, "If you cannot look at the sun, which is but one of the ministers that attends the Holy One, blessed be He, how then can you presume to look upon the Divine presence?"[XVI]

BANQUET FOR GOD (CHULLIN 60A)

On another occasion, the emperor said to Rabbi Yehoshua ben Chananya, "I wish to prepare a banquet for your God."

He replied: "You cannot undertake it."

"Why?" asked the emperor.

"Because His attendants are too numerous."

"Indeed, I will do it."

"Then go and prepare it on the spacious banks of the river Rebitha."

The emperor had spent six months of summer making preparations when a storm arose and swept everything into the sea.

He then spent the six months of winter making preparations when rain fell and washed everything into the sea.

"What is the meaning of this?" asked the emperor.

Rabbi Yehoshua ben Chananya answered: "They are but the sweepers and sprinklers that march before him!"

"In that case," said the emperor, "I cannot do it."[XVII]

How could the emperor request to feed God, something that a child knows is utter nonsense? And after the first six months, why didn't the emperor ask Rabbi Yehoshua what happened?

The *Ben Yehoyada* suggests that the emperor thought to prepare a meal for the angels who are God's soldiers, just as he might have heard how Avraham served a meal to the angels who visited him and Sarah.

Serving the angels is like serving God, similar to a sacrifice to God, which is eaten by the priests.

He requested that the angels come on a specified day to eat but before that day a strong wind came and swept all of the food into the river. So the emperor did not ask what happened but moved on to prepare another meal in a place where there would be no wind. For this meal, Rabbi Yehoshua prayed that rain should pour down and wash everything away. After this second feast was destroyed, the emperor now asked Rabbi Yehoshua the meaning of both events. Rabbi Yehoshua answered that these were unnatural events of the attendants of the angels. From this, the emperor understood that one cannot feed God in any way.[XVIII]

The emperor mistakenly thought that, as the mighty ruler of the entire Roman Empire, he should be the one to "see" God. Who else but the powerful caesar should be the one to "feed" God? Rabbi Yehoshua ben Chananya's retorts were aimed at destroying any heretical concepts regarding God.

While it does not appear that Rabbi Yehoshua engaged the emperor in a discussion as to how one truly forms an intimate relationship with God, Rabbi Aryeh Kaplan learns the following:

> *What this story is telling us is that God's power is infinite. Even if He had any needs He could supply them Himself. However, no such needs exist in the first place. God has absolutely no need for the world. We cannot even say that creation filled some inner need for God. Creation was an act of pure love and altruism, with God gaining absolutely nothing from it at all.*[2]

THE SPOOL (CHULLIN 60A)

The emperor's daughter once said to Rabbi Yehoshua ben Chananya, "Your God is a carpenter, for it is written: 'Who roofs His upper chambers with water' (Tehillim 104:3). Ask him to make me a spool!"

---

2   Rabbi Aryeh Kaplan, *The Infinite Light* (found in *The Aryeh Kaplan Anthology I*), p. 145.

> He replied: "Very well."
>
> He prayed for her and she was afflicted with leprosy.
>
> She was then removed to the open square of Rome and was given a spool [for so it was the custom in Rome, whoever was afflicted with leprosy was given a spool and removed to the open square, and was given threads of yarn to wind so that people may see them and pray for their recovery].
>
> One day, as Rabbi Yehoshua was passing by, he saw her sitting in the open square of Rome winding the yarn onto the spool.
>
> He remarked: "My God has given you a beautiful spool!"
>
> She said: "I pray, ask your God to take back what He has given me."
>
> He replied: "Our God grants a request, but once granted never takes it back."[XIX]

The non-Jews denied the concept of Divine providence, claiming that God is not involved in this world, but rather, the world runs on its own. The cardinal Jewish belief is that even though God created nature to run the world, nature is in God's providential Hand. For example, if God wants a certain person to earn a thousand dollars, He need not cause it to rain down but will set in motion a natural cause and effect. So it is in all matters: God rules the world in that He sets in motion natural causes and effects with His might and great providence.

The emperor's daughter challenged Rabbi Yehoshua to prove the providence of God by asking that she receive an item that was so far removed from her natural order, that it could only be attained by explaining that it was a result of Divine providence. Therefore, she ask for a "spool," something that was far from her and only attainable through "spinning" events in an unnatural way.[XX]

The leprosy, being placed in the marketplace, and getting the spool was the undeniable proof of Divine providence.

Once again, the empirical facts of the events made the arguments clear and incontrovertible.

THE LUZ BONE
(VAYIKRA RABBAH 18:1 AND BEREISHIT RABBAH 28:3)

The Roman Emperor Hadrian, may his bones rot, asked Rabbi Yehoshua ben Chananya: "From where does the Holy One, blessed be He, reconstruct man in the future?"

He answered him: "From the luz[3] of the spine."

He asked: "From where do you know this?"

He said: "It has come to me (as a tradition), and I will show you."

They tried to grind it in a mill but it was not ground, they burnt it in fire but it was not consumed, they put it in water but it was not softened, they put it on an anvil and he started to beat it with a hammer but the anvil slipped, the hammer was broken and it remained intact.[XXI]

Once more, the evidence brought by Rabbi Yehoshua ben Chananya was empirical and not subject to dispute.

RESURRECTION (SANHEDRIN 90B)

The Romans asked Rabbi Yehoshua ben Chananya: "From where do we know that the Holy One, blessed be He, will resurrect the dead and knows the future?"

He replied: "Both are deduced from this verse, "And the Lord said to Moshe: 'Behold you are about to sleep with your

---

3   The name of the bone is called the *"luz."* In the future, resurrection of the dead will begin with this bone (*Sefer Ta'amei Haminhagim* §425). Rabbi Chiya said: "It is written, 'Your dead will live again' (*Yeshayahu* 26:19). The Holy One will not create new bodies for the dead in the future, but rather resurrect their original bodies. For there is a single bone that remains of a person's body after it has decomposed in the ground. That bone does not rot or decompose. It remains intact forever. When the time comes [to resurrect the dead], the Holy One will soften that bone like yeast in dough. It will then rise up and expand in four directions. From it, He will reconstitute the body and all its limbs. Afterwards, the Holy One will infuse it with life (*Shaar Halikutim, Shmuel I* 2:19)." The *Shibolei Leket* (#130, Laws of Havdalah and Motza'ei Shabbat) writes that the *luz* bone receives its sustenance once a week at the *melaveh malkah*/Saturday night meal.

> *forefathers, and will rise up again; and this people will stray after the deities of the nations…'" (Devarim 31:16).*
>
> *[They replied:] "But perhaps 'will rise up, and stray after'?"*
>
> *He replied: "Then at least you have the answer to half of your question—that He knows the future."*[XXII]

It is not clear if the word "rise up" goes on the first part of the verse—"You will sleep with your fathers and rise up," i.e., the resurrection of the dead—or if the phrase relates to the second half of the verse—"And the nation will rise up again…and shall stray," i.e., God knows that in the future the people will go astray.

The philosophers are neither believers in the resurrection of the dead nor of God's knowledge of the future. They therefore inquired as to the Torah sources for these two fundamental Jewish beliefs.[XXIII]

The *Ben Yehoyada* questions: The Romans asked Rabbi Yehoshua two questions. How, then, did he make a compromise with his answer? Why did they ask those two questions together? How are they connected? Rabbi Yehoshua said there were two answers from the one verse and then backtracked?

The *Ben Yehoyada* proposes that the Romans did not really want a source proof for resurrection. They acknowledged that resurrecting the dead was possible, as seen by the actions of Eliyahu, Elisha, and Yechezkel. However, they thought that God will not resurrect the dead out of fear that those people will return and sin as they sinned before. If, on the other hand, God knows the future and sees that those people will not sin, then He will resurrect. The two questions are therefore connected. If you prove that God knows the future, then you've proven that God will resurrect the dead.[XXIV]

The *Rambam* sources this verse in *Hilchot Teshuvah* in a discussion on free will. If God knows that Israel will stray, where is the free choice? The *Rambam* answers that God was speaking generally about the nation of Israel, but each individual remains with free choice.

Elsewhere in *Hilchot Teshuvah*, the *Rambam* does touch upon the entire concept of free choice. If God knows what a person will do, where is the free choice? Judaism, however, believes in God's omniscient knowledge of past, present, and future, while at the same time man retains absolute free choice as to how to act. The *Rambam* writes that this paradox can not be completely understood.

An approach to somehow understand part of this is developed by the principle that time as we know it was created by God at the moment of creation of our world. In the heavenly spheres, there is past, present, and future, and God's knowledge of all time. Down in earth, we are limited and constricted by time, and the choice to act is in man's hands.[xxv]

BETTER THAN MOSHE (KOHELET RABBAH 9:3)

Hadrian (may his bones rot) said to Rabbi Yehoshua ben Chananya, "I am better than Moshe your teacher."

He asked: "Why?"

Hadrian: "I am alive and he is dead. And it is written that, 'A live dog is better than a dead lion'" (Kohelet 9:4).

Rabbi Yehoshua: "Can you decree that no fire be lit for three days?"

Hadrian: "Yes."

The decree was sent out, and as they stood at the palace they saw smoke coming from a house.

They asked, "What is this?"

"There is a sick person and the doctor came and said the sick person needed to drink a hot liquid."

Rabbi Yehoshua said: "You are still alive and your decree was voided. Moshe decreed that we cannot light fire on the Shabbat and until today, not one Jew lights a fire on the Shabbat.

Hadrian admitted: "He is better than me."[xxvi]

From this last encounter, and for most of the encounters, we witness Rabbi Yehoshua ben Chananya adroitly creating, maneuvering, or leveraging facts on the ground to present his arguments and answer the emperor's inquiries. In most of the episodes above, Rabbi Yehoshua ben Chananya is able to demonstrate his arguments with empirical evidence. These are not cases of sourcing Torah verses to prove a point. Philosophical reasoning is not used.

Rabbi Yehoshua ben Chananya is able to

- manipulate the emperor to experience a specific dream,
- show that fine wine should not be placed in gold vessels,
- frighten the emperor with the lion,
- reveal to the emperor the futility of trying to look directly at the sun,
- verify how the storms and winds prevent the emperor from "serving" God,
- place the emperor's daughter in a location where she was compelled to have a spool,
- demonstrate the indestructibility of the *luz* bone,
- prove that Moshe's laws are still adherently observed by the Jewish people.

Only in the episode regarding the resurrection do we encounter a shift in the debate. Here, Rabbi Yehoshua ben Chananya argues from within the verses of the Torah and is satisfied to prove at least one of two concepts to the emperor.

Through the sheer force of his extraordinary debating skills, Rabbi Yehoshua ben Chananya illustrates and elucidates cardinal Jewish principles:

- The eternal bond between God and the Jewish people
- The everyday working of Divine providence and God's presence
- The compatibility of free will with God's knowledge
- God's absolute independence from the world He created
- Omnipotence of God
- God's utter transcendence yet intimate involvement in mankind
- Uniqueness of the Shabbat for its observers
- The existence of life after death
- The primary role of the internal within man over the external and superficial

SECTION V
EMPEROR ANTONINUS

During one period of the long, tortuous history of the Roman exile, two leaders—one from Rome and one from Israel—formed an intimate, and almost mystical, bond. These two leading personalities were Emperor Antoninus and Rabbi Yehudah HaNasi.

Historians dispute the identity of Antoninus.

He has in turn been identified with Marcus Aurelius (Rapoport and Bodek), Septimius Severus (Graetz,), Caracalla (Jost and N. Krochmal), Elagabalus (Cassel), and Lucius Verus (Frankel).[1]

Traditional Jewish sources state that Antoninus mentioned by the Talmud was indeed a Roman Emperor, and was either Antoninus Fulvius Pius (reign 138–161) or Marcus Aurelius Antoninus (reign 161–180).

Seder Hadorot writes:

> *Antoninus Pius, meaning the righteous one, was the son-in-law [adopted heir] of Emperor Adrianas (Hadrian). He was wise and sought peace. He only went to war when absolutely necessary. He would say that it's better for one of his people to live than for one thousand of his enemies to die. He expanded the empire without fighting. His great modesty and righteousness caused other kingdoms to listen to him. He was the friend of Rabbeinu Hakadosh. He ruled in 3900 at the age of forty-seven.*[1]

---

1   Louis Ginsberg, *Antoninus in the Talmud*, Jewish Encyclopedia.

Sefer Hakabbalah concurs with this appraisal:

> Rabbeinu Hakadosh, Rabbi Yehudah the Prince, the son of Rav Shimon ben Gamliel, was the Rosh Yeshiva. God saw the poor state of the Jewish people and He fulfilled the verse, "When they stumble, they will be helped with a little help" (Daniel 11:34).
>
> And Hadrian died and Antoninus Pius ruled. And he loved Rabbeinu Hakadosh with all his soul and it is said that he secretly converted. And the days during Rebbi's life were all good days for the Jewish people and he lived long. Antoninus Pius died during Rebbi's life and then Marcus Aurelius and Commodus came after Antoninus and they both honored and elevated Rebbi all of his days.
>
> The rise of Antoninus brought relief to the relationship of the emperors with the Jewish people; he eliminated the decrees of Hadrian and permitted Jews to circumcise their sons on the condition that they wouldn't circumcise non-Jews, i.e., convert them to Judaism.[II]

In the history of *Historia Augusta*, it is mentioned that Antoninus Pius put down a Jewish rebellion that broke out during his rule. However, there is no clear evidence from other sources regarding such a rebellion during his reign. And if such a rebellion occurred, it probably would have happened during the first half of his rule as a result of the wars during Hadrian's time. The majority of researchers reject this matter as a result of the doubtful veracity of *Historia Augusta* as a reliable historical source.[2III]

Roman historians paint a positive picture of Antoninus Pius regarding his relationship with the Jews, buttressing the claims of those who say that he was Antoninus of the Talmud.

---

2   See, for example, Sir Ronald Syme, *Emperors and Biography: Studies in the Historia Augusta* (New York: Oxford University Press, 1971); and Anthony R. Birley, "Rewriting Second-and Third-century History in Late Antique Rome: *The Historia Augusta*," available at http://classica.org.br/revista/index.php/classica/article/viewFile/101/91.

The role of Antoninus Pius regarding the return to practice the mitzvot is also supported by Edward Gibbon:

> By the general indulgence of Polytheism, and by the mild temper of Antoninus Pius, the Jews were restored to their ancient privileges, and once more obtained the permission of circumcising their children, with the easy restraint that they should never confer on any foreign proselyte that distinguishing mark of the Hebrew race.[3]

Additionally, McLynn in his work on Marcus Aurelius echoes this fact:

> His [Antoninus Pius] Jewish policy also brought into this argument: while he lifted Hadrian's proscription on circumcision for Jews, he ordained that no Gentiles were to be circumcised which prevented proselytizing.[4]

Dorot Harishonim, on the other hand, clearly identifies Antoninus of the Talmud as Marcus Aurelius, and he quotes the historian Dio Cassius who says of Marcus Aurelius, "He very much loved to deal with matters of wisdom."

> And there is no doubt that he [Marcus Aurelius] read a copy of the Targum Shivim and knew of its great value; and he also had an idea concerning what the Torah was that Israel observed. And knew God's praiseworthy instructions which Israel kept and gave their lives on behalf.[IV]

Avodah Brurah summarizes this approach:

> According to Sefer Dorot Harishonim, Antoninus is the emperor Marcus Aurelius who ruled from 161 to 180. During his travels to the countries of the empire, he also visited in Judea and met Rav Yehudah HaNasi and became attached to him in friendship until his day of death.[V]

---

3   Gibbon, chap. 16.
4   McLynn, p. 136.

Rav Avigdor Miller agrees with the Marcus Aurelius position and expresses the relationship between Rabbi Yehudah HaNasi and Antoninus as follows:

> *Now took place one of the great miracles which God wrought for his people. While at Rome, Rebbi became acquainted with the son and eventual successor of the emperor Antoninus Pius. This gifted and noble Roman, who became the emperor Marcus Aurelius, came to admire the Jewish sage to such an extraordinary degree that his life was transformed thenceforth.*[5]

Accordingly, it seems that the Antoninus mentioned by the Talmud was either Antoninus Fulvius Pius or Marcus Aurelius Antoninus. Who were they?

---

5 Rav Avigdor Miller, *Exalted People*, p. 166.

1. ANTONINUS PIUS

ANTONINUS PIUS

Antoninus Pius was the fifteenth Roman emperor. "Ruling as a just and gentle man, under him, Rome reached its peak and his reign was known for its peace and prosperity."[1]

Titus Aurelius Fulvius Boionius Arrius Antoninus was born in the year 86 in the Italian town of Lanuvium. From a noble family, he entered the senate and took the usual career path of Roman leaders, moving from minor offices to provincial governor. Antoninus then became a trusted advisor to Emperor Hadrian. The emperor had adopted Lucius Aelius as his successor, but when Aelius died, Antoninus was adopted and earmarked for eventual rule.

When Hadrian died, Antoninus became emperor and the senate gave him the title "Pius," either because he had Hadrian declared a god, or because he freed senators whom Hadrian had planned to execute.

Unlike many other Roman rulers, Antoninus stayed near Rome and focused on governing the empire.

Internationally, Antoninus preferred diplomacy to fighting, and peacefully settled conflicts with Persia, although it was later claimed

---

1 https://study.com/academy/lesson/antoninus-pius-facts-quotes-accomplishments.html.

that his moves gave Persia time to rearm for a later war. He met ambassadors from India and sent a Roman trade mission as far as China.

Antoninus was involved in legal matters impacting the Empire during his reign. He had legal teams work on updating the Roman laws. Slaves and women were given some more rights, torture of prisoners was eased, and the police were told not to mistreat suspects. One important command he sent to all judges was to assume prisoners were innocent until proven guilty; another was that Roman law was to be applied equally throughout the empire.

With a strong, robust economy, funds were used to build roads, bridges, and water systems. When Roman cities were hit by fires or earthquakes, it was recorded that he sent them relief and forgave their taxes.

Emperor Marcus Aurelius, writing about his adoptive father Antoninus Pius:

> *I was subordinated to a ruler and a father capable of ridding me of all conceit, and of bringing me to recognize that it is possible to live in a Court and yet do without bodyguards and gorgeous garments and linkmen and statues and the like pomp; and that it is in such a man's power to reduce himself very nearly to the condition of a private individual and yet not on this account to be more paltry or more remiss in dealing with what the interests of the state require to be done in imperial fashion.*[2]

Edward Gibbon, in *The Decline and Fall of the Roman Empire*, writes:

> *Titus Antoninus Pius has been justly denominated a second Numa.*[3] *The same love of religion, justice, and peace, was the distinguishing characteristic of both princes. But the situation of the latter opened a much larger field for the exercise of those virtues…Antoninus diffused order and tranquility over*

---

2   *Meditations*, First Book, chap. 14.
3   "Numa Pompilius: reigned 715–673 BCE, was the legendary second king of Rome, succeeding Romulus. He was of Sabine origin, and many of Rome's most important religious and political institutions are attributed to him." https://en.wikipedia.org/wiki/Numa_Pompilius.

the greatest part of the earth. His reign is marked by the rare advantage of furnishing very few materials for history; which is, indeed, little more than the register of the crimes, follies, and misfortunes of mankind. In private life, he was an amiable, as well as a good man. The native simplicity of his virtue was a stranger to vanity or affectation. He enjoyed with moderation the conveniences of his fortune, and the innocent pleasures of society; and the benevolence of his soul displayed itself in a cheerful serenity of temper.[4]

The reign of Antoninus, although a relatively long one of twenty-three years, is known in history as the uneventful reign. Since much that is usually called "eventful" in history is made up of wars, tumults, calamities, and discords, it is to the greatest credit of Antoninus that his reign is called uneventful. We read of no conquests, no insurrections, no proscriptions, no extortions, and no cruelty. His reign is an illustration of the maxim, "Happy is the people which has no history." Although not so great a statesman as Hadrian, he was yet able to maintain the empire in a state of peace and prosperity. He managed the finances with skill and economy. He was kind to his subjects.[5]

On his deathbed, Antoninus Pius gave the tribune of the night-watch the password of the day as *aequanimitas* (equanimity) before lapsing into sleep and dying peacefully. As was often the case, this final phrase was taken as symbolic of his reign.

---

4   https://www.gutenberg.org/files/731/731-h/731-h.htm#link2HCH0001.
5   http://www.forumromanum.org/history/morey26.html.

2. MARCUS AURELIUS

MARCUS AURELIUS

Marcus Aurelius was born on April 26, 121, and as he grew up came to the attention of Hadrian, who promoted him to different positions of authority. The "circumstantial evidence that Hadrian wanted Marcus to succeed him, possibly around the time the young man was twenty-one, is overwhelming."[1]

Antoninus Pius himself was the adopted son of Hadrian (who in turn was the adopted son of Trajan). And Hadrian actually chose Antoninus Pius as his apparent heir (after his first choice was no longer in the running) and at the same time had him adopt the yet too young to be emperor, Marcus Aurelius, whom Hadrian eyed as a worthy future emperor.

Cassius Dio explains:

> *Marcus Antoninus, the philosopher, upon obtaining the throne at the death of Antoninus, his adoptive father, had immediately taken to share his power with Lucius Verus, the son of Lucius Commodus. For he was frail in body himself and devoted the*

---

1   McLynn, p. 37.

greater part of his time to letters. Indeed, it is reported that even when he was emperor, he showed no shame or hesitation about resorting to a teacher, but became a pupil of Sextus, the Boeotian philosopher, and did not hesitate to attend the lectures of Hermogenes on rhetoric, but he was most inclined to the doctrines of the Stoic school. Lucius, on the other hand, was a vigorous man of younger years and better suited for military enterprises. Therefore, Marcus made him his son-in-law by marrying him to his daughter Lucilla and sent him to conduct the war against the Parthians.[2]

Marcus Aurelius is portrayed as the personification of the ideal philosopher-king.

Edward Gibbon explains that to understand Marcus Aurelius, one needs to appreciate the fact that he was a Stoic from his youth.

The virtue of Marcus Aurelius Antoninus was of a severer and more laborious kind...At the age of twelve years he embraced the rigid system of the Stoics, which taught him to submit his body to his mind, his passions to his reason; to consider virtue as the only good, vice as the only evil, all things external as things indifferent. His meditations, composed in the tumult of the camp, are still extant; and he even condescended to give lessons of philosophy, in a more public manner than was perhaps consistent with the modesty of sage, or the dignity of an emperor...He was severe to himself, indulgent to the imperfections of others, just and beneficent to all mankind...War he detested, as the disgrace and calamity of human nature; but when the

COLUMN OF MARCUS AURELIUS

2   http://penelope.uchicago.edu/Thayer/E/Roman/Texts/Cassius_Dio/71*.html.

necessity of a just defence called upon him to take up arms, he readily exposed his person to eight winter campaigns, on the frozen banks of the Danube.³

Dio Cassius presents it this way:

> The emperor, as often as he had leisure from war, would hold court; he used to allow abundant time to the speakers, and entered into the preliminary inquiries and examinations at great length, so as to ensure strict justice by every possible means. In consequence, he would often be trying the same case for as much as eleven or twelve days, even though he sometimes held court at night. For he was industrious and applied himself diligently to all the duties of his office; and he neither said, wrote, nor did anything as if it were a minor matter, but sometimes he would consume whole days over the minutest point, not thinking it right that the emperor should do anything hurriedly.⁴

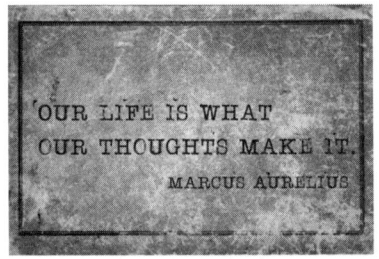

MARCUS AURELIUS—MEDITATIONS

A modern, highly favorable assessment of Marcus' *Meditations* is offered:

> *Meditations* is perhaps the only document of its kind ever made. It is the private thoughts of the world's most powerful man giving advice to himself on how to make good on the responsibilities and obligations of his positions. Trained in Stoic philosophy, Marcus Aurelius stopped almost every night to practice a series of spiritual exercises—reminders designed to make him humble, patient, empathetic, generous, and strong

---

3   Gibbon, pp. 89–90.
4   http://penelope.uchicago.edu/Thayer/e/roman/texts/cassius_dio/72*.html.

in the face of whatever he was dealing with. It is imminently readable and perfectly accessible. You cannot read this book and not come away with a phrase or a line that will be helpful to you the next time you are in trouble. Read it, it is practical philosophy embodied.[5]

---

5   https://dailystoic.com/meditations-marcus-aurelius/.

3. RABBI YEHUDAH HANASI

The demise of a righteous, moral, upright individual, a *tzaddik*, creates a huge vacuum in the world. God, in His beneficence and kindness, fills that emptiness. When a virtuous person passes on, the cycle of life continues and rejuvenates with the birth of a new righteous person.[1]

In the long history of the Oral Torah, the scholarship of many, many Sages contributed to the understanding, development, and wisdom of the Oral Torah. Scores of Tanna'im and Amora'im produced a legacy of erudition unmatched in any discipline.

Rabbi Akiva (50–135 CE) earned a unique position in Jewish history for his immeasurable contribution, scholarship, leadership, inspiration, and righteousness. It is hard to imagine the Mishnah and Talmud, Torah as the Jewish people know it and learn it, without Rabbi Akiva.

The Talmud in *Kiddushin* 72b declares:

> *As the Master said: While Rabbi Akiva was dying, Rabbi Yehudah HaNasi was born; while Rabbi Yehudah HaNasi was dying, Rav Yehudah was born…this teaches you that a righteous person does not leave the world before an equally righteous person is created, as it is stated: "The sun also rises and the sun also sets" (Kohelet 1:5).*[1]

---

1   See *Yoma* 38b and below, *Kiddishun* 72b.

What enormous shoes to fill! What a responsibility to be the one who would attempt to fill the vacuum and void left by Rabbi Akiva's demise. Who could possibly continue that legacy? But Rebbi, Rabbi Yehudah HaNasi, was such a man of destiny. The Guiding Hand of history created the opportunity and conditions; Rabbi Yehudah grabbed the bull by its horns and made his everlasting mark on the Torah world and by extension Jewish history.

What was the key to Rabbi Yehudah's historic greatness?

As seen in other major historical figures, it was a unique combination of skills, attributes, conditions, and timing.

A SYNOPSIS OF HIS LIFE

Rabbi Yehudah HaNasi (135–217 CE), known as HaNasi—The Prince (or head of the Sanhedrin); Rebbi—the teacher; and Rabbeinu Hakadosh—Our Holy Teacher, was born around sixty-five years after the Churban (destruction of the Second Temple); and during the time of the intense persecution, *shmad*. His father, Rabban Shimon ben Gamliel II, was the *Nasi* of the Sanhedrin, and Rebbi was brought up in the city of Usha, a leading center of Jewish life located in the northern Israel area of the Galilee.

BEIT SHEARIM

MOSAIC FLOOR—TZIPPORI

Rabbi Yehudah studied under his esteemed father and was raised with an eye to continue the leadership role as *Nasi*. His other teachers included the outstanding Sages Rav Yehudah ben Ilai, Rav Yaakov ben Kurshai, the Rashbi—Rabbi Shimon bar Yochai, Rabbi Yosi ben Chalafta, and Rabbi Elazar ben Shamua.

Rabbi Yehudah established an academy of learning in Sh'faram, later relocated to Beit Shearim and subsequently moved to Tzippori for health reasons. His stay in Tzippori lasted seventeen years, and the link is made between that stay and Yaakov's seventeen years in Egypt.[II]

ROYALTY

Rabbi Yehudah HaNasi descended from royalty. He was a scion of the House of David and the son of the *Nasi*.

Rebbi was the seventh generation from Hillel from the royal dynasty, and from the side of the mother of Hillel, was from Shaftia the son of Avital, King David's wife.[III]

SCHOLARSHIP

As noted above, Rabbi Yehudah had a number of illustrious teachers who passed on to him the full corpus of the Written and Oral Torah law.

Rava read the following verse about Rabbi Yehudah HaNasi: "One who draws water from deep wells" (*Mishlei* 20:5). This verse describes Rabbi Yehudah HaNasi, because by delving deeply into the Torah, he found a source that a *korban olah v'yored* (sliding-scale offering) atones for the unwitting defiling of sacrificial foods by partaking of them while ritually impure.[IV]

Rabbi Yehudah HaNasi himself testifies as to a source of his scholarship:

> *Rabbi Yehudah HaNasi said: The fact that I am more incisive than my colleagues is due to the fact that I saw Rabbi Meir from behind, i.e., I sat behind him when I was his student. Had I seen him from the front, I would be even more incisive, as it is written: "And your eyes shall see your teacher" (Yeshayahu 30:20).*[V]

Seeing the face of one's teacher increases one's understanding and sharpens one's mind. In Torah scholarship, the teaching passed down from teacher to pupil is the key to maintaining the authentic Sinai tradition.[VI]

WEALTH

Rabbi Yehudah HaNasi was an extremely wealthy man.

The Gemara relates: The stableman of the House of Rabbi Yehudah HaNasi was wealthier than King Shapur of Persia, due to Rabbi Yehudah HaNasi's abundant livestock.[VII]

> During his days, the Nasi's family came into control of wide assets in the Jezreel Valley, the Golan Heights, and probably in the Jordan Valley too, where they raised the precious persimmon fruit, from which perfumes and medical potions were produced. Besides the Nasi's industries that produced olives, wine, and perfume, he had many other industries and exports, such as fish, and flax for weaving linen.[2]

At the same time, the Talmud teaches us that Rabbi Yehudah HaNasi maintained his modesty and humbleness and used his wealth on behalf of the people of Israel.

> Despite his immense wealth, the luxury that surrounded him and the power that he wielded, it was all an external show, and when it came to himself, he lived frugally and even ascetically.[3]

The Gemara (*Ketubot* 104a) states that, at the time of his death, Rabbi Yehudah HaNasi extended his ten fingers upwards and declared:

> "Master of the World! It is revealed and known to You that I toiled with ten fingers for Torah and never benefitted from even my little finger. May it be Your will that there should be peace in my eternal rest." A heavenly voice declared: "Come in peace and rest in peace."[VIII]

---

2 www.hidabroot.com/article/90912/Rabbi-Judah-HaNassi.
3 Ibid.

HOLINESS

Rabbi Yehudah HaNasi was known as Rabbeinu Hakadosh, Our Rabbi, The Holy One.

The Gemara in *Shabbat* 118b says:

> *And they said to Rabbi Yehudah HaNasi: "Why did they call you Our Holy Rabbi?" He said to them: "It is because in all my days I never looked at my circumcision." If so, why wasn't Rabbi Yossi also called Our Holy Rabbi? The Gemara replies: "In the case of Rabbi Yehudah HaNasi, another matter of modesty was present in him, as he did not insert his hand below his belt due to his great modesty."*[IX]

The subjects of forbidden relations and holiness are mentioned side by side in the Torah, to teach us that in a place where we find purity in relations we find holiness. One who is pure in areas of relations is called holy.[X]

Livnat Sapir and the *Zohar* write that Rabbi Yehudah HaNasi was called Holy because his father sanctified him with *brit milah* during the days of the persecution/*shmad*.[XI]

Rabbi Yehudah HaNasi was sanctified at birth through the incredible sacrifice of his father; he was raised in sanctity and worked his entire life to perfect that trait.

The Gemara in *Bava Metzia* 85a relates:

> *When he heard that the greatness of Rabbi Elazar, son of Rabbi Shimon, was due to his suffering, Rabbi Yehudah HaNasi said to himself: "Afflictions are evidently precious." He accepted thirteen years of afflictions upon himself; six years of stones in the kidneys and seven years of scurvy. And some say it was seven years of stones in the kidneys and six years of scurvy.*[XII]

Megalei Amukot writes that Rabbi Yehudah HaNasi was from a spark of Yaakov, and he was called "Our Holy Master" because Yaakov instituted the third blessing in the *Amidah* prayer which reads "*HaKeil Hakadosh* [The Holy God]."[XIII]

Maharal reflects on Rebbi's piety:

> *The day Rebbi died, holiness disappeared, for they called Rabbeinu Hakadosh, "Our Rabbi, the Holy One." And that which it says in the end of Tractate Sotah, "When Rebbi died modesty and fear of Heaven left the world," this means that modesty and fear left the world, but those in that generation still had modesty and fear. But when Rebbi died, no holiness remained, therefore it says on the very same day that Rebbi died, holiness departed [from the world].*[XIV]

Rav Tzadok says:

> *Rabbi Yehudah was called Rabbeinu Hakadosh, Our Holy Teacher, because the most possible holiness to be achieved in this world was concentrated within him. He was a spark of Yaakov, as the Arizal explained. Therefore it is written in Ketubot 103a that every Shabbat eve, after his passing, Rabbi Yehudah HaNasi would come to his house as he had done during his lifetime, for Rebbi did not die. That means to say that he was the Nasi, supported the generation, and in him was included all of the souls of that generation. And he perfected his soul to such an extent that he merited the name "Holy"!*[XV]

CHESSED

The love and passion of Rabbi Yehudah HaNasi for Bnei Yisrael was heartfelt, overflowing, and simply outstanding.

In *Berachot* 16b, we read of the extra prayers composed and recited by leading Sages. After his morning prayer, Rabbi Yehudah HaNasi said the following:

> *May it be Your will, Our God, and God of our forefathers, that You save us from arrogant people and from arrogance, from evil men and bad events, from the yetzer hara, from evil companions or neighbors, from the destructive Satan, from harsh judgments and/or harsh opponents, whether he is a member*

> *of the covenant, (a Jew), or whether he is not a member of the covenant.*[XVI]

Rabbi Yehudah HaNasi would recite this prayer every day, despite the fact that royal officers stood watch over him for his protection. Nevertheless, he prayed to avoid conflict or hindrance resulting from arrogance.

Through his *chessed*, Rabbi Yehudah HaNasi provided the generations after him with this special daily prayer.

The Talmud learns that Rabbi Yehudah HaNasi suffered greatly during his lifetime as a result of an incident where he was deemed to show a lack of mercy and kindness. Particularly in the "criticism" of Rabbi Yehudah HaNasi do we get a glimpse of a huge and expansive soul imbued with feeling, kindness, and love.

The *Michtav M'Eliyahu* explains:

> *The attributes of the soul are very sensitive instruments especially the attribute of good deeds/chessed. And they are susceptible to be blemished for any reason. We can learn this idea from the wonderful story in the Talmud regarding Rabbi Yehudah HaNasi. He performed incredible amounts of chessed for the Jewish people for many generations in that he toiled and worked in organizing the Oral Torah, the Mishnah. He was such a tremendous giver that he gave everything to others and took nothing for himself. As the Sages teach us: the table of Rebbi was filled with extreme wealth; the guests benefitted from it and he didn't benefit from it at all. Nonetheless, the Talmud in Bava Metzia tells us: a calf that was designated to be ritually slaughtered cried in front of Rabbi Yehudah HaNasi. Rabbi Yehudah HaNasi said: "Go, because for this you were created."*
>
> *The Heavens said: "Because you [Rebbi] didn't have mercy on the calf, you will be afflicted with suffering."*[XVII]

This punishment transpired despite the fact that Rebbi undoubtedly understood the deeper meaning of ritual slaughtering and the ability to raise an animal to a higher level of existence.

The Gemara explains the statement:

> *The suffering stopped due to another incident. One day, the maidservant of Rabbi Yehudah HaNasi was sweeping the house. The maidservant was sweeping out young weasels lying around.*
>
> *Rabbi Yehudah HaNasi said to her: Let them be, as it is written: "The Lord is good to all; and His mercies are over all His works" (Tehillim 145:9).*
>
> *They said in Heaven: "Since he was compassionate, we shall be compassionate on him," and Rabbi Yehudah HaNasi was relieved of his suffering.*[XVIII]

This episode portrays Rebbi as the consummate *baal teshuvah*—put in a similar situation facing one of God's creatures, his compassion on the weasels alleviated his suffering!

And yet another incident from the Talmud:

> *The Gemara continues discussing Rabbi Yehudah HaNasi's relationship with Rabbi Elazar, son of Rabbi Shimon.*
>
> *Once Rabbi Yehudah HaNasi arrived at the home of Rabbi Elazar, son of Rabbi Shimon.*
>
> *He asked the local people: "Does that righteous person have a son?"*
>
> *They answered: "He has an errant son and any prostitute who hires herself out to others for two coins hires him for eight, as he is very handsome."*
>
> *Upon hearing this report, Rabbi Yehudah HaNasi resolved to free Rabbi Elazar's son from his plight.*
>
> *He brought the boy back to his home, ordained him as a rabbi, and gave him over to Rabbi Shimon ben Isi ben Lakonya (the brother of the boy's mother).*[XIX]

Rabbi Yehudah HaNasi demonstrated down-to-earth compassion by his actions. This was real-life caring and involvement in individuals from the man who was the leader of the entire nation. This event and others like it personify authentic Jewish leadership, such as that seen in Yaakov at the well; Moshe, in Egypt defending his brothers, and at the well in Midian advocating for the daughters of Yitro; and King David tending compassionately to his flock. Such practical, unassuming, but genuine concern for individuals is a hallmark of authentic Jewish leadership.

VISIONARY

Rabbi Yehudah HaNasi was blessed with great scholarship, having studied under the outstanding leaders of the previous generation, including Rabbi Shimon Bar Yochai. He was wise, wealthy, holy, modest, kind, and compassionate. He saw, understood, and empathized with the day-to-day struggles of the individual. And he recognized the big picture as well.

In fact, the Talmud in *Sanhedrin* 98b places Rabbi Yehudah HaNasi on the Mashiach level: "Rav says: 'If the Messiah is among the living in this generation, he is a person such as our saintly Rabbi Yehudah HaNasi, who was renowned for his sanctity, piety, and Torah knowledge.'"[XX]

Rav Tzadok explains:

> *He had no defects and perfected the souls of the generation that were attached to him; therefore, it says in Sanhedrin 98b, "Who from the living could be Mashiach? Rebbi!" For he perfected his soul to such an extent that he perfected his generation as well. But the generation was not yet worthy for such a revelation for they did not perfect the souls of those who preceded them. For, in the world of souls, the sons are included in the fathers. Rebbi perfected his soul completely but the souls until the end of the generations were not perfected. In any case, he merited not to die, but it wasn't clearly revealed to his generation. He established the Oral Torah, which is the primary Torah that revives, and that leads to the resurrection of the dead.*[XXI]

The Talmud in *Sanhedrin* 36a positions Rabbi Yehudah's stature in historical context: "From the time of Moshe until Rebbi we do not find Torah and greatness in one place (person)."[XXII]

The *Yad Ramah* elaborates:

> *That is to say we do not find anyone who was greater in his generation both in Torah and greatness. Such as Moshe Rabbeinu who was great and no one in Israel was like him in wisdom and malchut; and also Rebbi—Rabbeinu HaKadosh—was great and no one in his generation was like him in wisdom and leadership.*[XXIII]

But like all truly great historical leaders, Rabbi Yehudah HaNasi was a remarkable visionary. He understood the urgency of the times and was able to see the future dangers for the post-Churban Jewish people. He understood that the Jewish people stood at a pivotal, critical juncture and realized that he could possibly be the conduit to help ensure the future viability of Judaism and the Jewish people.

The result was not just leadership on a social, economic, and political playing field—which there was in abundance—but also the passion and love for the Jewish people—past, present, and future—that propelled Rebbi to codify in writing that which was actually prohibited to put pen to paper (or rather, reed brushes dipped in ink on papyrus).

The Talmud in *Gittin* 60b teaches that you may not transcribe those parts of the Torah that were given orally. Yet we see that the Oral Law was written! The Talmud there sources *Tehillim* (119:126): "Hashem has a set time to judge those who have nullified your Torah." The Talmud interprets this to mean that when it is a time to act for God, they may annul Your Torah. The Sages have permission (or rather a duty) to ignore or annul certain laws if they deem it necessary to preserve the Torah for the Jewish people.[XXIV]

The *Rambam*, in his introduction to the *Mishneh Torah*, writes:

> *Because Rebbi saw that the students were decreasing, and the persecutions were reappearing and the Roman Empire was spreading around the world and getting stronger, and Israel was going to the ends of the world, he therefore composed one work that would be accessible to everyone, so that they could quickly learn and not forget.*[XXV]

Sefer Yuchsin writes:

> When Rabbi Yehudah HaNasi saw the long length of the exile and that forgetfulness became commonplace, he said: "It is time to act for Hashem even though it will go against a precept of the Torah, for oral matters may not be written."[XXVI]

IN DEATH AS IN LIFE

Even the death of Rabbi Yehudah HaNasi is reported in extraordinary terms, as seen from *Ketubot* 103a:

> Rabbi Yehudah HaNasi commanded his sons: "My lamp should be lit in its usual place, my table should be set in its usual place, and the bed should be arranged in its usual place." The Gemara asks: What is the reason he made these requests? The Gemara explains: Every Shabbat eve, after his passing, Rabbi Yehudah HaNasi would come to his house as he had done during his lifetime, and he therefore wished for everything to be set up as usual.[XXVII]

Rabbeinu Bachya comments on Rebbi's death:

> "He expired and was gathered to his people" (Bereishit 49:33). The word "death" (מיתה) is not mentioned in connection with Yaakov. This prompted our Sages in Taanit 5b to say: "Our Patriarch Yaakov never died."
>
> Yet we see from the reports of the Torah here that he was treated as if dead—i.e., embalmed, buried, etc.—surely this is evidence that he did die!
>
> We must therefore understand the statement of our Sages who said, "He did not die," to mean that Yaakov's soul remained hovering over his body due to the degree of holiness he had attained. Whereas other righteous people, who did not attain the level of holiness that Yaakov attained, are forced to return their souls to celestial regions, and once they have returned there

they do not return to earth, Yaakov's soul was in a constant state of commuting between heaven and earth. Only extremely rarely did great men attain this degree of holiness in their lives, Rabbi Yehudah HaNasi being one of those select few.[XXVIII]

However one interprets the life-after-death episode and its precedents in Jewish History, Rabbi Yehudah HaNasi "lives on" like Yaakov and King David before him.[4]

---

4   As it states: "יעקב אבינו לא מת—Yaakov our father did not die"; "דוד מלך ישראל חי וקיים—King David lives and remains vibrant!"

4. THE ENCOUNTERS: PRINCE AND EMPEROR

There are numerous Torah sources describing the encounters and relationship between Rabbi Yehudah HaNasi and Antoninus. Yet, in so many ways, that historically unique bond remains enigmatic.

Their relationship was so "unusual," so one-sided, matching the leading Torah leader of his generation with an admiring Roman emperor.

Rabbi Yehudah HaNasi was the consummate teacher, with Antoninus the dutiful student.

Rabbi Yehudah HaNasi was the revered role model par excellence, and Antoninus the devoted admirer.

It's reasonable that historians might have difficulty accepting the Rabbi Yehudah HaNasi-Antoninus attachment. Standard preconceived notions would deny historians the ability to acknowledge such a remarkable historical match.

The Torah and its many classic commentators, however, clue us in early on.

FROM THE WOMB

By the pregnancy of Rivka, in *Bereishit* 25:23, we read:

> And the Lord said to her [Rivka], "Two nations are in your womb, and two kingdoms will separate from inside of you, and

one kingdom will become mightier than the other kingdom, and the elder will serve the younger."[I]

While the verse is clearly talking about the future Eisav and Yaakov safely ensconced in their mother Rivka's womb, the classical Torah commentators saw much more:

Yalkut Reuveni	Antoninus and Rebbi were the reincarnation of Eisav and Yaakov. Antoninus was the reincarnation of Eisav, and Rebbi the reincarnation of Yaakov, who instituted the blessing, "You Are Holy." Therefore, Rebbi is called "הנשיא—the Prince," which is the acronym for "ניצוץ של יעקב אבינו—the spark of Yaakov our father." In the merit of Yaakov, the Written Torah was given, and Rebbi compiled the Oral Torah.[II]
Rav Saadia Gaon	Two nations in your womb: These are Rebbi and Antoninus. He told her [Rivka] to comfort her and to speak to her heart. Even from the wicked Eisav will come Antoninus. And why did Antoninus come from a wicked one? Because he was the spark of Eisav that was taken from Yitzchak and Rivka. Antoninus was the fruit taken from the peel.[III]
Rashi	The word "nations" (גוים) is written as "mighty ones" (גיים); these are Antoninus and Rebbi for whom radishes and lettuce were always available in the summer and winter.[IV]
Meshech Chochmah	Sarah produced good while Hagar produced bad. And since Rivka felt the "boys" in her womb when Eisav was trying to get out when she passed a house of idol worship, she saw one was good and one was bad. Therefore, she asked, "Why isn't this like Sarah," for Rivka realized she was given good and the bad, and not just good like Sarah. The prophet answered her that she will produce two nations, including later in history, Antoninus. And so that even in the bad (Eisav) is mixed good (Antoninus) and therefore both are in your womb.[V]
Avodah Brurah	The word *geyim* (גיים) is linguistically rooted to "haughty/proud," for they [Rabbi Yehudah HaNasi and Antoninus] were extremely wealthy. And this is the comment of Rav Gedaliah Lifshitz: "From the language of גאים, that they acted with leadership and importance."[VI]

The *Maharal* connects the verse to the two, but broadens the scope beyond the relationship of two people:

> And it appears to me that this connection hints not only to Antoninus and Rebbi the individuals, but rather also to the entire two nations.
>
> Many kings came from Eisav, so why was this king singled out more than others?
>
> Rebbi and Antoninus were similar to Yaakov and Eisav. This one was a nasi in Yisrael and this one king of Edom at the same time.
>
> But both nations are unique in their importance.
>
> Even though there were emperors of one that were also important (like Antoninus), since it says "two nations in your womb," we interpret the verse as referring to two nations. Rebbi and Antoninus were singled out as more important and the rest of the kings and leaders in history are included in the interpretation of verse, each according to their level.
>
> The verse hints to the Jewish people and the Roman nation who have common unique attributes. They are refined and treat their food with importance. And this is what it means when it says that "Rebbi and Antoninus never ran out of radishes and lettuce." There are those people who eat like animals and don't have self-respect. But Yisrael and Eisav do not behave this way. They properly prepare themselves to be worthy.
>
> And Rome till this day honors itself with clothing and beautiful buildings more than other nation…And the Jewish people followed in the way of Rome because of their importance.
>
> Therefore, it says "two nations in your womb": two important nations.[VII]

The *Malbim* develops the concept of a national paradigm that began in the womb and played itself out throughout history. This comes to teach us four things:

- Two nations: each one will be a great nation, and the unusual pains of pregnancy show that it's a "tight squeeze" for both to live together.
- They each will have a unique religion and faith.
- The strength of one depends on the weakness of the other.
- The above paradigm will continue until the End of Days, and then the elder will serve the younger; and this is against the laws of nature, and it will not occur without a struggle and war.^{VIII}

Rav Hirsch writes:

> Rebecca was informed that she carried two nations in her womb who would represent two different forms of social government. The one state would build up its greatness on spirit and morals, on the humane in humans, the other would seek its greatness in cunning and strength. Spirit and strength, morality and violence oppose each other, and indeed, from birth onwards will they be in opposition to each other. One form of government will always be more powerful than the other. The scales will constantly sway from one to the other, between לאום ולאום. The whole of history is nothing else than the struggle as to whether spirit or sword, or, as our Sages put it, whether Caesarea or Jerusalem is to have the upper hand.[1]

AT BIRTH

The Rabbi Yehudah HaNasi-Antoninus bond formed in the womb through Eisav and Yaakov was replayed at their actual births.

The *Menorat Hamaor* 83 provides the details of the dramatic story:

> At that time, the Roman Empire prohibited Jews to circumcise their sons, and whoever circumcised his son would be killed. Rabban Shimon ben Gamliel, the father of Rabbi Yehudah the HaNasi, decided to circumcise his son anyway and did so

---

1 Hirsch, *Bereishit* 25:23.

> in secret. The governor heard about it and informed on him to the king. The king commanded Rabban Shimon ben Gamliel and his son to appear before him to determine if the accusation was true. The baby's parents took him and headed to the king's court, but on the way, they stopped at the house of Antoninus' parents. Antoninus' mother offered to switch her infant son Antoninus with their circumcised son. After they were switched, Antoninus cried and the rabbi's wife nursed him.
>
> When Rabbi Shimon ben Gamliel and his wife were called into the king and asked why they had transgressed the king's decree, Rabbi Shimon told the king to take the infant and check for himself whether or not he was circumcised. The king examined the infant and saw that he was uncircumcised. He was furious at the governor who had fooled him and harassed Rabbi Shimon for no reason. The governor was hanged at the king's command, and Rabbi Shimon was compensated with the cancellation of the decree. Thanks to Antoninus, Yehudah was saved from death.[IX]

The *Tosafot* (*Avodah Zarah* 10b) sources a midrash and says that when the infants were switched, Rabbi Yehudah HaNasi's mother nursed Antoninus (and apparently Antoninus' mother nursed the infant Rabbi Yehudah).[X]

Seder Hadorot confirms this extraordinary occurrence, saying that the Caesar's wife nursed Rabbi Yehudah and Rabbi Yehudah's mother nursed the infant Antoninus.[XI]

The commentators discuss the halachic issue of a Jewish child suckling from a non-Jewish woman. The midrash tells us that Moshe, who was to give over the Torah with his holy mouth, would not suckle from an Egyptian, and therefore Pharaoh's daughter employed Yocheved, Moshe's mother, to nurse the infant Moshe. But the halachah concurs that it is not prohibited when necessary.

The incident of the switched infants and the suckling leads to an interesting observation. How could Rebbi put the Mishnah teachings to writing when it was prohibited? One answer offered is that, yes, it was strictly wrong, though absolutely necessary, and that "wrongdoing" was the result of Rebbi nursing from Antoninus' mother!

Whether Antoninus of the Talmud was Antoninus Pius or Marcus Aurelius, both of these successive emperors ruled at the heels of catastrophic events for the Jewish people. And these events were concomitantly not minor ones for the Roman Empire. The Jewish revolt rocked the foundations of the Roman Empire.

Dio Cassius writes:

> Many Romans, moreover, perished in this war. Therefore Hadrian in writing to the senate did not employ the opening phrase commonly affected by the emperors, "If you and our children are in health, it is well; I and the legions are in health."[2]

In fact, according to historian Theodore Mannsen, "There is no parallel in all of the Roman history to this revolt in its strength and duration."[3]

The reigns of Antoninus Pius and Marcus Aurelius marked a change. And the Torah, already in *Bereishit*, informs us of just that—that something special and surprising will occur between perennial antagonists that will impact on Jewish history, to the extent that the *Seder Yaakov* remarks: "Rebbi was able to compile the Mishnah specifically during his time because the time was one of peace; Rebbi enjoyed his unique friendship with Antoninus and by extension the Jewish people benefitted."[XII]

Rashi commented on this point in *Bava Metzia* 33b:

> When the students of Shammai and Hillel began to differ and arguments arose in Israel, it was if there were two Torahs. This was a result of the persecutions, decrees, and harsh exile. These conditions made it difficult for matters to be properly clarified. This situation persisted until the time of Rabbi Yehudah HaNasi, when the Holy One, blessed be He, caused Rabbi

---

2   http://penelope.uchicago.edu/Thayer/E/Roman/Texts/Cassius_Dio/69*.html.
3   Theodore Mommsen, *The History of Rome* 1887 (vol. 1–5) ebook #10706, http://www.gutenberg.org/cache/epub/10706/pg10706.txt.

Yehudah HaNasi to find favor in the eyes of Emperor Antoninus. There was now quiet in Yisrael and Rabbi Yehudah HaNasi was able to gather the students of Eretz Yisrael together. Until now students would write down notes from the teachings of their rabbis, but there wasn't anything properly organized by topics. Rebbi gathered all of the material and organized it clearly with each subject in its place. He brought and included numerous sources and also decided the law/halachah.[XIII]

Dorot Harishonim elaborates, explaining how the Rebbi/Antoninus bond, coming as it did after the cruel period of destruction and *shmad*, became the key to Israel's fortune.

It was only because the Romans wanted to honor Rabbi Yehudah HaNasi, the "highly elevated one," that the Jewish people found "sweet honey" (Torah, Mishnah) "from the hive" (Roman rule). And therefore the *metivta* of learning was returned to its place under the leadership of Rabbi Yehudah HaNasi.

He quotes Rav Shrira Gaon who explains that quiet was achieved due to the mercy of the emperor to Rabbi Yehudah HaNasi. The outcome of this bond between Rabbi Yehudah HaNasi and Antoninus was that the entire structure of Jewish institutional life underwent a dramatic change all for the good of the nation.[XIV]

The *Megalei Amukot* reveals that Moshe himself prophetically prayed that God would cause Rabbi Yehudah HaNasi to find favor in the eyes of Antoninus.

When Moshe asks God to allow him to enter the Land of Israel, he uses the words, "אעברה נא—Please allow me to go over" (*Devarim* 3:25).

The letters of that expression—אעברה נא—stand for:

א—"אנטונינוס—Antoninus"

ע—"עשה—made"

ב—"בימי—in the days (of)"

ר—"רבי—Rabbi Yehudah HaNasi"

ה—"הקדוש—the Holy"

נ—"ניצוץ—spark"

א—"אחד—one."[XV]

The enigmatic meetings between Antoninus and Rabbi Yehudah HaNasi are described in *Avodah Zarah* 10b:

> *Antoninus had a certain tunnel that went from his house to Rebbi's house. Each day he would bring two servants to accompany him through the tunnel. He would kill one at the door of Rebbi's house, and he would kill the other who accompanied him back to his home at the door of his house.*
>
> *Antoninus told Rebbi: "When I come to your house nobody should be found with you."*
>
> *One day he found Chanina Bar Chama sitting there.*
>
> *Antoninus said to Rebbi, "Did I not tell you that when I come to you nobody should be with you?"*
>
> *Rebbi responded: "This is not a mortal."*
>
> *Antoninus said: "If so, let him tell the servant who is sleeping by the door to wake up and come in."*
>
> *Rabbi Chanina Bar Chama went and found that the servant had been killed.*
>
> *He said to himself: "What shall I do? If I return and tell Antoninus that his servant has been killed, I would violate the rule, one who is sent on a mission should not report back with bad news. But if I leave him and go I would be insulting the king."*
>
> *So Rabbi Chanina prayed for God to have mercy on the dead man. He revived him and sent him to Antoninus.*
>
> *Antoninus said: "I know that the least among you can resurrect the dead. Nevertheless, when I come no one should be found with you."*[XVI]

WHAT WAS THIS TUNNEL?

The *Tosafot Rid* suggests that since Rebbi lived in Tzippori and Antoninus had a palace on a high spot in Tiberias, there was a twelve-*mil*-long cave that went from Tiberias to Tzippori.[XVII]

Ben Yehoyada understands differently:

> It appears that the Roman emperors had a city in Eretz Yisrael, Caesarea, where they would visit when they came from the capital Rome. They would stay in Caesarea for a number of months so that their rule would be apparent. And this city was also known as their royal city and the king had a large estate appropriate for a king; and surrounding his large estate were other estates for his ministers so they could be close to the king; and when Antoninus would come to Caesarea he would send for Rebbi to come from Tiberius, and since Rebbi came as a guest, Antoninus would give him one of the estates that were close by. There was a cave from the king's estate to Rebbi's, and this cave was originally built when the estates were built in case it was needed for any matter, and therefore he would come to Rebbi via this cave.[XVIII]

Rav Miller describes the cave encounters:

> Marcus Aurelius resided for a time in the land of Israel at Caesarea, when Rabbi was at Zippori (where he spent the last seventeen years of his life, except for a short time before his death when he resided at Beth Shearim), and the most unusual episode in history transpired at that time. The Roman emperor became the devoted disciple of the Nasi. By means of one of the underground tunnels (which abounded in the land of Israel and which were famous in the war of Betar), Antoninus visited his teacher frequently and sought his counsel not only in matters of mind and soul, but also in the affairs of government. The relationship between these two was a perilous secret which was never divulged to anyone (except Rabbi's closest disciples) during the lifetime of these two participants."[4]

---

4   Miller, *Exalted People*, p. 167.

The *Tosafot Hashalem* says in the name of Rabbeinu Elazar from Gramaeza:

> *Rebbi and Antoninus had signs to show if there were people by Rebbi. If there was lettuce on the table, that was a sign for Antoninus to return, for the word for lettuce—chazeret, hints to chazor—go back, hinting that there were other people with Rebbi. If radishes were on the table, it was a sign that no one was there with Rebbi; tznon—radish, hints to tzane—shield, as found in Tehillim 5:13: "You shall surround...with a shield," as if to say it is safe for you to come, no one is with me.*[XIX]

However one learns the tunnel episodes, it is clear that the meetings were meant to be secret and hidden. That was the nature of their relationship.

The discussions and encounters between Rabbi Yehudah HaNasi and Emperor Antoninus can be divided as follows:

- Political/personal advice
- Spiritual matters
- The relationship

POLITICAL AND PERSONAL ADVICE

Antoninus highly valued the sagacious advice of Rabbi Yehudah HaNasi, both when dealing with political dilemmas as well as when facing sensitive personal matters.

Three examples include:

1. Let the dove fly
2. A radish a day
3. Lettuce of mercy

1. LET THE DOVE FLY

The Gemara in *Avodah Zarah* 10a describes a political issue Antoninus presented to Rabbi Yehudah HaNasi.

> Antoninus said to Rebbi: "I want that my son Asveirus should rule in my place and that Tiberius should be declared a free community.
>
> If I submit one of these requests to them [the authorities, the senate, in Rome], they will grant it, but both will not be granted."
>
> Rebbi brought a man and had him ride upon the shoulders of his fellow. He put a dove in the hand of the upper one and said to the lower one: "Tell the upper one to let the dove fly from his hand."
>
> Antoninus said: "Learn from it that Rebbi is telling me to ask them, 'Let Asveirus my son rule after me,' and then tell Asveirus to declare Tiberius a free community."[XX]

Antoninus' request for this political advice is answered enigmatically by Rebbi. The hidden nature of their relationship is reflected by the "hidden" messages Rebbi conveyed to Antoninus.

The *Iyun Yaakov* explains that Rebbi used the allegory of the dove since Yisrael is compared to a dove. Just as the wings of the dove protect it, so the Torah protects Israel.[XXI] Antoninus was concerned that the relationship between Rome and Yisrael would change after his reign, certainly if his son would not be next to rule.

Yad Eliyahu provides an esoteric explanation as to why Rebbi advised the emperor to ask for only one matter.

> The earthly kingship resembles the Divine Kingship, as we see from Taanit 8b: In the days of Rabbi Shmuel bar Nachmani there was a famine and a plague.
>
> The Sages said: "What should we do? Should we pray for mercy for two troubles, both the famine and the plague?
>
> "This is not possible, as it is improper to pray for the alleviation of two afflictions at once. And this is the ruling in the Tur, and we also see that by the Urim V'tumim, one did not ask for two things at once."[XXII]

Interestingly, this episode demonstrates the limits of the power of emperor during that period. The emperor had to contend with the senate, the powerful military and legions, and the people affectionately known as the "mob," who needed to be won over in Rome.

Antoninus realized that he couldn't ask for two requests. Rabbi Yehudah HaNasi advised him how one request could accomplish both intents.

2. A RADISH A DAY

Once again in *Avodah Zarah* 10a, Antoninus appeals to Rabbi Yehudah HaNasi, this time concerning a matter of political life and death.

> *Antoninus said to Rebbi: "The dignitaries of Rome are persecuting me."*
>
> *Each day Rebbi would bring Antoninus into a garden and each day he would pluck a single radish from its bed in front of Antoninus.*
>
> *Antoninus said to himself: "I learn from this that Rebbi is advising me to kill them off one at a time and not contend with all of them at once."*
>
> *But he should have spoken to him clearly!*
>
> *Rebbi said: "The dignitaries of Rome will overhear me and they will persecute him."*
>
> *So he should have spoken to him quietly!*
>
> *Rebbi avoided even this because it is written, "For a bird of the sky will carry the sound" (Kohelet 10:20).*[XXIII]

Ben Yehoyada quotes the *Aruch*, who teaches that Rebbi specifically pulled a radish, whose head is hidden in the ground while its leaves are seen above. This hints to us that the dignitaries of Rome, who persecute the emperor with bad advice, do this secretly and deviously with their thoughts. Their head is the home of their hidden devious advice, and therefore he suspects them and wishes to uproot them.[XXIV]

It is suggested in *Avodah Brurah* that perhaps the reason why the nobles in Rome were against Antoninus was a result of the historic "halachah" that "Eisav/Rome hates Yaakov/Israel." Antoninus decided to become attached to Rebbi and therefore engendered that hatred to be directed to himself.[XXV]

3. LETTUCE OF MERCY

A third incident recorded in *Avodah Zarah* 10b deals with a delicate issue involving Antoninus' daughter Gira.

> *Antoninus had a daughter named Gira who committed a transgression.*
>
> *He sent Rebbi a rocket herb [an edible annual plant used as a leaf vegetable for its fresh peppery flavor].*
>
> *Rebbi sent him a coriander [also known as cilantro or Chinese parsley].*
>
> *Antoninus sent Rebbi a leek.*
>
> *Rebbi sent him a lettuce.*[XXVI]

As seen before, this communication between Rabbi Yehudah HaNasi and Antoninus was also accomplished via hints.

Rashi explains that Gira was guilty of an illicit relationship, and the rocket herb symbolized that act. Rebbi sent a coriander, which hinted to Antoninus that his daughter deserved the death penalty. The retort of the leek sent by Antoninus told Rebbi that such a penalty would cut off his posterity. Rebbi's lettuce in turn told Antoninus that if that was the case, the emperor should have mercy on his daughter.[XXVII]

The *Tosafot* ask: What was Rebbi thinking when he initially said to kill her but then retracted? They answer that Rebbi's initial message, after he understood the nature of the transgression, was that Antoninus should cover up the matter and reprimand his daughter privately. Antoninus misunderstood the message and thought Rebbi had advised him to kill his daughter, so he sent a message that death would mean cutting off his progeny. Rebbi sent a new message clarifying what he initially meant and that Antoninus should have mercy on Gira.[XXVIII][5]

---

5   Based on the *Rabbeinu Chananel* and the *Aruch*.

We see that when Antoninus faced serious political or personal dilemmas, he knew he could turn to Rabbi Yehudah HaNasi for trustworthy, independent, and astute advice.

SPIRITUAL INQUIRIES

The back-and-forth between Antoninus and Rabbi Yehudah HaNasi demonstrates the emperor's deep thirst for wisdom beyond natural knowledge. Theirs was a bond focused on lofty spiritual matters.

1. The Tag Team: Body and Soul
2. Sunrise, Sunset…
3. The Evil Inclination

1. THE TAG TEAM: BODY AND SOUL

In *Sanhedrin* 91a–b, Antoninus attempts to understand the relationship between body and soul.

> *Antoninus, the Roman emperor, said to Rabbi Yehudah HaNasi: "The body and the soul are able to exempt themselves from judgment for their sins. How so? The body says: 'The soul sinned, as from the day of my death when it departed from me, I am cast like a silent stone in the grave, and do not sin.' And the soul says: 'The body sinned, as from the day that I departed from it, I am flying in the air like a bird, incapable of sin.'"*
>
> *Rabbi Yehudah HaNasi said to him: "I will tell you a parable. To what is this matter comparable? It is comparable to a king of flesh and blood who had a fine orchard, and in it there were fine first fruits of a fig tree, and he stationed two guards in the orchard: one lame, who was unable to walk, and one blind. Neither was capable of reaching the fruit on the trees in the orchard without the assistance of the other. The lame person said to the blind person: 'I see fine first-fruits of a fig tree in the orchard; come and place me upon your shoulders. I will guide you to the tree, and we will bring the figs to eat them.' The lame*

> person rode upon the shoulders of the blind person and they brought the figs and ate them.
>
> "Sometime later, the owner of the orchard came to the orchard. He said to the guards: 'The fine first-fruits of a fig tree that were in the orchard, where are they?' The lame person said: 'Do I have any legs with which I would be able to walk and take the figs?' The blind person said: 'Do I have any eyes with which I would be able to see the way to the figs?' What did the owner of the orchard do? He placed the lame person upon the shoulders of the blind person just as they did when they stole the figs, and he judged them as one.
>
> "So too, the Holy One, blessed be He, brings the soul on the day of judgment and casts it back into the body, as they were when they sinned, and He judges them as one, as it is stated: 'He calls to the heavens above and to the earth that He may judge His people' (Tehillim 50:4). 'He calls to the heavens above,' this is the soul, which is heavenly. 'And to the earth that He may judge His people,' this is the body, which is earthly."[XXIX]

Rav Saadia Gaon writes that the soul and body together act as one according to the beginning of their formation: And Hashem formed man dust from the earth and blew into him the soul of life. And these two have one recompense and one punishment.[XXX]

Oznaim L'Torah explains that the sins are attributed to the body and soul as one, for the body will argue on the Day of Judgment that from the time the soul left, it did not sin. And the soul argues that from the time the body left, it did not sin. And in order to judge, it will be necessary to return the soul to the body and judge them as they sinned. And the verse (*Devarim* 4:2) that attributed the sin just to the soul does so because through the action of the body, it is not possible to recognize if the act was done accidently or on purpose.[XXXI]

Antoninus was a believer. He accepted that God created man, body and soul. He sought to understand the nature of that paradoxical heavenly and earthly combination.

2. SUNRISE, SUNSET...

Antoninus probes Rabbi Yehudah HaNasi in *Sanhedrin* 91b in an effort to learn from God's heavenly creations.

> *Antoninus asked Rebbi: "Why does the sun rise in the east and set in the west?"*
>
> *Rebbi said to him: "If it were reversed, you would also have asked me this same question!"*
>
> *Antoninus said: "This is what I mean to ask you. Given that the sun rises in the east, why does it set in the west?"*
>
> *Rebbi said: "In order to offer greetings to its Creator, as it stated 'And the hosts of the heavens bow to you'" (Nechemiah 9:6).*
>
> *Antoninus said to Rebbi: "If that is why the sun does so, then it should travel in the middle of the sky, offer greetings and set there!"*
>
> *Rebbi answered him: "The sun proceeds to the end of the west on account of workers and travelers."*[XXXII]

The *Yad Ramah* explains the message Rabbi Yehudah taught his student Antoninus.

> *It appeared to Antoninus that the sun travels from east to west in the heavens, and in the evening sets in the west in the thickness of the heavens. And then it returns all night behind the heavens from west to east in the same arc it traveled during the day. And when it gets to the end of the night in the east, it rises and travels that arc until it gets back to the west.*
>
> *Therefore, Antoninus asked Rebbi, "Why does the sun set in the west?" Rather, should it not not travel all night until it returns to the place of its rising (the east, and set in the east) and rise again? And Rebbi answered him according to the reasoning of the questioner. In order to acknowledge the Creator, for the Divine presence rests in the west, and when it gets to the west it sets in acknowledgment, and the setting is its bowing. So Antoninus asked him, "Why doesn't it go to the middle of*

> the sky and bow there," for it is more honorable to bow at a distance! And Rebbi answered him, "Because of the workers and travelers"; if it (the sun) would set in the middle of the sky, it would set while the light of the sun was still strong, and people would not know that it is about to set, and workers would continue working in the field until the sudden nighttime, and travelers wouldn't know when to ask for lodging, before it would suddenly get dark for them.[XXXIII]

Antoninus asked this question because he was trying to understand God's reason for certain cosmological events. He clearly understood that there is a rationale and purpose for all of creation. Rabbi Yehudah taught him that all of nature is intended to reveal God and His *Malchut* to the world—the totality of creation and all of its parts.

3. THE EVIL INCLINATION

An additional question raised by Antoninus in *Sanhedrin* 91b deals with the origin of evil inclination. This question is particularly relevant to Antoninus and Rabbi Yehudah HaNasi as it takes us back to Eisav and Yaakov in the womb.

> *Antoninus also asked Rebbi: "From when does the evil inclination have influence over a person? Is it from the moment of the embryo's formation or from the moment of birth?"*
>
> *Rebbi said: "From the moment of the embryo's formation."*
>
> *Antoninus said: "If so, the fetus would kick against its mother's womb and leave the womb prematurely. Must it not rather be from the moment of birth?"*
>
> *Rebbi remarked: "Antoninus taught me this matter, and the Torah supports his view, as it is stated: 'Sin crouches at the door.'"*[6, XXXIV]

Rav Mordechai Levi references *Rashi*, who teaches in *Bereishit* that when Yaakov and Eisav were in the womb, the language of "running" is

---

6   Bereishit 4:7.

used. Yaakov tried to run when Rivka passed a house of Torah, and Eisav tried to run when Rivka passed a house of idol worship. So it appears that the evil inclination ruled Eisav while he was still in his mother's embryo. And this contradicts what Rebbi agreed to.

> *There appears to be a battle of the inheritance of two worlds.*
>
> *Why now was there a battle inside the womb for two worlds?*
>
> *And if one defeated the other, would he take the world in the embryo?*
>
> *Or the World to Come?*
>
> *One should know that Yaakov and Eisav are partners in this world, for their essences clash and therefore they could not be idle together in their mother's womb, so therefore even though they were in the womb they were pitted against each other for their essences clash, like fire and water; even though they don't have knowledge they will clash.*
>
> *Even if by nature they could be together, the essence of man is not in nature; so therefore even in the womb they clashed. The clash in the womb shows us the battle they would have in this world and in the World to Come.*
>
> *When they were in their mother's womb, they had no connection and theretofore they ran; they clashed as their essence clashed.*
>
> *The clash was in two worlds. Each one wanted to push the other and to claim complete existence without the other.* [xxxv]

The clash between Yaakov and Eisav is not an issue of whether or not the evil inclination is present in the womb. It is not present as Antoninus learned. The clash between Yaakov/Yisrael and Eisav/Rome is built into the nature of the world. The Antoninus/Rabbi Yehudah HaNasi paradigm ran counter to nature. It was an outstanding exception.

THE RELATIONSHIP

What made the relationship between these two great figures so unique?

According to Chazal, it was the recognition on Antoninus' part of the greatness inherent in Rabbi Yehudah HaNasi and the understanding of the role he, the Emperor of the Fourth Kingdom, was required to take vis-à-vis his "teacher."

From the encounters, one gets the sense that Rabbi Yehudah HaNasi not only taught Antoninus the wisdom of life and the profundities of Torah, but also showed him that the two of them had historical roles to fulfill. Not only did Antoninus realize that he was part of a historic rectification/*tikkun*, but he also apparently internalized that Yaakov and Eisav were the antecedents for his and Rabbi Yehudah HaNasi's *tikkun*.

A few examples illustrate the nature of their historically unique relationship.

1. Every Day
2. Gold and Wheat
3. My Master

1. EVERY DAY

The Talmud in *Avodah Zarah* 10b recounts a remarkable episode:

> *Every day, Antoninus would wait upon Rebbi. He would serve him food and drink. When Rebbi wished to climb into his bed, he would bend down before the bed and say to Rebbi: "Climb up on me to your bed."*
>
> *Rebbi protested: "It is improper to treat the throne so disrespectfully."*
>
> *He replied to Rebbi: "If only I would be the mat beneath you in the World To Come."*^{XXXVI}

The *Torat Chaim* explains that the prophecy relayed to a pregnant Rivka was fulfilled when Antoninus served Rabbi Yehudah HaNasi.

> *When it says, "The elder will serve the younger" (Bereishit 25:23), it is referring to a king, as the verse begins, "The might*

shall pass from one regime to the other." And we do not see that this prophecy occurred except in this case only.

And it appears that for this reason, because there was this prophecy, Rebbi allowed Antoninus to serve him and was not concerned that this was disparaging to the kingship.[xxxvii]

The *Maarit Ha'ayin* teaches that when Antoninus served Rabbi Yehudah HaNasi, he was engaging in an historical rectification/*tikkun*.

> Antoninus was the best of Eisav/Edom, and Rebbi was a spark of Yaakov Avinu. Antoninus came to rectify that which was wronged to Yaakov and therefore he served Rebbi.
>
> Rebbi accepted this but still he told Antoninus that it's not proper to disparage the royalty in this manner—not derech eretz, despite the prophecy. But Antoninus answered, "If only I could..."[xxxviii]

2. GOLD AND WHEAT

Avodah Zarah 10b teaches that Antoninus "served" Rabbi Yehudah with gifts. The commentators teach that these gifts represented much more than physical ones.

> Every day, Antoninus would send Rabbi Yehudah HaNasi crushed gold in leather sacks, with wheat at its opening to hide its contents.
>
> He would tell his messengers: "Bring this wheat to Rabbi Yehudah HaNasi."
>
> But Rebbi said to him: "I do not need the gold. I already have plenty."
>
> Antoninus replied: "Let it be for those who come after you, who will in turn give it to those who come after them, because those who will come after you and those who will come after them will need to pay my successors."[xxxix]

Ben Yehoyada connects the gold and wheat to the spiritual, God-given gifts of the Written and Oral Torah.

> *And that which Antoninus sent Rabbi Yehudah HaNasi sacks of gold with wheat at the openings hints to the Written Torah and the Oral Torah.*
>
> *The Oral Torah is called gold, as the Rabbis learned from the verse, "And the gold of that land is good" (Bereishit 2:12).*
>
> *And the Written Torah is called wheat, as the Rabbis learned in Makkot 10a on the verses, He who loves abundance, with increase [wheat]—this too is vanity" (Kohelet 5:9), and the verse, "Come, eat of my bread…" (Mishlei 9:5).*[XL]

Tzror Hamaor writes that the abundance of radishes and lettuce mentioned both by Antoninus and Rabbi Yehudah HaNasi hint at two types of learning—one is the revealed Torah and the second is the hidden, secret Torah. When you grow radishes, the head and leaves are revealed; but this is not the case when growing lettuce, which is totally covered inside the ground. Rebbi and Antoninus always had these foods on their tables—that is to say, they learned and dealt together with radishes, the revealed Torah, and also with lettuce hinting at the hidden Torah.[XLI]

Rabbi Yehudah was the teacher and Antoninus the student. Their actions and conversations revolved around Torah concepts.

3. MY MASTER

At the same time, Antoninus remained the Roman emperor with all of its historic implications, as seen in *Midrash Rabbah* (*Bereishit* 75:5):

> *Rabbi Yehudah HaNasi said to Rabbi Afas: "Write a letter in my name to my lord King Antoninus."*
>
> *He wrote: "From Yehudah the Nasi/Prince to my Lord King Antoninus."*
>
> *Rabbi Yehudah HaNasi said to him: "Write, from your servant Yehudah to my Lord King Antoninus."*

He said to him: *"Rabbi Yehudah, why do you disparage your honor?"*

He said to him: *"Am I better than my ancestor? Didn't Yaakov say: You should speak like this to my master to Eisav, 'Your servant Yaakov spoke like this?'"*^{XLII}

Rabbi Moshe HaLevi Spero writes:

> *Certain commentators have asked why Rabbi Yehudah HaNasi felt that the situation of Yaakov and Esau could serve as a justification for his actions, since the midrash also mentions that the consensus of Talmudic opinion did not look upon Yaakov's humility in that case with approval? The response offered is that once Yaakov opted to humble himself in the presence of Esau, the initial experience for the archetype of such behavior throughout Jewish history originated. Moreover, the archetype concretized itself with the repetition and reinforcement of this defensive attitude toward 'Eisav' throughout later Jewish history. Thus, Rabbi Yehudah HaNasi, though he lived some fifteen hundred years after Yaakov, acted as he was predisposed to act by a latent but powerful archetype for such action. He, after conscious reflection on this subliminal prompt, chose to follow its suggestion. Indeed, he could truly be able to say that he knew what Yaakov meant when the latter said "Your servant," for he had re-enacted a past patriarchal action.*[7]

Clearly, Rabbi Yehudah HaNasi felt that an aspect of Israel being subservient to Rome needed to be maintained despite his personal connection to Antoninus. Even the extraordinary relationship between Antoninus and Rabbi Yehudah HaNasi included elements of the ordinary Rome/Israel pathway.

---

7   Moshe HaLevi Spero, "Remembering and Historical Awareness," *Tradition*, vol. 15, N. 3 Fall 1975, pp. 48–49.

THE BUNDLE UNRAVELED

Avodah Zarah 10b tells of Rabbi Yehudah HaNasi's reaction to Antoninus' death:

> "When Antoninus died, Rebbi said, 'The bundle is unraveled.'"[XLIII]

The *Ben Yehoyada* has an interesting understanding of Rebbi's statement regarding Antoninus' death:

> What is this coming to teach us? Everyone knew that Antoninus died! Rather, Rebbi is saying: "Don't think that just as we were close friends and saw each other in this world, this will also be the case in the World to Come."
>
> The bundle has been unraveled, for how could Antoninus who was a righteous convert (!) enter the domain of Rebbi HaKadosh? Similar to what Antoninus himself said: "Rebbi, if only I would be the mat beneath you in the World to Come."[XLIV]

However we understand what it means to be in another's company in the World to Come, the *Ben Yehoyada* presents a forceful non-sentimental lesson: yes, the relationship was special, intimate, unique, and even historic. But regardless, one needs to understand and appreciate the difference between these two great men, which in eternity simply cannot be bridged.

On a more straightforward level, Rabbi Yehudah HaNasi declared upon Antoninus' death that the bond they enjoyed—the bundle—will now fade away and history will return to its normal Yisrael/Rome course.

There is a discussion recorded in the *Talmud Yerushalmi* (*Megillah* 3:2) that goes as far as to question whether or not Antoninus actually converted to Judaism.

Just the possibility of whether Antoninus converted is itself an indication of the uniqueness of the relationship these two colossal figures of history enjoyed and the impact of Rabbi Yehudah HaNasi on the emperor.

The *Chatam Sofer* portrays the special nature of the bond:

> *If you consider the mem as closed [i.e., using the gematria calculation where a final mem = 600], then the word geyim equals 623, the same as three crowns—כתר ג'—numerical value of 623. This means to say that both of them [Rebbi and Antoninus] were crowned with three crowns. The crown of kingship, the crown of Torah, and the crown of a good name. For Rebbi was like a king, as the prince of Israel and Antoninus also had the crown of Torah, as it says that he learned Torah by Rebbi. And the Tosafot quotes the Yerushalmi who says that Antoninus actually converted.*[XLV]

And the *Chatam Sofer* in *Torat Moshe* goes as far as to describe what could have been the historical Israel/Rome pattern:

> *The intention in the formation of these sons was for Yaakov and all of his descendants to be a nation of priests, a holy nation. And Eisav to be like Zevulun, providing for Israel like Zevulun [the commerce, business people]. And so all of Israel would be like Rebbi in his generation and all of Eisav would be like Antoninus. Rebbi was a prince of God and Antoninus honored him greatly like a student to a teacher. And Rebbi honored Antoninus like one honors all Roman emperors. But all of this was when they were in their mother's womb at the beginning of their formation in their womb.*[XLVI]

Whether Yisrael and Rome can ever return to the "intended" relationship remains in doubt.

In the words of Rav Hirsch:

> *Rabbi Judah the Prince, the friend of the Roman Emperor Antoninus, a ruler in whom the spirit of Esau showed respect and understanding for the spirit of Yaakov, for the **first time** and perhaps the **only time** for many centuries to come.*[8]

---

8   Hirsch, *Collected Writings*, vol. 2, p. 436.

SUMMARY

Alexander the Great, Ptolemy II, Vespasian, Hadrian, and Antoninus were five very different emperors who engaged the Jewish people in multiple ways.

Alexander was the Macedonian conqueror of the civilized world, who interacted with the Jewish nation and a range of Jewish representatives during his triumphant military campaigns in the early years of the Second Temple.

- Alexander the Great, prophesied about in *Sefer Daniel* as the originator of the Third Kingdom, Greece, was a once-in-history phenomenon.
- The Sages understood that Alexander had a unique historical role to fulfill.
- His relationship with the Jewish people was somewhat ambiguous, but overall, viewed as positive.
- Alexander's meeting with the leading Jewish figure of the time, **Shimon HaTzaddik**, was dramatic, effective, and consequential for the Jewish nation, and it resulted in the name Alexander (Sender) being adopted as a popular Jewish name.
- The **Elders of the South**, masters of the natural sciences, faced off with Alexander the philosopher in a bold yet respectful manner, avoiding discussions that could lead to metaphysical matters beyond the philosophical realm.
- **Geviha ben Pesisa** was the paradigm non-Rabbinic advocate

who, with the backing of the Sages, cogently presented Torah proofs in defense of the Jewish nation under attack.

Ptolemy II Philadelphus built on the foundation of his father, Ptolemy I Soter, the founder of a three-hundred-year Greek dynasty in Egypt. Those building blocks included positioning the Library of Alexandria as the leading intellectual center in the world. This ambitious endeavor brought him in direct contact with the Jewish people.

- The translation of the Torah from Hebrew to Greek under Ptolemy was part of an overall campaign to bring all works of scholarship and wisdom under one roof in Alexandria.
- At the same time, Ptolemy's motive in gathering the **seventy-two Sages** was not totally pure, as part of his agenda was to demonstrate that the Torah was not Divine but rather flawed.
- The translation of the Torah into Greek for King Ptolemy by the unidentified seventy-two translators was miraculous in that God's intervention resulted in one consistent translated text.
- At that moment in history, it created a sanctification of God's Name, a *Kiddush Hashem*. It was also a major contribution to Western civilization.
- The Sages, in their deeper wisdom, understood that in the long run, the translation was highly detrimental and injurious for the Jewish people and for the honor of the Torah. They memorialized the date of its completion negatively within the fast of the Tenth of Tevet.
- While the Torah is Israel's unique Divine gift, the nations of the world have access to Torah if they so choose.
- Israel has a responsibility to convey the morality, purity, and values of the Torah to mankind.

Vespasian typified the classical Roman emperor whose dominion was based on the raw brute power of the fierce legions. His encounter with **Rabban Yochanan ben Zakkai** took place as Vespasian was poised to capture Jerusalem, a task he ultimately left for his son, Titus.

- The Fourth Kingdom—Rome—differs from the first three—Babylon, Persia/Media, and Greece—in its length, brutality and intense hatred towards the descendants of Yaakov.
- Roman historians portray an overall positive picture of Vespasian and his son Titus. Jewish tradition clearly marks them as bitter, evil, and destructive foes.
- The approach among the Sages towards the Roman Empire and its emperors was not monolithic.
- Rabban Yochanan ben Zakkai, the leading Sage of his era, determined that a careful, circumspect, and moderate approach towards Rome could result in a pathway for Jewish survival.
- Rabban Yochanan chose a "small request"—Yavneh—in order to help continue the viability of Torah learning and adherence to the commandments.

Hadrian, may his bones rot, implemented a remarkable policy of military retreat as he looked inwards, focusing on the internal policies of the Roman Empire. Hadrian's emphasis on a domestic agenda did not prevent him from implementing the *shmad*/oppression vis-à-vis Yisrael.

- Hadrian's regime started off with a ray of hope for the Jewish people but eventually deteriorated to the point where he now ranks as one of the cruelest world rulers as it relates to the Jewish nation.
- **Rabbi Yehoshua ben Chananya** was raised for greatness and evolved into one of most outstanding debaters in Jewish history.
- He skillfully navigated the corridors of power in which he was welcomed by the emperor and family.
- He superbly defended the Jewish nation, the Torah, and the fundamental religious beliefs of Israel.

Antoninus had an amazing relationship with Rebbi Yehudah HaNasi. It is not completely clear who Antoninus actually was:

- **Antoninus Pius** ushered in an "uneventful" era where the mighty Roman legions did not fight any wars. He focused on the internal issues of the empire.
- **Marcus Aurelius,** an adherent of Stoic philosophy and author of *Meditations*, personified Western civilization's image of the philosopher-king.

The above attributes contributed to each one being earmarked as a leading candidate for the identity of Antoninus in the Talmud.

- The relationship between **Rabbi Yehudah HaNasi** and Antoninus was unique in the annals of world history, going contra to the axiom that Eisav/Rome hates Yaakov/Yisrael.
- Though unparalleled, the rapport between these two giants of history demonstrates the possibility of a positive Yisrael-Rome connection.
- The intimate bond between these two leaders was a gift from God and enabled Rabbi Yehudah HaNasi to fulfill the historic mission of compiling the magnum opus of the Oral Law, the Mishnah.

CONCLUSION

The great encounters in Jewish history between world leaders and representatives of the Jewish people are characterized by the following:

- A Jewish attitude of "Be respectful but be wary."

    Jewish advocates are cautious, they consider all possible consequences and they carefully weigh options. They show respect through the strength of their authentic Jewish values and convictions.

- Brevity, to avoid discussion of deeper Torah concepts and to preclude potential conflict.

    The goal of the Jewish representative when facing a powerful world leader is to get the intended job done quickly and efficiently. Politically, it is not meant to ingratiate oneself with royalty in an attempt to become part of the close inner circle of power. Theologically, it is not intended to be a part of an interfaith comparative religion symposium to discuss the merits of alternative religious beliefs. Spiritually, it is not calculated to reveal the deep and profound wisdom of the tradition.

- A modest, humble, and self-effacing approach.

  > *Self-confident Jewish leaders are not quick to speak publically nor are they headline seekers.*
  >
  > *They understand that modesty in action and speech is a hallmark of the Jewish people and that those attributes were the central dominating ones of Israel's most outstanding Jewish leader, Moshe Rabbeinu.*
  >
  > *In extraordinary scenarios, and when called for, pomp and ceremony are utilized to make a necessary strong impression.*

- Overall intellectual honesty, tempered by the sense of distance in values, ideology, and beliefs, in addition to fear of dire consequences that prevents total openness.

  > *All truly great Jewish leaders are known for their intellectual honesty and their being seekers of the truth. They internalize the overarching commandment to imitate God, whose defining attribute is Truth, as properly understood within a Torah framework.*
  >
  > *At the same time, they are prudent and use their common sense to avoid getting entangled in unsolvable theological conflicts.*

- Appreciation that there exists a huge unbridgeable chasm between Jews and non-Jews in worldviews, ideology, values, and history.

  > *Jewish advocates play their role because they promote and defend Jewish causes. They realize that Israel's historical mission vastly differs from the rest of mankind's charge. They are not wide-eyed utopians trying to bridge those differences.*

- Ability to clearly, cogently, and forcefully present Torah values.

  Jewish leaders are proud of their complete heritage and recognize that Torah values have preserved and nurtured the Jewish nation throughout history.

- An understanding and approach that the leading Sages steeped in Torah wisdom and worldly matters serve as the ideal representatives of the people.

  The Jewish agent needs to have a clear sense of what the Torah demands in dealing with other people, let alone when facing kings and emperors. They need to view Jewish history with a wide lens, past, present, and future, and must appreciate and emotionally connect to the ethos, tenuous conduits and pathos of Jewish history.

  The Jewish representative understands that world leaders value and respect the knowledge, wisdom, and insight of the Torah and Torah Sages.

- Flexibility, so that in certain unique cases positive results can be achieved by employing a non-Sage under the guidance and with the approval of the Sages.
- Courage, to defend the Jewish nation against unsubstantiated and malicious claims.

  The Jewish advocate possesses the moral certitude, commitment of character, and courage to go head-to-head with the powers that be.

- A unified Jewish front, articulating the Jewish cause by speaking with one voice, and with one compelling message.
- While the Jewish leader is fearless and is prepared to go at it alone if necessary, the true advocate knows that unity of purpose is not only an extremely effective "weapon," but also a deeply entrenched Jewish value.

- Understanding that earthly kingdoms are a reflection of the Divine *Malchut* and need to be treated with appropriate respect, honor, and even awe.
- Internalizing that the structure of the Four Kingdoms was built into the creation in order for Israel to sanctify God's Name globally.

> *The ideal Jewish defender recognizes that there exist enormous opportunities to make a Kiddush Hashem when dealing with the non-Jewish world. More so, the very purpose of interacting with the non-Jewish world might be in order to create a sanctification of God's Name. By interacting with the great emperors and kings of history, the Jewish advocate attempts to reveal God's Malchut by revealing earthly kingship.*

Like **Shimon HaTzaddik**, the Jewish advocate invests his stature, reputation, and position in society to meet the challenges facing the entire Jewish people.

Like the **Elders of the South**, the Jewish advocate is intellectually armed and prepared to push back and hands down win the Jewish case philosophically and theologically.

Like **Geviha ben Pesisa**, the Jewish advocate, as the simple man, can rise to the occasion, arguing from within the Torah sources to sway opinion.

Like the **seventy-two translators**, the Jewish advocate gets the job done quietly, modestly, and with deep faith that God is ever-present to assist.

Like **Rabban Yochanan ben Zakkai**, the Jewish advocate identifies with the individual, community, and the entire nation, and courageously makes extremely difficult decisions with one goal in mind: to ensure the spiritual continuity and vibrancy of Israel.

Like **Rabbi Yehoshua ben Chananya**, the Jewish advocate combines rare debating skills with lifelong scholarship to defend the Jewish people within the highest echelons of government.

Like **Rabbi Yehudah HaNasi**, the Jewish advocate is a forward-thinking visionary looking to uplift the entire Jewish nation to greater and greater heights.

The fascinating historic encounters between the emperors and the Jews are not meant to be the exclusive purview of outstanding leaders. Those encounters throughout history are meant to be a model and message for every Jew. They help guide every Jew, young and old, in interacting with the greater society. They illustrate for every Jew, in each generation, the pathway to fulfill the eternal mission of the Jewish people as it faces the world at large on the Divine stage of history.

APPENDIX A

TARGUM SHIVIM—THE CHANGES

These are the changes that the Sages made in the translation for Ptolemy:

	Verse:	Actual:	Changed To:
1	*Bereishit* 1:1	בראשית ברא אלהים In the beginning God created.	אלהים ברא בראשית God created in the beginning.
2	*Bereishit* 1:26	נעשה אדם בצלמנו כדמותנו Let us make man in our image and form.	אעשה אדם בצלם ובדמות I will make man in image and form.
3	*Bereishit* 2:2	ויכל אלקים ביום השביעי... וישבות ביום השביעי God ceased creating on the seventh day and then rested on the seventh day.	ויכל אלקים ביום הששי... וישבות ביום השביעי God ceased work on the sixth day and then rested on the seventh day.
4	*Bereishit* 5:2	זכר ונקבה בראם "Male and female created He them"; that God created them male and female—in the plural.	זכר ונקבה ברא אותם God created a male/female in the singular.

5	*Bereishit* 11:7	הבה נרדה ונבלה שם שפתם Let us go down and confuse their languages there.	הבה ארדה ובלה שם שפתם I will go down and confuse their languages there.
6	*Bereishit* 18:2	ותצחק שרה בקרבה Sarah laughed within herself.	ותצחק שרה בקרוביה Sarah laughed to those around her.
7	*Bereishit* 49:6	כי באפם הרגו איש וברצונם עקרו שור For in their anger they killed a man, and in their will they uprooted an ox.	כי באפם הרגו שור וברצונם עקרו אבוס For in their anger they killed an ox, and in their will they uprooted the feeding-trough.
8	*Shemot* 4:20	ויקח משה את אשתו ואת בניו וירכיבם על החמור Moshe took his wife and sons and rode on a donkey.	ויקח משה את אשתו ואת בניו וירכיבם על נושא בני אדם Moshe took his wife and sons and rode on an animal that carries people.
9	*Shemot* 12:40	ומושב בני ישראל אשר ישבו במצרים שלשים שנה וארבע מאות שנה The habitation of the Children of Israel, that they dwelled in Egypt, was four hundred and thirty years.	ומושב בני ישראל אשר ישבו במצרים ובשאר ארצות ארבע מאות שנה The habitation of the Children of Israel, that they dwelled in Egypt and in other lands, was four hundred years.
10a and 10b	*Shemot* 24:5, 11	וישלח את נערי בני ישראל...ואל אצילי בני ישראל לא שלח ידו He sent the lads of Bnei Yisrael. God did not unleash His power against the leaders of Bnei Yisrael.	וישלח את זאטוטי בני ישראל...ואל זאטוטי בני ישראל לא שלח ידו He sent the nobles of Bnei Yisrael. God did not unleash His power against the nobles of Bnei Yisrael.

		Actual	Changed To
11	*Bamidbar* 16:15	לא חמור אחד מהם נשאתי I did not take one donkey.	לא חמד אחד מהם נשאתי I did not take one desirable item.
12	*Devarim* 4:19	את השמש ואת הירח ואת הכוכבים כל צבא השמים וכו' אשר חלק ה' אלקיך אתם לכל העמים The sun, and the moon, and the stars, all the host of heaven…which Hashem, your God, assigned to all the nations.	את השמש ואת הירח ואת הכוכבים כל צבא השמים וכו' אשר חלק ה' אלקיך להאיר לכל העמים The sun, and the moon, and the stars, all the host of heaven…which Hashem, your God, assigned to illuminate all the nations.
13	*Devarim* 17:3	וילך ויעבד אלהים אחרים וכו' אשר לא צויתי And who will go and worship other gods…which I have not commanded.	וילך ויעבד אלהים אחרים וכו' אשר לא צויתי לעובדם And who will go and worship other gods…which I have commanded not to worship.
14	*Vayikra* 11:6	את הארנבת The hare	את צעירת הרגלים The short-legged one

CHANGE ONE—BEREISHIT 1:1

Actual:	Changed To:
בראשית ברא אלהים In the beginning God created.	אלהים ברא בראשית God created in the beginning.

The Torah's first word is: "בראשית—In the beginning," but the translated version starts instead with God's Name: *Elokim*.

Literally, the order of the words in the Torah are:

1. In the beginning;
2. created;
3. Elokim/God.

Rashi says that the change was made "in order that they wouldn't say that '*Bereishit*' is a name and that there are two divinities, with the first, '*Bereishit*,' creating the second, '*Elokim*.'"[I]

The *Tosafot* question *Rashi*:

> *Rashi's interpretation is difficult, as the word bereishit is not a name but rather means "beginning." And they wrote for him [Ptolemy] "beginning" in Greek! It appears to me that the Greeks knew that it is always appropriate to mention the Creator first, so if they would have written bereishit first, he would have said there are two divinities—the first was one creator and Elokim the second—so they switched the order.*[II]

The *Maharsha* expands on the reason for the change:

> *The non-believers would say that the Torah must start with God's Name.*
>
> *And the midrash explains that a king of flesh and blood mentions his name first and then his praises. But God is not like that; first He mentions the created world and only then His Name.*
>
> *And in Sefer Pa'aneach Razi, it gives a reason: Just as a person should not say, "For God is this sacrifice," but rather, "This sacrifice is for God," in case of a change of heart as it is said, and this prevents one from taking God's Name in vain. Here too, if God's Name is mentioned first, he might have paused after saying God's Name.*
>
> *Because the non-believers will deny all this and say it was appropriate to begin with His Name, and if they wrote "in the beginning" first they would claim there was, God forbid, something lacking in God.*
>
> *Or they would have [heretically] said that in the beginning of creation God acted, but all of the entities afterwards were not through His Hand but He let the forces of nature do the rest because He (God forbid!) left the world.*

> And therefore they changed the order for Ptolemy in order that there be no reason at all to interpret the verse according to these empty opinions, but simply, "God created." And to deny the approach of the non-believers, we say everyday, "In His goodness He rejuvenates every single day the act of creation."[III]

The *Torah Temimah* (*Bereishit* 1:1) asks: "Why indeed did the Torah not start with God's Name?" He points out that the *Yerushalmi*, *Chagigah* 2:1 says that the Torah did not want to start with the letter *aleph* for that is also the first letter of the word *arur*, cursed! The *Torah Temimah* explains this to mean that the Torah did not start with God's Name, Elokim, which starts with the letter *aleph*, because that Name connotes the attribute of *Din*/Justice.

He goes on to explain *Rashi*:

> *Proper honor dictates that the Torah should begin with God's name. And why wasn't it done so? [See previous paragraph.]*
>
> *Rashi says that the reason they changed the order was so that one would not say that there are two divinities and the first created the second. The Tosafot ask: But the word bereishit is not a name but rather means "in the beginning," and furthermore, the translated word in Greek would mean "in the beginning." And the way to understand Rashi is that it would have been more honorable to start with God's Name, and by not doing so, one might say that the name Elokim is one of the creations, and the verse could mean, "In the beginning the first cause created Elokim and the heavens and the land!"*[IV]

The *Nachalat Yaakov* stresses that it was necessary to begin with God's Name since Ptolemy II the "Greek" was a follower of Aristotle, his father's teacher, who held that the world did not really have a beginning.[V]

This heretical idea, negating the sacrosanct belief of creation ex nihilo, needed to be smashed to pieces at the very outset of the translation, and the change was critical to uphold the most basic of Jewish principles.

The idea of always mentioning God's Name first makes sense, and one would think that this especially applies to the Torah. But the deeper wisdom of the Torah says otherwise. The *Ramban*, in his introduction to *Bereishit*, writes: "We have a truthful tradition that the entire Torah is the Names of the Holy One, blessed be He."[VI] Therefore, mentioning God's Name first in the Torah is not as critical as it would be in a non-Torah document; but this esoteric concept could not have been explained to, and accepted by, Ptolemy.

Similarly, the Hebrew word *bereishit* has many deep meanings and permutations, making it an appropriate word with which to begin the Torah. Explaining all of those hidden teachings to Ptolemy would have been difficult and most likely not accepted by him.

CHANGE TWO—BEREISHIT 1:26

Actual:	Changed To:
נעשה אדם בצלמנו כדמותנו	אעשה אדם בצלם ובדמות
Let us make man in our image and form.	I will make man in image and form.

When discussing Hashem's plan to create man, the Torah employs the plural version: "Let us make man in our image and form." The translation instead used the singular: "I will make man in image and form."

Also, the Torah says, "in our image and form," while the translation reads, "in image and form."

The *Maharsha* explains:

> And Ptolemy would not have accepted the explanation given to refute the non-believers—that immediately afterwards it says that God created (in the singular). And the reason it is written here in the plural is because God doesn't act unless He consults with His heavenly ministers. As Rashi explains, this is the attribute of modesty in God whereby the Great One consults with the minor ones. Rashi adds that as man is created in God's image, the heavenly angels were "jealous," so God conferred with them. And Rashi brings both explanations that merge as one.[VII]

The *Torah Temimah* views this change as a continuation of the issue aimed at preventing any claim that God is not the sole Divinity:

> *The translation did not use the plural so that Ptolemy would not say that there are two divinities. And the reason why the verse is written in the plural is because that's the way of royalty, and even a human king speaks in the "royal we" plural. However, Ptolemy might not have accepted that reason because he might have been looking to find fault in the Torah of Moshe. And even though they could have brought him a proof from a nearby verse as it says: "And God created (singular) man," in any case they did not want to argue with him too much; similarly as it states in Tamid 32a regarding Alexander the Great and the Elders of the South, who also didn't want to engage Alexander too much in discussion.*[VIII]

The idea of not wanting to engage the other side in too much discussion is an ongoing theme in the historic encounters between Jewish representatives and non-Jewish figures. The motto of the Jewish emissaries was always, "Keep it short! Honor the other side but stay alert and wary."

These encounters were not a relaxing, "Let's shoot the breeze and compare notes among friends." They were often forced upon the Jewish representatives. They are a clash of hopes, ideals, beliefs, and dreams. They are intense disputes centered on the purpose of life and the role of respective nations in history. We find that the Sages and Elders could be sharp, incisive, even daring; but always brief, to the point, avoiding excess conversation and discussion. In this case, what was good for the interaction between the Elders of the South and Alexander was also good for the seventy-two elders and Ptolemy, Alexander's heir.

CHANGE THREE—BEREISHIT 2:2

Actual:	Changed To:
ויכל אלקים ביום השביעי...וישבות ביום השביעי God ceased work on the seventh day and then rested on the seventh day.	ויכל אלקים ביום הששי...וישבות ביום השביעי God ceased work on the sixth day and then rested on the seventh day.

The Torah literally reads that "God ceased work on the seventh day and then rested on the seventh day." The translation reads that "God ceased work on the **sixth day** and then rested on the seventh day."

Rashi explains in *Megillah* that they wrote "on the sixth day" and not "on the seventh," in order that Ptolemy not say that God worked on the seventh day, and accordingly the Jews should also be working on their "Shabbat." The Elders did not think Ptolemy would accept the midrash of the Sages which taught: "What was the world missing? Rest! The Shabbat came and rest came."

The *Torah Temimah* teaches that without the change, Ptolemy would not have accepted any explanation for the words, "seventh day."

> *They changed "on the seventh" to the "sixth day" in order that Ptolemy not say that the work was completed on the seventh day. And in fact, the explanation of "and the work was completed on the seventh day" means that by the seventh day the work was completed. And the reason they did not explain this to Ptolemy was because perhaps he would not accept this reason.*[IX]

CHANGE FOUR—BEREISHIT 5:2

Actual:	Changed To:
זכר ונקבה בראם	זכר ונקבה בראו אותם
Male and female created he them; that God created them male and female—in the plural.	God created a male/female—in the singular.

The Torah reads: "Male and female created He them; that God created them [in the plural] male and female."

The translation reads in the singular.

Rashi explains:

> *It reads as if God created two bodies: each one both male and female. Therefore the translation reads in the singular as man was created one body, two faces (male and female).*[X]

We see in another verse (*Bereishit* 1:27) that God created man in his image: "And God created man in His own image, in the image of God created He him; male and female He created them."[XI] One body, one person, male and female, was created.

So the word בראם implies two bodies, and the other verse implies one body. And Ptolemy would not have accepted the teaching of the Sages that initially, in thought, God intended to create two and in the end created only one.[XII]

The *Torah Temimah* similarly learns that the word בראם implies that two entities were created, each one male and female.[XIII]

Ben Yehoyada asks:

> Why would this have been a problem if Ptolemy thought there were two bodies each one male and female? It seems to me that the issue would have been as follows: In the Torah, it only says the names Adam and Chavah, and if there were two bodies, then Ptolemy would ask: "Where are the names of the other two—the male and female from the other body? It must be missing from the Torah! And if you took this out from the Torah then other things are also missing from the Torah!"[XIV]

CHANGE FIVE—BEREISHIT 11:7

Actual:	Changed To:
הבה נרדה ונבלה שם שפתם Let us go down and confuse their languages there.	הבה ארדה ובלה שם שפתם I will go down and confuse their languages there.

The Torah reads in the plural, "Let us go down and confuse their languages," while the translation uses the singular: "I will go down."

The *Torah Temimah* deals with the switch from the plural to the singular:

> As we've seen before, the plural was used because that is the great and honorable way like a mortal king who employs the

royal "we." And once again the explanation is that even though they could have pointed out that the singular is immediately used—"God went down"—they were concerned that they could not show this in the translation and that Ptolemy might not accept this reason.[XV]

On the surface it appears that one could counter and say that as a king himself, Ptolemy could very well understand the concept of the "royal we." Also, Ptolemy respected other religions and cultures, and he learned from his father to take counsel from others.

Clearly the translators understood that if Ptolemy was looking for an excuse to find fault in the Torah, then they could not take the chance that he would accept their explanation for the usage in plural.

CHANGE SIX—BEREISHIT 18:2

Actual:	Changed To:
ותצחק שרה בקרבה	ותצחק שרה בקרוביה
Sarah laughed within herself.	Sarah laughed to those around her.

The Torah says that "Sarah laughed *inside of her*," while the translation was changed to read: "And Sarah laughed to those around her."

The *Torah Temimah* teaches that *Rashi* learns that the change was made so that Ptolemy would not say that by Avraham it also says that he laughed, and in his case, God was not strict with him, but with Sarah, God was strict. Therefore, they wrote that Sarah laughed out loud. And if not for these words, we could say that the reason for the change was that, truthfully, it's hard to understand since she laughed "inside"; why does it even write that she laughed? And the midrash sensed this and says that we know she laughed through Divine inspiration.[XVI]

They were also concerned that Ptolemy would ask how they knew she laughed (if it was inside) and they sensed that Ptolemy would not accept the explanation of Divine inspiration so they wrote she laughed publicly.

The *She'erit Yaakov* asks how they could make such a change, given that the translators stuck faithfully to the truthful meaning of the Torah and only made changes in the words they translated.[1] Sarah did not laugh publicly—it's not true!

He explains that whenever a righteous person falls down from his/her lofty level, it causes the entire world to fall down from its position. It was clear to the wise translators that when Sarah laughed "inside of her," it caused those close to her, i.e., those souls she impacted in her work together with her husband Avraham, to also "spiritually" fall. Therefore Sarah's internal laugh was indeed a "public" laugh with a "public" impact.[XVII]

CHANGE SEVEN—BEREISHIT 49:6

Actual:	Changed To:
כי באפם הרגו איש וברצונם עקרו שור For in their anger they killed a man, and in their will they uprooted an ox.	כי באפם הרגו שור וברצונם עקרו אבוס For in their anger they killed an ox, and in their will they uprooted the feeding-trough.

Yaakov, in his blessing to his sons Shimon and Levi, mentioned that "In their anger they killed men," while the translation says that "They killed oxen."

They also changed the words of the second half of the verse from "They uprooted the ox," to "They uprooted the feeding-trough."

Rashi teaches that the translators needed to defend Shimon and Levi:

> So that he shouldn't say that "Your ancestors were murderers, for their father [Yaakov] testified that they killed men"; therefore they wrote "oxen" instead of "men," as they weren't important in their eyes like animals and weren't particular about the animals.[XVIII]

---

1 See *Tosafot, Megillah* 9a.

The *Maharsha* asks:

> *Why did they change the second part of the verse? What forced them? And in the first part why did they write oxen and not just animals?*
>
> *And it appears that the whole verse is referring to Shechem and his city, as per the Targum. "Or in their anger they killed a man," that is Shechem who was the ruler of the city, as a result of his defiling their sister Dinah; and without anger they killed the people of the city who did not sin.*
>
> *That which they changed was good; "They killed an ox," refers to Shechem, the person who was like an ox; "And they uprooted the trough" means the place of the ox, the people of the city.*
>
> *And in order not to change the language so much, since in the second part of the verse it says ox, they used that same word in the first part of their change; and that which Rashi said to prevent Ptolemy from saying, "Yaakov called his sons murderers," they certainly were not murderers for all the people deserved death, as according to the Ramban.*[XIX]

The *Torah Temimah* says that because Ptolemy was looking to find fault in the Torah, the Sages made the change so that Ptolemy would not say that they, the sons of Yaakov, were murderers.[XX]

There is no denying the Shechem episode and the action taken by Shimon and Levi in the killings of Shechem and the men of the city. It is clearly written in the Torah and the translators certainly would not change the story itself. Ptolemy would have accepted those actions as a legitimate response to the forced kidnapping and abduction of an innocent Dinah. The perpetrators and those who allowed it, those who accepted it, were also guilty. Rather, the translators were concerned that a literal translation would have led Ptolemy to say that Yaakov himself viewed his sons as illegitimate murderers.

CHANGE EIGHT—SHEMOT 4:20

Actual:	Changed To:
ויקח משה את אשתו ואת בניו וירכיבם על החמור	ויקח משה את אשתו ואת בניו וירכיבם על נושא בני אדם
Moshe took his wife and sons and rode on a donkey.	Moshe took his wife and sons and rode on an animal that carries people.

The Torah writes that Moshe took his wife and sons and rode on a *donkey* [to go from Midian to Egypt].

The translation changes it to read that Moshe took his wife and sons and rode on an *animal that carries people*!

The *Maharsha* explains according to *Rashi* that an animal that carries people could be interpreted as a camel. But the Sages did not want to write "camel" because that would be untrue (and this is the same reasoning brought down by the *Tosafot* in change #10—see below). The midrash tells us that it is written "**the** donkey" to tell us that this is the same donkey Avraham rode to the *Akeidah* and it is the same one that Mashiach will ride. But Ptolemy would not have accepted such a reason.[XXI]

The *Torah Temimah* writes:

> *Rashi and the Tosafot explain the change of riding a donkey in the original, as opposed to riding on an animal that carries people in the translation, was so that one wouldn't say that Moshe did not have a horse or a camel. And that reason is not at all clear, for we see that by Avraham who was rich and who had horses and camels, nonetheless it says that he rode a donkey! And it is more reasonable to say that it isn't proper to mention riding by a woman and it is offensive to say riding on a donkey by a woman; they therefore changed it to riding on an animal that carries people. This language is more honorable and would be accepted by Ptolemy. And the simple idea here shows that Ptolemy was trying to find fault in the Torah.*[XXII]

The *Ben Yehoyada* writes:

> Rashi explains that it refers to a camel, so that one would not say, "Moshe your teacher did not have a horse or camel." The Tosafot wrote in case he [Ptolemy] would say to them: "Did Moshe your teacher not have a horse or camel?"
>
> And I found written on a piece of worn-out paper that the great Gaon, Rav Moshe Chaim [Luzzatto, i.e., the Ramchal] asked: "What did the Tosafot add to Rashi?"
>
> Rashi learns that the word was changed from "donkey" to "animal carrying people" so that Moshe would not be criticized, saying that he was poor and didn't have a horse or camel. On the other hand, the Tosafot learns that Ptolemy would reason that Moshe did have a horse or camel and would have put his wife and children on them; therefore the words of the Torah, on a donkey, would be untruthful![XXIII]

Both *Rashi* and the *Tosafot* are learning this change based on how they think the translators attempted to anticipate Ptolemy's thought process. They were concerned that he would question an inconsistency or fact that did not make sense to him.

The *Ben Yehoyada* continues:

> And Rashi specifically mentioned a camel because had they written "donkey," then Ptolemy could have claimed that it was cruelty to animals to have three people ride on a donkey. Therefore, they wrote "animal carrying people," implying it was a camel. And one could ask why the translators weren't worried about Avraham's honor when it says in Bereishit that Avraham rode on a donkey? Couldn't he have questioned: "Didn't Avraham have a camel or horse?" And it appears to me that by Avraham it specifically records in the Torah that he had flock, sheep, slaves, donkeys, and camels. It's apparent that Avraham was rich! So it is clear that he rode the donkey by choice; he was comfortable riding it or that it was a Libyan donkey, which is an important animal.

But it is difficult according to Rashi, for why would Ptolemy care if Moshe was poor? And it appears that even the nations of the world know the principle that prophecy only occurs on the wise, mighty, and wealthy. And if they translated "donkey," Ptolemy would have said that the Torah is a fraud.

CHANGE NINE—SHEMOT 12:40

Actual:	Changed To:
ומושב בני ישראל אשר ישבו במצרים שלשים שנה וארבע מאות שנה The habitation of the Children of Israel, that they dwelled in Egypt, was four hundred and thirty years.	ומושב בני ישראל אשר ישבו במצרים ובשאר ארצות ארבע מאות שנה The habitation of the Children of Israel, that they dwelled in Egypt and in other lands, was four hundred years.

The Torah writes that the Bnei Yisrael lived "In Egypt for four hundred and thirty years."

The translation says they lived "In Egypt and in other lands for four hundred years."

Torah Temimah writes that "they changed the number of years [and added the words, 'and in other lands'] because perhaps Ptolemy would say that the numbers aren't correct."

And, indeed, the Children of Israel were not in Egypt for four hundrend and thirty years.

> Kehat [son of Yaakov] was one that went down to Egypt and when you add up the years of Kehat and [his son] Amram and [his son] Moshe, all of them combined don't equal four hundred!
>
> Rather, the Torah calculates the decree of the Egyptian exile from the time of the Covenant of the Parts. And from that time to Yitzchak's birth is thirty years, and from Yitzchak's birth to the Exodus from Egypt is four hundred years. And if you take away the thirty years of Yitzchak and also Yaakov's one hundred and thirty years—his age when he went down to Egypt—you get a total of two hundred and ten years.

And this was the decree, which said that the Jewish people would be strangers "In a land that would not be theirs," and it doesn't say in Egypt. And from when Yitzchak was born, Avraham was a stranger in the land of the Plishtim, and until the Exodus from Egypt, Yitzchak and his descendants were strangers in the Land of Canaan and not rulers of the land. The thirty years—bringing the total to 430—don't count because it says: "In your descendants [starting from Yitzchak]."[XXIV]

- 210—The years the Jewish people were in Egypt
- 400—From the birth of Yitzchak until the Exodus
- 430—From the Covenant of the Pieces until the Exodus

Ensuring historical accuracy in the Torah was critical to preserving the authenticity of the Torah. This was especially true when determining the history of the Jewish people in Egypt, the country where the Ptolemies established their dynasty.

Additionally, Ptolemy II himself was the son of the historian general who fought with Alexander and wrote a military history of Alexander. He certainly would have disparaged any writing that he thought lacked historical accuracy.

CHANGE TEN, A AND B—SHEMOT 24:5,11

Actual:	Changed To:
וישלח את נערי בני ישראל...ואל אצילי בני ישראל לא שלח ידו	וישלח את זאטוטי בני ישראל...ואל זאטוטי בני ישראל לא שלח ידו
He sent the lads of Bnei Yisrael. God did not unleash His power against the leaders of Bnei Yisrael.	He sent the nobles of Bnei Yisrael. God did not unleash His power against the nobles of Bnei Yisrael.

The Torah says: "And he sent the lads [נערי]." The translation uses the word "nobles [זאטוטי]."

In explaining that Moshe sent the lads (of the Bnei Yisrael) to bring the offerings, the Torah employs the word נערי. In their translation for Ptolemy, the Sages used the word זאטוטי instead.

Similarly, in a later verse, the translation also changes the word אצילי (leaders) to זאטוטי (nobles), as well.

These verses take place the day before the giving of the Torah on Mount Sinai.

> And Moshe wrote all the words of Hashem, and he arose early in the morning and built an altar at the foot of the mountain and twelve monument-stones for the twelve tribes of Yisrael.
>
> And he sent the youths of the Children of Yisrael, and they offered up burnt-offerings, and they slaughtered peace-offerings to Hashem, bulls.

The *Torah Temimah* sources *Rashi* and adds that the reason for the change is because the word נערי means small (young lads), and Ptolemy would say that Moshe sent the most inferior to receive the Divine presence. זאטוטי, however, is a word of importance. The second change wasn't really necessary, as the original word did not denote smallness, but the translators wanted to be consistent.[XXV]

The translators' change reflects their understanding of the essential mistake that Ptolemy would have made in this case. From his Greek perspective, the value of young lads, seen as non-productive members of society, was marginal and was not appropriate for the event. The Jewish view differs.[2] The Gemara in *Shabbat* 119b states:

> Reish Lakish said in the name of Rabbi Yehudah HaNasi: The world endures only for the sake of the breath of schoolchildren. Said Rav Papa to Abaye: What about mine and yours? Breath in which there is sin is not like breath in which there is no sin, replied he.[XXVI]

---

2   *Siftei Chachamim, Megillah*, p. 32.

CHANGE ELEVEN—BAMIDBAR 16:15

Actual:	Changed To:
לא חמור אחד מהם נשאתי	לא חמד אחד מהם נשאתי
I did not take one donkey.	I did not take any desirable item.

The Torah quotes Moshe as saying: "I did not take one *donkey*." The translation reads: "I did not take any desirable *item*." *Rashi* says:

> *They made the change from "I didn't take a donkey" to "I didn't take any desirable item," so that Ptolemy would not say that perhaps Moshe did not take a donkey but he might have taken other items.*[XXVII]

Siftei Chachamim adds:

> *This incident was by the rebellion of Korach and his assembly against Moshe, and through derash it needed to make this change because "Not one donkey did I take" even when I went from Midian to Egypt and placed my wife and sons on the donkey; as if to say, that I only took my donkey not theirs. And since earlier [in change #8] they did not translate that Moshe took his wife and sons on a donkey, but on "An animal that carries people," therefore per Rashi they were forced to make this change and not mention a donkey.*[XXVIII]

The translation needed to be absolutely clear as to Moshe's far-reaching yet truthful claim that he did not take absolutely anything for himself during his entire forty-year tenure as leader of the Jewish people. For a king such as Ptolemy, this would have been an astounding assertion, given the accepted norm that everything captured in war (and peace) belongs by right to the king. Any reason to challenge Moshe's claim and to impugn an untruthful or exaggerated assertion on Moshe's part needed to be struck down and eliminated.

CHANGE TWELVE—DEVARIM 4:19

Actual:	Changed To:
את השמש ואת הירח ואת הכוכבים כל צבא השמים וכו' אשר חלק ה' אלקיך אתם לכל העמים	את השמש ואת הירח ואת הכוכבים כל צבא השמים וכו' אשר חלק ה' אלקיך להאיר לכל העמים
The sun, and the moon, and the stars, all the host of heaven…which Hashem, your God, assigned to all the nations.	The sun, and the moon, and the stars, all the host of heaven…which Hashem, your God, assigned to illuminate all the nations.

In the original, it reads: "Which Hashem, your God, assigned to all the nations."

In the translation, it's changed to: "Which Hashem, your God, assigned to illuminate all the nations."

The *Torah Temimah* explains: Without the addition of this word—"illuminate"—he [Ptolemy] would have ruled that it is permitted for non-Jews to worship idols. He would have interpreted "assigned" as that God allotted the idols to worship. And even though the previous explanation [that the *Torah Temimah* brought down] explained that the word "assigned" means "with words to remove them from the world," such an explanation could not be said to Ptolemy.[XXIX]

CHANGE THIRTEEN—DEVARIM 17:3

Actual:	Changed To:
וילך ויעבד אלהים אחרים וכו' אשר לא צויתי	וילך ויעבד אלהים אחרים וכו' אשר לא צויתי לעובדם
And who will go and worship other gods…which I have not commanded.	And who will go and worship other gods…which I have commanded not to worship.

In the actual text it reads: "And who will go and worship other gods…which I have not commanded."

In the translation, they added: "Which I have commanded not to worship."

Rashi explains:

> *If the word "to worship" would not have been added, it would appear that the words "I have not commanded" would mean that these are gods that were created against Hashem's will.*[xxx]

After bringing down *Rashi*'s interpretation, the *Maharsha* adds that in the *Talmud Yerushalmi* the change reads, "That I not command to the nations of the world to worship." And according to this text, if the translators had not made the change and added the words "to worship," Ptolemy would have thought that the nations of the world were not commanded to avoid the worship of idolatry.[xxxi]

CHANGE FOURTEEN—VAYIKRA 11:6

Actual:	Changed To:
את הארנבת The hare.	את צעירת הרגלים The short-legged one.

In the Torah passage discussing non-kosher creatures that may not be eaten, the Sages changed the word "הארנבת—the hare," to "צעירת הרגלים—the short-legged one."

The Talmud explains:

> *And they wrote for him "the short-legged one" and did not write "the arnevet (the rabbit)" because Ptolemy's wife's name was Arnevet. [They did so] in order that he wouldn't say that the Jews are making fun of me and placed my wife in the Torah.*[xxxii]

Siftei Chachamim notes that in the *Yerushalmi* it states that this change was made because Ptolemy's mother's name was *Arnevet*; and one is more forgiving on the honor of one's mother than the honor of one's wife, and sometimes the opposite is the case.

Indeed, this reading is borne out by studying the etymology of Ptolemy's full name, which was Ptolemy son of Lagos:

λαγός • (lagós) m (plural λαγοί, feminine λαγουδίνα or λαγίνα)

1. hare, male hare

Derived terms

λαγάς m (lagás, "hare hunter")

λαγουδάκι n (lagoudáki, "small hare, bunny")

λαγουδίνα f (lagoudína, "female hare")

The *Siftei Chachamim* explains why the Gemara, in this change, says that Ptolemy would have said that the translators "placed" the word and not "wrote" the offensive word. Since the Torah was written many years before there was a Ptolemic family in the world, how could one say that they wrote that specific word? Rather, Ptolemy would claim that on their own they "placed" the name among the letters and even worse, among the impure animals.[XXXIII]

Rashi explains that instead of rabbit, they wrote "short-legged one" because his wife's hands were shorter and smaller than her legs.[XXXIV]

Ben Yehoyada challenges *Rashi* and argues that:

> This is problematic, because if so they should have written "short hands" [instead of short legs] because Ptolemy's wife had unusual hands, for they were extremely short. And when she was born they called her "rabbit" for a rabbit is unusual for its hands are much shorter than its legs. And it was common to name an infant based on an event or a novelty found in the infant, for example Yaakov, who was holding on to his brother's heel, or Eisav, who had a full mantle of hair and was complete. And perhaps the nation of Ptolemy's wife was called Arvenet. They needed to write "short-legged one" because if they wrote "short hands," he would say they intended his wife.[XXXV]

The *Torah Temimah*, on the other hand, had access to a different text:

> *I found another version that instead of "short-legged one" reads "hairy-legged one," and this is the correct version. For the naturalists wrote that it's the nature of rabbits to grow long hair on their legs. And they made this change so that Ptolemy could not say that the Jews are making fun of me and placed my wife in the Torah.*[XXXVI]

The *Ben Yehoyada* asks why this last "rabbit" change was not written in the order as the verses appear in the Torah as were the previous thirteen changes. The rabbit verse is from *Sefer Vayikra* and should have come before the previous three changes which were from *Bamidbar* and *Devarim*!

He explains that all of the previous changes were done so that Ptolemy would not argue about what was written in the Torah. This change, however, was not about the words of the Torah but rather to prevent him from saying that the Jews are making fun of me [of my wife] by placing her name among the impure animals.[XXXVII]

APPENDIX B

THE FOUR KINGDOMS—TORAH SOURCES

The primary Biblical source for the Four Kingdoms is the Book of Daniel, where various prophecies and dreams describe those kingdoms. The Sages understood that the structure of the Four Kingdoms is built into the blueprint of creation and history. Accordingly, they realized that the Torah, the ultimate blueprint of creation and history, includes sources detailing the nature of the Four Kingdoms.

The Torah passages which the Sages expounded to be discussing the Four Kingdoms include the following:

- Torah Source 1—Descriptions of Chaos
- Torah Source 2—Rivers from Eden
- Torah Source 3—A World War
- Torah Source 4—Covenant with Avraham
- Torah Source 5—Eisav Goes Hunting
- Torah Source 6—Yaakov's Ladder
- Torah Source 7—The Mishkan
- Torah Source 8—The Camel and Friends
- Torah Source 9—Types of Tzaraat
- Torah Source 10—The Red Heifer

TORAH SOURCE 1—DESCRIPTIONS OF CHAOS

Bereishit 1:2—"The earth was without form and empty with darkness on the face of the depths but God's spirit moved on the water's surface."[I] Rav Shimon ben Lakish in *Bereishit Rabbah* 2:4 interprets this verse of the Torah as referring to the Four Kingdoms.

- "Without form" refers to **Babylon**, as it says, "I saw the land and it was unformed" (*Yirmiyahu* 4:23).
- "Empty" refers to **Persia/Media**, as it says, "And they hurried to bring Haman" (*Esther* 6:14)—"hurried" being a play on the Hebrew word *vohu*—בוהו.
- "Darkness" is **Greece**, who darkened the eyes of Yisrael with their decrees, saying to them, "Write upon the horn of the ox[1] that you have no connection to the God of Israel."
- "On the face of the deep" is the evil kingdom (**Rome/Edom**) that has no limit, like the deep.
- "And God's spirit" is the spirit of the **King Mashiach**, as it says, "And the spirit of God rests upon him" (*Yeshayahu* 11:2).[II]

Rabbeinu Bachya learns that the separation between light and darkness described in *Bereishit* 1:4 refers to the distinction between Yisrael and the nations. That cosmological separation finds historical expression in the division between the Four Kingdoms and Yisrael as alluded to in verse two above.[III]

From the primordial chaos of creation, from the forces of utter negativity, the Torah derives the Four Kingdoms. And from that chaos inexorably emerges a deep spirit that ultimately sustains the world.

TORAH SOURCE 2—RIVERS FROM EDEN

The utter mystery of Creation and man's ultimate goal to return to the source of life is exemplified by the Torah's description of the Garden of Eden and the body of water that came out of Eden.

---

1 Greece references the horn of an ox as a bitter reminder to Israel of the sin of the Golden Calf.

Bereishit 2:10–14 describes:

> And a river flowed out of Eden to water the garden, and from there it separated and became four heads. The name of one is Pishon; that is the one that encompasses all the land of Havilah, where there is gold. And the gold of that land is good; pearls and precious stones are also found there. The name of the second river is Gichon and it surrounds the land of Cush. And the name of the third river is Tigris, which flows east of Assyria, and the fourth river is the Euphretes.[IV]

In these verses, the number four is explicit and is connected to the Four Kingdoms.

In *Bereishit Rabbah* 16:4, Rav Tanchum said in the name of Rav Yehoshua ben Levi: In the future, God will pour the cup of poison on the nations from the place where judgment comes. "And a river flowed out of Eden to water the garden; and from there it separated, and became four heads." It does not say "became four rivers" but rather four "heads," alluding to the four exiles.

- The name of the first is Pishon. This is **Babylon**, as it says, "For the horsemen shall spread throughout" (*Chavakuk* 1:8), referring to Kasdin/Babylon.
- And the name of the second river is Gichon which is **Persia/Media**, for Haman attacked the nation (Yisrael) like a snake, as it says, "On your belly you will crawl" (*Bereishit* 3:14), a play on the word "belly"—גחנך.
- Chidekel (Tigris) is **Greece**, which was quick and sharp with its edicts and which said to Yisrael, "Write for me on the horn of an ox that you have no part with the God of Yisrael."
- And the fourth river is Parat (Euphrates), **Edom (Rome)**, which broke and oppressed the sons (of Yisrael)—a play on the word פרת—Parat.[V]

Rav Tanchum teaches that the verse should have said, "And the one river became four rivers." The fact that the verse instead reads "And became four **heads**" hints that the verse is referencing "heads," four rivers corresponding to the "heads" of history, i.e., the four empires of world history.

The *Alshich Hakadosh* is troubled by how Chazal recognized that the four rivers corresponded to the exiles. He understands that the water in Gan Eden represents the Torah that protects the Jewish people. But when the nation abandons the Torah, when the river of Torah leaves Gan Eden, then the river turns to four heads; i.e., Yisrael loses its protection and becomes subjugated under the four kingdoms of the world.[VI]

TORAH SOURCE 3—A WORLD WAR

The Torah in *Bereishit* (14:1) tells the story of how a number of ancient kings undertook a military expedition, conquered their enemies' land, and attempted to maintain control. The subdued kings eventually revolted, but their rebellion ended up crushed. These events are recorded early in the Torah, involve Avraham, and are connected to the Four Kingdoms.

"Now it came to pass in the days of Amraphel king of Shinar, Arioch king of Ellasar, Chedorlaomer king of Elam, and Tidal king of Goyim."[VII]

Bereishit Rabbah 42:2 explains:

> *Rav Avun said: Just as history starts with the four kings in Bereishit, so too will it develop and close with four kingdoms.*
>
> *It starts with Chedorlaomer king of Elam, Tidal king of Goyim, Amraphel king of Shinar and Arioch king of Ellasar. And so it closes with the four kingdoms, Babylon, Persia/Media, Greece and Rome/Edom [which conscripted soldiers from all of the nations].*[VIII]

The *Ramban* explains that this event happened to Avraham to demonstrate that the Four Kingdoms will rule the world, and in the end Avraham's sons [Yisrael] will overcome them, the nations will fall into their hands, and they will get back captives and property.

The *Ramban* continues:

- The first one is the King of **Babylon**, as it says, "You (Nevuchanezzar, Babylon) are the head of gold" (*Daniel* 2:38).

- And perhaps Elassar is the name of a city in **Media** or **Persia**.
- And Elam, in this city the first king of **Greece** ruled and from there he spread his kingdom when he (Alexander the Great) defeated King Darius; afterwards he expanded his kingdom throughout the entire world.
- And the King of Goyim was the king of different nations who placed him as the head; this alludes to **Rome** who ruled over groups of different nations.[IX]

The *Ramban* develops, fine-tunes, and extensively utilizes the concept of "The actions of the Patriarchs are a sign to the children":

> I will tell you a principle by which you will understand all the coming portions of Scripture concerning Avraham, Yitzchak, and Yaakov. It is indeed a great matter which our Rabbis mentioned briefly, saying: "Whatever happened to the Patriarchs is a sign to the children." It is for this reason that the verses narrate at great length the account of the journey of the Patriarchs, the digging of the wells, and other events…[X]

Rav Hirsch elaborates:

> The events described in these verses are significant also from another standpoint, as already noted by our Sages. On the very first page of recorded political history, four victorious kingdoms are mentioned analogous to the course of world history, which likewise divides into four world powers ultimately destined to fall into the hands of Mashiach, who will triumph by the power of God…[2]

TORAH SOURCE 4—COVENANT WITH AVRAHAM

The Covenant of the Pieces is the history-defining pact between God and Avraham, the progenitor of the Jewish people. The Sages taught

---

[2] Hirsch, *Collected Writings*, vol. 2, p. 325.

that this private, albeit riveting, seminal event is yet another example in the Torah that reveals the pattern of world history.

In *Bereishit* 15:8–12 it states:

> And he [Avraham] said: "O Lord God how will I know that I will inherit it?"
>
> He said to him: "Take for Me three **heifers** and three **goats** and three **rams** and a turtle-**dove** and a **young pigeon**."
>
> And he brought all these for Him and he divided them in the middle and placed each part opposite the other but he did not divide the birds.
>
> Vultures descended on the carcasses and Avram drove them away.
>
> When the sun was setting, a deep sleep fell upon Avram, and behold, a fright, a great darkness was falling on him.[XI]

Bereishit Rabbah 44:15 explains these verses:

- Three heifers: This is **Babylon** who had three kings: Nevuchadnetzar, Evil-Marodach, and Belshazzar.
- Three goats: This is **Persia/Media** who had three kings: Koresh, Darius, and Achashveirosh.
- Three rams is **Greece**.

    > Rabbi Elazar said: "The children of Greece captured all directions except for the east."
    >
    > Rabbi Yochanan asked him: "But it says in Daniel 8:4, 'I saw the ram pushing westward, northward, and southward and no beasts who could stand before him, and no one could save anyone from its hand and it did according to his will, and became great.'"
    >
    > The verse does not say east and this is the opinion of Rav Elazar.

- A turtle-dove and young pigeon is **Edom [Rome]**; it appears [pure] as a turtle-dove, but is really a thief.[XII]

The midrash follows the interpretation that משולשת means three animals[3] of each kind mentioned, and not animals who are three years old.

Accordingly, it states that the three heifers refer to Babylon's three kings: Nevuchadnetzar, Evil-Marodach, and Belshazzar. The three she-goats symbolize three Persian/Media kings: Koresh (Cyrus), Darius, and Achashveirosh.

The midrash is not saying that each of these empires only had three kings, but rather points out those kings who significantly impacted the Jewish people.

The midrash then shifts gears with its analysis. The three rams signify Greece, but not with three Greek kings. Rather, three there refers to the directions that Greece captured: north, south, and west. Perhaps when it comes to Greece the midrash can't connect the three animals to three Greek kings, since the only ruler of significance, the only one that really counts, was Alexander. And there were too many Greek kings after the death of Alexander and the division of his empire. So the three must connect to Alexander specifically and therefore it relates to the three directions of his conquests.

Rabbi Elazar's statement that Greece only captured territory in three directions is difficult, as Alexander moved eastwards all the way to India. In fact, the Abarbanel learns that the ram in *Daniel* represents Persia/Media and not Greece, because it was the Persian Empire that didn't capture land eastwards.[4]

The verse ends with a turtle-dove and a young pigeon, designating Rome/Edom. The thought behind this is that Rome often appears civilized and cultured on the outside (תור) while it is inherently like a thief (גוזל), which is a play on the Hebrew word גזל, which means thief.

The midrash continues: "When the sun was setting, a deep sleep fell upon Avram and behold, a fright, a great darkness was falling on him."

- "Fright" is **Babylon**, as it states, "Then was Nebuchadnezzar filled with fury" (*Daniel* 3:19).

---

3   See *Rashi* and also *Oznaim L'Torah*.
4   *Abarbanel*, Commentary on Daniel, *Hamaayan Hayeshua* 9:4.

- "Darkness" is **Persia/Media** who darkened the eyes of Israel with fasting (fast of Esther).
- "Great" is **Greece**; Rav Shimon says there were 120 ministers, 120 regional heads, and 120 army officers [in Greece]; the Rabbis say there were sixty of each. As it says, "Who led you through the great and dreadful wilderness, where there were serpents, fiery serpents, and scorpions, and thirsty ground where there was no water" (*Devarim* 8:15).
- "Fell upon him" is **Edom (Rome)** as it says,"From the sound of their fall, the earth quaked; a cry whose sound was heard in the Red Sea" (*Yirmiyahu* 49:21), referring to Rome/Edom.[XIII]

As the birds of prey swoop down, attacking the covenantal pieces, Avraham drives them away. The vultures of history during the four kingdoms were too often ready and able to sweep down on the Jewish people, who were too often not ready and not able to drive them away.

TORAH SOURCE 5—EISAV GOES HUNTING

The future of the Jewish people and the course of world history hung in the balance. The patriarch Yitzchak was ready to bless his two sons, Eisav and Yaakov, with the spiritual and material blessings enabling them to carry out their historic missions. It was a pivotal moment fraught with danger and opportunity. The patriarch Yitzchak and matriarch Rivka held vastly different views connected to those blessings and the four kingdoms.

Bereishit 27:1–3 recounts the episode:

> *Yitzchak had grown old and his eyes were too dim to see. He called his elder son Eisav and said, "My son," and he said, "Here I am."*
>
> *And he said, "I am old and I do not know when I will die. So, now, sharpen your implements, your sword [and take] your bow, and go forth to the field, and hunt game for me."*[XIV]

Bereishit Rabbah 65:13 states:

- "Sharpen your **implements**" is **Babylon**, as it states, "And he (Nevuchanezzar) brought the vessels (implements) from the Temple to his treasury" (*Daniel* 1:2).
- "Your **sword**" is **Persia/Media**; "And they hung (*vayitlu*) Haman on the tree" (*Esther* 7:10), *vayitlu* being a play on words.
- "Your **bow**" is **Greece**, as it says, "For I bend Judah for Me, like a bow I filled [the hand of] Ephraim; and I will arouse your sons, O Zion, against your sons, O Yavan (Greece), and will make you as the sword of a mighty man" (*Zechariah* 9:13).
- "**Go out to the field**" is **Edom (Rome)**; "And Yaakov sent messengers before him to Eisav his brother unto the land of Seir, the field of Edom" (*Bereishit* 32:4).[xv]

The *Alshich* fascinatingly elaborates:

What does Eisav's hunting for foods have to do with Babylon, Persia/Media, Greece, and Edom?

And according to our approach, what did Rivka recognize that she thwarted her husband's intentions and in the process endangered Yaakov for perhaps his father would feel him and know from the smooth skin that he wasn't Eisav?

Or that before Yitzchak could eat and bless Yaakov, Eisav would come from the field and catch Yaakov as a thief in the night and perhaps kill him, and his father would curse him? However, Yitzchak and Rivka differed in their intentions.

Yitzchak knew in his heart that Yaakov alone would inherit the World to Come, while Eisav would inherit this world in its entirety. The control of this world was divided among the Four Kingdoms—Babylon, Persia/Media, Greece, and Edom—the four kingdoms alluded to in Nevuchadnetzar's dream of the idol.

And after the four, an everlasting kingdom (Yisrael) would appear.

Yitzchak said in his heart that Eisav only has a portion in the here and now. And therefore let it be a complete control through the four kingdoms. Eisav is Edom under whom Yisrael will be subjugated, and this is the understanding of Bereishit 27:10 that Eisav's control would be accomplished through this mitzvah of hunting.

It was through these four actions:

- *By taking the vessels, Eisav would gain the future control of **Babylon**.*
- *Through the sword he would rule **Persia**.*
- *Through the mitzvah of taking the bow, Eisav would be blessed with the control that **Greece** merited.*
- *By going out to the field, Eisav would get his own empire (**Rome**).*

But Rivka was guided by a different spirit. She said in her heart: "If Yitzchak's intention comes to pass, how will Yaakov rise up after such a fall in the first exile? What will happen?!

"And this last exile is to be very different from the first one; he will never be redeemed until all of Israel returns to God!"

There was a profound difference between Yitzchak and Rivka. Both understood that Eisav's mission was of this world, while Yaakov was destined to build towards the World to Come. But for Yitzchak, "this world" meant the entire "this world", and this world is controlled by the four kingdoms. Eisav should take his "weapons" (Babylon), his sword (Persia), his bow (Greece), and thereby inherit all of the heretofore power of the three kingdoms as he goes out to the field—the combined power of the three in Rome.

Rivka saw such a blessing in this world and asked, "How could Yaakov/Yisrael survive in such a totally dominated Eisav/ Rome world?!"[XVI]

Today, looking back at Jewish history, can one imagine the consequences if Rivka had not prevailed?

What course would history have taken had Eisav received the entire unmitigated power of the four kingdoms?

TORAH SOURCE 6—YAAKOV'S LADDER

In Yaakov's prophetic dream, described in *Bereishit* 28:10–12, the mystical ladder connects Heaven to earth with *malachim*, spiritual entities, ascending and descending the rungs. And Yaakov, the apex of the patriarchs, is given a glimpse of the deepest secrets of creation.

> *Yaakov left Beer Sheva and he headed to Charan. And he arrived at the place and spent the night there because the sun had set. And he took some stones, he placed them at his head and lay down in that place. And he dreamed, and behold! A ladder set up on the ground and its top reached to heaven. Angels of God were ascending and descending upon it.*[XVII]

Bereishit Rabbah 68:14 elaborates:

> "And behold a ladder"; this is Nevuchadnetzar's dream: "O king, you saw and behold a great image. An image, which was mighty, and with unusual splendor, was standing before you; and its appearance was frightening" (Daniel 2:31).

And the angels of God, two are going up and two are going down. These are the archangels of the four kingdoms. It says "up and down," not "down and up." They will go up and have ascension, but each one is inferior to the preceding one.

It says: "As for that image, its head was of fine gold" (Daniel 2:32).

- **Babylon** is higher than all of them, as it says, "You are the head of gold" (ibid., v. 38).
- And then it says, "And after you will arise another kingdom inferior to you [**Persia**]" (ibid., v. 39).
- And another, a Third Kingdom of copper, which shall rule over the entire earth [**Greece**].

- And in the end, Daniel reveals, "And the toes of the feet were partly iron, and partly clay, so part of the kingdom shall be strong, and part of it will be broken [**Rome**]" (ibid., v. 42).

"And Hashem is standing over him (Yaakov)"; as it says, "And in the days of these kings the God of heaven will set up a kingdom forever, it will not be be destroyed; and the kingdom will not be left to another people; it shall crumble and consume all these kingdoms, but it will stand forever" (ibid., v. 44).[XVIII]

The midrash connects, through a homophonic play on the words, "The ladder of Yaakov"—**Sulam**, with Nevuchadnetzar's dream of the mighty image—**Tzelem**. The going up and down of the angels teaches that each succeeding kingdom of the four will be "lower," inferior to the preceding one. The plural of "going up and going down" indicates two angels plus two more angels, a total of four, representing the archangels of the four kingdoms.

The *Midrash Mevuar* explains: "God showed Yaakov in the dream the entire future prophesy [Daniel's] of the four kingdoms."[XIX]

Yaakov is fully tuned into the future course of Jewish history, the Four Kingdoms. And it is Yaakov who institutes the evening/night Maariv prayer, the prayer of darkness and exile. That prayer is ultimately the prayer of our faith, our hopes, our dreams, and our personal and national redemption.

Midrash Tanchuma (*Vayeitzei* §3) teaches:

> *Rabbi Shmuel ben Nachman said: These are the archangels of the nations of the world.*
>
> - *God showed Yaakov the archangel of **Babylon** ascending seventy (**70**) steps on the ladder and falling.*
> - *And the archangel of **Persia/Media**—fifty-two (**52**) steps up and then falling.*
> - *And of **Greece** (**180**) one hundred and eighty.*
> - *And he showed him Edom (**Rome**) going up, but he didn't know how many steps.*

> Yaakov became afraid and said: "Maybe this one will not fall!" God said to him, "Do not be afraid...fear not, O My servant Yaakov, says the Lord, and do not be dismayed, O Yisrael" (Yirmiyahu 30:10).
>
> "Even if you can't see, I will cause him to fall, as it says, 'If you go up high like an eagle, and if you place your nest among the stars, I will bring you down, says the Lord.' (Ovadiah 1:4)."[xx]

TORAH SOURCE 7—THE MISHKAN

The *Mishkan*/Tabernacle is the earthly structure constructed of materials, such as gold, silver, and copper, that paradoxically contains the Divine. The *Mishkan* is a microcosm of the world. The activities in building the *Mishkan* define the creative acts forbidden on the Shabbat—the culmination of weekday activity and life.

The request to bring the material for the Tabernacle is found in *Shemot* 25:1–8:

> God spoke to Moshe saying: "Speak to the children of Yisrael and have them take for Me an offering; from every person whose heart inspires him to generosity, you shall take My offering. The offering you shall take from them: gold, silver, and copper; blue, purple, and crimson wool; linen and goat hair; ram skins dyed red, tachash skins, and acacia wood; oil for lighting, spices for the anointing oil and for incense; shoham stones and filling stones for the ephod and for the choshen. And they shall make Me a sanctuary and I will dwell among them."[xxi]

Midrash Tanchuma (Terumah §7) explains how this connects to the Four Kingdoms:

- Gold corresponding to **Babylon**, as it states, "You are the head of gold" (Daniel 2:38).
- Silver corresponding to **Media** as it states, "Ten thousand pieces of silver" [that wicked Haman gave to King Achashveirosh] (Esther 3:9).

- Copper corresponding to **Greece**, which is inferior to all.
- Ram skins dyed red corresponding to **Rome/Edom**, as it states, "And the first one [Eisav] emerged ruddy" (*Bereishit* 26:25).
- God said: "Even though you see the four kingdoms on top of you, I will plant the seeds of redemption within the exile." It is written afterwards, "Oil for the lamp"; this is Mashiach the King, as it says, "There I will make David's horn to sprout, I have set up a lamp for my anointed" (*Tehillim* 132:17)."[XXII]

Daat Sofrim takes an interesting approach in explaining why copper, the lower of the three metals (gold and silver), represents Greece:

> "*Copper corresponding to Greece which is the most inferior of them.*" The danger of Greece was less. The political greatness of Greece itself was insignificant compared to the greatness of Babylon and Media. Greece was never a singular nation. It benefited from political recognition thanks to a man—Alexander the Macedonian—whose culture was considered Greek, who was from Macedonia adjacent to Greece. He established cities where Greek culture ruled.[XXIII]

Alexander's strategic plan was not to make the world purely a Greek nation. Yes, the influence of Greek culture would be significant. The new Egyptian cosmopolitan city Alexandria would face Greece (or Macedonia for that matter), but Alexander always incorporated local traditions, customs, and cultures. He aimed to create a global world culture.

Originally, the Greek world was composed of independent city-states with plenty of wars between them. Subsequent to Alexander the Great, the Greek Empire was split into four, once again with wars between the successors. The intellectual/spiritual challenge to Yisrael was enormous, more than the other kingdoms. The power of Greece as a world power, though, was inferior.

TORAH SOURCE 8—THE CAMEL AND FRIENDS

The animal world has its own hierarchy and is in fact referred to as the animal kingdom. The Torah specifies clean as well as impure animals in *Vayikra* 11:4–7 and the midrash connects the latter to the Four Kingdoms.

- However, among the cud-chewing, hoofed animals, there are ones that you may not eat. The **camel** shall be unclean to you although it brings up its cud, since it does not have a true hoof.
- The **hyrax** shall be unclean to you although it brings up its cud, since it does not have a true hoof.
- The **hare** shall be unclean to you although it brings up its cud, since it does not have a true hoof.
- The **pig** shall be unclean to you although it has a true hoof which is cloven, since it does not chew its cud.[XXIV]

The *Midrash Rabbah* (*Shemini* 13:5) expounds these verses in several ways, giving several explanations regarding their allusion to the Four Kingdoms.

FIRST EXPLANATION OF VERSES[XXV]

Empire	Animal	Source	Explanation
Babylon	Camel גמל	Tehillim 137:8	"O Daughter of Babylon, who is destined to be plundered, praiseworthy is he who repays you your recompense that you have done to us."[XXVI] Play on Hebrew word *gamal* (camel) and *gamul* (recompense)
Persia/Media	Hyrax שפן	Mordechai/ Haman	Rabbis: Just as the hyrax has kosher and non-kosher signs, so Persia had a *tzaddik* and an evil man. Rav Yehudah: The last Darius, the son of Esther, was pure from his mother Esther and impure from his father Achashveirosh.

Greece	Hare ארנבת	The mother or wife of Ptolemy was named Arnevet.[5]	
Rome	Pig חזיר	Power of Rome	In *Devarim*, Moshe put the first three in one verse and the pig separately. Why? Rav Yochanan said: "The pig is equal to all three combined." Why is Rome compared to a pig? Just as a pig when it rolls around it shows its hoofs saying, "Look, I'm kosher and pure," so Rome steals, oppresses, and claims to be pure.

TORAH SOURCE 9—TYPES OF TZARAAT

The Torah describes four types of spiritual diseases called *tzaraat* and the procedures enabled by the *Kohen* for purification of these afflictions. More than a punishment, these external symptoms are a direct consequence of man's actions and can actually be viewed as blessings. They enable a person to focus on the spiritual reasons behind the physical occurrence and allow for intense introspective repentance.

The midrash connects the four types of "*tzaraat*/leprosy" to the four kingdoms of history based on *Vayikra* 13:2: "If a man has a rising, or a scab, or a bright spot in the skin of his flesh, and it forms a lesion of *tzaraat* on the skin of his flesh, he shall be brought to Aharon the *Kohen*, or unto one of his sons the Kohanim."[XXVII]

The midrash (*Vayikra Rabbah* 15:9) elaborates:

- "Rising"—This is **Babylon**, as it says, "You shall take up this parable against the king of Babylon...How has the oppressor ceased! The haughty (gold) one ceased!"

---

5   See Appendix A above, change #14, for further discussion.

> (Yeshayahu 14:4). Our Rabbis say, as it says, "You are the head of gold" (Daniel 2:38).
>
> - "Scab"—this is **Media [Persia]**, referring to Haman who was like a snake, "On your belly you will crawl" (Bereishit 3:14).
> - "Bright spot"—This is **Greece**, who shined with their decrees against Yisrael saying: "Write for us on the horn of an ox that you have no portion in the God of Yisrael."
> - "Plague of leprosy"—This is **Edom [Rome]**.
>
> In this world, the Kohen sees the afflictions, but in the World to Come, the Holy One, blessed be He, says: "I will purify you," as it says, "And I will sprinkle clean water upon you, and you shall be clean" (Yechezkel 36:25).[XXVIII]

TORAH SOURCE 10—THE RED HEIFER

The classic example of a *chok*—an unexplained "irrational" law—is the paradox of the Red Heifer as taught in *Bamidbar* 19:1–2: The impure become pure; while at the same time the pure become impure.

> God spoke to Moshe and Aharon saying: "This is the statute of the Torah which God commanded, saying, 'Speak to the children of Yisrael and have them take for you a perfectly red unblemished cow which never had a yoke on it.'"[XXIX]

Yalkut Shimoni (Chukat §19):

- "Heifer" is Egypt, as it says, "Egypt is a very fair heifer" (Yirmiyahu 46:20).
- "Red" is **Babylon**, as it says, "You are the head of gold" [Red] (Daniel 2:38).
- "Faultless" is **Persia /Media**. Rabbi Chiyah Bar Ava says, "The kings of Persia were faultless. God only faults them for the idol worship that they received from their ancestors."
- "No blemish" is **Greece**. When Alexander the Macedonian

bowed down to Shimon HaTzaddik, [and] his entourage asked: "Why are you bowing down to a Jew?" he answered, "An image in the likeness of this man gains victory before me on all my battlefields."

- "Upon which never came a yoke" is the **Fourth Kingdom** [**Rome**], who did not accept God's yoke, and if that isn't enough, they curse and reject God, [as it says], "For whom do I have in heaven…" (Tehillim 73:25).[xxx]

The *Maharal* in *Ner Mitzvah* asks: What could possibly be the connection between the Red Heifer and the Four Kingdoms?

The commandment and laws of the Red Heifer are lofty; they are found on the "highest level," to the point that they are so inscrutable, so unfathomable that even Shlomo HaMelech could not fully grasp them. If one understands this idea, then one can understand how the exile, the Fourth Kingdom, Rome, could be so long. It too has a strength on a high level so that it is almost impossible to envision its end. As Yaakov saw Rome ascend the ladder in his dream/prophecy but not descend! So too we can not understand the depth of the Red Heifer.

The nullification of the Four Kingdoms and the return of the Kingdom of Israel are hinted specifically in the mitzvah of the Red Heifer. For the negation of the Four Kingdoms is on so high a lofty level that such a power that rules the world should lose its high status. Similarly we see that the mitzvah here is on the loftiest of levels; it is very deep beyond our understanding. Since the mitzvah is so unknown, so too was the timing of Israel's return not revealed to the Prophets.[xxxi]

ENDNOTES

SECTION I: ALEXANDER THE GREAT

I. BIOGRAPHY

I **צמח דוד, חלק שני, שנה תכג**
אלכסנדרוס מוקדון נולד בשנת תכג (324) ובעת ההוא נראה ברקיע כוכב נורא ונתגעשה הארץ וירגזו מוסדות תבל והיו ברקים ורעמים וקור גדול במוקדוניה אשר לא נודע ליושביה כמוהו.

II **סדר הדורות, אלף הרביעי עמוד סח**
אריסטוטלו הפילוסוף וראש החכמים היה רבו של אלכסנדר ותלמיד סוקרטו ופלטוני, ונולד במצידוניא וחי כ' שנים אחר מיתת אלכסנדר תלמידו והיו ימי חייו ס"ב שנים, וכתב שדבר עם שמעון הצדיק על חכמת אלקות והשתומם מאוד ממעלת חכמת שמעון.

III **רבי צדוק הכהן מלובלין, פוקד עקרים פרק ו**
ואריסטו ראש לחכמי יון היה בזמן שמעון הצדיק משירי אנשי כנסת הגדולה והוא בימי אלכסנדר מוקדון ראש מלכות יון כנודע וממנו התפשטות חכמת יונית וגזירותיהם שהחשיכו עיניהם של ישראל וכו'.

IV **רמ"ע מפאנו, גלגולי נשמות אות ת**
אריסטוטלוס היה ניצוץ אבטליון שלמד תלמידים שאינם מהוגנים ונעשים צדוקים, וכן אריסטוטלוס היה מבחינתם, לכן לבסוף חזר בתשובה ונתגלגל באנטונינוס שלמד מרבינו הקדוש.

V **מהר"ל, נצח ישראל פרק א**
וזה אין ספק כי הגלות הוא שנוי ויציאה מן הסדר, שהשם יתברך סדר כל אומה במקומה הראוי לה, וסדר את ישראל במקום הראוי להם, שהוא ארץ ישראל, והגלות מן מקומם הוא שנוי ויציאה לגמרי. וכל הדברים כאשר הם יוצאים ממקום הטבעי והם חוץ למקומם, אין להם עמידה במקום הבלתי טבעי להם...

VI **דניאל, ב, לט**
ובתרך תקום מלכו אחרי ארעא מנך ומלכו תליתאה אחרי די נחשא די תשלט בכל ארעא.

VII **מלבי"ם, שם**
ומלכו, מלכות שלישית אחרת של נחשת, אשר תמשול בכל הארץ, רצה לומר והחלק השלישי שהוא הבטן והירכים שהיו נחשת, מרמז על מלכות הג' שהוא מלכות יון, שהיא ג"כ מלכות אחרת ממין אחר, כמו שהנחושת מתכות אחר, ומה שהוא של נחשת מפני שתמשול על כל הארץ, שהנחושת מורה על תוקף המלכות, וכן כמו שהשרש כולל כל הגוף, כי ממנו צומח כל הגוף בעת ההויה, והוא שורש האדם מצד שהוא עץ השדה בנפש הצומחת שלו, כן תמלא מלכות אלכסנדר את כל הארץ.

VIII	**מהר"ל, ספר נר מצוה, חלק א (עמוד נד, הרטמן)**
	ויראה כי בשביל כך היה לנמר שראה דניאל ד' גדפין של עוף, שבשביל שהיו עזים הלכו לכבוש את כל העולם, כי מי שאינו עז יש לו כובד הטבע ומבקש ההנחה ואינו מבקש התנועה, אבל מי שהוא עז הוא כמו אש...שאין לו ההנחה כלל, ולכך היה המלכות הזה משוטט בכל העולם, ולפיכך אלכסנדר שהוא עיקר במלכות רביעית הלך לכבוש את כל העולם, מה שלא עשה שום מלך.

2. THE BATTLES

I	**מלבי"ם, דניאל ח, ו**
	ויבא עד האיל: שקרב לעיר בירת המלך אשר ראיתי עומד לפני האובל: רצה לומר שדרוש לא זה ממקומו לצאת לקראתו שהיה אלכסנדר כאין בעיניו ושלח לנגדו שר צבאו וצוה שיביאנו לפניו אסור בזיקים. וירץ אליו בחמת כחו: שנצח את שר צבאו במלחמה ורץ אליו בעצמו.
II	**צמח דוד, חלק שני, שנה תמט-תנד (ראה סדר הדורות תכ"ג)**
	חידש המלך אלכסנדר את העיר הגדולה אמון מנוא וקרא אותה אלכסנדריה עד היום הזה...היה חכם ונבון גדול בכל שבע חכמות, אוהב את החכמים מכבדם ומספיקן, רחמן על עמו, אוהב אמת ומשפט וכבד וחבב את ישראל.
III	**סדר הדורות, ג' אלפים, תכ"ג**
	יום מולד אלכסנדר בחודש אייר יום ד' בזרוח השמש ובו ביום באייר בד' בבוא השמש מת, ושני חייו היו ל"ב שנה וימי מלכותו י"ב שנה כי בן כ' מלך.
IV	**פרקי דרבי אליעזר, פרק יא**
	מלך השמיני הוא אלכסנדרוס מוקדון שמשל מסוף העולם ועד סופו שנאמר (דניאל ח, ה) ואני הייתי מבין והנה צפיר העזים בא מן המערב, על פני הארץ אין כתיב כאן אלא על פני כל הארץ. לידע מה בקצוות הארץ, ולא עוד אלא שרצה לעלות לשמים לידע מה שבשמים, ולירד לתהומות ולידע מה בתהומות וחצה המלכות לארבע רוחות השמים, שנאמר (דניאל יא, ד) וכעמדו תשבר מלכותו ותחץ לארבע רוחות השמים.

3. ALEXANDER AND SHIMON HATZADDIK

I	**רמב"ם, הקדמה למשנה תורה, פסקה ז**
	בית דינו של עזרא הם הנקראים "אנשי כנסת הגדולה". והם חגי זכריה ומלאכי, דניאל וחנניה ומישאל ועזריה, ונחמיה בן חכליה, ומרדכי בלשן וזרובבל, והרבה חכמים עמהם תשלום מאה ועשרים זקנים. האחרון מהם הוא שמעון הצדיק, והוא היה מכלל המאה ועשרים, וקבל תורה שבעל פה מכולם. והוא היה כהן גדול אחר עזרא.
II	**אבות, א, ב**
	שמעון הצדיק היה משיירי כנסת הגדולה. הוא היה אומר, על שלשה דברים העולם עומד, על התורה ועל העבודה ועל גמילות החסדים.
III	**תולדות תנאים ואמוראים, חלק ג עמוד 1217**
	בדברי ימי הגדול בענקים הלזה אשר הוא היחיד והמיוחד מכל חכמי ישראל שזכה לשם גדול כזה.
IV	**בן סירא, שמעון בן יוחנן הגדול**
	(א) גדול אחיו ותפארת עמו, שמעון בן יוחנן הכהן (*א) אשר בדורו נפקד הבית, ובימיו חזק היכל. (ב) אשר בדורו נכרה מקוה, ושיח כים בהמונו. (ג) אשר בימיו נבנה קיר / פנות, מעון, כהיכל מלך. (ד) הדואג לעמו מחתף, ומחזק עירו מצר. (ה) מה נהדר בהשגיחו מאהל, ובצאתו מבית הפרכת.
V	**דורות הראשונים, התקופה האמצעית פרק ו**
	התקופה האמצעית הזאת היינו התקופה אשר בין ימי אנשי כנסת הגדולה ובין ימי התנאים, אשר הותחלו עם הלל ושמאי והבתים אשר יסדו.

VI	**יומא, לט, א**
	תנו רבנן ארבעים שנה ששמש שמעון הצדיק היה גורל עולה בימין מכאן ואילך פעמים עולה בימין פעמים עולה בשמאל והיה לשונו של זהורית מלבין מכאן ואילך פעמים מלבין פעמים אינו מלבין והיה נר מערבי דולק מכאן ואילך פעמים דולק פעמים כבה...
VII	**אברבנאל, מעיני הישועה, מעין ט, תמר ב**
	ופני אדם רומז למלכי מדי ופרס לפי שהם לא הרעו לישראל בממשלתם והיו שאר האומות בערך הבעלי חיים הטורפים האכזרים מדי ופרס רחמנים כבני אדם. הלא תראה שהם השיבו את ישראל על אדמתם ונתנו להם עזר רב ורשות לבנות את בית ה' והשיבו שמה הכלים הקדושים אשר הגלה נ"נ וכן כתב יוסף בן גוריון שעבודת ישראל למלכי מדי ופרס היתה עבודה מתוקה.
VIII	**יומא, סט, א**
	והתניא בעשרים וחמשה בטבת יום הר גרזים הוא דלא למספד,יום שבקשו כותיים את בית אלקינו מאלכסנדרוס מוקדון להחריבו, ונתנו להם, מה עשה, באו והודיעו את שמעון הצדיק, מה עשה, לבש בגדי כהונה ונתעטף בבגדי כהונה ומיקירי ישראל עמו ואבוקות של אור בידיהן, וכל הלילה הללו הולכים מצד זה והללו הולכים מצד זה, עד שעלה עמוד השחר, כיון שעלה עמוד השחר אמר להם, מי הללו, אמרו לו יהודים שמרדו בך, כיון שהגיע לאנטיפטרס זרחה חמה ופגעו זה בזה, כיון שראה לשמעון הצדיק ירד ממרכבתו והשתחוה לפניו, אמרו לו מלך גדול כמותך ישתחוה ליהודי זה, אמר להם דמות דיוקנו של זה מנצחת לפני בבית מלחמתי, אמר להם למה באתם, אמרו אפשר בית שמתפללים בו עליך ועל מלכותך שלא תחרב יתעוך עובדי כוכבים להחריבו, אמר להם מי הללו, אמרו לו כותיים הללו שעומדים לפניך, אמר להם הרי הם מסורין בידיכם.
IX	**דורות הראשונים, התקופה האמצעית פרק יא**
	ויאזעפוס אשר ידע כי ידוע היה אז כהן גדול חשב שהוא היה גם היוצא לקראת אלכסנדר.
X	**תולדות תנאים ואמוראים, חלק ג, אות ש שמעון הצדיק**
	ולפי דעת חז"ל יצא לקראתו נכדו שמעון הצדיק, אך דברי שניהם אמת כי הכה"ג-הנשיא היה באמת ידוע אבי אביו דשמעון, ושמעון היה אז...לכן הוקם לשמש במקדש בתור כה"ג המשמש, וזה כונת הרמב"ם ששמעון הצדיק שימש בכה"ג אחר עזרא.
XI	**בן יהוידע, יומא שם**
	לבש בגדי כהונה ונתעטף בבגדי כהונה. פירוש בגדי כהונה כשהיה לובשם כה"ג בבהמ"ק היה שורה עליהם זיו של אורה שכל אדם הרואה אותם מרגיש במראה עיניו בהארה זו ובודאי הארה זו לא תהיה עליהם אלא רק בבהמ"ק, אך עתה ראה שמעון הצדיק השעה צריכה לכך שתהיה הארה זו עליהם גם כשהוא לובשם חוץ למקדש לכך בצאתו בהם המשיך אותה ההארה ע"י כונות ידועות לו, ולזה אמר לבש בגדי כהונה הם בגדים העיקרים ונתעטף בבגדי כהונה קאי על אותו זיו ההארה שלהם שהמשיך על הבגדים. ומ"ש ואבוקות של אור בידם, נ"ל בס"ד שתפסו בידם אבוקות של אור זכר לזכות התורה שיש להם כמ"ש נר מצוה ותורה אור שתגין עליהם. ועוד נ"ל בס"ד שתפסו אבוקות של אור בידם לזה עשו כונה על שם קדוש הנקרא אדי"ר רו"ן שיוצא מפסוק ימינך ה' נאדרי בכח...ושם זה יש בו אותיות או"ר ואותיות י"ד ואותיות נ"ר ולכן תפסו אבוקו"ת או"ר ביד"ם שיש כאן אור ויד ונר שכיונו בזה על שם אדי"ר רו"ן הנזכר לשמירתם. ומה שהיו מהלכין כל הלילה כולה נראה כיונו לילך רק בחצי השני שנקרא לילה שהוא את רצון וכיון שזרחה חמה פגעו זה בזה ומן השמים נעשה כך לסימן טוב שבזריחת החמה יהיה נס הישועה ע"ד וזרחה לכם יראי שמי ומרפא בכנפיה.
XII	**ספר יוחסין, מאמר ראשון**
	וביקש שהבנים שיולדו להם בשנה ההיא שיקראו אלכסנדרוס על שמו ושימנו חשבונו מן השנה ההיא.
XIII	**טיב גיטין, אות מ"ב**
	מ"ש הרבה הי' נקראים אלכסנדרוס ונשתרבב בינינו ע"ש אלכסנדר מוקדון כמו שנמצא ביוסיפין שהכה"ג הבטיח לו לעשות לו זכרון בהיכל ה' שכל הכהני' אשר יולדו בשנה ההיא יהיו נקראים על שמו והוטב בעיניו.

XIV	**אגרות משה, אורח חיים ה, סימן י'**

ומש"כ ששם אלכסנדר היה זה מתוך לחץ, שהוצרכו לפצותו על שלא הרשו לו להכניס את תמונתו למקדש, היא עובדא בדויה לגמ' שלנו. דשמעון הצדיק היה חשוב מאד בעיניו, כמפורש ביומא דף ס"ט ע"א, דכיון שראה לשמעון הצדק ירד ממרכבתו והשתחוה לפניו ואמר שהוא מפני שדמות דיוקנו של זה מנצחת לפני בית מלחמתי, אלא היה זה לכבודו להכרת טובה. ומה שראיתי בטיב גיטין אות מ"ב שאיתא ביוסיפון שהכ"ג הבטיח לו שהכהנים אשר יוולדו בשנה ההיא יהיו נקראים על שמו, וגם זה הוא טעם נכון, מאחר שאינו ענין איסור אף שהוא דבר גנאי, שייך לעשות זה להכרת טובה. ואדרבה עשו זה בשמחה, והכניסו שם אלכסנדר בכלל שמות העברים.

4. THE TEN QUESTIONS

I	**ולא עוד אלא, (על פדר"א) להג"ר אליהו הכהן האיתמרי (עמוד עה א)**

וכיון שכן בהיות אלכסנדרוס מוקדון חכם שבחכמים ופלוסוף לחקור בנסתרות לידע אמיתות הדברים, רצה לחקור בידיעת האלהות הן כדי להשיג האמת הן כדי להיות הוא ג"כ ראש המעידים בהיות הוא מן השמים ומן האויר ומן הארץ ומארבע קצוות שלה ומתהומות, שהן כל אלה ראתה עינו. ומסיבה זאת מלאו לבו לחזור בכל מקום ולעלות בשמים ולירד בתהום לראות היש אלוה בלעדי ה' חלילה וחס, ואחר החיפוש בתר חיפוש להיות דבוק באמונת האחדות כראוי כי כוונתו היה להשגת האמת, כי על זה נברא האדם.

II	**רבינו בחיי, בראשית יב, ט**

ויסע אברם הלוך ונסוע הנגבה—וכל מסעות אלו כדי להשיג השגת נבואתו של קל שקי הוא כנוי של אל"ף דל"ת שהשיג שכולל אותו הנגבה. ["הנגבה" כמנין "אדנ"י".]

III	**בבא בתרא, כה, ב**

אמר רבי יצחק הרוצה שיחכים ידרים ושיעשיר יצפין, וסימניך שלחן בצפון ומנורה בדרום, ורבי יהושע בן לוי אמר לעולם ידרים, שמתוך שמתחכם מתעשר, שנאמר (משלי ג, טז) "אורך ימים בימינה בשמאלה עושר וכבוד".

IV	**עירובין, נג, ב**

אמרי ליה לרבי אלעאי הצפינו הכין רבי אבהו [צפון] אמר להן נתייעץ במכתיר והנגיב למפיבשת. רש"י—לפני זקני דרום שהן חכמים מאד, ע"ש שהיה מפיבשת אדם גדול קרי להו הכי.

V	**יבמות, סב, ב**

והיה העולם שמם עד שבא רבי עקיבא אצל רבותינו שבדרום ושנאה להם רבי מאיר ורבי יהודה ורבי יוסי ורבי שמעון ורבי אלעזר בן שמוע והם העמידו תורה אותה שעה.

VI	**תמיד, לא, ב, לב, א**

עשרה דברים שאל אלכסנדרוס מוקדון את זקני הנגב אמר להן מן השמים לארץ רחוק או ממזרח למערב אמרו לו ממזרח למערב, תדע שהרי חמה במזרח הכל מסתכלין בה, חמה במערב הכל מסתכלין בה, חמה באמצע רקיע אין הכל מסתכלין בה, וחכמים אומרים זה וזה כאחד שוין שנאמר (תהילים קג, יא) כגבוה שמים על הארץ וגו' כרחוק מזרח ממערב ואי חד מינייהו נפיש נכתבו תרוייהו כי ההוא דנפיש. ואלא חמה באמצע רקיע מאי טעמא אין הכל מסתכלין בה משום דקאי להדיא ולא כסי ליה מידי.

VII	**רש"י, שם**

מן השמים לארץ רחוק—כלומר איזה רחוק יותר.
אמרו לו ממזרח למערב—רחוק יותר משמים לארץ. ותדע שהרי חמה במזרח הכל מסתכלים בה חמה באמצע רקיע אין הכל מסתכלין. ולמה לפי שהחמה כשהיא במזרח או במערב היא רחוקה ובשביל שהיא רחוקה יכולים להסתכל בה שאין האורה מזיק לעינים אבל כשהיא באמצע הרקיע קרובה ואורה מזיק כ"כ שאין יכולין לראות.
וחכ"א וזה וזה מדתם שוה—כדמוכחי קראי, כתוב אחד אומר כגבוה שמים על הארץ וכתוב אחד אומר כרחוק מזרח ממערב. ואם לא היתה מדתן שוה אלא מזרח ומערב רחוק יותר למה

אחז הכתוב במועט במדה לא היה לו כלל לומר אלא המרובה אלא ודאי שניהם שוין במדה לכך אחז את שניהן.
אלא מאי טעם חמה באמצע הרקיע אין הכל מסתכלין בה—כמו שהם מסתכלין כשהיא במזרח או במערב.
משום דקאי להדיא—בגילוי היא עומדת ולא כסי לה מידי ובשביל כך אורה מזהיר ומזיק לעינים המביטות שם.

חתם סופר, תמיד לב, א — VIII

מספקא אי הכדור כדוריי או בציי והיא פלוגתא ישנה בין החכמים.

הרב יצחק שוראקי, אלכסנדר מוקדון וזקני הנגב, תשע"ג, עמ' 395-408 — IX

זקני הנגב, שהתעלו בחכמה מתוך מרחב גיאוגרפי פחות משופע, משיבים באופן ברור, שהמרחק לשמים קטן יותר מהמרחק שבין מזרח ומערב. האדם קרוב יותר לשמים מאשר לקצוות הארץ, למרחב הרוחני מאשר למרחב הגיאוגרפי וההשתלשלות הצבאית והפוליטית בעולם. הקירבה לשמים כבר מוכנה בנפשו, רוח ומהותו של האדם הדומה לעליון. ויש אפילו מקום שבו קירבה זו נראית באופן מורגש, ששם 'נשקי שמיא וארעא' כחוט שערה (תענית כה ע"ב; בבא בתרא עד ע"א), מקום שמעביר אותנו לעולם עליון מן העולם הגשמי שבו אנו חיים.

מאמרי הרב יגאל אריאל, רוח הגולן, אלכסנדר וזקני הנגב https://rgl.org.il — X

אך אפשר לפרש שאין מדובר רק בממדיו הפיזיים של העולם אלא בהשקפת העולם על ממדיו הרוחניים. הקו האופקי מתאר תנועה ואחיזה במה שלפנינו, את צירי הפעילות של האנשים והצבאות הפועלים במרחב, מזרח וממערב, את יעילותם. הקו האנכי של ארץ-שמים, מתאר את הגובה, את קווי הרוח, של מה שמעלינו, השירה, החזון, התבוננות מעבר ליש הממשי. חכמים הם אנשי רוח, מאמינים, המישור שבין השמים לארץ בוודאי עניין אותם, אולם הם עונים: יש להתמקד בקו האופקי. נראה שהתמקמו מדיון עמוק וענו תשובה שבוודאי תמצא חן בעיני אלכסנדר...אולם זקני הנגב לא אמרו את כל העולה על ליבם. הם לא הזכירו את שיטת חכמים. וחכמים אומרים: זה וזה כאחד שוין שנאמר (תהילים ק"ג יא-יב) כי כגבה שמים על הארץ גבר חסדו על יראיו. כרחק מזרח ממערב הרחיק ממנו את פשעינו. ואי חד מיניהו נפיש נכתבו תרווייהו כי ההוא דנפיש...החסד האלוהי מקרב את בני האדם לא רק לשמים, אלא גם זה לזה.

רנן לבקר, תמיד לב, א — XI

הערה—מן השמים לארץ רחוק או ממזרח למערב, אולי שאל על עניני הצלחה שהם בהשגחה וצריכין ג"כ להשתדלות כמ"ש העקדה פ' וישלח שכ"ו ומי משתיהם רחוק להביא הענין הנרצה כי שמים הוא ההשגחה ומזרח ומערב הוא ההשתדלות...

תמיד, לב, א — XII

אמר להן שמים נבראו תחלה או הארץ, אמרו שמים נבראו תחלה, שנאמר בראשית ברא אלקים את השמים ואת הארץ.

חגיגה, יב, א — XIII

ת"ר ב"ש אומרים שמים נבראו תחלה ואח"כ נבראת הארץ שנאמר בראשית ברא אלהים את השמים ואת הארץ וב"ה אומרים ארץ נבראת תחלה ואח"כ שמים שנאמר (בראשית ב, ד) ביום עשות ה' אלהים ארץ ושמים אמר להם ב"ה לב"ש לדבריכם אדם בונה עלייה ואח"כ בונה בית שנאמר (עמוס ט, ו) הבונה בשמים מעלותיו ואגודתו על ארץ יסדה אמרו להם ב"ש לב"ה לדבריכם אדם עושה שרפרף ואח"כ עושה כסא שנאמר (ישעיהו סו, א) כה אמר ה' השמים כסאי והארץ הדום רגלי וחכ"א זה וזה כאחת נבראו שנאמר (ישעיהו מח, יג) אף ידי יסדה ארץ וימיני טפחה שמים קורא אני אליהם יעמדו יחדו ואידך מאי יחדו דלא משתלפי מהדדי קשו קראי אהדדי אמר ר"ל כשנבראו ברא שמים ואח"כ ברא הארץ וכשנטה נטה הארץ ואחר כך נטה שמים.

צל"ח, שם — XIV

ומעתה נוכל לומר שפלוגתא בית שמאי ובית הלל אם שמים קדמו או ארץ קדמה, הוא עצמו הפלוגתא שבין הפילוסופים, ודעת בית שמאי שגרמי השמים אין בהם שום חיות ותנועתם

בטבע הוטבע בהם בתחלת הוייתם, וכמו שהאש יתנועע תמיד למעלה והאבן יפול תמיד למטה, ואין זה מצד חיות ורצון שבהם, כן הוטבע בגרמי השמים התנועה הסיבובית, ולכן אין לתעות בהם לחשבם לאלהות ולכן סבר בריאת שמים קודם. ובית הלל סוברים שיש בהם חיות ונפש שכלי ותשוקה, והיא דעת הרמב"ם במורה נבוכים חלק ב' פ"ז, ולכך סברי בית הלל בריאת הארץ קודם מפני שפלותה.

XV **אפיקי ים, תמיד לב, א**
...אבל לדעתי יש בזה כוונה נפלאה, שהנה שאלת אלכסנדר היה סתירת הכתובים שבשמים וארץ כתיב בתחילה שמים ואח"כ ארץ...וכמו דאיתא בזה מחלוקת ב"ש וב"ה וחכמים...ששמים שנזכר בפ' ראשון הם ה' שמים עליונים מז' רקיעים, ושמים שנזכר ביום שני יהי רקיע וכו' הם שמי השמים והם ב' תחתונים רקיע וווילון שנבלל בו. וה' שמים עליונים הם קדמו לארץ שהרי הם רוחניים מאוד ואינם מושגים כלל מהותם.

XVI **חתם סופר, תמיד לב, א**
וצ"ע מ"ט לא ניחא לי' בפשיטות אי ארץ תחלה דבהכי פליגי ב"ש וב"ה ר"פ אין דורשין (חגיגה יב, א) ותו מאי קא מייתי ליה מבראשית ברא דלמא לעולם כא' נבראו וא"א להוציא שתי תיבות באחת היה צריך לכתוב שמים וארץ...ונ"ל דלא ניחא לי להרב המפרש למימר דהשיג אלכסנדרוס סוד ה' ליראיו ב"ש וב"ה כי דבריהם נוגעים ברומו של עולם בסתרי בראשית ומרכבה...

XVII **תמיד, לב, א**
אמר להן אור נברא תחלה או חשך, אמרו לו מלתא דו אין לה פתר, ונימרו ליה חשך נברא תחלה, דכתיב והארץ היתה תהו ובהו וחשך, והדר ויאמר אלקים יהי אור ויהי אור, סברי דילמא אתי לשיולי מה למעלה מה למטה מה לפנים ומה לאחור. אי הכי שמים נמי לא נמרו ליה, מעיקרא סבור אקראי בעלמא הוא דקא שייל, כיון דחזו דקהדר שאיל סברי לא נימא ליה, דילמא אתי לשיולי מה למעלה מה למטה מה לפנים ומה לאחור.

XVIII **משנה חגיגה, ב, א**
אין דורשין בעריות בשלשה ולא במעשה בראשית בשנים ולא במרכבה ביחיד אלא אם כן היה חכם ומבין מדעתו כל המסתכל בארבעה דברים ראוי לו כאילו לא בא לעולם מה למעלה מה למטה מה לפנים ומה לאחור.

XIX **מאמרי הרב יגאל אריאל, רוח הגולן, אלכסנדר וזקני הנגב https://rgl.org.il**
אלא שהדברים מורכבים יותר שהרי ישעיהו מדבר על בריאת החושך: יוֹצֵר אוֹר וּבוֹרֵא חֹשֶׁךְ עֹשֶׂה שָׁלוֹם וּבוֹרֵא רָע אֲנִי ה' עֹשֶׂה כָל אֵלֶּה. אם מייחסים לחושך בריאה, מתבוונים לחושך מסוג אחר, לא רק העדר אור אלא חושך שיש בו ממשות . אפשר להגדיר זאת בכמה אופנים: א. משהו פיזי כמו 'חור שחור', הבולע כל ישות אחרת. ב. לפני הבריאה היה האור אין סוף, שאינו מותיר מקום וזמן.... ג. האור מסמל את החכמה, הדעת או את התורה...ד. אור וחושך הם גם סמל לטוב ולרע...

XX **תמיד, לב, א**
אמר להם אידין מתקרי חכים, אמרו ליה איזהו חכם הרואה את הנולד.

XXI **קהלת, ב, יד**
החכם עיניו בראשו והכסיל בחשך הולך וידעתי גם אני שמקרה אחד יקרה את כלם.

XXII **תמיד, לב, א**
אמר להן אידין מתקרי גבור, אמרו לו איזהו גבור הכובש את יצרו.

XXIII **משלי, טז, לב**
טוב ארך אפים מגבור ומשל ברוחו מלכד עיר.

XXIV **תמיד, לב, א**
אמר להן אידין מתקרי עשיר, אמרו ליה איזהו עשיר השמח בחלקו.

XXV **קדושין, מט, ב**
על מנת שאני חכם אין אומרים כחכמי יבנה כר' עקיבא וחבריריו אלא כל ששואלים אותו דבר חכמה בכל מקום ואומרה.

XXVI	שם

על מנת שאני גבור אין אומרים כאבנר בן נר וכיואב בן צרויה אלא כל שחביריו מתיראים ממנו מפני גבורתו.

XXVII	שם

על מנת שאני עשיר אין אומרים כרבי אלעזר בן חרסום וכרבי אלעזר בן עזריה אלא כל שבני עירו מכבדים אותו מפני עושרו.

XXVIII	מהרש"א, שם

ונראה דאלו השאלות כלפי עצמו שאלם שישבחו ויהללו אותו בהן, לפי שהיה חכם בחכמת הפילוסופיא שהיה תלמידו של אריסטוטלוס, והיה גבור כובש כמה ארצות, וגם עושר בנכסים שאסף במלחמה. אבל הם השיבו לו על פי מה שאמר הכתוב (ירמיהו ט, כב) "אל יתהלל חכם בחכמתו וגו', כי אם בזאת יתהלל המתהלל המתהלל השכל" וגו', דהוא תכלית ואושר האמיתי.

XXIX	ירמיהו, ט, כב-כג

כה אמר ה' אל יתהלל חכם בחכמתו ואל יתהלל הגבור בגבורתו אל יתהלל עשיר בעשרו. כי אם בזאת יתהלל המתהלל השכל וידע אותי כי אני ה' עשה חסד משפט וצדקה בארץ כי באלה חפצתי נאם ה'.

XXX	חתם סופר, מסכת תמיד, לב, א

אידין מתקרי חכים—אפשר כיון להתלוצץ בהם כי ידוע שהיה פלוסוף גדול וכל אלו השאלות ששאל לא היו מסופקים אצלו כי היה לו חקירות על כולם עם מופתי הפלוסופים רק בא לנסותם בחדות לידע חכמת היהודים וסברתם בענינים הללו וכיון שהשיבו מילתא דא אין להם פתר שאל להם איזה חכם כלומר איך תקראו חכמים ולא תדעו לפתור לי מילתא דא במופת והם בחכמתם השיבו איזהו חכם הרואה את הנולד רמזו לו כי הם יודעים האמת רק להיותם רואים הנולד לכן לא השיבוהו כי ישאלם מה למעלה וכו'.

XXXI	עקדת יצחק, שער ס"ה

מבאר שהלומד מכל אדם הוא חכם כי חכם הוא מי שמבין את חסר ידיעתו ומבין שעליו ללמוד, ומתוך כך הוא למד מכל אדם. ולדעת חכמי הנגב חכם הוא הרואה את הנולד, כי המתעצל בחכמה שקוע בהווה ואינו יכול לראות את העתיד, אבל חכם אינו שקוע בעניני ההווה. וכן הוא אומר שהכובש את יצרו הוא גבור כי גבור הוא מי ששולט בעצמו. ובאבריו תחלה ואח"כ ימשול בזרים. וכן העשיר הוא תבונתו של מי שדי לו במה שיש לו, והוא מבין שאם ה' ברא אותו עם זה, זה נחוץ לו ולא עוד. ולכן זה נלמד מהפסוק יגיע כפיך כי תאכל, כלומר, ה' נתן לך כפים ולא זהב, כי די לך בכפיך.

XXXII	תמיד, לב, א

אמר להן מה יעביד איניש ויחיה, אמרו ליה ימית עצמו.

XXXIII	תמיד, לב, א

מה יעביד איניש ימות, יחיה את עצמו.

XXXIV	רש"י, שם

ימית את עצמו—ישפיל את עצמו. יחיה את עצמו—יגבה את עצמו ומתוך כך יתנו בו הבריות עין רעה ויקנאו בו וימות ולימדום חכמים שאדם הרוצה שיחיה ישפיל את עצמו וירחמו עליו הבריות ויחיה ויראה שנים הרבה ומגאוה ימנע עצמו שלא יקצרו ימיו וימות בלא עתו.

XXXV	רבינו יונה, אבות ב, טו

רבי יהושע אומר עין הרע, פירושו מי שאינו שמח בחלקו ועויין את חברו העשיר ממנו מתי יעשר עושר גדול כמוהו, והוא גורם רע לעצמו ולחברו, כאשר אמרו חכמי הטבע, החומד מכל אשר לרעהו אויר עולה מן המחשבה ההיא ושורף את הדברים שעויין בהם עינו הרע, גם בקרבו ישרף אחר שמתאוה לדברים שאין יכולת להיות מצוי בידו, והמחשבה ההיא מקלקלת גופו כי יתקצר רוחו ומוציאתו לדברים מן העולם. וזהו עין הרע שאמר ר' יהושע, וראיה לזה הפירוש על שאמר בכאן עין הרע בלשון זכר, שזהו העויין ברע, ולמעלה אמר עין רעה, שפירשנוה על מדה הכילות.

XXXVI	מכתב מאליהו, חלק ד עמוד 5-6

לפני הרבה שנים ביארנו שפעולת עין הרע מושרשת בעובדה שנפשות כל בני אדם קשורות

ומעורות זו בזו וחייהם תלויים זה בזה בשורשם הרוחני, ואם אחד מקנא בחברו ועינו צרה בו, היינו שעצם מציאותו של חבירו מטרידה אותו והיה רוצה לראותו בכל רע, (שזוהי גדר עין רעה, כמו שביארנו בראש דברינו), אז—במדה וחיי חברו תלויים בו, כנ"ל, יתכן ויוכל לגרום על ידי זה למעט מחברו שפע החיים, וממילא יהיה יותר עלול לנזקים ולאסון. ומהר"ל ז"ל מלמד לנו שגם אם לא איכפת לו צרכי חברו יכול זה להחשב כעין הרע, כי כל מי שרואה לחברו צרכים חיוניים ויש בידו לעזור ולא איכפת לו, הריהו מכריז בזה שמציאותו של חברו אינה מעניינת אותו, היא מיותרת בשבילו, והרי זה גדר עין הרע.

XXXVII מהרש"א, תמיד לב, א

אמר להן מה יעביד איניש ויחיה כו'. רש"י פירשו לענין גאה ושפלות ובהאי גוונא כתב הערוך בערך חי (עיין שם) ויותר נראה לפרשו כמשמעו 'מה יעביד איניש ויחיה'? והשיבו לו 'ימית את עצמו'—בעולם הזה להרחיק מתענוגי עולם הזה, כדי שיחיה לעולם הבא כמו שנאמר 'אדם כי ימות באהל' ואמר להם מה יעביד איניש וימות? א"ל יחיה את עצמו בעולם הזה בתענוגים וימות בעולם הבא.

XXXVIII תמיד, לב, א

אמר להן מה יעביד איניש ויתקבל על בריתא, אמרו יסני מלכי ושלטן, אמר להו דידי טבא מדידכו ירחם מלכו ושלטן ויעבד טיבו עם בני אינשא.

XXXIX אבות, א, י

שמעיה ואבטליון קבלו מהם שמעיה אומר אהוב את המלאכה ושנא את הרבנות ואל תתודע לרשות.

XL אבות, ב, ג

הוו זהירין ברשות—שאין מקרבין לו לאדם, אלא לצורך עצמן, נראין כאוהבין בשעת הנאתן, ואין עומדין לו לאדם בשעת דחקו.

XLI תוספות יום טוב, שם

הוו זהירין ברשות וכו'. כתב הר"ב אע"פ שאתם צריכים להתודע לרשות כדי לפקח וכו' דעל כיוצא בזה לא אמר שמעיה [בפרק דלעיל משנה י'] כי זו מצוה רבה היא להתודע להם לפקח על עסקי צבור ומרדכי ורבינו הקדוש יוכיחו. מד"ש בשם רשב"ץ.

XLII רנן לבקר, תמיד לב, א

כתב המפרש יסני מלכי ויתקבלו דבריו ויאהבו אותו, יעביד טיבו עם בני אינשא ויבאו בני העיר לעבדו, נראה דעצת זקני הנגב לענין שיתקבל מאהבה, אבל עצת הפילוסוף לבדו מיראה, א"כ בחנם התפאר דידי טבא דהא נחל ושקר כי זו אהבה עדיפא, וגם כשלא יגיע להם טובה ממנו לא יעבדוהו, ומהרש"א כ' עוד שאי אפשר להטיב לכל אדם...ולי נראה עוד שזקני נגב לא חשו לדבריו מפני שברחימו מלכי ושלטן ימנע מלעסוק בחכמה כדאי' במגילה במרדכי שנאמר בו רצוי לרוב אחיו ולא לכל אחיו, שפרשו ממנו סנהדרין שנתבטל מתלמוד תורה.

XLIII תמיד, לב, א

אמר להן בימא יאי למידר או ביבשתא יאי למידר, אמרו ליה ביבשתא יאי למידר, דהא כל נחותי ימא לא מיתבא דעתיהון עד דסלקין ליבשא.

XLIV פירוש הגר"א, ספר יונה, א, ה

אל הים—הוא עולם הזה שנמשלת לים ועולם הבא ליבשה ולכך שאל אלכסנדרוס מוקדון את זקני הנגב...לפי ששהיה לו כל תאוות עולם הזה ומלך על כל העולם...

XLV **הרב עדין אבן-ישראל, אנחנו יצורים של יבשה, ובכל זאת אנו מחויבים לגלות גם את הים**

https://he.chabad.org/library/article_cdo/aid/3594154

המושגים 'ים' ו'יבשה' מבטאים את שני המצבים הכוללים של המציאות. הים נקרא בלשון הזהר (זהר א יח, א; בשינוי פתח אליהו, הקדמה לתיקוני זהר יז, ב. ובכ"מ) "עלמא דאתכסיא" (העולם המכוסה, הנסתר) והיבשה נקראת "עלמא דאתגליא" (העולם הנגלה). היבשה היא המציאות שמעל לפני השטח, מציאות גלויה לעין, שהחיים שבה נמצאים על פניה. לעומתה,

XLVI **מאמרי הרב יגאל אריאל, רוח הגולן, אלכסנדר וזקני הנגב https://rgl.il/?section=22**
חכמי הדרום ענו לו שאמנם טוב להרחיק בים, טוב לחלום חלומות גדולות ונצורות, טוב לאדם למצות את כל כוחותיו ולהתקדם אף מעבר לגבולותיו. אבל עליו לזכור שזו חריגה מן המסגרת, שבים הוא אורח, וסופו לחזור הביתה אל ביתו, אל היבשה, ורק שם דעתו תתיישב. טוב אפוא לחלום אבל רק כאשר הרגליים ניצבות מוצקות על האדמה. אין ללכת בעקבות החלום ולבנות מגדל הפורח באוויר שאין בו ממש.

XLVII **מדרש רבה, במדבר יג, יד**
אמר רבי יונה אלכסנדרוס מקדנוס כד בעי מיסק לעיל הוי סליק וסליק עד שראה את העולם ככדור ואת הים כקערה בגין כן ציירין ליה כדורא בידיה וצורינין קערה בידיה אינו שליט בים אבל הקדוש ברוך הוא שליט בים ושליט ביבשה מציל בים ומציל ביבשה ולכך הביאו קערה כנגד הים ומזרק כנגד היבשה.

XLVIII **אוצרות מהרש"א , חלק א עמוד 121**
א"ל אידין מנבון—שהייה לו לב עליהם בכל הדברים אלה שהתריסו נגדו וביזו כל ענייני חכמתו וגבורתו ועושרו ומלכותו, ועל כן אמר איזה מנבון חכם יתיר, דודאי על פיו השיבו לו כך. ואמרו דאינו כן, דאתה רואה דכחדא שווי, דהא נתכוונו לדבר אחד, ואם תשים אשמה עלינו, על כולנו הוא! ועל זה אמר להם, על מה דין אתריסתנו נגדי ולבזות את כל מעלתי, חכמתי, ועושרי, וגבורתי, ומלכותי. ורש"י פירש לעניין אמונה וקבלת אלהותו, והוא דחוק, שלא נזכר זה שהתריסו בזה נגדו, ושביקש מהם על זה להפך אמונתם.

XLIX **תמיד, לב, א**
אמר להן אידין מנבון חכים יתיר, אמרו לו כולנא כחדא שווין, דהא כל מילתא דאמרת לנא בחד פתרנא לך, אמר להן על מה דין אתריסתון לקבלי (מפרש-ואינבם מחזיקים יראתנו, הלא אתם יודעים כי אנחנו הרבים ואתם תחתינו), אמרו ליה סטנא נצח. אמר להן הא אנא מקטילנא יתכון בגזירת מלכין, אמרו ליה שלטן ביד מלכא ולא יאי למלכא כזב, מיד אלביש יתהון בלבושין דארגוון ושרי מניכא דדהבא (-שרשרת זהב) על צואריהון.

5. AFRICA, GAN EDEN

I **תמיד, לב, א**
אמר להן בעינא דאיזל למדינתא דאפריקי, אמרו ליה לא מצית אזלת דפסקי הרי חשך, אמר להן לא סגיא דלא אזילנא, אמטו הכי משיילנא לכו, אלא מאי אעביד, אמרו ליה אייתי חמרי לובאי דפרשי בהברא (מפרש-שיודעים לילך בחושך), ואייתי קיבורי דמתני וקטר בהאי גיסא, דכי אתית נקטת בגווייהו ואתית לאתרך (תחזור על פיחם).

II **ערוך השלם, חלק א, אפריקי עמוד רמג**
ובתמיהו הנ"ל יש להביו צפונית של אפריקא. ואלכסנדרוס מוקדון רצה לילך למצרים תחתונה לעם שיושב בהר קצייא עיין ערך אלכסנדרוס. ובויק"ר פכ"ז א' אלכסנדרוס מוקדן אזל לגבי מלכא קציא לאחוריהי הרי חושך אזל להדא מדינתא דשמא קרטיגנא...וא"כ מה שקרא התלמוד אפריקי נקרא בויק"ר קרטיגינא.

III **מהר"ל, חידושי אגדות, תמיד לב, ב**
רק מפני שהעה"ז אשר בו האנשים עיקר יש לו סוף והעדר במקום ההוא, ולכך ראוי שיהיה שם הרי חושך שהחושך הוא העדר המציאות, ואחר הרי החושך כאלו שם הויה לעולם חדש הוא.

IV **תמיד, לב, א-ב**
עבד הכי ואזל מטא לההוא מחוזא דכוליה נשי, בעי למיעבד קרבא בהדייהו, אמרו ליה, אי קטלת לן יאמרו נשי קטל, ואי קטילנא לך יאמרו מלכא דקטלוהו נשי. אמר להן אייתו לי נהמא, אייתו ליה נהמא דדהבא אפתורא דדהבא, אמר להו מי אכלי אינשי נהמא דדהבא, אמרו ליה אלא אי נהמא בעית לא הוה לך באתרך נהמא למיכל דשקלית ואתית להכא. כי

נפיק ואתי כתב אבבא דמחוזא, אנא אלכסנדרוס מוקדון הויתי שטייא עד דאתיתי למדינת אפריקי דנשיא ויליפת עצה מן נשיא.

V **תמיד, לב, ב**
כי שקיל ואתי יתיב אההוא מעיינא, קא אכיל נהמא, הוו בידיה גולדני דמלחא (מפרש-דגים מלוחים), בהדי דמחוורי להו נפל בהו ריחא, אמר שמע מינא האי עינא מגן עדן אתי, איכא דאמרי שקל מהנהו מיא טרא באפיה, איכא דאמרי אידלי כוליה עד דמטא לפתחא דגן עדן, רמא קלא פתחו לי בבא, אמרו ליה זה השער לה' וגו', אמר להון אנא נמי מלכא אנא מיחשב חשיבנא, הבו לי מידי, יהבו ליה גולגלתא חדא. אתייה תקליה לכוליה דהבא וכספא דידיה בהדיה (שקל נגדו), לא הוה מתקליה, אמר להון לרבנן מאי האי, אמרי גולגלתא דעינא דבישרא ודמא דלא קא שבע, אמר להו ממאי דהכי הוא, שקלי קלילי עפרא וכסייה, לאלתר תקלא, דכתיב שאול ואבדון לא תשבענה וגו'.

VI **מהר"ל, נתיבות עולם, נתיב העושר, ב, ט**
האדם אשר הוא תמיד רודף אחר העושר עינו לא תשבע עושר, וכדכתיב (קהלת ד, ח) גם עינו לא תשבע עושר. ותלה זה בעין מפני כי העין רואה ממזרח עד מערב והוא מקבל הכל, וכאשר דבק בו החסרון אינו מלא כלל והוא רוצה וחפץ תמיד לקבל ואינו שבע. ולכך אמרו במסכת תמיד (לב, ב) על אלכסנדר מוקדון שהיה הולך לכבוש את כל העולם עד שהגיע לסוף העולם והגיע לג"ע ולא פתחו לו שערי גן עדן שאמרו לו צדיקים יבאו בו ואמר אנא מלכא מחשב חשיבנא הבו לי מידי יהבו ליה גלגלתא דעינא אתקליה לכולי כספא ודהבא ולא תקיל אמר להו מאי האי א"ל גלגלתא דעינא דבישרא ודמא דלא שבע אמר להו ממאי דהכי הוא אמרי דלא שבע שקלי עפרא ולאלתר תקיל ע"כ. פירוש זה, כי אלכסנדר היה הולך וכובש כל העולם, ולא די לו במלכות שלו אשר כבר כבש עד שהיה רוצה אף לכנוס לגן עדן אשר דבר זה אינו ראוי לו, ומפני שהיה סבור אלכסנדר כי דבר זה שהולך לכבוש הכל הוא חשיבותו ומעלתו, שהיה כובש אף דבר שאינו ראוי שיהיה אדם בא שם, ובשביל זה אמר מחשב חשיבנא כי מלכא אנא ולכך ראוי לו לבא אף לגן עדן. ובודאי אילו זה מלכותו היה כראוי שהיה מלכות הש"י חפץ בו, לא היה דבק בו חסרון והיה שבע ולא היה הולך לכבוש אף דבר שאינו ראוי, אבל מפני שהיה המלכות שלו מלכות שאינו שלם לכך לא היה שבע. ולכך נתנו לו גלגלתא דעינא כלומר מה שאתה הולך וכובש כל כך אף דבר שאינו ראוי לך, זהו שיש לך מדת העין שאינו שבע מפני כי הוא בשר ודם גוף חמרי ובשביל כך דבר בו ההעדר והחסרון לכך אינו שבע בשביל ההעדר שדבק בעין. ומפני כך תקל בנגדו כל כסף וזהב ולא תקל, כי בשביל ההעדר שבו אינו מלא כלל. ולא האמין כי גלגלא דעינא אינו שבע ומיד שהניחו כנגדו עפר היה שבע כי העפר הוא ראוי לכסוי, ודבר זה ידוע כי המת שהוא צריך גניזה נטמון בעפר, והדם שהוא צריך כסוי מכסין אותו בעפר...ורמזו לו מן גן עדן כי כאשר עינו אינו שבע א"א להשביע אותו רק בעפר דהיינו שיהיה העין טמון בעפר ע"י מיתה כי דבר זה כאשר הוא חסר תמיד ואין לו שביעה אי אפשר להשביע אותו כי אם על ידי העפר שהוא בטול לעין, ודבר זה גורם המיתה אליו עד שיהיה בעפר. וכך אירע לאלכסנדר מוקדן שמת קודם חצי ימיו כמו שכתבו המפרשים עליו בפירוש דניאל על הכתוב (דניאל ח,) וכעצמו נשברה הקרן...

VII **רב פעלים, חלק ב, אורח חיים שאלה א**
ועוד דרך אגב רצינו לדעת מ"ש בגמרא דתמיד פ"ד על אלכסנדרוס מוקדון דמטא לפתחא דג"ע ורמא קלא פתחו לי בבא, ואמרו ליה זה השער לה' צדיקים יבאו בו, אם הדברים כפשוטן דמטא לג"ע ממש ודפק על הפתח והשיבו לו כך, וכן מ"ש בגמרא דכתובות דף ע"ז, שבקש ריב"ל מן מלאך המות שיראהו מקומו בג"ע...ואם הוליכו למקום שהגיע לו אלכסנדרוס מוקדון או לצד אחר...ואשר שאלת על אלכסנדרו' מוקדון שדפק על פתח ג"ע אם הוא כפשוטו ממש, דע כי ג"ע יש לו חצר סובב אותו, ופתח ג"ע העקרי הוא בתוך החצר ההוא, אך לאותו חצר כ"ב יש לו פתח, ועומדים בתוך החצר ההיא הכרובים ולהט החרב לשמור דרך עץ החיים, וכשבא אלכסנדרוס ודפק על הפתח, דפק על פתח החצר ההוא של ג"ע, ולא על פתח העקרי של ג"ע שהוא בתוך החצר, ודברים אלו שהשיבו לו המה מן הכרובים שבחצר, והם אשר נתנו לו דבר הדומה לעינים, כי כן נצטוו מן השמים...

VIII   ולכאורה יפלא הלא אלכסנדר מוקדון חזר מאפריקה בדיוק בדרך שהלך לשם דהלא קשר חבל בחבל כדי לחזור בלעומת שבא לפי עצמו של זקני הנגב, וא"כ איך זה שלא הריח ריח גן עדן בהליכתו אלא בחזרתו. ושמעתי בצעירותי ביאור נחמד בדרך הנ"ל. כאשר אלכסנדר הלך למדינה זו היה מלא תאות הכיבוש ובהרגשת כוחי ועוצם ידי הלך לבטחה, אדם בזה אינו ראוי ואינו מסוגל להריח ריח גן עדן, אך כאשר הוא חזר משם לאחר שלמד עצה ובינה מנשות אפריקי וחזר משם שפל ברך או אז היה יכול להריח ריח גן עדן.

6. THE ACCUSATIONS

I   **תולדות תנאים ואמוראים חלק א, אות ג, גביא בן פסיסא; מרגליות הים סנהדרין צא, א**
ובערוך...פ' חכם היה והיה גבן...
מרגלית הים—במגילת תענית פ"ג גביהה בן פסיסא שוער הבית. ובה"ע' שם של שהיה גיבן שהיינו "גביע" בארמית, לכן נקרא כן, ולחזק את הרשם כינו את אביו בהיפכו "פסיסא" דהיינו ארוך...

II   **סנהדרין, צא, א**
תנו רבנן בעשרים וארבעה בניסן איתמטילו דימוסנאי מיהודה ומירושלים (רש"י-עוררין בעלי חמס), כשבאו בני אפריקיא לדון עם ישראל לפני אלכסנדרוס מוקדון, אמרו לו ארץ כנען שלנו היא, דכתיב ארץ כנען לגבולותיה, וכנען אבוהון דהנהו אינשיה הוה, אמר להו גביהא בן פסיסא לחכמים תנו לי רשות ואדון עמהן לפני אלכסנדרוס מוקדון, אם ינצחוני אמרו הדיוט שבנו נצחתם, ואם אני אנצח אותם אמרו להם תורת משה נצחתכם. נתנו לו רשות והלך ודן עמהם. אמר להם מהיכן אתם מביאים ראייה, אמרו לו מן התורה, אמר להן אף אני לא אביא לכם ראייה אלא מן התורה, שנאמר ויאמר ארור כנען עבד עבדים יהיה לאחיו, עבד שקנה נכסים עבד למי ונכסים למי, ולא עוד אלא שהרי כמה שנים שלא עבדתונו. אמר להם אלכסנדרוס מלכא החזירו לו תשובה, אמרו לו תנו לנו זמן שלשה ימים, נתן להם זמן, בדקו ולא מצאו תשובה, מיד ברחו והניחו שדותיהן כשהן זרועות וכרמיהן כשהן נטועות, ואותה שנה שביעית היתה.

III   **בן יהוידע, שם**
אף אני לא אביא לכם ראייה אלא מן התורה—קשא כיון דהם יודעים מה שכתיב בתורה, והביא טענה מן התורה שכתוב בה ארץ כנען לגבולותיה, איך לא ידעו מה שכתוב בתורה עבד עבדים יהיה לאחיו. ונ"ל בס"ד דחשבו שלא ישיבו להם תשובה זו דעבד עבדים יהיה לאחיו, מפני כי בדבר זה יפלו בחמתו של אלכסנדרון מוקדון שהוא מן יפת, דאז אומר להם איך לקחתם הכל לעצמכם, כיון דכתיב עבד עבדים יהיה לאחיו שהם שם ויפת, וא"כ חצים הוא לבני יפת, אמנם באמת גביהה נרגש בזה הטענה של המלך ועשה לה תקנה בתשובתו, דאחר אומרו עבד למי ונכסים למי, אמר ולא עוד אלא שהרי כמה שנים שלא עבדתונו כונתו בזה למצוא מקום לפני אלכסנדרוס שיגבה ממנו חלקו של יפת והיינו לומר לו אנחנו לקחנו מה שלקחנו בעבור חלקינו מן קרקע דוקא, ואתה יש לך לגבות עכשיו חלק יפת הממון שהרויח כל אותם שנים שלא עבדוני, וגם ארצם החדשה של עתה שהיא אפריקה שהיא יקרה מאד תהיה שלך.

IV   **סנהדרין, צא, א**
שוב פעם אחת באו בני מצרים לדון עם ישראל לפני אלכסנדרוס מוקדון, אמרו לו, הרי הוא אומר וה' נתן את חן העם בעיני מצרים וישאילום, תנו לנו כסף וזהב שנטלתם ממנו, אמר גביהא בן פסיסא לחכמים תנו לי רשות...אמר להן מהיכן אתם מביאין ראיה, אמרו לו מן התורה, אמר להן אף אני לא אביא לכם ראיה אלא מן התורה, שנאמר ומושב בני ישראל אשר ישבו במצרים שלשים שנה וארבע מאות שנה, תנו לנו שכר עבודה של ששים ריבוא ששיעבדתם במצרים שלשים שנה וארבע מאות שנה, אמר להן אלכסנדרון מוקדון החזירו לו תשובה, אמרו לו תנו לנו זמן שלשה ימים, נתן להם זמן, בדקו ולא מצאו תשובה, מיד הניחו שדותיהן כשהן זרועות וכרמיהן כשהן נטועות וברחו, ואותה שנה שביעית היתה.

V **משך חכמה, בראשית, מז, כג**
קניתי היום אתכם ואת אדמתכם לפרעה—ספרה התורה לנו זאת. מפני דהתורה אמרה ושאלה אשה משכנתה וכו' כלי כסף וזהב ושמלות, וכבר צעקו אנשי מצרים לפני אלכסנדר מוקדון תנו לנו כסף וזהב שלקחתם והשיב להם גביהה בן פסיסא בפ' חלק צ"א תנו לנו שכר עבודה של ששים רבוא שעבדתם עמהם במצרים רד"ו שנה יעו"ש ובמדרש רד"ו היא עבודה עבדו למלך מצרים כמו שכתוב ויבנו את פיתום וכו' לפרעה וכו' ואיך נטלו מאת העם כלי כסף וזהב. אך כיון שפרעה קנה אותם והמה ומה שלהם שייך למלך מצרים והכל שלו אז שפיר נטלו דמי עבודתם ודו"ק.

VI **תורה תמימה, שמות, יב, מ**
ומושב בני ישראל וגו'—ת"ר, כשבאו בני מצרים לדון עם ישראל לפני אלכסנדר מוקדון אמרו להם, תנו לנו כסף וזהב שנטלתם, אמר להם גביהא בן פסיסא, הא כתיב ומושב בני ישראל וגו' במצרים שלשים שנה וארבע מאות שנה, תנו לנו שכר עבודה של ששים רבוא בת"י שנה, ולא מצאו תשובה וברחו. ועיין בתהלים ק"ה ל"ז ויוציאם בכסף וזהב ואין בשבטיו כושל, וז"ל התרגום שם, ואפקינון בסימא ובדהבא ולא אתדנו עם מצראי למתקלי, ע"כ. ופשוט דכוון לאגדה זו, ור"ל דאף שיצאו בכסף וזהב בכ"ז לא נשכלו בדינים עם המצרים שיצאו זכאים בדין כמבואר הכא, ועיין מש"כ בפ' נח בפסוק כנען עבד עבדים.

VII **סנהדרין, צא, א**
ושוב פעם אחת באו בני ישמעאל ובני קטורה לדון עם ישראל לפני אלכסנדרוס מוקדון, אמרו לו ארץ כנען שלנו ושלכם, דכתיב ואלה תולדות ישמעאל בן אברהם, וכתיב אלה תולדות יצחק בן אברהם. אמר להם גביהא בן פסיסא לחכמים...הלך ודן עמהן, אמר להם מהיכן אתם מביאין ראייה, אמרו לו מן התורה, אמר להן אף אני לא אביא ראייה אלא מן התורה, שנאמר ויתן אברהם את כל אשר לו ליצחק ולבני הפילגשים אשר לאברהם נתן אברהם מתנות, אב שנתן אגטין לבניו בחייו ושיגר זה מעל זה כלום יש לזה על זה כלום.

VIII **תולדות תנאים ואמוראים; מרגליות הים שם**
וכיון שהגיע לבית קה"ק א"ל אדוני המלך עד כאן יש לנו רשות להכנס מכאן ואלך אין לנו רשות לכנס...

מרגליות הים—...וכשהגיע למקום שאי אפשר ליכנס ממנו אמר לו מכאן ולפנים אי אפשר לך לכנוס שאתה ערל...

IX **תלמוד ירושלמי, בבא מציעא, פ"ח ה"א**
אלכסנדרוס מוקדון סליק לגבי מלכא קציא חמא ליה דהב סגין כסף סגין, אמר ליה לא דהבך ולא כספך אנא צריך, לא אתית אלא מיחמי פרוכסין דידכון (המנהג), היך אתון יהבין היך אתון דיינין. עד דו עסוק עימיה אתא בר נש חד דאין עם חבריה דזבן חדא חלקא וחספתה ואשכחון בה סימא דדינרי, (קנה חלקא שדה אחת עם האשפה והחורבה שבתוכה ומצא אוצר), אהן דזבין הוה מר, קיקילתא זבינית סימא לא זבנית (האוצר לא קניתי), אהן דזבין הוה מר, קיקילתא וכל דאית בה זבינית (כל מה שבו מכרתי), עד דאינון עסיקין דין עם דין אמר מלכא לחד מיניהון אית לך בר דכר, אמר ליה אין, אמר לחבריה אית לך ברת נוקבא, אמר ליה אין, אמר לון אסבון דין לדין וסימא יהוי לתרויהון. שרי גחיך (אלכסנדר צחק), אמר ליה למה את גחיך, לא דנית טבאות, אמר ליה אילו הוה הדין דינא גבכון היאך הויתון דנין, אמר ליה קטלין דין ודין וסימא עלת למלכא, (הייתי הורג שניהם והאוצר היה למלך). אמר ליה הכי אתון רחמין דהב סוגיי, (אתם אוהבים זהב), עבד ליה אריסטון אפיק קומיי קופד דדהב (בשר), תרנגולין דדהב, אמר ליה דהב אנא אכיל, אמר ליה תיפח רוחיה דההוא גברא דהב לית אתון אכלין, ולמה אתון רחמין דהב סוגין, אמר ליה דנחא עליכון שמשא, אמר ליה אין, נחת עליכון מיטרא, אמר ליה אין, אמר ליה דילמא אית גביכון בעיר דקיק (יש לכם צאן), אמר ליה אין, תיפח רוחיה דההוא גברא לית אתון חיין אלא בזכות בעירא דקיקא, דכתיב אדם ובהמה תושיע ה'.

X **דעת חכמה ומוסר, חלק ג' סימן צ**
מזה יצא לנו הערה גדולה, כשנתבונן בכל דיני התורה נראה וניכר שהיסוד הוא עולם חסד

יבנה (תהלים פט, ג), ומיסוד החסד נובעים כל דיני התורה. האדם והתורה המה רק חסד, תחילת היצירה היא חסד, מפני שרצה הקב"ה להיטיב עם ברואיו ולא אחרת...כל דמות האדם ותבניתו וכל הנהגתו ודיניו נובעים מהשורש של חסד, כל דיני בין אדם לחברו המה מהיסוד של קיום העולם, כמו גזל, וכל קיום העולם בנוי על חסד, נשמת התורה היסוד היא חסד.

SECTION II: PTOLMEY

1. PTOLEMY SOTER

I	**תולדות ישראל, חלק רביעי עמודים 25-26** ויקומו דברי החוזה על מלכות אלכסנדר הגדולה והרחבה: וצפיר העזים הגדול עד-מאד ובעצמו נשברה הקרן הגדלה ותעלינה חזות ארבע תחתיה לארבע רוחות השמים
II	**צמח דוד, חלק שני, שנה תנד** בטולמיאוס הוא המלך הראשון שמלך אחר אלכסנדר על מצרים בשנת תנ"ד ונקרא בלשון חז"ל תלמי בן לאגו או בן אוגלוס אשר על שמו נקראו אחריו שאר מלכי מצרים בטולמיאוס ותלמי. והוא צוה להתתיל ולהעתיק את התורה אך מעשיהו לא עלה בידו כראוי והיה מלך זה צורר היהודים והגלה שבי יותר ממאה אלף יהודים למצרים. ומלך שלשים שנה עד שנת תפ"ד.
III	**דורות הראשונים, חלק א, פרק יב** כבר בראשית ימי מלכותו במצרים בא תלמי לאגו בראש חילו לירושלים ויקח מבני יהודה שבי גדול מאד יותר ממאה אלף אנשים ויביאם אל ארץ מצרים....
IV	**תולדות ישראל, חלק רביעי עמוד 24** ויבחר מתוכם שלשים אלף איש גבור חיל, ויפקד בידם את ערי המבצר, וישבע אותם להיות נאמנים גם לבניו...ויפקד בידם את משמרת מבוא הים והנהרות ומפקד האניות העוברות.
V	**תולדות ישראל, חלק רביעי עמודים 22-24** וירגש גם העריץ החנף היוני הזה, כי ישראל הוא העם האחד הנאמן בימים ההם... ...ומהם כשלשים אלף בחורי חיל הבדיל בעת ההיא לגדוד...

2. PTOLEMY PHILADELPHUS

I	**צמח דוד, חלק שני שנה תפד** בטולמיאוס השני הנקרא פילידולפוס בנו של בטולמיאוס הראשון מלך על מצרים בשנת תפ"ד והיה מופלג בכל החכמות אוהב את החכמים ומספיקים והיה לו בית ועד לחכמים בעיר אלכסנדריאה של מצרים ובנה מגדול פארון אשר בנמל אלכסנדריא נראה בו נפלאות כמוזכר ביוספון ספר ג פרק י"ד. וכתב בספר יוחסין בדף י"ד שהיו לו שלש מאות אלף ספרים מהחכמות. ובספר מאור עינים פרק ה' גם בפ' מ' כתב ע"ש סופר יונ"י שהיו לו לבטולמיאוס יותר מת"ש אלף ספרים מכל החכמות ומכל הלשונות מארבע כנפות הארץ אשר אחרי ימים רבים במלחמות יוליס ופומפיוס כולם נשרפו מאנשי הצבא נגד רצון הקיסר.
II	**תולדות ישראל, חלק רביעי עמודים 26-27** ...ויאהב המלך הזה מאד את הדעת וישם את אלכסנדריא עיר מלכותו, גם לעיר מושב המדעים...

3. THE TARGUM SHIVIM

I	**מגילה, ט, א** א"ר יהודה אף כשהתירו רבותינו יונית לא התירו אלא בספר תורה ומשום מעשה דתלמי המלך דתניא מעשה בתלמי המלך שכינס שבעים ושנים זקנים והכניסן בשבעים ושנים בתים ולא גילה להם על מה כינסם וכנכס אצל כל אחד ואחד ואמר להם כתבו לי תורת משה רבכם נתן הקב"ה בלב כל אחד ואחד עצה והסכימו כולן לדעת אחת וכתבו לו.

II	**מסכת סופרים, א, ז**
	מעשה בחמשה זקנים שכתבו לתלמי המלך את התורה יונית והיה היום קשה לישראל כיום שנעשה העגל שלא היתה התורה יכולה להתרגם כל צרכה.
III	**מסכת סופרים, א, ח**
	שוב מעשה בתלמי המלך שכנס ע"ב זקנים והושיבם בע"ב בתים ולא גלה להם על מה כנסם נכנס לכל אחד ואחד מהם אמר להם כתבו לי תורת משה רבכם נתן המקום עצה בלב כל אחד ואחד והסכימו דעתן לדעת אחת וכתבו לו תורה בפני עצמה וי"ג דבר שינו בה ואלו הן וכו'.
IV	**שפתי חכמים למסכת מגילה, שם**
	מעשה בתלמי המלך עי' (במס' סופרים פ"א ה"ז וה"ח) דמשמע התם ב' מעשים היו, וב' פעמים תרגמו התורה יוונית, פעם ראשונה ה' זקנים תרגמו התורה יוונית, ולא עלתה להם לתרגמה כהוגן, לכן אח"כ נתעורר להביא אסיף של ע"ב זקנים, לעמוד על אמיתה של תורה, ובסוף מגילת תענית אית' ח' בטבת נכתבה התורה יונית בימי תלמי המלך, ובא חושך לעולם שלשה ימים עי"ש וכן אית' בש"ע או"ח תק"פ ובסליחות לי' בטבת עיי"ש.
V	**שפתי חכמים למסכת מגילה, שם**
	כתבו לי תורת משה רבכם. באגדה שרצה בזה "לפקור" כאילו תורה אינה מן השמים, אלא כתבו לי שהיא תורת משה רבכם דייקא, אבל מה עשה הקב"ה נתן בלב כל א' וא', והסכימו כולם לדעת אחת, וכתבו לו ט"ו שינויים, והסכמה זו שהיא רק גילוי משמים דהא מעשה בזה אי אפשר בבשר ודם, ומזה לך ראיה ברורה שתורה נתינתה כולה מסיני משמים, ולא כמו שאמרת כתבו לי אותה שהיא רק תורת משה רבכם.
VI	**בן יהוידע, שם**
	נ"ל היה דבר זה קשה יותר מפני שהיתה העלילה על ידי תלמי שישמו מספר לילית שנתלבשה בו הסט"א לעשות סכסוכים לה ולבא על ישראל בעלילה ובעקיפין, ואז השי"ת לא עזבם בידו שהגין עליהם זכות תלמוד תורה, כי תלמוד ג' תלמי שאם תשבר אות י' דתלמי לשתי אותיות דו יהיו אותיות תלמוד ממש. ומה שכינס שבעים ושנים זקנים נ"ל מאת ה' היתה זאת לסימן טוב להורות כי גובר חסדו יתברך, כי חסד עולה ע"ב שגבר לעשות להם נס זה שיהיו כולם מתכוונים לדבר אחד, וגבר ישראל.
VII	**ספר התודעה, דף קצד**
	אלמלא ביקש לו תואנה, היה מתחלה מגלה לחכמים את רצונו, ומועיד להם מקום וזמן אחד כדי שישבו בחבורה ויהיו נושאים ונותנים יחד בכל דבר של ספק תרגום, עד שמכוונים כלם לדעה אחת. תלמי לא עשה כן אלא ביקש תואנות והיה מתכוון להכשילם...והיה בדבר זה קידוש השם הגדול וקידוש שם ישראל וחכמיו.
VIII	**תורה תמימה, בראשית א, א**
	ומה שכנס ע"ב זקנים—פשוט הוא שכוון למספר הסנהדרין, ויתכן שכוון בזה להיות בטוח באמונת ההעתקה, ואע"פ דסתם סנהדרין הם במספר ע"א איש כמבואר במשנה ריש סנהדרין ב' א', אך זה נבאר אי"ה במק"א, דלבד העע"א איש הי' עוד אחד על גביה והי' נקרא מופלא שבסנהדרין, ובס"ה היו ע"ב איש [ע' לפנינו בפ' בהעלתך י"א ט"ז], והנה גם ממעשה זה דתלמי שכנס ע"ב זקנים רא"י לזה, וכ"מ ממשנה זבחים י"ד ב' מקובלני מפי שנים ושבעים זקן, ואין כאן המקום להאריך בזה.
IX	**תורה תמימה, בראשית א, א**
	ותכלית ומטרת תלמי המלך בהעתקה זו אולי [כפי שמשמע מכל השנויים שעשו ומסדר האספה שעשה הוא], היתה למצוא עילה בתורת משה, ולכן הכניסם בע"ב בתים ולא גילה להם מקודם על מה כנסם כדי שלא ישוו דעותיהם בנוסח ההעתקה, והי' זה ההשגחה מאת ה' כי אע"פ שהיו מוכרחים לעשות איזו שנויים בהעתקה כדי שלא יתאנה להם, כפי שיתבאר אי"ה לפנינו בהמשך החבור בכל המקומות ששינו, בכ"ז יצאה העתקת כל אחד שוה ומכוונת זו לזו.
X	**דברים, א, א-ה**
	אלה הדברים אשר דבר משה אל כל ישראל בעבר הירדן במדבר בערבה מול סוף בין פארן ובין תפל ולבן וחצרת ודי זהב. אחד עשר יום מחרב דרך הר שעיר עד קדש ברנע. ויהי בארבעים

שנה בעשתי עשר חדש באחד לחדש דבר משה אל בני ישראל ככל אשר צוה ה' אתו אלהם. אחרי הכתו את סיחן מלך האמרי אשר יושב בחשבון ואת עוג מלך הבשן אשר יושב בעשתרת באדרעי. בעבר הירדן בארץ מואב הואיל משה באר את התורה הזאת לאמר.

XI **דברים, כז, א-ג, ח**
ויצו משה וזקני ישראל את העם לאמר שמר את כל המצוה אשר אנכי מצוה אתכם היום. והיה ביום אשר תעברו את הירדן אל הארץ אשר ה' אלהיך נתן לך והקמת לך אבנים גדלות ושדת אתם בשיד. וכתבת עליהן את כל דברי התורה הזאת בעברך למען אשר תבא אל הארץ אשר ה' אלהיך נתן לך ארץ זבת חלב ודבש כאשר דבר ה' אלהי אבתיך לך. וכתבת על האבנים את כל דברי התורה הזאת באר היטב.

XII **יהושע, ח, ל-לב**
אז יבנה יהושע מזבח לה' אלהי ישראל בהר עיבל. כאשר צוה משה עבד ה' את בני ישראל ככתוב בספר תורת משה מזבח אבנים שלמות אשר לא הניף עליהן ברזל ויעלו עליו עלות לה' ויזבחו שלמים. ויכתב שם על האבנים את משנה תורת משה אשר כתב לפני בני ישראל.

XIII **רש"י שם**
באר את התורה—בשבעים לשון פירשה להם.

XIV **שפתי חכמים, דברים, א, ה**
מדכתיב כאן באר את התורה, ובפ' כי תבא (להלן כז ח) כתיב וכתבתם וגו' דברי התורה הזאת באר היטב, והיטב מתגלגל בציורופו שבעים ה' ה"י הי"ט היטב.

XV **העמק דבר, דברים, א, ה**
אבל ברור שאין זה פשט המקרא אלא כונה שני' ודרש שהיה בה בכלל באר משה, אבל לא היה נצרך זה אלא בשביל אוה"ע ולא לישראל. וכאן עיקר הביאור הי' לישראל וע"ז הוכיחן ברוב דברים.

XVI **אזנים לתורה, דברים, א, ה**
בע' לשון פירשה להם רש"י. קשה להבין, לאיזה צורך פירש להם את התורה בשפות לא ידעו ולא שמעו מעולם? ובשלמא על האבנים כתבו "באר היטב" את התורה בע' לשון כדי שיבואו או"ה ויעתיקו אותה בלשונם ובכתבם (סוטה ל"ה) אבל לבאר בע"פ לב"י את התורה בלשונות זרות להם אין תועלת. וראיתי מפרשים בע' פנים לתורה. ונכון.

XVII **טעם ודעת, דברים, א, ה**
וזו כוונת רש"י שפירש להם התורה באר היטב, עד שהיו הדברים מתבארים מעצמם בלא שום קושי בתרגומם לשבעים לשון.

XVIII **לבוש האורה, דברים, א, ה**
הואיל משה באר את התורה רש"י בשבעים לשון פרשה להם ע"כ. נ"ל דהכי פי' הואיל באר משמע שהתחיל לבאר אותה להם עכשיו כדי שיבינה והרי כבר למד אותה עמהם כל פרשה ופרשה בפני עצמה כדאמרינן כיצד סדר משנה כו' שהיו באים כל ישראל ולמד עמהם תחלה הוא ואחר כך אהרן כו' אלא על כרחך לומר דבאר זה רצה לומר שהתחיל לבאר להם עכשיו מה שלא באר להם כבר זה הוא ומה זה שעד עכשיו ביאור להם הכל בלשון הקדש ועכשיו התחיל לבאר אותה בלשונות אחרים דחשש אולי אינם כולם בעלי לשון הקדש ולא הבינוהו כולם דודאי עם רב כזו שהם יותר מששים רבוא יש בהם בעלי לשונות הרבה לכך אמר רש"י בשבעים לשון כלומר כיון שחשש שמא יש בהן בעלי שאר לשונות חוץ מלשון הקדש והוצרך לפרש להם ודאי הוצרך לפרש להם בכל השבעים לשונות דהי מנייהו מפקת שמא מאותו לשון שישאר לא לפרש יש בהם והם לא יבינוה.

XIX **אמרי שפר על רש"י, כי תבוא, טז, ח**
שמפני שראה משה רבינו ע"ה שישראל לבין שבעים יגלו שבעים אומות לפיכך באר אותה בשבעים לשון, שבאיזה מקום שישראל יבואו ילמדו באותו לשון ע"כ.

XX **סוטה, לב, א**
ואחר כך הביאו את האבנים ובנו את המזבח וסדוהו בסיד וכתבו עליו את כל דברי התורה בשבעים לשון שנאמר באר היטב.

XXI	**סוטה, לה, ב**
	תנו רבנן כיצד כתבו ישראל את התורה רבי יהודה אמר על גבי אבנים כתבוה וכתבת על האבנים את כל דברי התורה הזאת וגו' ואחר כך סדו אותן בסיד אמר לו רבי שמעון לדבריך היאך למדו אומות של אותו הזמן תורה אמר לו בינה יתירה נתן בהם הקב"ה ושיגרו נוטירין שלהן וקלפו את הסיד והשיאוה.
XXII	**תוספות, שם ד"ה כיצד**
	בתוספתא רבי יהודה אמר על גבי המזבח כתבוה אבל בירושלמי תני על אבני המלון נכתבו דברי ר' יהודה ר' יוסי אמר על אבני מזבח נכתבו מאן דאמר על אבני המלון בכל יום ויום אומות העולם היו משלחין נוטירין ומשיאין את התורה שהיתה כתובה בשבעים לשון.
XXIII	**עיון יעקב, שם**
	נמצאת אתה אומר שלשה מיני אבנים היו אחד שהקים משה, נראה לי הטעם שעשאן כן שלש פעמים לפי שכתבו כן כדי שהאומות בארץ ישראל ילמדו התורה ושלש ארצות חלוקות בא"י יהודה ועבר הירדן והגליל לכן כתבו כן על שלשה מיני אבנים במקומות חלוקים כדי שאם יבואו האומות מכל שלש הארצות שיכולין ללמוד את התורה והיינו לדעת התוספות שקודם התחלת המלחמה אף מא"י מקבלין...מ"מ קודם שצוה להחרימם היו יכולין לומר שהיו רוצים להתגייר ולחזור בתשובה לקבל עליהם עול התורה והמצוות אך לא היה להם מהיכן ללמדה לכך באר להם בשבעים לשון.
XXIV	**אזנים לתורה, דברים, כז, ב**
	ובכלל רבו השיטות במיני האבנים ומקומן. אבל יש להתפלא מה בצע בכתיבה זו לאו"ה, ההיתה תקוה, שיקבלו את התורה ע"י ישראל, שנואי נפשם, אחרי שמאנו לקבלה מידי הקב"ה, שחזר בעצמו ובכבודו על כל אומה ולשון בשעת מ"ת ולא קבלוה?!
XXV	**רש"י, בראשית א, א**
	אמר ר' יצחק לא הי' צריך להתחיל את התורה אלא מהחודש הזה לכם......ומה טעם פתח בבראשית משום כח מעשיו הגיד לעמו לתת להם נחלת גוים שאם יאמרו אומות העולם לישראל לסטים אתם שכבשתם ארצות שבעה גוים הם אומרים להם כל הארץ של הקב"ה היא הוא בראה ונתנה לאשר ישר בעיניו ברצונו נתנה להם וברצונו נטלה מהם ונתנה לנו.
XXVI	**סוטה, לה, ב**
	אמר לו בינה יתירה נתן בהם הקב"ה ושיגרו נוטירין שלהן וקלפו את הסיד והשיאוה.
XXVII	**בן יהוידע, סוטה, שם**
	בינה יתירה נתן הקב"ה באומות, ושגרו נוטירין וכו' פירוש כיון שהיו האבנים מוסדים בסיד, מהיכן ידעו האומות שיש כאן כתיבה תחת הסיד, ולכן אמר בינה יתירה נתן בהם להבין דבר מתוך דבר, כי אמרו למה זה בסיד, אלא ודאי שם יש דברים שרצו לכסותם בסיד, ושלחו סופרים שלהם שהם בקיאים במלאכת הכתיבה, ופקחים במעשיהם, וקלפו הסיד בדרך חכמה שלא יתקלקל הכתב שתחתיו אפילו אות א' מחמת הקילוף, וע"י כ"ב העתיקו אותה כולה בלתי שום חסרון אות כלל, ועכ"ז לא למדו אותה, אע"פ שהיתה מועתקת כולה אצלם.
XXVIII	**אזנים לתורה, דברים כז, ב**
	ואם היו ב"י כותבים את התורה על האבנים, כדי שיבואו או"ה להעתיק אותה הי' הדבר נראה כאלו מלמדים אותם להם בפועל ממש.
	סנהדרין נט, א
	ואמר ר' יוחנן עובד כוכבים שעוסק בתורה חייב מיתה שנאמר (דברים לג, ד) תורה צוה לנו משה מורשה לנו מורשה ולא להם.
XXIX	**שו"ת אגרות משה, יו"ד חלק ג, סימן צ'**
	ויש מקום לחלק בין תורה שבכתב לתורה שבע"פ, דאולי תורה שבכתב לא נאסר דהרי נתחייבו ישראל כשנכנסו לארץ לכתוב את התורה על גבי האבנים בשבעים לשון כדי שכל אומות העולם יעתיקו את התורה וילמדו אותה כמפורש בסוטה דף לה, ב, ואם אסור ללמדם אף תורה שבכתב הרי היה זה דבר אסור ונצטרך לומר שהיה זה הוראת שעה לעבור על האיסור בשביל שלא יהא פתחון פה להאומות לומר לא היה לנו מהיכן ללומדה שאם אין לנו הכרח לא נימא

XXX	כן, שלכן אולי ליכא האיסור בתורה שבכתב והכתיבה הא היה זה רק על תורה שבכתב שהוא דבר מותר ונתחייבו בדבר היתר באותו זמן כשנכנסו לארץ אבל ראיה גדולה ליכא דהא אפשר שלמצוה זו שלא יהא להם פתחון פה נתחייבו אף שהיה דבר איסור.
	אגרת הראיה, חלק א, עמוד קג
	ומה שהעירות מענין איסור לימוד תורה לנכרי, ממה שאמרה תורה לכתוב על האבנים את דברי התורה, כדי שילמדו או"ה, אין למדין דורות משעה. אותו ההכשר, שהוכשר העולם בעת יציאת מצרים ומ"ת,...זה היה מאורע שאינו נמשך.
XXXI	**בן יהוידע, מגילה ט, ב**
	נמצא הם עשו שינוי בי"ד פרשיות, כי יש שתיים שהם בפרשה אחת, ונראה כי יד שנשתלחה בבהמ"ק כמ"ש במוסף מפני היד שנשתלחה בבית מקדשך, גרמה שיהיו נצרכים לשלוח יד בי"ד פרשיות מפני פחדן מן האויב ההוא, שאם לא הי' חרבן וגלות לא היו חוששין ולא היו נמסרים בידו.

4. THE RESULT

I	**שפתי חכמים, מגילה ט, א**
	כשהתירו רבותינו יוונית לא התירו אלא בס"ת ומשום מעשה דתלמי המלך וכו'. לכאורה וכי משום אותו מעשה, התירו לכתוב התורה ביוונית לדורות, ושאלתי הדבר לתלמידי חכמים, ויש מהם שפירשו לי, מדנעשה להם נס משמים בזה הדבר, נמצא שהסכימו למעלה להתיר לכתוב התורה יוונית. ומפי' המשניות לרמב"ם משמע לפי שעל ידי מעשה דתלמי מלך, היה ידוע ומפורסם אף בישראל התורה בלשון יון, לכן התירו רבותינו כן רק תורת משה היינו חמשה חומשי תורה.
II	**סליחות לעשרה בטבת, (בימי הביניים).**
	אזכרה מצוק אשר קְרָאָנִי
	בשלוש מכות בחודש הזה הכני
	גָּדְעֵנִי הֱנִיאָנִי הִכְאָנִי
	אךְ עתה הֶלְאָנִי
	דְּעָכַנִי בשמונה בו שמאלית וימנית
	הלא שלשתן קבעתי תענית
	ומלך יון אנסני לכתוב דת יוונית
	על גבי חרשו חורשים האריכו מענית.
III	**רבי צדוק הכהן מלובלין, רסיסי לילה עמוד קסז**
	והתחלת שמד יוונים היה על ידי העתקת התורה יונית שזה היה על ידי הרגשת ההוד דכנסת ישראל, עד שגם מלכי עמים הודו להם. כי בקשת העתקת התורה היה בשביל שהכירו מעלתה, וכבוד גדול כיבדם תלמי על זה, ועל כן זה ההעתקה על ידי כהנים, אבל חכמי ישראל הרגישו שזה היה הפיכת ההוד למשיחת וגזרו תענית על זה.
IV	**מנחת יצחק, חלק ג סימן צח עמוד קסג**
	שכבר צווחי קמאי, עפ"י המבואר במגילת תענית וטור (או"ח סי' תק"פ) (הביאו בשם ה"ג, כי ביום ח' טבת, נכתבה התורה לתלמי המלך, והי' ג' ימים חושך בעולם...והלא מצינו בספר יוסיפון ובספר מאור עינים שהי' אורה ושמחה ליהודים, והשיגו עי"ז כבוד גדול, והמלך והעמים הכירו יקר התורה כי רבה, ובאר שם החת"ס באריכות, כי בהעתקת התורה יונית, או לכל לשון, אז החילו עם בני ישראל לטעום טעם פשוטו של מקרא, ומאז החל האפיקורסות להתנוצץ, ולא אבו שוב שמוע לקול דברי חז"ל ולפירושיהם.
V	**תורת משה, חתם סופר, פרשת ויחי**
	הנה בימים האלו ובזמן הזה הועתקה התורה יונית בימי תלמי המלך ונתכבדו ישראל כבוד גדול והיה ג' ימים חשך בעולם כמו ג' ימים של מתן תורה וג' ימים שהתענו בימי אסתר כשקבלו תורה מאהבה בימי אחשורוש וליהודים היתה אורה אז ג' ימי חשך בעו"ה כי עי"ז למדו יוונית ונהפכו למינות...

VI **אונ' בר-אילן, דר. אריה רייך, תרגום השבעים אור או חושך, דף שבועי, מספר 529, פרשת ויגש, תשס"ד**

תורה זו ניתנה לישראל בלשון הקודש, ורק בלשונה המקורית היא יכולה לשמור על משמעויותיה הרבות. באופן שבו היא נדרשה על-ידי חכמי ישראל במהלך הדורות—כל פסוקיה, תיבותיה, אותיותיה ואפילו תגיה היוו בסיס לתלי תלים של הלכות ורעיונות. כל מי שבא לתרגם את התורה ללשון אחרת לא יוכל לעולם לשמור על כל המשמעויות הרבות הללו, אלא ייאלץ בעל-כורחו לבחור במשמעות אחת בלבד—בדרך כלל אחת מן הפשטות—ולהניח את כל השאר. בכך הוא בהכרח יהפוך את התורה לטקסט רדוד ושטוח, ללא העומק המיוחד והרבגוני הטמון בטקסט המקורי. זו כנראה המשמעות של דברי מגילת תענית שעם תרגום התורה "החושך בא לעולם שלושה ימים".

VII **הרב משה אדלר, עשרה בטבת—תרגום השבעים**
https://nahariya.co.il/GetLesson.aspx?lesid=5044

התורה הקדושה מסובבת יותר לתרגום: שבעים פנים לתורה יש, כל משפט משמעויות רבות יש בו המשולבות יחד למשפט אחד. תרגום התורה ע"י משה, יהושע ועקילס לא הוו תחליף ללימוד התורה הקדושה, אלא רק כחומר עזר למתקשה, לגויים, ולכל שרצה להתקרב לתורה. ברור היה כי הרוצה להעמיק עליו ללמוד את המקור. לא היה ניסיון לתרגם במדויק את התורה אלא להפך, המטרה היתה לוודא שכל קוראי התרגום יידעו שזה אינו אלא תחליף. לא כן היה בתקופה תלמי: בידודים של שבעים ושניים הזקנים מראה כי רצה תלמי לוודא שהתרגום נאמן למקור, שיהווה תחליף לתורה הקדושה, שאפשר יהיה ללמוד את התרגום במקום התורה. זו הסיבה ליום האבל והצום ולהסבר המילים "שלא היתה התורה להתרגם כל צרכה".

VIII **ספר התודעה, דף קצד**

ואילו כל מי שבא לתרגם התורה בלשון אחרת, לא ימצא בעולם שום לשון שדומה ללשון הקודש בהוראות המרובות של התיבות ובנטיותיהן השונות, מה הוא עושה? מניח את כל אוצרות הדרוש והרמז והסוד הגנוזים בתיבה זו, ותופס רק את הפשט שבה ואותו הוא מתרגם. נמצא שהמתרגם את התורה, ללשון אחרת, הרי כאלו מציג אותה ככלי ריק...משל, למה הדבר דומה? לארי שניצוד וכלאוהו בסוגר. קודם שנבלא היו הכל יראים מפניו ובורחים, עכשיו הכל באים ומציצים בו ואומרים: היכן גבורתו של זה? כך התורה, כל זמן שהיא נתונה ביד ישראל ומתפרשת ע"י חכמיו בלשונה, לשון הקודש, הכל חרדים מפניה ומתיראים להטיל בה דופי...ולפיכך דימו החכמים מאורע יום זה, ליום שנעשה בו העגל, שכשם שהעגל לא היה בו ממש ועובדיו חשבוהו לממש, כך אין בתרגום ממשה של תורה, ואעפ"כ כל הגוים שרואים אותו מדמים בנפשם שכבר יודעים את התורה ואומרים על התרגום: זאת התורה, והרי כבר ידענוה.

IX **תולדות ישראל, חלק רביעי עמוד 82**

ויהי התרגום הזה לאוצר חמדה בעיני בני ישראל היושבים במצרים, וישימו אותו בראשונה למליץ לתורה בבתי הכנסת, כי נשכחה מעט מעט הלשון העבריה מפיהם מפני היוונית...ויתהללו בה יושבי מצרים מאד...ויצאו ביום ההוא אל פרו השקט הקרוב לאלכסנדריה, אשר אותו פנה תלמי לזקנים לתרגם את התורה והתפללו ביום ההוא, ושמחו שם ואכלו ושתו וחגגו עד הערב.

SECTION III: VESPASIAN

2. TITUS

I **גיטין, נו, ב**

אזל שדריה לטיטוס הרשע ואמר (דברים לב, לז) אי אלהימו צור חסיו בו טיטוס הרשע שחירף וגידף כלפי מעלה מה עשה תפש זונה בידו ונכנס לבית קדשי הקדשים והציע ספר תורה ועבר עליה עבירה ונטל סייף וגידר את הפרוכת ונעשה נס והיה דם מבצבץ ויוצא וכסבור

הרג את עצמו שנאמר (תהלים עד, ד) שאגו צורריך בקרב מועדיך שמו אותותם אותות אבא חנן אומר (תהלים פט, ט) מי כמוך חסין יה מי כמוך חסין וקשה שאתה שומע ניאוצו וגידופו של אותו רשע ושותק דבי רבי ישמעאל תנא (שמות טו, יא) מי כמוכה באלים ה' מי כמוכה באלמים מה עשה נטל את הפרוכת ועשאו כמין גרגותני והביא כל כלים שבמקדש והניחן בהן והושיבן בספינה לילך להשתבח בעירו שנאמר (קהלת ח, י) ובכן ראיתי רשעים קבורים ובאו וממקום קדוש יהלכו וישתכחו בעיר אשר כן עשו אל תיקרי קבורים אלא קבוצים אל תיקרי וישתכחו אלא וישתבחו איכא דאמרי קבורים ממש דאפילו מילי דמטמרן איגלייא להון עמד עליו נחשול שבים לטובעו אמר כמדומה אני שאלהיהם של אלו אין גבורתו אלא במים בא פרעה טבע במים בא סיסרא טבעו במים אף הוא עומד עלי לטובעני במים אם גבור הוא יעלה ליבשה ויעשה עמי מלחמה יצתה בת קול ואמרה לו רשע בן רשע בן בנו של עשו הרשע בריה קלה יש לי בעולמי ויתוש שמה אמאי קרי לה בריה קלה דמעלנא אית לה ומפקנא לית לה עלה ליבשה ותעשה עמה מלחמה עלה ליבשה בא יתוש ונכנס בחוטמו ונקר במוחו שבע שנים יומא חד הוה קא חליף אבבא דבי נפחא שמע קל ארזפתא אישתיק אמר איכא תקנתא כל יומא מייתו נפחא ומחו קמיה לנכרי יהיב ליה ארבע זוזי לישראל אמר ליה מיסתייך דקא חזית בסנאך עד תלתין יומני עבד הכי מכאן ואילך כיון דדש דש תניא אמר רבי פנחס בן ערובא אני הייתי בין גדולי רומי וכשמת פצעו את מוחו ומצאו בו כצפור דרור משקל שני סלעים במתניתא תנא כגוזל בן שנה משקל שני ליטרין אמר אביי נקטינן פיו של נחושת וצפורניו של ברזל כי הוה קא מיית אמר להו ליקליוה לההוא גברא ולבדרי לקיטמיה אשב ימי דלא לשכחיה אלהא דיהודאי ולוקמיה בדינא.

באר הגולה, באר ו

דע, כי טיטוס הוא אשר החריב ושרף והשחית את בית אלוקינו, ואין אדם כמוהו בעולם שהיה מתנגד אל השי"ת כמו זה הרשע.

שעורי דעת, חלק ב, חיי העולמות, עמוד פה

וכן הוא ענין מה שמצינו בטיטוס הרשע, שתפס זונה בידו ונכנס לבית קדשי הקדשים......והיינו מפני שחפצו היה להגביר כח הטומאה, ובגודל החטא ורשעתו הנוראה בחללו את קדשי הקדשים חשב שיתגבר כח הטומאה וישליט אותו בעולם, כי ידע שבמעשה הרע הוא נותן כח למרכבת הטומאה ונותן שליטה לרע בכל העולמות...ולכן חשבו כל אלה שנתכוונו למרוד בבורא יתב', כי בהגבירם כח הטומאה והרע ינצח גם בעליונים.

גיטין, נו, ב

אונקלוס בר קלוניקוס בר אחתיה דטיטוס הוה בעי לאיגיורי אזל אסקיה לטיטוס בנגידא אמר ליה מאן חשיב בההוא עלמא אמר ליה ישראל מהו לאידבוקי בהו אמר ליה מילייהו נפישין ולא מצית לקיומינהו זיל איגרי בהו בההוא עלמא והוית רישא דכתיב (איכה א, ה) היו צריה לראש וגו' כל המיצר לישראל נעשה ראש.

3. RABBAN YOCHANAN BEN ZAKKAI

ראש השנה, לא, ב   I

והתניא כל שנותיו של רבן יוחנן בן זכאי מאה ועשרים שנה מ' שנה עסק בפרקמטיא מ' שנה למד מ' שנה לימד.

סוכה, כח, א   II

אמרו עליו על רבן יוחנן בן זכאי מימיו לא שח שיחת חולין ולא הלך ד' אמות בלא תורה ובלא תפילין ולא קדמו אדם בבית המדרש ולא ישן בבית המדרש לא שינת קבע ולא שינת עראי ולא הרהר במבואות המטונפות ולא הניח אדם בבית המדרש ויצא ולא מצאו אדם יושב ודומם אלא יושב ושונה ולא פתח אדם דלת לתלמידיו אלא הוא בעצמו ולא אמר דבר שלא שמע מפי רבו מעולם ולא אמר הגיע עת לעמוד מבית המדרש חוץ מערבי פסחים וערבי יום הכפורים.

ברכות, יז, א   III

אמרו עליו על רבן יוחנן בן זכאי שלא הקדימו אדם שלום מעולם ואפילו נכרי בשוק.

IV	**ברכות, כח, ב**

וכשחלה רבי יוחנן בן זכאי נכנסו תלמידיו לבקרו כיון שראה אותם התחיל לבכות אמרו לו תלמידיו נר ישראל עמוד הימיני פטיש החזק מפני מה אתה בוכה אמר להם אילו לפני מלך בשר ודם היו מוליכין אותי שהיום כאן ומחר בקבר שאם כועס עלי אין כעסו כעס עולם ואם אוסרני אין איסורו איסור עולם ואם ממיתני אין מיתתו מיתת עולם ואני יכול לפייסו בדברים ולשחדו בממון אעפ"כ הייתי בוכה ועכשיו שמוליכים אותי לפני ממ"ה הקב"ה שהוא חי וקיים לעולם ולעולמי עולמים שאם כועס עלי כעסו כעס עולם ואם אוסרני איסורו איסור עולם ואם ממיתני מיתתו מיתת עולם ואיני יכול לפייסו בדברים ולא לשחדו בממון ולא עוד אלא שיש לפני שני דרכים אחת של גן עדן ואחת של גיהנם ואיני יודע באיזו מוליכים אותי ולא אבכה אמרו לו רבינו ברכנו אמר להם יהי רצון שתהא מורא שמים עליכם כמורא בשר ודם אמר לו תלמידיו עד כאן אמר ולואי תדעו כשאדם עובר עבירה אומר שלא יראני אדם.

V	**סוטה, מט, ב**

משמת רבן יוחנן בטלה החכמה.

4. YAVNEH

I	**דורות הראשונים, חלק ג, רבי יוחנן בן זכאי וחבריו, פרק י**

בימי חרבן הבית הראשון היה כל מעשי הבבליים נגד בני ישראל רק דבר מדיני כללי...בחרבן הבית הראשון מצאה האומה בכללה מנוחה שלמה על נהרות בבל ויתישבו שם בערים אשר בנו להם לבדם, ויבנו בתים ויטעו כרמים, ובניהם שרים בהיכל מלך בבל.

II	**דורות הראשונים, שם**

על הדבר הזה חדרה עתה עין חכמי ישראל וראש הדור רבן יוחנן בן זכאי בראשם, ותהי עינם ולבם איך להוציא את העם מתוך המהפכה ואיך לקומם את הריסות העם, על ידי מקום חדש בלב האומה, על ידי בריאה חדשה אשר יברא עתה בתוך ימי המלחמה...מקום חדש אשר משם יצאו כל קוי האור אל כל המקום אשר נפוצו שם בני ישראל, מקום חדש עם עמודים חדשים אשר ישוב ישראל וישען עליהם.

III	**גיטין, נו, א**

אבא סקרא ריש בריוני דירושלים בר אחתיה דרבן יוחנן בן זכאי הוה שלח ליה תא בצינעא לגבאי אתא א"ל עד אימת עבדיתו הכי וקטליתו ליה לעלמא בכפנא א"ל מאי איעביד דאי אמינא להו מידי קטלו לי א"ל חזי לי תקנתא לדידי דאיפוק אפשר דהוי הצלה פורתא א"ל נקוט נפשך בקצירי ולייתי כולי עלמא ולישיילו בך ואייתי מידי סריא ואגני גבך ולימרו דנח נפשך וליעיילו בך תלמידך ולא ליעול בך איניש אחרינא דלא לרגשון בך דקליל הוא דיעד דחייא קליל ממיתא עביד הכי נכנס בו רבי אליעזר מצד אחד ורבי יהושע מצד אחר כי מטו לפיתחא בעו למדקריה אמר להו יאמרו רבן דקרו בעו למדחפיה אמר להו יאמרו רבן דחפו פתחו ליה בבא נפק כי מטא להתם אמר שלמא עלך מלכא שלמא עלך מלכא א"ל מיחייבת תרי קטלא חדא דלאו מלכא אנא וקא קרית לי מלכא ותו אי מלכא אנא עד האידנא אמאי לא אתית לגבאי א"ל דקאמרת לאו מלכא אנא איברא מלכא את דאי לאו מלכא את לא מימסרא ירושלים בידך דכתיב (ישעיהו י, לד) והלבנון באדיר יפול ואין אדיר אלא מלך דכתיב (ירמיהו ל, כא) והיה אדירו ממנו וגו' ואין לבנון אלא ביהמ"ק שנאמר (דברים ג, כה) ההר הטוב הזה והלבנון ודקאמרת אי מלכא אנא אמאי לא קאתית לגבאי עד האידנא בריוני דאית בן לא שבקינן אמר ליה אילו חבית של דבש ודרקון כרוך עליה לא היו שוברין את החבית בשביל דרקון אישתיק קרי עליה רב יוסף ואיתימא רבי עקיבא (ישעיהו מד, כה) משיב חכמים אחור ודעתם יסכל איבעי ליה למימר לה שקלינן צבתא ושקלינן ליה לדרקון וקטלינן ליה וחביתא שבקינן לה אדהכי אתי פריסתקא עליה מרומי אמר ליה קום דמית ליה קיסר ואמרי הנהו חשיבי דרומי לאותיבך ברישא הוה סיים חד מסאני בעא למסיימא לאחרינא לא עייל בעא למשלפא לאידך לא נפק אמר מאי האי אמר ליה לא תצטער שמועה טובה אתיא לך דכתיב (משלי טו, ל) שמועה טובה תדשן עצם אלא מאי תקנתיה ליתי איניש דלא מיתבא דעתך מיניה ולחליף קמך דכתיב (משלי יז, כב) ורוח נכאה תיבש גרם עבד הכי עייל ליה

ומאחר דחכמיתו כולי האי עד האידנא אמאי לא אתיתו לגבאי אמר ליה ולא אמרי לך אמר
ליה אנא נמי אמרי לך אמר ליה מיזל אזילנא ואינש אחרינא משדרנא אלא בעי מינאי מידי
דאתן לך אמר ליה תן לי יבנה וחכמיה ושושילתא דרבן גמליאל ואסוותא דמסיין ליה לרבי
צדוק קרי עליה רב יוסף ואיתימא רבי עקיבא (ישעיהו מד, כה) משיב חכמים אחור ודעתם
יסכל איבעי למימר ליה לשבקינהו הדא זימנא והוא סבר דלמא כולי האי לא עביד והצלה
פורתא נמי לא הוי.

אבות דרבי נתן, פרק ד

אמר לו, אתה הוא רבי יוחנן בן זכאי, שאל מה אתן לך. אמר לו, איני מבקש ממך אלא יבנה.
אלך ואשנה בה לתלמידי, ואקבע בה תפלה, ואעשה בה את כל מצות האמורות בתורה. אמר לו,
לך, וכל מה שאתה רוצה לעשות עשה. אמר לו, רצונך שאומר לפניך דבר אחד? אמר לו, אמור.
אמר לו, הרי את עומד במלכות.—מניין אתה יודע? אמר לו, כך מסור לנו, שאין בית המקדש
נמסר ביד הדיוט, אלא ביד המלך, שנאמר, (ישעיה י, לד)"וּנְקַף סִבְכֵי הַיַּעַר בַּבַּרְזֶל, וְהַלְּבָנוֹן
בְּאַדִּיר יִפּוֹל". אמרו, לא היה יום אחד שנים ושלשה ימים, עד שבא אליו דיופלא מעירו שמת
קיסר, ונמנו עליו לעמוד במלכות.

IV

מהר״ל, חידושי אגדות גיטין נו, ב

תן לי יבנה וכו', יש לדקדק למה בחר באלו ג' דוקא. דע כי כוונת ר״י היה כאשר אלו שלשה
נגד ג' מדות שהקב״ה מנהיג עולמו בהן, והיה רוצה ריב״ז שיהיה עומדים כל מדותיו של הקב״ה,
וזה שהקב״ה נוהג עולמו על ידי חסד שעושה עם בריותיו, והשני מדת היושר והדין, והשלישי
מדת הרחמים לרחם על ברואיו. וידוע כי החכמים דביקים במדת החסד...ולפיכך רצה ביבנה
וחכמיה, ואחר כך רבי צדוק משלים המדה השנית מדת הדין בתעניתו, ודבר זה תבין כי מפני
שמרחם על אחד הוא דבק בו לגמרי והוא אחד עמו...ולכך שושלת דר״ג שהם זרע מיוחס
ואין בהם פסולת אז השם יתברך מרחם עליהם, כי הם עם הקב״ה כאשר הם זרע כשר בלי
פסולת...וכאשר יש להם אלו שלשה דהיינו יבנה וחכמיה ורבי צדוק ושושילתא דר״ג, אז היו
דבקים בכל מדותיו יתברך ויצילו אותם על הכל, כי אלו ג' דברים הם כל מדות שהוא יתברך
מנהיג את עולמו בהן, והבן הדברים היטב.

V

ירושלמי דמאי, פ״ג, ה״ד

אמר רבי יהושע בן קבסוי כל ימי הייתי קורא הפסוק הזה (במדבר יט, יט) והזה הטהור על
הטמא טהור א' מזה על טמא א' עד שלמדתיה מאצרה של יבנה.

VI

SECTION IV: HADRIAN

2. HADRIAN

דורות הראשונים, ימי אושא וראשית ימי אדריאנוס פרק ב

ויהי ההיפר מטראיאן, כי תחת אשר טראאן הי' איש מלחמה וחי על חרבו, וירגיז את כל
העמים במלחמותיו, השתדל אדריאנוס להשלים עם כל העמים, וגם בארץ בבל תחת אשר
טראיאן הכין את חילו להלחם עמהם שנית משך אדריאנוס את ידו מהם.

I

דורות הראשונים, ימי אושא וראשית ימי אדריאנוס

בראשית ימי אדריאנוס נראה כמו אור לבני ישראל, ואף כי לא ארכו הימים וקו אור חלף
הלך לו, והשמים החלו להתקדר, עד כי היה לעב ענן והחשך כסה ארץ...

II

דורות הראשונים, ימי אושא וראשית ימי אדריאנוס

...אבל חכמי ישראל אשר עינם לטובת עמם מיד כאשר נראה שביב אור התחזקו
ויהפכוהו למעטה אורה ומקור חיים. וגם בפעם הזאת מהרו להקים מחדש את דבר המתיבתא
הכללית אשר כבר נתבטלה מימים רבים...ויקימו אותה בעיר אושא...ובכל זה הזיק מאד לכל
חיי העם...כי בני ישראל בכל מקומות מושבותיהם קבלו משם כל אור ואמתות...וכן הדבר
כי בראשית ימי אדריאנוס בשנת 711 שזה הוא בשנת שבע וארבעים לחרבן ירושלים צוה
אדריאנוס לבנות את ירושלים מחדש...כי אדריאנוס עשה אז גם לטובת יהודי אלכסנדריא ויצו

III

להקים מחדש את בתיהם ההרוסים ואת היכליהם...כי בעלות אדריאנוס לכסא רומא הקריבו יהודי אלכסנדריא לפניו משפטם ודינים, והיונים נתחייבו ממנו בדין...

3. RABBI YEHOSHUA BEN CHANANYA

I **ערכין, יא, ב**

מעשה בר' יהושע בר חניה שהלך לסייע בהגפת דלתות אצל ר' יוחנן בן גודגדא אמר לו בני חזור לאחוריך שאתה מן המשוררים ולא מן המשוערים.

II **פרקי אבות, ב, ח**

יהושע בן חנניה, אשרי יולדתו.

III **ירושלמי יבמות, פ"א, ה"ו**

ראה את רבי יהושע וקרא עליו (ישעיהו כח, ט) את מי יורה דעה, זכור אני שהיתה אמו מולכת עריסתו לבית הכנסת בשביל שיתדבקו אזניו בדברי תורה.

IV **סנהדרין, יז, ב**

אמר רב יהודה אמר רב כל עיר שאין בה שנים לדבר ואחד לשמוע אין מושיבין בה סנהדרי ובביתר הוו שלשה ובינה ארבעה רבי אליעזר ורבי יהושע ור"ע ושמעון התימני דן לפניהם בקרקע.

V **גיטין, נח, א**

תנו רבנן מעשה ברבי יהושע בן חנניה שהלך לכרך גדול שברומי, אמרו לו תינוק אחד יש בבית האסורים יפה עינים וטוב רואי וקוצותיו סדורות לו תלתלים, הלך ועמד על פתח בית האסורים, אמר, מי נתן למשיסה יעקב וישראל לבוזזים, ענה אותו תינוק ואמר, הלא ה' זו חטאנו לו ולא אבו בדרכיו הלוך ולא שמעו בתורתו, אמר מובטחני בו שמורה הוראה בישראל, העבודה שאיני זז מכאן עד שאפדנו בכל ממון שפוסקין עליו, אמרו לא זז משם עד שפדאו בממון הרבה, ולא היו ימים מועטין עד שהורה הוראה בישראל, ומנו רבי ישמעאל בן אלישע.

VI **עירובין, נג, ב**

אמר רבי יהושע בן חנניה מימי לא נצחני אדם חוץ מאשה תינוק ותינוקת מאי היא פעם אחת נתארחתי אצל אכסניא אחת עשתה לי פולין ביום ראשון אכלתים ולא שיירתי מהן כלום שנייה ולא שיירתי מהן כלום ביום שלישי הקדיחתן במלח כיון שטעמתי משכתי ידי מהן אמרה לי רבי מפני מה אינך סועד אמרתי לה כבר סעדתי מבעוד יום אמרה לי לך למשוך ידיך מן הפת אמרה לי רבי שמא לא הנחת פאה בראשונים ולא כך אמרו חכמים אין משיירין פאה באילפס אבל משיירין פאה בקערה. תינוקת מאי היא פעם אחת הייתי מהלך בדרך והיתה דרך עוברת בשדה והייתי מהלך בה אמרה לי תינוקת רבי לא שדה היא זו אמרתי לה לא דרך כבושה היא אמרה לי ליסטים כמותך כבשוה. תינוק מאי היא פעם אחת הייתי מהלך בדרך וראיתי תינוק יושב על פרשת דרכים ואמרתי לו באיזה דרך נלך לעיר אמר לי זו קצרה וארוכה וזו ארוכה וקצרה והלכתי בקצרה וארוכה כיון שהגעתי לעיר מצאתי שמקיפין אותה גנות ופרדיסין חזרתי לאחורי אמרתי לו בני הלא אמרת לי קצרה אמר לי ולא אמרתי לך ארוכה נשקתיו על ראשו ואמרתי לו אשריכם ישראל שכולכם חכמים גדולים אתם מגדולכם ועד קטנכם.

VII **בראשית רבה, סד, ח**

בימי ר' יהושע בן חנניה גזרה מלכות הרשעה שיבנה בית המקדש, הושיבו פפוס ולוליאנוס טרפיזין מעכו עד אנטוכיא והיו מספקין לעולי גולה כסף וזהב וכל צרכם, אזלון אילין כותאי ואמרין ידיע להוי למלכא דהדין קרתא מרדתא תתבנא ושוריא ישתכללון מנדה ובלו לא יתנון...ואמר להון הון מה נעביד וגזירית, אמרין ליה שלח ואמר להון או ישנון יתה מאתריה או יוספון עליה חמש אמין או יבצרון מיניה חמש אמין, מן גרמיהון אינון חזרין בהון. והוון קהליא מצתין בהדה בקעתא דבית רימון, כיון דאתון כתיבא שרון בכיין, בעיין לממרד על מלכותא, אמרין יעול חד בר נש חכימא וישדך (פי'-ישקיט) צבורא, אמרין יעול רבי יהושע בן חנניה, דהוא אסכלוסטיקא (-אדון) דאורייתא. עאל ודרש ארי טרף טרף ועמד עצם בגרונו, אמר כל דאתי מפיק ליה אנא יהיב ליה אגריה, אתא הדין קורא מצראה דמקוריה (-מקורו)

אריך יהיב מקוריה ואפקיה, א"ל הב לי אגרי, א"ל זיל תהא מלגלג ואומר דעלית לפומא דאריה בשלום ונפקת בשלום, כך דייגו שנכנסנו לאומה זו בשלום ויצאנו בשלום.

VIII **סוטה, מט, ב**
משמת רבי יהושע בטלה עצה ומחשבה, רש"י, שהיה זהיר בדרשות ובקי בהלכות ובתשובת האפיקורסים ולהבין ברמזיהם כדאמרי' בפ"ק דחגיגה (ה, ב).

IX **חגיגה, ה, ב**
כי קא ניחא נפשיה דרבי יהושע אמרו ליה רבנן מאי תיהוי עלן מאפיקורסין, אמר להם אבדה עצה מבנים נסרחה חכמתם, כיון שאבדה עצה מבנים נסרחה חכמתן של אומות העולם.

4. IN THE EMPEROR'S HOME

I **שפתי חכמים, ברכות נו, א**
והנה משם קצת משמע, דהאי סתם קיסר הוא היה אדריאנוס...

II **דורות הראשונים, אדריאנוס בעלותו למלוכה**
...אבל היה כל זה בימי היותו בסוריא אשר ככל הגמוני סוריא עמדה גם ארץ ישראל תחת פקודתו.

III **חגיגה, ה, ב**
ר' יהושע בן חנניה הוה קאי בי קיסר אחוי ליה ההוא אפיקורסא עמא דאהדרינהו מריה לאפיה מיניה (-החזיר פניו מהם), אחוי ליה ידו נטויה עלינו, אמר ליה קיסר לר' יהושע מאי אחוי לך, עמא דאהדרינהו מריה לאפיה מיניה, ואנא מחוינא ליה ידו נטויה עלינו. אמרו ליה לההוא מינא מאי אחויית ליה, עמא דאהדרינהו מריה לאפיה מיניה, ומאי אחוי לך, לא ידענא, אמרו גברא דלא ידע מאי מחוו ליה במחוג יחוי קמי מלכא, אפקוהו וקטלוהו.

IV **תענית, ז, א**
כדאמרה ליה ברתיה דקיסר לר' יהושע בן חנניה אי חכמה מפוארה בכלי מכוער, אמר לה אביך רמי חמרא במני דפחרא (-יין בכלי חרס), אמרה ליה אלא במאי נירמי, אמר לה אתון דחשביתו רמו במאני דהבא וכספא. אזלה ואמרה ליה לאבוה, רמייא לחמרא במני דהבא וכספא ותקיף (-החמיץ), אתו ואמרו ליה, אמר לה לברתיה מאן אמר לך הכי, אמרה ליה רבי יהושע בן חנניה, קריוהו, אמר ליה אמאי אמרת לה הכי, אמר ליה כי היכי דאמרה לי אמרי לה, והא איכא שפירי דגמירי, אי הוו סנו (-אם היו מכוערים) טפי הוו גמירי.

V **בן יהוידע, שם**
...על בן נ"ל דלאו על יין דקאים לשתיה הוא אומר, אלא הכוונה הוא על יין שדרכם לנסכו בכל יום לע"ז...והשיב לה דאתם החשובים צריך לשמרו בכלי זהב...ומצא אביה טעם בדבריה, וצוה שכך יעשו והחמיץ היין, ואחר ששאל מבתו מי הגיד לך עצה זו וא"ל ריב"ח, ושאל מאי אמרת ליה, והשיבה הכי והכי אמרת ליה, חשד את ריב"ח דלאו בשביל הוכוח אמר לה כן, אלא אמר כן כדי לקלקל את המוכן לע"ז...אך היא אמרה לו כך, והוכרחתי להשיב לה כך, לסתור דבריה שהיתה מגנה אותי, ואמרתי לה שיש הוכחה מן שמירת היין בכלים שאינו נשמר אלא רק בכלי פחות ולא נתכונתי בדרך עצה...

VI **שבת, קנב, א**
א"ל קיסר לר' יהושע בן חנניה מ"ט לא אתית לבי אבידן א"ל טור תלג סחרוני גלידין כלבוהי לא נבחין טחנוהי לא טוחנין.

VII **ברכות, נו, א**
אמר ליה קיסר לר' יהושע בר' חנניא אמריתו דחכמיתו טובא אימא לי מאי חזינא בחלמאי, אמר ליה חזית דמשחרי לך פרסאי וגרבי בך, ורעיי בך שקצי בחוטרא דדהבא (-עושים בך עבודת המלך), הרהר כוליה יומא ולאורתא חזא.

VIII **שפתי חכמים, שם**
אמריתו דחכימו טובא—אפשר דכונת הקיסר היה, על דכתיב (דברים ד, ל) ואמרו רק עם חכם ונבון הגוי הגדול הזה. ובס' סמיכות חכמים פי', משום דאמרינן חכם עדיף מנביא, ועל זה

סמך הקיסר, וא"ל אמירתו דחכמימו, ר"ל דחכמתכם הוא יותר מנבואה, לכן שאל להם שידעו העתיד, מה שיראה בחלום...

IX **אמרי נועם, שם**
לזה נצרך חכמה להכיר היטב טבע של אדם להבין מאיזה דבר הוא מתפעל ואיזה כח מהד' יסודות מתגבר בו אז נוכל לידע איזה דבר לומר לו שיחלום אותו הדבר בלילה וז"ש דחכמיתו טובא משום דצריך לזה חכמה גדולה.

X **בן יהוידע, ברכות נו, א**
אמר לו דברים מורים מעניינים הנעשים במלחמה כי הדרך אם נצח מלך זה למלך אחר במלחמה אינו מבטל מלכותו לגמרי אלא מניחו להיות מלך על עמו כמו שהיה ורק משהו מטיל עליו מס קצוב שיקחהו מעמו וז"ש משחרי לך פרסאי שיכבשו אותך ותשאר תחת ידם לרעות חזיריי אלו הרומיים שנקראים חזירים על שם קליפת חזיר.

XI **שבת, קיט, א**
א"ל קיסר לר' יהושע בן חנניא מפני מה תבשיל של שבת ריחו נודף, אמר לו תבלין אחד יש לנו ושבת שמו שאנו מטילין לתוכו וריחו נודף, אמר לו תן לנו הימנו, אמר לו כל המשמר את השבת מועיל לו, ושאינו משמר את השבת אינו מועיל לו.

XII **בן יהוידע, שבת, קיט, א**
שם תבלין אחד יש לנו ושבת שמו לא דבר שקר ח"ו אלא התבלין הוא ההארה של קדושת שבת הנמשכת בשבת על התבשיל ג"כ על אשר נתבשל לכבוד שבת וההארה זאת נקראת שבת כי היא נמשכת מקדושת השבת ונרמזה התבלין באותיות שבת במילוי שלהם...ובזה יובן בס"ד ושמרו בני ישראל את השבת לעשיות את השבת פירוש כדי לעשיות את השבת הם התבלין שנקראים שבת שהם לא יהיו אלא רק אצל שומרי שבת. או לעשיות את השבת ר"ל תבלים הרמוזים באותיות שבת כאמור...

XIII **חולין, נט, ב**
אמר ליה קיסר לר' יהושע בן חנניה אלקיכם כאריה מתיל דכתיב אריה שאג מי לא יירא, מאי רבותיה, פרשא קטיל אריא, אמר ליה לאו כהאי אריא מתיל, כאריא דבי עילאי מתיל, אמר ליה בעינא דמיחזית ליה ניהלי (-הראיני אותו), אמר ליה לא מצית חזית ליה, אמר ליה איברא חזינא ליה, בעא רחמי אתעקר מדוכתיה, כי הוה מרחיק ארבע מאה פרסי ניהם חד קלא, אפילו כל מעברתא ושורא דרומי נפל, אדמרחיק תלת מאה פרסי ניהם קלא אחרינא, נתור כבי ושיני דגברי, ואף הוא נפל מכורסיא לארעא, א"ל במטותא מינך בעי רחמי עליה דלהדר לדוכתיה, בעא רחמי עלוה ואהדר ליה לאתריה.

XIV **מהרש"א, שם**
כאריה מתיל כו'. הנה זה הקיסר כפר ביכולת ושיש אחד שיש לו כח ויכולת יותר ממנו דהא פרשא קטיל אריה וא"ל דמתיל לאריה דבי עילאי דעל ההוא אריה נאמר אריה שאג מי לא יירא שאין הפרש יכול לו מיראת שאגתו כמו שהראה לו דבמרחק ד' מאות וג' מאות פרסי אפי' מעברתא ושורא נפל ונתור כבי כו', כך ה' דיבר מי לא ינבא שלא יראה מאותה הנבואה שיש יכולת ביד ה' להענישו כמ"ש בעניינו אם תהיה רעה בעיר וה' לא עשה.

XV **מהר"ל, חדושי אגדות חולין שם**
...שהגיע פחד ורעדה אליו, ואמר לו כי זה היה בשביל שהוא רוצה לדעת ולעמוד על כח הקב"ה וגבורתו.

XVI **חולין, נט, ב (ס, א)**
אמר ליה קיסר לר' יהושע בן חנניה בעינא דאיחזי לאלהיכו א"ל לא מצית חזית ליה א"ל איברא חזינא ליה אזל אוקמיה להדי יומא בתקופת תמוז א"ל איסתכל ביה א"ל לא מצינא א"ל יומא דחד משמשי דקיימי קמי דקודשא בריך הוא אמרת לא מצינא לאיסתכלא ביה שכינה לא כל שכן.

XVII **חולון, ס, א**
אמר ליה קיסר לרבי יהושע בן חנניה בעינא דאיצבית ליה נהמא לאלהיכו אמר ליה לא מצית מאי נפישי חילוותיה א"ל איברא אמר ליה פוק צבית לגידא דרביתא דרויחא עלמא טרח

	שיתא ירחי קייטא אתא זיקא כנשיה לימא טרח שיתא ירחי דסיתוא אתא מיטרא טבעיה בימא א"ל מאי האי אמר ליה הני כנושאי זלוחאי דאתו קמיה א"ל אי הכי לא מצינא.
XVIII	בן יהוידע, שם
	קשא איך ס"ד שטות זו ואפילו תנוק בן יומו יודע דאין שייך אכילה אצל הקב"ה, ועוד קשא אחר ששה חודשים הראשונים אמאי לא א"ל מאי האי...וני"ל בס"ד דהקיסר חשב להכין הסעודה למלאכים שהם חייליותיו של הקב"ה, כי שמע וידע שהמלאכים אכלו אצל אברהם אע"ה ובשביל שעושה לחיילות השי"ת לבכודו אמר אצבי נהמא לאלייכו כמו שתמצא בקרבנות דכתיב בהו קרבן לה' והכהנים הם אוכלים...
XIX	חולין ס, א
	א"ל בת קיסר לר' יהושע בן חנניה אלהיכון נגרא הוא דכתיב (תהלים קד, ג) המקרה במים עליותיו אימא ליה דנעביד לי חדא מסתוריתא אמר לחיי בעא רחמי עלה ואינגעה אותבה בשוקא דרומי ויהבי לה מסתוריתא דהוו נהיגי דכל דמנגע ברומי יהבו ליה מסתוריתא ויתיב בשוקא וסתר דולילי כי היכי דליחזו אינשי וליבעי רחמי עליה יומא חד הוה קא חליף התם הות יתבא וסתרה דולילי בשוקא דרומאי אמר לה שפירתא מסתוריתא דיהב ליך אלהי אמרה ליה אימא ליה לאלהיך לשקול מאי דיהב לי אמר לה אלהא דידן מיהא יהיב משקל לא שקיל.
XX	בן יהוידע, שם
	נ"ל בס"ד הכונה כי הגוים הקדמונים היו כופרים בהשגחה ואומרים שאין הקב"ה משגיח בעוה"ז אלא העולם מתנהג מאליו בטבע, אך אנחנו בית ישראל מאמינים דאע"פ שברא הקב"ה הטבע שיתנהג בו העולם, עב"ז הטבע הוא בידו יתברך והולך ע"פ השגחתו יתברך, שאם רוצה הקב"ה שזה האדם ירויח היום הזה אלף דינרים אינו מוריד לו אלף דינרים מן השמים אלא יעשה לו סיבה טבעית שבעבור אותה הסיבה יסבב לו להרויח אלף דנרים...ועל זאת דברה ברמז לריב"ח לפי דבריכם שאתם אומרים הסיבות מסתובבים מן הקב"ה אימא ליה דלעביד לי חדא מסתוריתא פירש שיתן לי איזה דבר שהוא רחוק ממני שאין אני יכולה להשיגו ויתנהו לי על ידי סיבה רחוקה.....
XXI	ויקרא רבה, יח, א
	אדריינוס שחיק עצמות שאל את רבי יהושע בר חנינא אמר לו, מהיכן הקב"ה מציץ את האדם לעתיד לבא, אמר לו מלוז של שדרה, אמר לו מן הן את מודע לי, אייתי יתיה קומוי, נתנו במים ולא נמחה, טחנו בריחים ולא נטחן, נתנו באש ולא נשרף, נתנו על הסדן התחיל מקיש עליו בפטיש, נחלק הסדן ונבקע הפטיש ולא הועיל ממנו כלום.
XXII	סנהדרין, צ, ב
	שאלו רומיים את ר' יהושע בן חנניה מניין שהקב"ה מחיה מתים ויודע מה שעתיד להיות, אמר להו תרוויהו מן המקרא הזה, שנאמר ויאמר ה' אל משה הנך שוכב עם אבותיך וקם העם הזה וזנה, ודילמא וקם העם הזה וזנה, אמר להו נקוטו מיהא פלגא בידייכו, דידעו מה שעתיד להיות.
XXIII	בן יהוידע, שם
	מניין שהקב"ה מחיה מתים ויודע כו'. הפילוסופים הם מן הכופרים בידיעה ובתחיית המתים והם שאלו על שניהם מנין מן התורה. ואמר להו נקוט מיהא פלגא בידייכו וכו'. יש לדקדק לכאורה בהאי לישנא דהוה ליה למימר נקוט מיהא חדא בידייכו דהיינו הידיעה, ואפשר לפרש דהכי קאמר נקוט מיהא פלגא בשאלת תחיית המתים בידייכו שהרי הכתוב הזה וקם אין לו הכרע כדלעיל והוי הראיה כמחצה על מחצה ונקיט נמי בידייכו הך כולה מלתא דידעו מה כו' וק"ל.
XXIV	בן יהוידע, שם
	קשה הם שאלו שתים ואיך עשה להם פשרה באחת, ועוד למה שאלו שתי שאלות אלו ביחד מה שייכות יש להם זע"ז, ועוד הוא אמר תחלה דילמדו תרוויהו מהמקרא הזה, ואח"כ איך אומר נקוטו מיהא פלגא דנמצא לא עמדו דבריו בכך, וני"ל בס"ד דהם מעיקרא לא רצו לידע ראיה שיש יכולת להקב"ה להחיות מתים, דעל זה אין צורך להביא ראיה מן הכתוב, מאחר דהם מודים דאליהו זכור לטוב ואלישע הע"ה ויחזקאל הע"ה החיו מתים, וכ"ש הקב"ה יכול

להחיות מתים, אך הם חושבים שאין הקב"ה מחיה המתים לעתיד מחשש שמא חוזרים וחוטאים כאשר חטאו בראשונה, אך אם יתברר להם שהקב"ה יודע מה שעתיד להיות אפשר שיחיה את המתים לעתיד, מפני שהוא יודע מה שעתיד להיות והוא יודע שלא יחטאו עוד, ולכן אין לו ספק בדבר זה כדי שיבטל התחיה מחמת ספק זה דשמא יחטאו, ונמצא שתי שאלות אלו תלויים זב"ז...

XXV **טעם ודעת, פרשת וילך לא, טז**
...והזמן שאנו יודעים אותו הוא בריאה שנברא עם בריאת זה העולם...

XXVI **קהלת רבה, ט, ג**
אנדריאנוס שחיק טמיא שאל את ר' יהושע בן חנניה, א"ל אנא טב ממשה רבך, א"ל למה, דאנא חי והוא מת, וכתיב כי לכלב חי הוא טוב מן האריה המת, א"ל לית יכיל את לגזור דלא ידלק בר נש נור תלתא יומין, א"ל אין, לעידן רמשא דיומא קמו סלקו תרויהון על איגר פלטין, חמי תננא סליק מן רחיק (-ראו עשן עולה), א"ל מה כן, אמר איפרכא ביש (-חולה), ועאל אסיא ובקר יתיה ואמר ליה עד דשתי חמימי לא מיתסי, אמר ליה תיפח רוחיה, עד דאת בחיים בטלה גזירתך, ומשה רבינו בשעה שגזר עלינו לא תבערו אש בכל מושבותיכם ביום השבת לא מדליק יהודאי נור בשבתא מיומוהי, ועדיין לא נתבטלה גזירתו מכמה שנים עד השתא, אמרת את כן דאנא טב מיניה.

SECTION V: ANTONINUS

I **סדר הדורות, ג' אלפים תת"ק (צמח דוד)**
אנטונינוס פיאוס—פירוש חסיד חתן אדריאנוס קיסר, איש חכם ומבקש שלום, ולא יצא למלחמה רק ע"י הכרח גדול. ומורגל בפיו לומר מוטב שיחיה אחד מעמי משימותו אלף שונאי והרחיב מלכותו בלא חרב, רק לרוב ענוותנותו וחסידותו שמעו בקולו כל המלכים. היה ידידו של רבינו הקדוש מלך ג' אלפים תת"ק בן מ"ז שנה.

II **ספר הקבלה להראב"ד, עמוד טו**
רבינו הקדוש הוא רבי יהודה הנשיא בן רבן שמעון בן גמליאל והיה ראש ישיבה כי ראה השם יתעלה את עני ישראל מורה מאד וקים להם מקרא שכתוב ובהכשלם יעזרו עזר מעט. ומת אנדריינוס ומלך ברומי אנטונינוס בן אסיורוס והיה אוהב את רבינו הקדוש בנפשו ואומרים שגיירו בסתר. והיו בימי רבינו הקדוש כולם ימים טובים לישראל והאריך ימים ובימיו מת אנטונינוס ומלך אנטיפוס ואחריו קומודוס וכולם כבדו ונשאו את רבינו הקדוש כל ימיו. (עלייתו של אנטונינוס הביא הקלה ביחסיו הקיסרות עם היהודים, הוא ביטל את גזירות אדריאנוס ואישר ליהודים למול את בניהם בתנאי שהם לא ימולו נוכרים כלומר לא יעסקו בגיור.

III **אנטונינוס פיוס /https://he.wikipedia.org/wiki**
בהיסטוריה אוגוסטה נזכר שאנטונינוס פיוס דיכא מרד יהודי שפרץ בתקופת שלטונו אולם אין מידע ברור ממקורות אחרים על מרד כזה בתקופת שלטונו, ואם מרד כזה אכן התרחש, ייתכן שמדובר על המחצית הראשונה של שלטונו וניתן לראות זאת כתולדה של המלחמה של ימי אדריאנוס. רוב החוקרים דוחים את הידיעה הזאת בשל איכותה המפוקפקת של ההיסטוריה אוגוסטה כמקור היסטורי.

IV **דורות הראשונים, המאורע הכללי וראשית ימי רבי, פרק מה**
ועל כן אין ספק כי גם קרא את העתקת השבעים מהתורה וידע גודל ערכה, וגם הי' לו איזה מושג מה הוא התורה הזאת אשר יעסקו בה בני ישראל, ומה הם פקודי ה' ישרים אשר ישמרו בני ישראל ויתנו נפשם עליהם.

V **עבודה ברורה, עבודה זרה י, א**
אנטונינוס—לפי ספר דורות הראשונים אנטונינוס זה הוא הקיסר מרקוס אנטונינוס שמלך בשנת 161 עד 180 למספרם, תוך מסעותיו בארצות ממלכתו ביקר אף במחוז יהודה ופגש את רבי יהודה הנשיא, ונקשר אליו בידידות עד יום מותו.

3. RABBI YEHUDAH HANASI

I	**קדושין, עב, ב**
	דאמר מר כשמת ר' עקיבא נולד רבי כשמת רב יהודה נולד רב יהודה נולד רבא כשמת רבא נולד רב אשי כשמת רב אשי צדיק נפטר מן העולם עד שנברא צדיק כמותו שנאמר (קהלת א, ה) וזרח השמש ובא השמש עד שלא כבתה שמשו של עלי זרחה שמשו של שמואל הרמתי שנאמר (שמואל א ג, ג) ונר אלהים טרם יכבה ושמואל שוכב וגו'.
II	**בראשית רבה, צו, ה**
	בחייו היה דר בציפורי שבע עשרה שנה והיה קורא על עצמו ויחי יעקב בארץ מצרים שבע עשרה שנה, וחיה יהודה בציפורי שבע עשרה שנין.
	ספר יוחסין, מאמר ראשון
	וי"ז שנים היה בציפורי כמו יעקב במצרים כדאיתא בב"ר.
III	**ספר יוחסין, מאמר ראשון**
	והוא ז' להלל מזרע המלוכה מצד אמו של הלל משפטיה בן אביטל אשת דוד המלך.
IV	**שבועות, ז, א**
	קרי רבא עליה דרבי דולה מים מבורות עמוקים.
V	**עירובין, יג, ב**
	אמר רבי האי דמחדדנא מחבראי דחזיתיה לר' מאיר מאחוריה ואילו חזיתיה מקמיה הוה מחדדנא טפי דכתיב (ישעיהו ל, כ) והיו עיניך רואות את מוריך.
VI	**מהרש"א, שם**
	דהסברת פנים הוה מחדדי טפי דיש להבין בקריצת עינים וברמיזת שפתים והיינו רואות את מוריך שמראה לו פנים טפי וק"ל.
VII	**בבא מציעא, פה, א**
	אהוריירי'ה דבי רבי הוה עתיר משבור מלכא כד הוה רמי כיסתא לחיותא.
VIII	**כתובות, קד, א**
	בשעת פטירתו של רבי זקף עשר אצבעותיו כלפי מעלה אמר, רבונו של עולם גלוי וידוע לפניך שיגעתי בעשר אצבעותי בתורה ולא נהניתי אפילו באצבע קטנה, יהי רצון מלפניך שיהא שלום במנוחתי. יצתה בת קול ואמרה יבא שלום ינוחו על משכבותם.
IX	**שבת, קיח, ב**
	והאמרו ליה לרבי מאי טעמא קראו לך רבינו הקדוש אמר להו מימי לא נסתכלתי במילה שלי ברבי מילתא אחריתי הוה ביה שלא הכניס ידו תחת אבנטו.
X	**ויקרא רבה, כד, ו**
	אמר רבי יהודה בן פזי מפני מה נסמכה פרשת עריות לפרשת קדושים אלא ללמדך שכל מקום שאתה מוצא בו גדר ערוה אתה מוצא קדושה...כל מי שהוא גודר עצמו מן הערוה נקרא קדוש.
XI	**ספר יוחסין, מאמר ראשון**
	ובספר לבנת הספיר ובזוהר שנקרא קדוש שקדשו אביו במילה בשעת השמד.
XII	**בבא מציעא, פה, א**
	אמר רבי חביבין יסורין קבל עליה תליסר שני, שית בצמירתא ושבע בצפרנא ואמרי לה שבעה בצמירתא ושית בצפרנא.
XIII	**מגלה עמוקות, ואתחנן, אופן פג**
	ולכן נקרא רבי רבי יהודה נשיא, נוטריקון נ'יצוצו ש'ל י'עקב א'בינו. [וכתב עוד בפרשת תזריע כי מטעם זה נקרא "רבנו הקדוש" כי יעקב אבינו תיקן ברכה שלישית של שמונה עשרה "הא-ל הקדוש".]
XIV	**מהר"ל, חידושי אגדות כתובות קג, ב**
	אותו יום שמת רבי בטלה קדושה, שהיו קורין אותו רבינו הקדוש, והא דאמר בשלהי סוטה משמת רבי בטלה ענוה ויראה, התם כך פירושו משמת רבי בטלה ענוה ויראה, אך אותם שהיו בדורו והיו חיים אחריו היה בהם יראה וענוה, רק משמת רבי בטלה ענוה ויראה שלא היה בדור אחר דורו יראי שמים וענוים, וזהו שאמר כשמת רבי בטלה ענוה ויראה, אבל לא שייך לומר באותו

יום שמת רבי, דלאו באותו יום ממש בטלה ענוה ויראה, אבל קדושה לא הניח רבי אחריו כלל שום קדושה, ולכך אמר אותו היום בטלה קדושה.

XV **רבי צדוק הכהן מלובלין, ישראל קדושים, עמוד 64**
וכן רבינו הקדוש שנקרא כן בסתמא כי נתייחד בתוקף הקדושה שאפשר להשיג בעולם הזה, היה ניצוץ יעקב אע"ה כידוע מהאריז"ל, דעל כן אתי כל בי שמשי לביתיה כמ"ש בכתובות (קג, א) דגם כן לא מת, והיינו שהוא היה נשיא ופרנס הדור וכולל כל נפשות דורו, וכשהשלימים נפשו כל כך שיזכה לשם קדוש סתם...

XVI **ברכות, טז, ב**
רבי בתר צלותיה אמר הכי, יהי רצון מלפניך ה' אלהינו ואלהי אבותינו שתצילנו מעזי פנים ומעזות פנים מאדם רע ומפגע רע מיצר רע מחבר רע משכן רע ומשטן המשחית ומדין קשה ומבעל דין קשה בין שהוא בן ברית בין שאינו בן ברית.

XVII **מכתב מאליהו, חלק ג עמוד קג**
כלים רגישים מאד הן מדות הנפש, וביחוד מדת החסד, והן עלולות להפגם גם בסיבה כשלהי. דבר זה נוכל ללמוד ממעשה שנפלא המובא בגמרא על רבי יהודה הנשיא, הלא הוא חסדו עם כלל ישראל לדורות, בזה שעמל וטרח בסידור וכתיבת התורה שבעל פה, המשניות. הוא היה בעל חסד שאף נתן את הכל לאחרים ולעצמו לא נטל כלום, כאמרם רז"ל שאף ששולחנו של רבי היה בעשירות מופלגת, נהנו מזה רק הארחים, והוא לא נהנה מהעולם אפילו באצבע קטנה, ולמרות כל זאת איתא בגמרא (ב"מ פה א), "ההוא עגלא דהוו ממטו ליה לשחיטה, אזל תליא לרישיה בכנפיה דרבי וקא בכי, אמר ליה זיל לכך נוצרת, אמרי (ברקיע), הואיל ולא קא מרחם, ליתו עליה יסורין".

XVIII **בבא מציעא, פה, א**
וע"י מעשה הלבו יומא חד הוה קא כנשא אמתיה דרבי ביתא הוה שדיא בני כרכושתא וקא כנשא להו אמר לה שבקינהו כתיב (תהלים קמה, ט) ורחמיו על כל מעשיו, אמרי הואיל ומרחם נרחם עליה.

XIX **בבא מציעא, פה, א**
איקלע רבי לאתריה דר' אלעזר בר' שמעון א"ל יש לו בן לאותו צדיק אמרו לו יש לו בן וכל זונה שנשכרת בשנים שוכרתו בשמנה אתייה אסמכיה ברבי ואשלמיה לר' שמעון בן איסי בן לקוניא אחות דאמיה.

XX **סנהדרין, צח, ב**
אי מן חייא הוא כגון רבינו הקדוש.

XXI **רבי צדוק הכהן מלובלין, ישראל קדושים, עמוד 64**
...היינו כשלא יגיע לו שום פגם עוד, ועל כן שהשלים גם נפשות כל דורו האחוזים בו, ולפיכך איתא בסנהדרין (צח, ב) אי מן חיי הוא כגון רבינו הקדוש שחשבו עליו שהוא משיח, כי כבר תיקן נפשו כל כך עד שהמשיך ותיקן כל דורו עמו, אלא שעדיין לא היה הדור כדאי שיהיה גם אצלם בהתגלות כן, כי עדיין לא נתקנו גם הדורות הבאים הכלולים בהם, דלעולם נפשות הבנים כלולים באבותם, ורבינו הקדוש תיקן נפשו לגמרי עם כל הנתלה בו מזרעו עד סוף כל הדורות וכן מנפשות כל בני דורו, אבל מה שנתלו בנפשות דורו מדורותיהם אחריהם עד סוף כל הדורות זה לא נתקן עדיין...ומכל מקום הוא זכה לנפשיה דמצד עצמו לא מת אלא שלא היה בהתגלות ברור מצד הדור, והוא יסד התורה שבעל פה שזהו עיקר הטל תורה המחייה ורוח הקדש דחכמים המביא לתחיית המתים.

XXII **סנהדרין, לו, א**
ואמר רבה בריה דרבא ואיתימא רבי הלל בריה דרבי וולס, מימות משה ועד רבי לא מצינו תורה וגדולה במקום אחד.

XXIII **יד רמה, שם**
מימות משה ועד רבינו לא מצינו תורה וגדולה במקום אחד כלומר לא מצינו מי שהיה גדול יותר מכל בני דורו בין בתורה בין בגדולה כגון משה רבינו שהיה גדול בישראל ואין כמותו לא בחכמה ולא במלכות וכן רבינו הקדוש היה גדול ולא היה בדורו כמוהו לא בחכמה ולא בנשיאות.

XXIV	**גיטין, ס, א-ב**

דרש רבי יהודה בר נחמני מתורגמניה דרבי שמעון בן לקיש כתיב (שמות לד, כז) כתוב לך את הדברים האלה וכתיב (שמות לד, כז) כי ע״פ הדברים האלה הא כיצד דברים שבכתב אי אתה רשאי לאומרן על פה דברים שבעל פה אי אתה רשאי לאומרן בכתב.

דר׳ יוחנן ור״ש בן לקיש מעייני בספרא דאגדתא בשבתא והא לא ניתן ליכתב אלא כיון דלא אפשר (תהלים קיט, קכו) עת לעשות לה׳ הפרו תורתך ה״נ כיון דלא אפשר עת לעשות לה׳ הפרו תורתך.

XXV	**רמב״ם, הקדמה למשנה תורה**

לפי שראה שהתלמידים מתמעטים והולכים, והצרות מתחדשות ובאות, וממלכת הרשעה פושטת בעולם ומתגברת, וישראל מתגלגלים והולכים לקצוות, חיבר חיבור אחד להיות ביד כולם, כדי שילמדוהו במהרה, ולא יישכח.

XXVI	**ספר יוחסין, מאמר ראשון**

וכשראה רבי ע״ה אורך הגלות והשכחה מצויה אמר עת לעשות לה׳ אע״פ שהפירו תורתך לפי שדברים שבעל פה אי אתה רשאי לכותבן.

XXVII	**כתובות, קג, א**

ת״ר בשעת פטירתו של רבי אמר לבני אני צריך נכנסו בניו אצלו אמר להם הזהרו בכבוד אמכם, נר יהא דלוק במקומו שולחן יהא ערוך במקומו מטה תהא מוצעת במקומה....... נר יהא דלוק במקומו שולחן יהא ערוך במקומו מטה תהא מוצעת במקומה-מאי טעמא כל בי שמשי הוה אתי לביתיה ההוא בי שמשא אתאי שבבתא קא קריה אבבא אמרה אמתיה שתיקו דרבי יתיב כיון דשמע שוב לא אתא שלא להוציא לעז על צדיקים הראשונים.

XXVIII	**רבינו בחיי, בראשית, מט, לג**

ויגוע ויאסף אל עמיו–והנה הפרשה הזאת מעידה שמת וכי חנטו אותו מצריים ובכו אותו שבעים יום ואחר כך קברוהו בניו במערת המכפלה מקום קבורת אבותיו. אבל פירוש לא מת לא מת טעם מיתה, או יהיה ענין לא מת כי נפשו של יעקב היה מרחפת על גופו תמיד לתוקף קדושתו כי שאר נפשות הצדיקים שאינם במדרגת הקדושה כמוהו חוזרות לשרשן ולערן וכיון שעלו לא ירדו, אבל יעקב לקדושת גופו ומעלתו היתה נפשו עולה ויורדת והכח הגדול הזה אינו נמצא רק לקדושים אשר בארץ יחידי הדורות כגון רבינו הקדוש, ומזה דרשו רז״ל בכתובות פרק הנושא (דף ק״ג) כל בי שמשי הוה אתי לביתיה יומא חד אתיא שבבתיה וקא קריא אבבא אמרה לה אמתיה שתיקו דרבינו יתיב כששמע רבי תו לא אתא שלא להוציא לעז על הצדיקים הראשונים, כלומר שחזרה נשמתה לשרשה ולא הגיעו אל המעלה הזאת להיות להם כח גדול כל כך כמו רבינו הקדוש.

4. THE ENCOUNTERS: PRINCE AND EMPEROR

I	**בראשית, כה, כג**

ויאמר ה' לה שני גויים בבטנך ושני לאומים ממעיך יפרדו ולאום מלאום יאמץ ורב יעבד צעיר.

II	**ילקוט ראובני, תולדות, כה, כג**

ויאמר ה' לה... עשו ויעקב היו גלגולי אנטונינוס ורבי, אנטונינוס היה גלגולו דעשו, ורבי היה גלגולו דיעקב שתיקן אתה קדוש, ולכן נקרא ר' יהודה נשי״א, ר״ת ניצוץ ש׳ל י׳עקב א׳בינו, ובזכות יעקב ניתנה תורה שבכתב, ור׳ סידר תורה שבעל פה.

III	**רבינו סעדיה גאון—ראה שפתי כהן שם**

שני גוים בבטנך אלו רבי ואנטונינוס, אמר לה כן לנחם אותה ולדבר על לבה, שאפילו עשו הרשע יוצא ממנו אנטונינוס, ולמה יצא ממנו אנטונינוס מרשע, הניצוץ שהיה מעשו שלקח מיצחק ומרבקה, וממש יצא אנטונינוס פרי מקליפה.

IV	**רש״י, שם ד״ה שני גוים בבטנך**

גיים כמו גאים אלו אנטונינוס ורבי שלא פסקו מעל שלחנם לא צנון ולא חזרת לא בימות החמה ולא בימות הגשמים.

V **משך חכמה, בראשית, כה, כג**
שני גוים בבטנך זה אנטונינוס ורבי כו'. הענין דרשה ברירה חלק הטוב, וחלק הרע נטלה הגר וכמו שאמר עד יעקב אבינו לא פסקה זוהמה (שבת קמו,א) וכיון שראתה שהבנים מתרוצצים וכשהולכת לבית ע"ז עשו מפרכס לצאת הרי כאן האחד טוב והאחד רע ולמה זה אנכי שלא כדרך שרה שלרבקה ניתן גם את הטוב גם הרע ולא בררו לה בירור הטוב לעצמו והשיבו לה שני גוים זה אנטונינוס הרי שבחלק הרע שלך מעורבב גם הטוב ולבן המה שניהם בבטנך ודו"ק.

VI **עבודה ברורה, עבודה זרה י, א**
גוים מלשון גאוה שהיו עשירים מופלגים. וז"ל הגהות הג"ר גדליה ליפשיץ, מלשון גאים שהתנהגו בשררות וחשיבות.

VII **מהר"ל, גור אריה בראשית כה, כג**
אנטונינוס ורבי—ונראה לא שהיה זה מרמז על אנטונינוס ורבי בלבד, אלא על כללות שתי האומות מרמז, כי כמה וכמה מלכים עמדו מעשו (ראה להלן לו, לא-לט), ומה בא לומר במלך זה בלבד יותר מכל המלכים, רק כי רבי ואנטונינוס היו יחד דומה ליעקב ועשו, זה נשיא ישראל וזה מלך אדום (ב"ר עה, ו), והיו בזמן אחד שנראה זה יותר בהם, שהם היו ראש לאומתם, והחשוב שבאומה ראוי להיות חשיבות זה יותר, ובשאר אומה אומר לפי מדריגה כל אחד ואחד נראה בו חשיבות זה. סוף סוף יש בשתי אומות שהיה דבר זה שהם מיוחדים בחשיבות. אף על גב דהוי כמה וכמה קסריים באדום שהיו גם כן חשובים, כיון שאמר "שני גוים בבטנך" אם כן פירוש הכתוב שני גאים שהיו יחד, כי כך משמע לשון "שני גאים", וזהו רבי ואנטונינוס שהיו יחד כמו יעקב ועשו, והיה נראה בהם חשיבות זה יותר, ובשאר—לפי מדריגת כל אחד ואחד. ומרמז על כלל ישראל ואדום שיש להם ענין מיוחד, שהם גיים, ורוצה לומר כי נפש חשוב יש להם, ונוהגים במאכל שלהם בחשיבות, וזהו שאמרו כי 'לא פסקו מעל שלחנם לא צנון ולא חזרת'. ורוצה בזה כי יש אוכל אכילתן כבהמה ואינו מחשיב עצמו, אבל ישראל ועשו אין נוהגין כך, רק מתקנין תקון הראוי לאדם להחשיב עצמו. וכן יש במסכת עבודה זרה (ב ע"ב) שאמרו אדום הרבה שווקים תקנינו, הרבה מרחצאות תקננו, והכל לעדן את נפשם. וכן אדום נוהגין עד היום במלבושיהם להתכבד מאד יותר משאר אומות, וגם בבניינים נאים...

VIII **מלבי"ם, שם**
שני גוים—ובא להורות ד' דברים, א] כי שני גוים בבטנך, שכל אחד יהיה גוי גדול, והורה כאלו כבר צר להם המקום לשבת יחדו מפני רבוים, ב] ושני לאומים...לאום מורה שיש להם דת ואמונה מיוחדת...ג] אחר כך ולאם מלאם יאמץ—רוצה לומר חוזק כל אחד יהיה נתלה בהחלשת כח השני...וזה ימשך עד עת קץ, ד] ואז רב יעבד צעיר...וזה גורם גם כן הפרוד, שעבודת הרב להצעיר הוא נגד טבע העולם, ולא יהיה זה מבלי ריב ומלחמה.

IX **מנורת המאור, סימן פג**
תנו רבנן, פעם אחת גזרה מלכות עכו"ם (רומי) גזרה על ישראל שלא למול את בניהם, ובאותו זמן נולד רבנו הקדוש, ואמר רבי שמעון בן גמליאל אביו, הקב"ה ציונו למול ורשעים הללו גזרו עלינו שלא למול, כיצד אנו מבטלים גזירתו של הקב"ה ונקיים גזרתו של אותו רשע?! מיד עמד רבי שמעון בן גמליאל ומל את בנו, כשהודיעו הדבר בפני ההגמון שהיה בעיר, שלח וקרא את רבי שמעון בן גמליאל, אמר לו, מפני מה עברת על גזירתו של מלך ומלת את בנך? אמר לו, כך ציונו הקב"ה, אמר לו אותו הגמון, הרבה כבוד יש לך עלי שאתה ראש לאומתך, אלא גזירתו של מלך היא ואיני יכול להניחך, אמר לו, ומה אתה מבקש? אמר לו אני רוצה שנשלח את הילד ואת אמו אצל המלך, ומה שהוא רוצה לעשות יעשה, אמר לו, עשה כל מה שאתה חפץ. מיד שלח את רבנו הקדוש ואת אמו והלכו כל היום בדרך, לערב הגיעו למלון של אביו של אנטונינוס בן אסוירוס, ובאותו הזמן נולד אנטונינוס, נכנסה אמו של רבינו הקדוש אצל אמו של אנטונינוס, אמרה לה, מה טיבך? אמרה לה, כך וכך גזרו עלינו שלא למול, ועכשיו מלתי את בני, ולכך מוליכין אותנו אל המלך באחד, כיון ששמעה כן אמרה לה, אם רצונך קחי את הילד שלי שאינו מהול, ותני לי את הילד שלך, ולכי ומלטי את נפשך ואת נפש בנך מאת המלך. מיד עשתה כן, והלכה למלך. נכנס אותו הגמון למלך אמר לו, אדוני המלך זו עברה על גזרתך

ומלה את בנה, ועכשיו הבאתי אותה אצלך, ומה שתרצה לעשות עשה, אמר להם המלך, ראו בנה אם הוא מהול, נמצא שאינו מהול. באותה שעה כעס המלך על אותו הגמון, אמר לו אני גוזרת על מהול ואתה הבאת לי שאינו מהול! באותה שעה היו גדולים יושבין לפני הקיסר ואמרו לו, אדוננו המלך, אנו מעידין בודאי שבנה של זו מהול היה, אלא אלהיהם של אלו קרוב הוא להם, וכיון שהם קוראים אליו מיד הוא עונה להם, שנאמר (דברים ד, ז) "כי מי גוי גדול אשר לו אלהים קרובים אליו כה' אלהינו בכל קראנו אליו", מיד ציוה המלך ונהרג אותו הגמון, וביטל את הגזרה, ושלח את רבנו הקדוש ואת אמו לשלום. כיון שחזרו לביתה של אנטונינוס אמרה אמו, הואיל ועשה לך הקב"ה נס על ידי ולבנך על ידי שיהיו בני שושבינים (-אוהבים וחברים) לעולם, ובשכר אותו חלב ששינק אנטונינוס מאמו של רבנו הקדוש, זכה ולמד תורה ושמש את רבינו הקדוש ונעשה מלך לאומתו וירש העולם הזה והעולם הבא ע"כ.

תוספות ד"ה אמר, עבודה זרה, י, ב   X

אמרינן במדרש חלב מטמא, חלב מטהר, כשנולד רבי גזרו שלא למול, ואביו ואמו מלוהו, שלח קיסר והביאו לרבי ולאמו לפניו, והחליפתו אמו באנטונינוס והניקתו עד שהביאתו לפני קיסר, ומצאוהו ערל ופטרום לשלום. ואמר אותו הגמון אני ראיתי שמלו את זה, אלא הקב"ה עושה להם נסים בכל עת, ובטלו הגזרה, ואמרינן נמי בירושלמי שלסוף למד אנטונינוס תורה ונתגייר ומל עצמו.

סדר הדורות, ג' אלפים תת"ק   XI

ואשת הקיסר הניקה את רבי ואמו של רבי הניקה את אנטונינוס.

סדר יעקב, עבודה זרה י, ב   XII

מציין רש"י במסכת בבא מציעא לג, ב שכתב דמשום הכי נתחברה אז המשנה, שהיה זמן שלום.

רש"י, בבא מציעא לג, ב   XIII

בימי רבי נשנית משנה זו—הא דקתני גמרא אין לך מדה גדולה מזו לפי שמשרבו תלמידי שמאי והלל שהיו לפניו שלשה דורות רבו מחלוקות בתורה ונעשית כשתי תורות מתוך עול שעבוד מלכיות וגזירות שהיו גוזרין עליהן ומתוך כך לא היו יכולים לתת לב לברר דברי החולקים עד ימיו של רבי שנתן הקב"ה לו בעיני אנטונינוס מלך רומי כדאמרינן בעבודה זרה (דף י:) ונחו מצרה ושלח וקבץ כל תלמידי ארץ ישראל ועד ימיו לא היו מסכתות סדורות אלא כל תלמיד ששמע דבר מפי גדול הימנו גרסה ונתן סימנים הלכה פלונית ופלונית שמעתי משם פלוני וכשנתקבצו אמר כל אחד מה ששמע ונתנו לב לברר טעמי המחלוקת דברי מי ראוין לקיים וסידרו המסכתות דברי נזיקין לבדם ודברי יבמות לבדם ודברי קדשים לבדם וסתם נמי במשנה דברי יחידים שראה רבי את דבריהם ושנאן סתם כדי לקבוע הלכה כמותם לפיכך אמרו בגמרא אין לך מדה גדולה מזו ושיתנו לב לטעמי המשנה.

דורות הראשונים, ר' יהודה הנשיא והמתיבתא פרק מג   XIV

ורק על ידי אשר רצו הרומיים לעשות יהודה יקר וגדולה לר' יהודה והממשלה עצמה פקדה על היהודים "יהודה שעילה יתעלה" רדו היהודים דבש מפקודה זו ויקיימו מעז יצא מתוק, וישיבו על ידי זה את דבר המתיבתא למקומה תחת יד ר' יהודה...

ושקטו רבנן ביומו דרבי משום שמדה רחמנותא דאיכא בין אנטונינוס ורבי ואסכים לתרוצי הלכתא...אבל על ידי מאורע כללי גדול מאד נשתנו אז פני הדברים, ור' יהודה הנשיא נתקרב אל הקיסר החדש, וכל הדברים נשתנו שינוי גדול לטובה.

מגלה עמוקות, אופן פג   XV

והתפלל משה בעת ההיא על אותו את שיתן הקב"ה חן לרבי אנטונינוס—"אעברה נא" נוטריקון א'נטונינוס ע'שה ב'ימי ר'בינו ה'קדוש נ'יצוץ א'חד, נמצא שיעקב ועשו שהיו תאומים היו ניצוץ אחד ונחלקו אחר כך לשתיים, וכבר אמרו רז"ל (ברכות נז:) שהשיב הקב"ה לרבקה שני גוים בבטנך על אנטונינוס ורבי שאז נתן עשו ויעקב.

עבודה זרה, י, ב   XVI

הוה ליה ההיא נקרתא דהוה עיילא מביתיה לבית רבי, כל יומא הוה מייתי תרי עבדי חד קטליה אבבא דבי רבי וחד קטליה אבבא דביתיה, א"ל בעידנא דאתינא לא נשכח גבר קמך

(-לא יהיה איש אצלך). יומא חד אשכחיה לר' חנינא בר חמא דהוה יתיב, אמר לא אמינא לך בעידנא דאתינא לא נשכח גבר קמך, א"ל לית דין בר איניש, א"ל אימא ליה לההוא עבדא דגני אבבא דקאים וליתי. אזל ר' חנינא בר חמא אשכחיה דהוה קטיל, אמר היכי אעביד אי איזיל ואימא ליה דקטיל, אין משיבין על הקלקלה, אשבקיה ואיזיל קא מזלזלינן במלכותא בעא רחמי עליה ואחייה ושדריה, אמר ידענא זוטי דאית בכו מחיה מתים, מיהו בעידנא דאתינא לא נשכח איניש קמך.

XVII **תוספות רי"ד, עבודה זרה י, ב**
רבי היה דר בציפורי ואנטונינוס היה הפלטורין שלו בראש טבריא על פסגה אחת, ושם יש מערה ההולכת מטבריא לציפורי מהלך י"ב מיל.

XVIII **בן יהוידע, שם**
נראה הענין כך, דהיה למלכי רומי עיר אחת בארץ ישראל ששמה קסרי שהם היו באים מרומי עיר המלוכה שלהם ויושבים שם בקסרי כמה חדשים ידועים בכל שנה כדי שתהיה ניכרת שליטה שלהם, וזו קסרי גם כן נחשבת עיר המלוכה שלהם, והיה שם המלך חצר גדול הראוי למושב המלך, וסביבותי' כמה חצרות למושב השרים שלו שהם קרובים לחצר המלך וסמוכים לו, ובזמן שאנטוטינוס בא בדרכו לעיר המלוכה זו קסרי שבארץ ישראל היה שולח אחר רבי לבוא מעיר טבריא שישב בעיר המלוכה, וכיון שהוא בא בתורת אורח היה נותן לו חצר מן החצירות הסמוכים לחצר המלך לדור בו, והיה מעיקרא נקירתא מחצר המלך לזה החצר שיושב בו רבי, כך היה בני מעיקרא כשבנו המקום הזה לאיזה סיבה או צורך אחד, ולכך היה בא אצל רבי דרך אותה נקירתא.

XIX **עבודה ברורה, עבודה זרה י, א**
בתוס' השלם שם מביא מרבינו אלעזר מגרמייזא דרבי ואנטונינוס עשו סימנים בזה אם יש אנשים אצל רבי. דאם היה על השלחן חזרת הסימן היה לאנטונינוס "חזור בך", דיש שם אנשים אחרים. ואם היה שם צנון הסימן היה דאין איש אצלי ואין איש עמדי בלשון "כצנה רצון תעטרנו" (תהלים ה, יג) כלומר בא אצלי ואין איש עמדי, עכ"ד. והקשה בסדר יעקב, דא"כ הול"ל מעל "שולחנו" והיינו מעל שולחן רבי, ולא מעל "שולחנם".

XX **עבודה זרה, י, א**
א"ל אנטונינוס לרבי בעינא דימלוך אסוירוס ברי תחותי ותתעביד טבריא קלניא, ואי אימא לה חדא עבדי תרי לא עבדי, אייתי גברא ארכביה אחבריה ויהב ליה יונה לעילאי בידיה, וא"ל לתתאה אימר לעילאי דלמפרח מן ידיה יונה, אמר שמע מינה הכי קאמר לי, את בעי מיניהו דאסוירוס ברי ימלוך תחותי, ואימא ליה לאסוירוס דתעביד טבריא קלניא.

XXI **עיון יעקב, שם**
...כי כנסת ישראל ליונה משולים...

XXII **עבודה ברורה, שם בשם יד אליהו**
ואי אימא להו חדא עבדי תרי לא עבדי—כי מלכותא דארעא כעין מלכותא דרקיעא והרי אנו רואין בימי ר' שמואל בר נחמני הוה כפנא ומותנא, אמרי היכי נעביד—ניבעי רחמי, אתרתי לא אפשר, הרי דאין מבקשין רחמים על שני דברים כאחד; וכן נפסק בטוש"ע, וע' ביומא דגם באורים ותומים אין שואלים על שני דברים כאחד, עכ"ל.

XXIII **עבודה זרה, י, א**
א"ל מצערין לי חשובי רומאי, מעייל ליה לגינא, כל יומא עקר ליה פוגלא ממשרא (-צנון מערוגה) קמיה, אמר שמע מינה הכי קאמר לי את קטול חד חד מינייהו ולא תתגרה בהו בכולהו. ולימא ליה מימר בהדיא, אמר שמעי חשובי רומי ומצערו ליה. ולימא ליה בלחש, משום דכתיב כי עוף השמים יוליך את הקול.

XXIV **בן יהוידע, שם**
ונ"ל בס"ד כי פוגלא הוא צנון כמ"ש הערוך וזה דרכו להיות הראש טמון בארץ והעלים נגלים למעלה, ורמז לו בזה על חשובי דרומאי שהיו מצערים את הקיסר בעצות רעות שמיעצים עליו בסתר וכל העצות הם יוצאים במרמות מהשכל שהוא במוח שבראשם שלהם וזה הראש שלהם שהוא מעין נובע העצות הוא טמון ונסתר ולכך הוא חושש מהם ורוצה לעוקרם.

XXV	**עבודה ברורה, עבודה זרה שם**
	מצערין לי חשובי [רומאי]—הטעם שציערוהו אולי י"ל משום שהלכה בידוע שעשו שונא ליעקב, ואנטונינוס שכבר נתן דעתו להיות מחובר לרבי הוליד לרבי שנאה אצלם מפני זה.
XXVI	**עבודה זרה, י, ב**
	הוה ליה ההוא ברתא דשמה גירא, קעבדה איסורא, שדר ליה גרגירא, שדר ליה כוסברתא (-כוס ברתא, שחוט הבת), שלח ליה כרתי (-יכרת זרעי), שלח ליה חסא (-חוס עלה).
XXVII	**רש"י, שם**
	עבדה איסורא—זנתה. שדר ליה—אנטונינוס לרבי עשב ששמו גרגירא רוק"א בלע"ז והבין רבי מה לי ולעשב הזה ודאי סימנא הוא דשלח לי גרגירא נגרר' ונמשך לב גירא עם הנואפים יודע היה ללמוד אנטונינוס. שדר ליה—רבי כוסברתא בלע"ז אלינאר"א כלומר שחוט הבת כוס ברתא שתי מלות. הדר שדר ליה—אנטונינוס כרתי בלע"ז פורי"ש כלומר אם כן יכרת זרעי. הדר שדר ליה חסא—לייטוג"א בלע"ז כלומר חוס עלה.
XXVIII	**תוספות, שם**
	שדר ליה כוסברתא. לפ"ה קשה מה עלה בדעתו של רבי מתחלה לומר שישחטנה ועוד קשה שלבסוף חזר בו רבי מעצמו לכך נראה כפירוש ר"ח והערוך שדר ליה גרגירא כלומר נאפה גירא הנואפת והנואפת תרגום ירושלמי גיירא וגיירתא שדר ליה כוסברתא כסה על קלונה והוכיחנה בסתר ואנטונינוס לא הבין מה ששלח לו והיה סבור שאמר שחוט הבת ושדר ליה כרתי כלומר וכי תתן לי עצה שיכרת זרעי שדר ליה חסא כלומר לא שלחתי לך אלא שתחוס עליה כלומר וכסה אותה אמרתי לך.
XXIX	**סנהדרין, צא, א-ב**
	אמר ליה אנטונינוס לרבי גוף ונשמה יכולין לפטור עצמן מן הדין ביצד גוף אומר נשמה חטאת שמיום שפירשה ממני הריני מוטל כאבן דומם בקבר ונשמה אומרת גוף חטא שמיום שפירשתי ממנו הריני פורחת באויר כצפור אמר ליה אמשול לך משל למה הדבר דומה למלך בשר ודם שהיה לו פרדס נאה והיה בו בכורות נאות והושיב בו שני שומרים אחד חיגר ואחד סומא אמר לו חיגר לסומא בכורות נאות אני רואה בפרדס בא והרכיבני ונביאם לאכלם רכב חיגר על גבי סומא והביאום ואכלום ושקטו רבן ביומו דרבי מכל שמדה משום רחמנותא דאיכא בין אנטונינוס ורבי ואסכים לתרוצי הלכתא...אבל על ידי מאורע כללי גדול מאד נשתנו אז פני הדברים, ור' יהודה הנשיא נתקרב אל הקיסר החדש, וכל הדברים נשתנו שינוי גדול לטובה...לימים בא בעל פרדס אמר להן בכורות נאות היכן הן אמר לו חיגר כלום יש לי רגלים להלך בהן אמר לו סומא כלום יש לי עינים לראות מה עשה הרכיב חיגר על גבי סומא ודן אותם כאחד אף הקב"ה מביא נשמה וזורקה בגוף ודן אותם כאחד שנאמר (תהלים נ, ד) יקרא אל השמים מעל ואל הארץ לדין עמו יקרא אל השמים מעל זו נשמה ואל הארץ לדין עמו זה הגוף.
XXX	**רס"ג, אמונות והדעות מאמר הששישי מהות הנפש**
	כי הנפש והגוף יחדיו פעל א', כאשר קדם בתחלת היצירה, (בראשית ב, ז) וייצר יי' אלהים את האדם עפר מן האדמה ויפח באפיו נשמת חיים. וכן המה שניהם גמול אחד ועונש א'.
XXXI	**אזנים לתורה, ויקרא ד, ב**
	דבר אל בני ישראל לאמר נפש כי תחטא—החטאים מתיחסים לגוף ולנשמה כאחד, שהרי הגוף יטעון ביום הדין, שמיום שיצאה ממנו הנשמה אינו חוטא, והיא גם היא תטעון, שמיום שנפרדה מהגוף אינה חוטאת, וכדי לדון אותם יהי' צורך להחזיר את הנשמה אל הגוף ולדון אותם כמו שחטאו, ולמה יחס כאן הכתוב את החטא רק אל הנפש? מפני שבמעשי הגוף א"א להכיר אם הדבר נעשה בשוגג או במזיד.
XXXII	**סנהדרין, צא, ב**
	א"ל אנטונינוס לרבי מפני מה חמה יוצאה במזרח ושוקעת במערב, א"ל אי הוה איפכא נמי הכי הוה אמרת לי, א"ל הכי קאמינא לך מפני מה שוקעת במערב, א"ל כדי ליתן שלום לקונה, שנאמר וצבא השמים לך משתחוים, א"ל ותיתי עד פלגא דרקיע ותתן שלמא ותיעול, משום פועלים ומשום עוברי דרכים.

XXXIII **יד רמה, סנהדרין צ"א, ב**

אמר ליה אנטונינוס לרבי חמה מפני מה שוקעת במערב כך היה נראה לאנטונינוס שחמה מהלכת ביום ממזרח למערב על פני הרקיע כלפי הארץ ובערב שוקעת במערב בעביו של רקיע וחוזרת וסובבת כל הלילה אחורי הרקיע ממזרח למזרח על גבי הקשת שהלכה על פניו ביום כלפי הארץ וכשמגעת בסוף הלילה למזרח בוקעת ברקיע ויוצאה ומהלכת על פני הקשת ההיא עד שמגעת למערב—ולפיכך שאל אנטונינוס את ר' מפני מה שוקעת במערב ואינה סובבת את הרקיע אחורי הרקיע כיפה כל הלילה למקום שתחזור לבקר ותזרח ור' השיב לו תשובה לפי דעת השואל וסברתו והיינו דאמר ליה כדי ליתן שלום לקונה שהשכינה במערב וכיון שהיא מגת למערב היא שוקעת שם ליתן שלום ושקיעתה זו היא השתחותה ואקשי ליה ותיתי עד פלגא דרקיעא ותן שלום ותיעול שכן דרך כבוד להשתחות מרחוק ואי משום דבציר יומא תשהה בהילוכה טפי אמר ליה משום פועלים ומשום עוברי דרכים אלו היתה שוקעת בחצי השמים נמצאת שוקעת מתוך חוזק אורה ולא היה אדם מרגיש בשעת שקיעתה והיו פועלין שוהין במלאכתן בשדות עד שחשיכה ועוברי דרכים מהלכין בדרך ולא היו מבקשין בית לינה מבעוד יום לפי שהיו סבורין שעדיין היום גדול ונמצא היום מחשיך עליהם פתאום.

XXXIV **סנהדרין, צ"א, ב**

ואמר ליה אנטונינוס לרבי מאימתי יצר הרע שולט באדם משעת יצירה או משעת יציאה, א"ל משעת יצירה, א"ל אם כן בועט במעי אמו ויוצא, אלא משעת יציאה, אמר רבי דבר זה למדני אנטונינוס ומקרא מסייעו, שנאמר לפתח חטאת רובץ.

XXXV **ר' מרדכי לוי, מחוברת אדר תשס"א סימן יט**
http://www.ateret4u.com

ושמעתי באומרים לי להעיר בזה ממה שכתב רש"י בפ' תולדות על הפסוק "ויתרוצצו הבנים בקרבה" שרבותינו דרשוהו לשון ריצה, כשהיתה עוברת על פתחי תורה וכו' עוברת על פתחי עבודת אלילים עשו מפרכס לצאת. ע"ש. הרי שיצה"ר שלט על עשו גם בהיותו בתוך מעי אמו. וזה עומד מנגד למה שהסכים רבנו הקדוש. על כן אמרתי לשנות פרק זה כפי אשר תשיג ידי בס"ד. מריבים בנחלת שני עולמות. יש מקשים למה היו עתה מריבים בתוך הבטן בשני עולמות, ועוד אם האחד נצח השני—וכי יקח בבטן העולם ממנו, ועוד עולם הבא—אשר יחפוץ ויבחר בו השם הוא הקדוש ויקרב אותו לו (עפ"י במדבר ט"ו, ה), ויש לך לדעת כי יעקב ועשו אינם משותפים יחד בעולם, לפי שהם מציאות מצד עצמם מתנגדים יחד, ולכך לא היו יכולים לעמוד יחד בבטן אמם, כי בטן אמם הוא דבר אחד משותף לשני דברים שהם מתנגדים זה לזה, ולפיכך אף שעדיין היו בבטן אמם היו מתנגדים זה לזה, כי מאחר שבעצם מציאות הם מתנגדים—אין להם שתוף ביחד, כמו אש ומים, שאף על גב שאין דעת ורצון בהם הם מתנגדים בצד עצמם, ואין עמידה להם.

XXXVI **עבודה זרה, י, ב**

כל יומא הוה משמש לרבי מאכיל ליה משקי ליה, כי הוה בעי רבי למיסק לפוריא (-למטה) הוה גחין קמי פוריא א"ל סק עילוואי לפורייך, אמר לאו אורח ארעא לזלזולי במלכותא כולי האי, אמר מי ישימני מצע תחתיך לעולם הבא.

XXXVII **תורת חיים, שם**

נראה דהיינו הא דכתיב ורב יעבוד צעיר פשטא דקרא משמע דבמלך איירי מדכתיב ברישא ולאום מלאום יאמץ קאי ועליה עבד צעיר ורב ולא אשכחן בשום מקום שנתקיימה נבואה זו שהיה מלך עשו עבד ליעקב אם לא בהך עובדא…ונראה דמהאי טעמא קבל מיניה רבי שישמשנו, ולא חש לזלזולא דשלטון.

XXXVIII **מראית העין, שם**

אנטונינוס היה הטוב שהיה בעשו ורבינו הקדוש היה ניצוץ יעקב אבינו, ובא אנטונינוס עתה לתקן אשר עיות עם יעקב ולכן היה משמש לו וזה היה תיקונו ולכך היה מקבל ממנו רבינו הקדוש, ומיהו אמר לו לאו אורח ארעא לזלזולי במלכותא כולי האי—אורח ארעא דייקא שאינו דרך ארץ, והשיבו מי יתנני.

XXXIX	**עבודה זרה, י, ב**
	כל יומא הוה שדר ליה דהבא פריכא במטראתא (-שק גדול) וחיטי אפומייהו, אמר להו אמטיו חיטי לרבי, אמר ליה רבי לא צריכנא אית לי טובא, אמר ליהו למאן דבתרך דיהבי לבתראי דאתו בתרך ודאתי מינייהו ניפוק עלייהו (-היוצאים מבניך יוציאו הוצאות למלכי רומי העומדים אחרי על סמך הממון הזה).
XL	**בן יהוידע, שם**
	ומה שהיה שולח לו מטרתא דדהבא פריכא וחיטי אפומייהו רמז לו בזה על תורה שבכתב ותורה שבעל פה אשר בקרבו כי התורה שבעל פה נקראת זהב כמו שאמרו רז"ל על פסוק וזהב הארץ ההיא טוב, ותורה שבכתב נקראת תבואה כמו שאמרו רז"ל (מכות י, ב) על פסוק (קהלת ה, ט) מי בהמון לא תבואה וכן הוא אמר (משלי ה, ט) לבו לחמו בלחמי.
XLI	**צרור המור, בראשית כה, כב; במדבר יא, טז**
	בצרור המור כתב, דיש כאן רמז לשני סוגי הלימוד, האחד תורת הנגלה, והשני תורת הנסתר והסוד, כי בעת גידול הצנון נשארים ראשו ועליו מגולים, משא"כ בעת גידול החזרת היא מכוסה לגמרי ונטמנת בתוך הקרקע, ובזה פירש שאנטונינוס ורבי שלא פסקו מעל שולחנם דהיינו שלמדו ועסקו ביחד ב"צנון" הרומז לתורת הנגלה כצנון שהוא מגולה, וב"חזרת" הרומזת לתורה הנסתר כחזרת הנטמנת ונסתרת תוך הקרקע עכ"ד.
XLII	**בראשית רבה, פרשה עה סימן ה**
	כה תאמרון לאדוני לעשו—רבינו אמר לרבי אפס, כתוב חד אגרא מן שמי למרן מלכא אנטונינוס. קם וכתב, מן יהודה נשיאה למרן מלכא אנטונינוס. נסביה וקריה וקרעיה(-נטלה וקראה וקרעה). אמר ליה, כתוב מן עבדך יהודה למרן מלכא אנטונינוס. אמר ליה, רבי, מפני מה אתה מבזה על כבודך? אמר ליה, מה אני טב מן סבי? לא כך אמר [יעקב], כה תאמרו לאדוני לעשו, כה אמר עבדך יעקב.
XLIII	**עבודה זרה, י, ב**
	כי שכיב אנטונינוס אמר רבי נתפרדה חבילה.
XLIV	**בן יהוידע, שם**
	קשה מאי קמ"ל. דהא כ"ע ידעי לה, ונ"ל בס"ד בא להודיע אל תחשבו כשם שהיינו חברים בעוה"ז ורואין זא"ז כן יהיה בעוה"ב, אלא נתפרדה חבילה, דאיך יבא אנטונינוס גר צדק למחיצתו של רבינו הקדוש, וכאשר אמר הוא עצמו מי ישימני מצע תחתיך לעוה"ב.
XLV	**חתם סופר, בראשית כה, כג**
	שני גוים בבטנך גיים כתיב זה אנטונינוס ורבי, ר"ל כי גיים אם תחשוב מ"ם סתומה לשש מאות יעלה כמו ג' כתר לומר ששניהם נבחרו בשלשה כתרים כתר מלכות ותורה ושם טוב, כי רבי היה ג"כ כמו מלך נשיא בישראל...ואנטונינוס היה לו גם כן כתר תורה...
XLVI	**תורת משה (לחתם סופר), בראשית כה, כג**
	והנה תחלת כוונת יצירת הבנים האלו הי' שיהי' יעקב וכל זרעו לעולם ממלכת כהני' וגוי קדוש נשיא אלקי' בעולם, ועשו כזבולון, נותן לתוך פיו של ישראל כזבולון, וא"כ יהיה כל ישראל לעולם כמו רבי בדורו וכל עשו לעולם כאנטונינוס, רבי נשיא אלקים ונהג בו אנטונינוס כבוד גדול כתלמיד לרבי ורבי נהג כבוד באנטונינוס כמו לכל קיסר רומי, אך כל זה הי' כל זמן שהיה בבטן אמם בתחלת יצירה שני גיים זה אנטונינוס ורבי ב'ב'ט'נ'ך' דייקא.

SECTION VI: SUMMARY

APPENDIX A: TARGUM SHIVIM

I	**רש"י, מגילה, ט, א**
	אלהים ברא בראשית—את השמים, שלא יאמר בראשית שם הוא, ושתי רשויות הן, וראשון ברא את השני.

II	**תוספות, שם**

אלהים ברא בראשית—פירש הקונטרס שאם כתבו בראשית ברא היו אומרים בראשית שם הוא ושתי רשויות הן. וקשה שהרי בראשית אין שם כלל אלא בתחלה. ועוד שכתבו לו בלשון יונית בתחלה. ונ"ל שהיונים היו יודעים שלעולם יש להזכיר הבורא בתחילה ואם כן אלו כתבו בראשית קודם היה אומר דעת שתי רשויות הן והתיבה הראשונה הוי בורא אחד ואלהים הוי השני משום הכי הפכו לו.

III	**מהרש"א, מגילה, ט,א**

ובספר פענח רזי בשם ספר לקח טוב נתן טעם לענין כדאמרינן שלא יאמר האדם לה' קרבן אלא קרבן לה' דשמא יתחרט בתוך דבורו ולא יסיים ונמצא מוציא שם שמים לבטלה הכי נמי הכא אם היה אומר אלהים ברא והיה פוסק ולכך התחיל בראשית עכ"ל. ולפי שהמינים יכחישו כל זה ויאמרו דראוי להתחיל בשמו ואילו כתבו בראשית ברא אלהים יבא זה להכריחם שיאמרו ודלכך לא פתחה התורה בשמו על שיש חסרון בחקו ח"ו. וכפי דעות המופסדות אשר למינים שיהיה פי' בראשית בתחלה ברא מי שברא אלהים שהא' ברא את הב' ושני רשויות הן ח"ו והמקרא קצר וחסר ממנו אלהים הפועל שאלתים הכתוב בקרא הוא אלהים הפועל ומצינו במקראות שחסר מהם הפועל או שיפרשו כי בתחלה ברא אלהים ולבסוף ברא אלהים אחר וב' רשויות הן או שיפרשו כי בתחלה וראשית הבריאה עשה אבל כל התולדות אח"כ אינו בידו ונתן ביד המערכות כי עזב את הארץ. ומשום הכי הפכו לו לכתוב אלהים ברא בראשית כדי שלא יהא להם שום מכריח לפרש הכתוב בכל דעות המופסדות הללו אלא כפשטיה אלהים ברא בראשית ולהכחיש דעות אלו המינים אנו אומרים בכל יום ובטובו מחדש בכל יום תמיד מעשה בראשית.

IV	**תורה תמימה, בראשית א, א**

מפני שכבוד הוא להתחיל התורה בשם ה', ועיין מש"כ בדרשא הקודמת למה באמת לא התחילה התורה כן.

וטעם השינוי כאן שכתבו לו אלהים ברא בראשית פירש"י שלא יאמר בראשית שם הוא ושתי רשויות הן וראשון ברא את השני, עכ"ל, והתוס' הקשו שהרי בראשית אינו שם כלל אלא באורו בתחלה, ועוד הלא כתבו לו בלשון יונית בתחלה, עיי' מש"כ בזה. ונראה לפרש דברי רש"י עפ"י דרכו, דהכוונה היא כמש"כ למעלה דכבוד הוא להתחיל התורה בשם ה', ומדלא התחילה כן יש לחוש שלא יאמר דהשם אלהים הוא מהנבראים כמו שמים וארץ, ויהי' שיעור הכתוב בראשית ברא [הסבה הראשונה] את אלהים ואת השמים ואת הארץ.

V	**נחלת יעקב, בראשית א, א**

...ששינו הזקינים לתלמי המלך וכתבו אלקים ברא בראשית. ופי' רש"י שלא יאמרו שני רשויות הם, ובראשית שם הוא, וברא אלקים עיי"ש. והקשו בתוספות שם דהא כתבו הפי' של בראשית בלשון יונית......ולפענ"ד נראה לפרש, דהנה במורה נבוכים הביא דעת אריסטו שהעולם קדמון.

VI	**רמב"ן, בהקדמתו לספר בראשית**

עוד יש בידינו קבלה של אמת כי כל התורה כולה שמותיו של הקדוש ברוך הוא.

VII	**מהרש"א, מגילה ט, א**

כתבו לו אעשה אדם כו'. כפרש"י שלא יאמרו ב' רשויות הן והוא לא יקבל מ"ש ר"י פ"ד דסנהדרין כ"מ שפקרו המינים תשובתן בצידן נעשה אדם וגו' ויברא אלהים וגו' הנה נרדה וגו' וירד אלהים וגו' ונכתבו מעיקרא בלשון רבים דא"ר' אין הקב"ה עושה דבר אא"כ נמלך בפמליא של מעלה כו' וענינו כפרש"י בחומש שהוא ממדת הענוה שיהא הגדול נמלך בקטן והוא ע"פ ב"ר ע"ש אך מה שהוסיף רש"י בחומש ולפי שהאדם בדמות המלאכים ויתקנאו בו לפיכך נמלך בהם כו' הוא ע"פ מ"ש במסכת סנהדרין שם בשעה שבקש הקב"ה לבראות האדם כו' א"ל' רצונכם נעשה אדם אמרו מה אנוש כי תזכרנו וגו' ע"ש מזה נראה כי מפני קנאת המלאכים נמלך עמהם לפי שנברא כדמותם ורש"י הרכיב בפירוש החומש דברי התלמוד ודברי הב"ר לענין אחד לפי שב' הטעמים קרובים לענין אחד.

VIII	**תורה תמימה, בראשית א, כו**

ולא ככתוב בלשון רבים כדי שלא יאמר שתי רשויות הן. ומה שבאמת כתיב בלשון רבים הוא משום דמדרך הכבוד והגדולה כך הוא, וכמו במלך בו"ד שמדבר בלשון רבים, אלא שתלמי לא

היה מקבל זה מפני שאולי היה רוצה למצוא עילה בתורת משה. ונראה דאע"פ שהיו יכולים להביא לו ראיה דרשות אחת בבריאה מדכתיב בפסוק הסמוך ויברא אלהים את האדם וכמ"ש בדרשא הבאה, בכ"ז לא היו רוצים להתוכח אתו הרבה וכמ"ש כהאי גונא בתמיד ל"ב א' באלכסנדר מוקדון וזקני הנגב, יעו"ש ולפנינו לעיל בפסוק א'. ומה שנוגע עוד לאגדה זו לעיל בפ' בראשית ברא אלהים, יעו"ש וצרף לכאן.

IX — תורה תמימה, בראשית ב, ב

כדי שלא יאמר דביום השביעי גמר מלאכתו, ובאמת הוי באור הלשון ויכל ביום השביעי—שליום השביעי כבר כלתה המלאכה, וכמו באור הלשון אך ביום הראשון תשביתו שאור (פרשת בא) שפירושו שליום הראשון של חג כבר יהיה נשבת, ומה שלא בארו בזה לפני תלמי הוא משום דאולי לא הי' מקבל פירוש זה, מפני שאולי הי' רוצה למצוא עילה בתורת משה כמש"כ ריש פרשה הקודמת.

X — רש"י, מגילה, ט, א

זכר ונקבה בראו ולא כתבו בראם—דמשמע שני גופין בכל אחד זכר ונקבה שני פרצופין לכך כתבו בראו שכך נברא אדם בשני פרצופים.

XI — בראשית א, כז

ויברא אלהים את האדם בצלמו בצלם אלהים ברא אותו, זכר ונקבה ברא אותם.

XII — מהרש"א, מגילה, ט, א

זכר ונקבה בראו ולא כתבו בראם כו'. פרש"י דבראם משמע שני גופין ברא כ"א זכר ונקבה ב' פרצופין כו' עכ"ל. ר"ל דאינך קראי לא משתמעי כן דכתיב ויברא אלהים את האדם בצלמו וגו' בצלם אלהים ברא אותו דמשמע דגוף א' האדם נברא מתחלה כדאמרינן פרק הרואה ובפרק קמא דכתובות. ולפי זה נראה לפרש בפשיטות טפי דבראם משמע שני גופין ואינך קראי משמעם דגוף א' נבראו מתחלה וכדאמרינן קראי בפרק הרואה ובפ' עושין פסין ובפ"ק דכתובות, כתיב בצלם אלהים ברא אותו וכתיב זכר ונקבה בראם כו'. ותלמי לא יקבל מדרש חכמים שם כיצד עלה במחשבה לבראות שנים ולבסוף נברא אחד ולכך שינו לו לכתוב בראו דמשמע נמי דנברא גוף א' וקרוב לזה פי' בע"י בשם התוס'.

XIII — תורה תמימה, בראשית, ה, ב

דבראם משמע שני גופין ברא כל אחד זכר ונקבה, וע' בירושלמי מגילה פ"א ה"ט ובפי' קרבן עדה, ודבריו צ"ע. ובדבר תכונת זה המלך וכונתו בהעתקת התורה בארנו בר"פ בראשית, יעו"ש.

XIV — בן יהוידע, מגילה, ט, א

וקשה מה תואנה ומה עלילה הי' לו למצוא, אי הוה משמע הכי, ונ"ל בס"ד כי בתורה לא כתיב אלא שם אדם לזכר ושם חוה לנקבה, ואם הי' מניח במנוחה ששני גופים כל אחד מהם יש בו זכר ונקבה, הי' אומר שמות אדם וחוה המה של זכר ונקבה בגוף אחד, וצריך שיש ב' שמות אחרים לזכר ונקבה של גוף השני ואיה הם השמות בתורה, וא"כ מוכרח לומר שהחסרת דברים מן התורה, דודאי הי' כתוב שתי שמות עוד לזכר ונקבה של גוף השני והחסרת אותם, וא"כ כמו שהחסרתם זה החסרתם דברים אחרים, והי' עושה עי"כ עלילות ברשע לומר כו"כ הי' כתוב בתורה, ואתם עקרתם דברים אלו ממנה.

XV — תורה תמימה, בראשית, יא, ז

ומה דכתיב באמת בלשון רבים, הוא משום דמדרך הגדולה והכבוד כך הוא, וכמו במלך בו"ד שמדבר בעדו בלשון רבים, כנודע, אלא שתלמי לא הי' מקבל זה הבאור, מפני שאולי הי' רוצה למצוא עילה בתורת משה, ואע"פ שהיו יכולים להוכיח לו מדכתיב מיד וירד ה' לשון יחיד [עי' בדרשא הבאה], אך בנוסחת ההעתקה לא היו יכולים לברר זה, ובין כה הי' מתאנה להם, ומה שנוגע עוד לדרשא זו ולענין הכינוס בכלל עיין מש"כ לעיל ר"פ בראשית.

XVI — תורה תמימה, בראשית, יח, יב

פירש"י שלא יאמר תלמי כי על אברהם דכתיב בי' (פרשת לך) ויצחק, לא הקפיד, ועל שרה הקפיד, ולכן כתבו לו ותצחק בקרוביה, ולכן הקפיד, עכ"ל. ולולא דבריו י"ל בטעם ששינו לשון זה משום דבאמת קשה דכיון דצחקה בקרבה מניין להכתוב כל עיקר דבר זה שצחקה, ובאמת במ"ר הרגישו בזה ואמרו שברוח הקודש נודע שצחקה, ולפי"ז חששו שמא ישאל תלמי שאלה

זו מאין ידעו זה, ואת דרשת המ"ר שברוה"ק נודע לא יקבל, ולכן כתבו לו בקרוביה הרי צחקה בפרהסיא. ובדבר תכונת זה המלך והעתקת התורה ע"י כתבנו לעיל בריש פרשת בראשית.

XVII **שארית יעקב, מגילה, ט, א**
...וביאר דבזמן שהצדיק נופל ממדרגתו זה גורם שכל העולם ג"כ נופלים ממדרגתן...ולפ"ז י"ל דהיה פשוט לחכמים המתרגמים לתלמי המלך דבזמן שצחקה שרה בקרבה זה גרם דגם קרוביה דהיינו הנשמות המקושרים לה ג"כ נפלו ממדרגתם...

XVIII **רש"י, מגילה, ט, א**
הרגו שור—שלא יאמר רצחנים היו אבותיכם שהרי אביהם מעיד עליהם שהם הרגו איש לכך כתבו שור שלא היו חשובין בעיניו אלא כבהמות ולא הקפיד על הבהמות.

XIX **מהרש"א, מגילה, ט, א**
כי באפם הרגו שור וברצונם וגו'. כפרש"י דלפי שינוי נמי ודאי דלא נתבוננו נמי רק על שכם ואנשי עירו דודאי לא כתבו לו דבר שקר שלא היה כמ"ש התוס' לקמן גבי זאטוטי כו'. ויש לדקדק גם שמטעם זה כפרש"י שינו רישא דקרא מ"מ סיפא דקרא ששינו וברצונם עקרו אבוס מי הכריחם לכך, וע"ק ברישא דקרא שכוונו על שכם למה שינו לקרוא שור ולא בהמה סתם. והנראה בזה כי פי' הכתוב לדעתם כולו על שכם ועירו כפי' התרגום ברוגזיהון קטלו קטול וברעותיהון תרעו שור שנאה א"נ פי' הכתוב הוא כי באפם הרגו שכם הוא איש ושכם הוא משל עיר הרגו באף על שטמא דינה אחותם וברצונם שלא באף עקרו שור דהיינו אנשי עירו שלא פשעו כך נראה לפרש בפ' הוציאו גבי ארור דאין לו הכרע שפרש"י על הרגע עקרו שור ארור שור על שכם שהוא מארור כנען או כו' ע"ש. והשתא ניחא דלפי מה ששינו לו נמי יתפרש כן כי באפם הרגו שור הוא שכם דנחשב כשור וברצונם עקרו אבוס הוא מקום השור שהם אנשי עירו וכדי שלא לשנות הרבה מלשון הכתוב כתיב בסיפא דקרא שור כתבו לו מלת שור בריש דקרא ולא לשון בהמה ועניו שלא יאמר רצחנים היו כו' כפרש"י דודאי לא היו רצחנים על הריגתם שהיו כולם חייבים מיתה כדברי הרמב"ן שהי"ז"ע"ז אלא דאי הוו כתבו לו הרגו איש היה לו לבעל דין לחלוק ולומר שע"כ היה יעקב מקפיד על ההריגה כאילו הרגו איש וע"כ שינו לו הרגו שור גו' שלא היה מקפיד רק כאילו הרגו בהמה ועקרו אבוס בהמה.

XX **תורה תמימה, בראשית מט, ו**
כי הוא כוון למצוא עילה בתורת משה, ולכן כתבו לו עקרו אבוס ולא איש, שלא יאמר רוצחים הם. ובפרטיות מתכונת ומטרת תלמי בהעתקה זו כתבנו לעיל ר"פ בראשית.

XXI **מהרש"א, מגילה, ט, א**
ויקח משה וגו' נושא בני אדם כו'. פרש"י דמשמע גמל שלא יאמר כו' ע"ש פי' דמשמע נמי גמל דאי הוה דוקא משמע גמל ולא חמור א"כ הוו כתבו לו שקר והתוס' כתבו לקמן גבי זאטוטי וגו' שלא רצו לשקר לו דאי הוה רצו לשקר לו ה"ל לכתבו וירכיבם על הגמל ובמדרשות יש לכך כתיב החמור בה"א הידיעה שזהו החמור שחבש אברהם לעקידת יצחק והוא שעתיד להגלות עליו מלך המשיח אבל תלמי לא יקבל זה.

XXII **תורה תמימה, שמות, ד, כ**
פירשו רש"י ותוס' בטעם שנוי זה שלא יאמר וכי לא היה למשה רכבכם סוס או גמל, עכ"ל ואין זה מבואר כלל, דהא מצינו גם באברהם שהיה עשיר והיו לו סוסים וגמלים ובכ"ז כתיב ביה ויחבוש את חמורו, ויתכן קצת לומר ע"פ הדרשה הקודמת, שאין נאות להזכיר רכיבה באשה, ויותר מזה מגונה רכיבה על החמור, לכן שינו לכתוב וירכיבם על נושא בני אדם, דלשון זה מורה יותר לשון מכובד. ודע שפשטות העניין מורה שיראו שמא הוא מבקש למצוא עילה בדברי התורה, וע"ע מש"כ בענין זה ר"פ בראשית.

XXIII **בן יהוידע, מגילה, ט, א**
...פירש רש"י דמשמע גמל. ובתוספות כתבו פן יאמר להם וכי לא היה לו למשה רכבכם סוס או גמל ע"ש...מה הוסיפו ומה חידשו התוספות על פירוש רש"י ז"ל. ופירש להם דרש"י לא כתב וכי לא היה לו וכו' אלא כתב שלא יאמר משה רכבכם לא היה לו סוס או גמל.

XXIV **תורה תמימה, שמות, יב, מ**
אולי כוון זה המלך למצוא עילה בתורת משה וכמש"כ בפרשת שמות בפסוק וירכיבם על

החמור, עיי"ש, ושינו כאן כדי שלא יאמר שאין החשבון מכוון, שהרי קהת מיורדי מצרים היה וכשאתה מונה שנותיו של קהת ועמרם ומשה כולן ביחד אין מגיעות לארבע מאות שנה, וכש"כ שהרבה משנות הבנים נבלעות בתוך שני האבות, אלא שמנה הכתוב מיום שנגזרה גזירת גלות מצרים בין הבתרים ומשה עד שנולד יצחק שלשים שנה ומשנולד יצחק עד שיצאו ממצרים ארבע מאות שנה, צא מהם שלשים של יצחק וק"ל שחי יעקב כשבא למצרים נשארו מאתים ועשר, וכן היתה הגזירה כי גר יהיה זרעך בארץ לא להם ולא כתוב בארץ מצרים וכשנולד יצחק היה אברהם גר בארץ פלשתים ומאז עד שיצאו ממצרים נמצא יצחק וזרעו שהם זרעו של אברהם גרים ושלשים שנה קודם לכן לא נמנו בגזירה דהא זרעך כתיב.

XXV **תורה תמימה, שמות, כד, ה**

משום דנערי הוא לשון קטנה ויאמר גרועים שבכם שלחתם לקבל פני שכינה, וזאטוטי הוא לשון חשיבות כמו זוטו של ים [ב"מ כ"א ב' ועיי"ש ברש"י] ומבואר בגמרא גם בפסוק י"א דכתיב לפנינו ואל אצילי בני ישראל שינו ג"כ ואל זאטוטי, ואע"פ דשם אין מוכרח הדבר, אך רצו להתאים הלשונות שהם ענין אחד, וע"ע מש"כ בעניני תכונת זה המלך תלמי ותכלית העתקת התורה ע"י הזקנים לעיל ס"פ שמות בפסוק וירכיבם על החמור.

XXVI **שבת, קיט, ב**

אמר ריש לקיש משום רבי יהודה נשיאה אין העולם מתקיים אלא בשביל הבל תינוקות של בית רבן א"ל רב פפא לאביי דידי ודידך מאי א"ל אינו דומה הבל שיש בו חטא להבל שאין בו חטא.

XXVII **רש"י, מגילה, ט, א**

לא חמד אחד מהם נשאתי—כדי שלא יאמר תלמי חמור לא לקח אבל חפץ אחר לקח וענין הדבר בכלל.

XXVIII **שפתי חכמים, שם**

והוא במחלקותו של קרח ועדתו עם משה ובדרש י"ל שהיו צריכין לשנות כאן, שהרי פרש"י לא חמור אחד מהם נטלתי, אפילו כשהלכתי ממדין למצרים, והרכבתי את אשתי ואת בני על החמור, והיה לי ליטול אותו חמור משלהם, לא נטלתי אלא משלי עכ"ל וא"כ מאחר שהם לא כתבו ויקח משה אשתו ובניו וירכיבם על החמור, אלא שינו וכתבו וירכיבם על נושאי בני אדם עיי"ש לכן על כרח' לפרש"י היו צריכין לשנות כאן חמד והכוונה כמו שפרש"י.

XXIX **תורה תמימה, דברים, ד, יט**

ולולא הוספת מלה זו היה דן שמותר לב"נ לעבוד עבודה זרה, דהיה מפרש אשר חלק שהחליק להם את העבודה זרה כחלק לשם אלהות, ואע"פ דבדרשה הקודמת נתבאר פירוש המלה אשר חלק שהחליקן בדברים כדי לטורדן מן העולם, אך כמובן לא היה אפשר לבאר זה לתלמי.

XXX **רש"י, מגילה, ט, ב**

אשר לא צויתי לעובדם—שאם לא כתבו לעובדם משמע אשר לא צויתי שיהיו א"ב אלהות הן שעל כורחו נבראו.

XXXI **מהרש"א, מגילה, ט, ב**

אשר לא צויתי לעובדם כו'. פרש"י שאם כתבו לעובדם הוה משמע ליה אשר לא צויתי שיהיו כו' ע"ש דמצינו לשון צווי גבי בריאה כי הוא צוה ונבראו, ובירושלמי איתא הגירסא אשר לא צויתי לאומות לעובדם ולפי זה יש לפרש דאם לא שינו לכתוב מלת לאומות היה קשיא ליה מאי אשר לא צוה לעבדם הא בישראל בדרבה מיניה שצוה להם בכמה כתובים באזהרה גם שלא לעבדם ולכך שינו לו לכתוב לאומות שלא צוה להם לעבדם ומיהו שלא לעבדם נמי אינו מפורש באומות דתלמי לא יאמין שהנכרים מצוה על ע"ז.

XXXII **מגילה, ט, ב**

וכתבו לו את צעירות הרגלים ולא את הארנבת מפני שאשתו של תלמי ארנבת שמה שלא יאמר שחקו בי היהודים והטילו שם אשתי בתורה.

XXXIII **שפתי חכמים, שם**

מפני שאשתו של תלמי וכו' ובירושלמי איתא מפני שאמו של תלמי ארנבת שמה עי"ש והנה יש מוחל יותר על כבוד אמו מכבוד אשתו, ויש ג"כ להיפך. שלא יאמר שחקו בי היהודים

XXXIV	והטילו שם אשתי בתורה. י"ל בדיוק נקט 'הטילו' ולא נקט 'וכתבו' דלכאורה מאחר שהתורה היא כבר כתובה מכמה שנים רבים קודם היות משפחת תלמי המלך בעולם, וא"כ האיך יכול לומר כן, לכן נקט בדיוק שיאמר 'שהטילו' שם אשתו בתורה ר"ל מעצמם הטילו כן בין התיבות ובין החיות הטמאות ודו"ק. **רש"י, שם**
XXXV	וכתבו—במקום ואת הארנבת ואת צעירת הרגלים לפי שידיה קצרות וקטנות מרגליה. **בן יהוידע, שם** וקשה לפי"ז הו"ל לכתוב צעירת הידים. ונ"ל בס"ד דאשתו של תלמי היתה משונה בידיה שהיו קצרות הרבה לפי שלא כדרך בני אדם, ומחמת השינוי הזה שהיה בידיה קראוה כשנולדה בשם ארנבת, מפני שהארנבת משונה בידיה שהם קצרות מרגליה, והיה דרכם לקרות את הילד הנולד על שם המאורע שאירע בעת לידתו או על שם חידוש הנמצא בו בעצמו, כמו שם יעקב על שם שאחז בעקב אחיו, ושם עשו על שם שהיה כולו כאדרת שער שהוא עשוי ונגמר כאנשים גדולים בשערותיו, ואפשר שגם אותה האומה של אשת תלמי היו קורין את הארנבת בשם ארנבתא בלשון תורה, ועל כן הוכרחו לכתוב צעירת הרגלים שאם יכתבו צעירת הידים היה אומר על אשתו הם מתכוונים שהיא היתה צעירת הידים שיש בה שינוי בידיה מחמת קצרותם.
XXXVI	**תורה תמימה, ויקרא, יא, ו** מצאתי כתוב גירסא אחרת במקום צעירת הרגלים—שעירת הרגלים, והיא גירסא נכונה, שכן כתבו הטבעיים שטבע הארנבת לגדל שער ארוכות ברגליה. ומפרש בגמרא שעשו כן כדי שלא יאמר צחקו בי היהודים והטילו שם אשתי בתורה, ואף כי האמת היא שיש חיה בשם ארנבת, י"ל דחששו משום דכתיב ארנבת הנקבה ולא הזכר כמו בשארי החיות, וטעם הדבר באמת שכתוב המין הנקבה כתב הראב"ע משום דחיה זו אין ממנה זכר אלא נקבה, ובתשבי שורש גלגול כתב הטעם מפני שהוא רובע ונרבע, ואין טעם זה מספיק.
XXXVII	**בן יהוידע, מגילה, ט, א** ברם הא קשיא לי למה הברייתא הביא פסוק ואת הארנבת הכתוב בספר ויקרא, אחר פסוקים שהביא מספר דברים, ונ"ל בס"ד דכל אותם השינויים הוצרכו לעשות כדי שלא יעשה עמהם ויכוח בדברי תורה, משא"כ שינוי פסוק הארנבת לא הי' שם סיבת ויכוח בד"ת, אלא רק משום שלא יאמר שחקו בי היהודים.

APPENDIX B: FOUR KINGDOMS

I	**בראשית, א, ב** והארץ היתה תהו ובהו וחשך על פני תהום ורוח אלהים מרחפת על פני המים.
II	**בראשית רבה, ב, ד** ר"ש בן לקיש פתר קריא בגלויות, והארץ היתה תהו זה גלות בבל שנאמר(ירמיה ד, כט) ראיתי את הארץ והנה תהו. ובוהו זה מלכות מדי (אסתר ו, יד) ויבהילו להביא את המן. וחושך זה מלכות יון שהחשיכה עיניהן של ישראל בגזירותיהן שהיתה אומרת להם כתבו על קרן השור שאין לכם חלק באלהי ישראל. על פני תהום זה גלות ממלכת הרשעה שאין להם חקר כמו התהום, מה התהום הזה אין לו חקר אף הרשעים כן. ורוח אלקים מרחפת זה רוחו של מלך המשיח היאך מה דאת אמר (ישעיה יא, ב) ונחה עליו רוח ה'.
III	**רבינו בחיי, בראשית, א, ד** ויבדל אלהים בין האור ובין החושך—כי בו יבדיל הקב"ה בין ישראל שקוו לישועה ובין האומות השרוים בחשך.
IV	**בראשית ב, י-יד** ונהר יצא מעדן להשקות את הגן ומשם יפרד והיה לארבעה ראשים. שם האחד פישון הוא הסובב את כל ארץ החוילה אשר שם הזהב. וזהב הארץ ההוא טוב שם הבדלח ואבן השהם. ושם הנהר השני גיחון הוא הסובב את כל ארץ כוש. ושם הנהר השלישי חדקל הוא ההלך קדמת אשור והנהר הרביעי הוא פרת.

V **בראשית רבה, טז, ד**

אמר רבי תנחום בשם רבי יהושע בן לוי עתיד הקב"ה להשקות כוס תרעלה לאומות ממקום שהדין יוצא, מאי טעמא, ונהר יוצא מעדן להשקות את הגן ומשם יפרד, והיה לד' נהרים אין כתיב כאן אלא לד' ראשים, אלו ד' גליות כנגד ד' ראשים. שם האחד פישון, זו בבל על שם (חבקוק א, ח) ופשו פרשיו...ושם הנהר השני גיחון, זו מדי היה המן שף עמה כנחש על שם על גחונו תלך. חדקל, זו יון שהיתה קלה וחדה בגזירותיה, שהיתה אומרת לישראל כתבו על קרן השור שאין לכם חלק באלהי ישראל....והנהר הרביעי הוא פרת, זו אדום. פרת, שהפירה והציירה לבניו (נ"א לפניו).

VI **אלשיך, בראשית ב, י**

והנה אין נראה פה ייחס אל המלכויות, ואפשר לדבריהם יהיה רמז הפסוק...נהר השפע יוצא מהמתעדן על דברי תורה, להשקות את הגן אלו ישראל...אמנם כאשר ומשם יפרדו שיתפרד העם מן התורה, שהוא עון בטול תורה...אז יהיה לארבעה ראשים הם ארבע גליות.

VII **בראשית יד, א**

ויהי בימי אמרפל מלך שנער אריוך מלך אלסר כדרלעמר מלך עילם ותדעל מלך גוים.

VIII **בראשית רבה, מב, ב**

ויהי בימי אמרפל...אמר ר' אבון כשם שפתח בארבע מלכויות כך אינו חותם אלא בארבע מלכויות, את כדרלעמר מלך עילם ותדעל מלך גוים ואמרפל מלך שנער ואריוך מלך אלסר כך אינו חותם אלא בארבע מלכויות, מלכות בבל ומלכות מדי ומלכות יון ומלכות אדום.

IX **רמב"ן, בראשית, יד, א**

המעשה הזה אירע לאברהם להורות כי ארבע מלכויות תעמודנה בעולם ובסוף יתגברו בניו עליהם ויפלו כלם בידם וישיבו כל שבותם ורכושם והיה הראשון מהם מלך בבל, כי כן העתיד, כדכתיב (דניאל ב, לח) אנת הוא רישא די דהבא ואולי אלסר שם עיר במדי או בפרס, ו"עילם" בעיר ההיא המלך מלך יון הוא המלך הראשון ומשם נתפשט מלכותו כשנצח דריוש. וכבר הזכירו זה רבותינו (ע"ז, י, א) רבי יוסי אומר שש שנים מלכו בעילם ואחר כך נתפשטה מלכותם בכל העולם כולו. ו"מלך גוים" המלך על עמים שונים אשר שמוהו עליהם לראש ולקצין רמז למלך רומי אשר המלך על עיר מקובצת מעמים רבים כתיים ואדום ויתר גוים.

X **רמב"ן, בראשית, יב, ו**

ויעבר אברם בארץ עד מקום שכם. אומר לך כלל תבין אותו בכל הפרשיות הבאות בענין אברהם יצחק ויעקב, והוא ענין גדול הזכירוהו רבותינו בדרך קצרה, ואמרו כל מה שאירע לאבות סימן לבנים, ולכן יאריכו הכתובים בספור המסעות וחפירת הבארות ושאר המקרים, ויחשוב החושב בהם כאלו הם דברים מיותרים אין בהן תועלת.

XI **בראשית, טו, ח-י"ב**

ויאמר אדני אלקים במה אדע כי אירשנה. ויאמר אליו קחה לי עגלה משלשת ועז משלשת ואיל משלש ותר וגוזל. ויקח לו את כל אלה ויבתר אתם בתוך ויתן איש בתרו לקראת רעהו ואת הצפר לא בתר. וירד העיט על הפגרים וישב אתם אברם. ויהי השמש לבוא ותרדמה נפלה על אברם והנה אימה חשכה גדלה נפלת עליו.

XII **בראשית רבה, לך לך, מד, טו**

דבר אחר קחה לי עגלה משלשת זו בבל שהעמידה שלשה מלכים נבוכדנצר ואויל מרודך ובלשצר, ועז משלשת זו מדי שהיתה מעמידה ג' מלכים כורש ודריוש ואחשורוש, ואיל משלש זו יון ר' אלעזר ור' יוחנן, ר"א אמר כל הרוחות כבשו בני יון ורוח מזרחית לא עמדו א"ל ר"י והכתיב (דניאל ח, ד) ראיתי את האיל מנגח ימה וצפונה ונגבה וכל חיות לא יעמדו לפניו ואין מציל מידו ועשה כרצונו והגדיל, הוא דעתיה דר"א דלא אמר מזרחית, ותור וגוזל זו מלכות אדום, תור הוא אלא שגזלן הוא.

XIII **בראשית רבה, לך לך, מד יז**

והנה אימה חשכה גדולה נופלת עליו. אימה זו בבל דכתיב (דניאל ג, יט) באדין נבוכדנצר התמלי חמא. חשיכה זו מדי שהחשיכה עיניהם של ישראל בצום ובתענית. גדולה זו יון ר' סימון ורבנן, רבי סימון אמר מאה ועשרים דוכסים מאה ועשרים אפרכון מאה ועשרים

אסטרטליטין ורבנן אמרי מס' ס' דכתיב (דברים ח, טו) נחש שרף ועקרב נחש זו בבל. שרף זו
מדי עקרב זו יון מה עקרב זו יולדת לס' ס' כך העמידה מלכות יון מששים ששים...נפלת עליו
זו אדום שנאמר (ירמיהו מט, כא) מקול נפלם רעשה הארץ.

XIV **בראשית, כז, א-ג**
ויהי כי זקן יצחק ותכהין עיניו מראת ויקרא את עשו בנו הגדל ויאמר אליו בני ויאמר אליו
הנני. ויאמר הנה נא זקנתי לא ידעתי יום מותי. ועתה שא נא כליך תליך וקשתך וצא השדה
וצודה לי ציד(ה).

XV **בראשית רבה, סה, יג**
דבר אחר שא נא כליך זו בבל, ואת הכלים הביא בית אוצר אלהיו (דניאל א, ב), תליך זו מדי,
ויתלו את המן על העץ (אסתר ז, י), קשתך זו יון, שנאמר כי דרכתי לי יהודה קשת (זכריה ט,
יג), וצא השדה זו אדום, ארצה שעיר שדה אדום (בראשית לב, ד).

XVI **אלשיך, בראשית, לב, ד**
...מאמר אחד שאמרו בב"ר וז"ל שא נא כליך זו בבל ואת הכלים הביא בית אוצר אלהיו. תליך
זו מדי ויתלו את המן על העץ. קשתך זו יון כי דרכת לי יהודה קשת. וצא השדה זו אדום ארצה
שעיר שדה אדום. ע"כ. וראוי לשים לב מה ענין מטעמיו אל בבל ומדי ויון ואדום. ועל פי דרכנו
נשקיף ונראה מה ראתה רבקה להפר כונת אישה. או יקרה
שבעודו יצחק אוכל טרם יברכנו, יבא עשו מן השדה ויתפס כגנב במחתרת ויפול בחרב אחיו
ויחרה אף אביו עליו להביא עליו קללה...אמנם הנה יצחק ורבקה חלקו בכוונותיהם. והוא כי
הנה יצחק היה עם לבבו כי כאשר יעקב לבדו הוא הנוחל עולם הבא. כן עשו ינחל העולם
הזה בהחלט. והוא כי הנה שליטת העה"ז נחלקה לד' מלכיות בבל ומדי ויון ואדום והם ד'
מלכיות הרמוזים בצלם נבוכדנאצר. שבתריהון יקום אלהא שמיא מלכודי לעלמין לא תתחבל
ואמר יצחק בלבו אחרי שאין לעשו חלק רק פה. יהי לו אשר לו לגמרי ותתקיים שליטת הד'
מלכיות בולם בעשו היא אדום היא שיתעבדו תחתיו ישראל ד"פ מה שהתעתדו לגלות לד' מלכיות
והן זאת כונת מאמרם ז"ל (שם) שא נא כליך זו בבל כו' כי ע"י עשותו מצוה זו. ע"י ד' דברים
אלה. על יד לקיחת הכלים. תבורך בשליטת המעותדת לבבל. וע"י תליך תבורך בשליטת מדי.
וע"י כן לא יפול המן להיות נתלה. כי שם לא נפל שדוד. רק על כי הממשלה לא לאדום היתה
רק למדי...אך רבקה רוח אחרת עמה. הלא הוא כי אמרה בלבה אם עצת יצחק היא תקים. מי
יקום יעקב אחרי נפלו בגלות הראשון ואוי מי יחיה...ועוד ראוי להשית לב מה נשתנה גלות
הזה האחרון מן הראשון. כי בזה לא נגאל עוד. עד נשוב עד ה' כל איש ישראל אז מאלינו
טרם עת הקץ.

XVII **בראשית, כח, י-יב**
ויצא יעקב מבאר שבע וילך חרנה. ויפגע במקום וילן שם כי בא השמש ויקח מאבני המקום
וישם מראשתיו וישכב במקום ההוא. ויחלם והנה סלם מצב ארצה וראשו מגיע השמימה והנה
מלאכי אלהים עלים וירדים בו.

XVIII **בראשית רבה, סח, יד**
ד"א והנה סלם זה חלומו של נבוכדנצר (דניאל ב, לא) ואלו צלם חד שגיא וגו', מוצב ארצה,
(דניאל ב, לא) וזיויה יתיר קאם לקבלך, וראשו מגיע השמימה, (דניאל ב, לא) צלמא דכן רב,
והנה מלאכי אלהים, עולים שנים ויורדים שנים, אלו שרי ארבע מלכיות ששלטנותנו גומרת
בהן, עולים ויורדים, יורדים ועולים אין כתיב כאן אלא עולים ויורדים עולין הם ועליה תהא
להם אלא שכל אחד ירוד מחבירו, כתיב (דניאל ב, לב) הוא צלמא רישיה די דהב טב חדוהי
ודרעוהי די כסף וגו', בבל למעלה מכולם (דניאל ב, לח) כדכתיב אנת הוא רישא די דהבא,
וכתיב (דניאל ב, לט), ובתרך תקום מלכו אחרי ארע מינך וכתיב (דניאל ב, לט) ומלכו תליתאה
אחרי די נחשא, וכתיב בסיפא (דניאל ב, מב) ואצבעת רגליא מנהן פרזל ומנהן חסף מן קצת
מלכותא תהוי תקיפא ומינה תהוי תבירה, והנה ה' נצב עליו, כתיב (דניאל ב, מד) וביומיהון די
מלכיא אינון יקים אלה שמיא מלכא די לעלמין וגו'.

XIX **מדרש מבואר, שם**
ואת כל החזון העתיד הזה על ארבעה המלכיות הראה הקב"ה ליעקב בחלומו.

XX	**מדרש תנחומא, פרשת ויצא**
	ויחלום והנה סולם מוצב ארצה וראשו מגיע השמימה והנה מלאכי אלוקים עולים ויורדים בו. א"ר שמואל בר נחמן אלו שרי אומות העולם דא"ר שמואל בר נחמן מלמד שהראה לו הקב"ה לאבינו יעקב שרה של בבל עולה שבעין עוקים ויורד. ושל מדי חמשים ושנים ויורד. ושל יון מאה [ושמונים] ויורד. ושל אדום עלה ולא ידע כמה. באותה שעה נתירא יעקב אבינו ואמר שמא לזה אין לו ירידה. א"ל הקב"ה (ירמיהו ל, י) ואתה אל תירא עבדי יעקב ואל תחת ישראל כביכול אפילו אתה רואהו עולה אצלי משם אני מורידו שנאמר (עובדיה א, ד) אם תגביה כנשר ואם בין כוכבים שים קנך משם אורידך נאם ה'.
XXI	**שמות, כה, א-ח**
	וידבר ה' אל משה לאמר. דבר אל בני ישראל ויקחו לי תרומה מאת כל איש אשר ידבנו לבו תקחו את תרומתי. וזאת התרומה אשר תקחו מאתם זהב וכסף ונחשת. ותכלת וארגמן ותולעת שני ושש ועזים. וערת אילם מאדמים וערת תחשים ועצי שטים. שמן למאר בשמים לשמן המשחה ולקטרת הסמים. אבני שהם ואבני מלאים לאפד ולחשן. ועשו לי מקדש ושכנתי בתוכם.
XXII	**מדרש תנחומא, תרומה ז**
	וזאת התרומה אשר תקחו וגו'. זהב כנגד מלכות בבל דכתיב בה (דניאל ב, לח) אנת הוא ראשה די דהבא. כסף כנגד מלכות מדי דכתיב (אסתר ג, ט) ועשרת אלפים ככר כסף. נחושת כנגד מלכות יון שהיא פחותה מכולם. וערות אילים מאדמים כנגד מלכות אדום שנא' (בראשית כה, כה) ויצא הראשון אדמוני. אמר הקב"ה אע"פ שאתם רואין ארבע מלכויות מתגאות ובאות עליכם אני מצמיח לכם ישועה מתוך שעבוד. מה כתיב אחריו שמן למאור זה מלך המשיח שנא' (תהלים קלב, יז) שם אצמיח קרן לדוד ערכתי נר למשיחי.
XXIII	**דעת סופרים, תרומה**
	בין העצמה הרוחנית שהמשכן נועד לנסוך בתוך עם ישראל היה הכושר לעמוד בין אומות העולם, תהיה התנגשות תמידית עם העמים האלה בכל התנאים, בעתות של מלחמה, וביותר בזמני שלום וידידות, בהיותם עם קטן בעל הרבה תכונות משותפות לאנושות, יידרש ממנו מאמץ בלתי פוסק לשמור על מה שנמסור להם מה? בעוד שכניו הקרובים והרחוקים יבנו מסגרות חיים...הקדושה שתנוסך בהם על ידי אהל מועד, המשכן, תסיע לעם ישראל להתחזיק מעמד מול העמים המיוחדים...נחשת כנגד מלכות יון שהיא פחותה מכולם, הסכנה של יון היתה פחותה לא היתה מדינה אחידה. היא נהנית מפירסום מדיני הודות לאדם של פי תרבותו היה נחשב כיווני, הוא אלכסנדר מוקדון, ממקדוניה הסמוכה ליון. הוא ייסד ערים בית ששלטה בהם תרבות יון.
XXIV	**ויקרא, יא, ד-ז**
	אך את זה לא תאכלו ממעלי הגרה וממפריסי הפרסה את הגמל כי מעלה גרה הוא ופרסה איננו מפריס טמא הוא לכם. ואת השפן כי מעלה גרה הוא ופרסה לא יפריס טמא הוא לכם. ואת הארנבת כי מעלת גרה הוא ופרסה לא הפריסה טמאה הוא לכם. ואת החזיר כי מפריס פרסה הוא ושסע שסע פרסה וגרה לא יגר טמא הוא לכם.
XXV	**מדרש רבה, שמיני, יג, ה**
	את הגמל זו בבל שנאמר אשרי שישלם לך את גמולך שגמלת לנו. את השפן זו מדי. רבנן ורבי יהודה ב"ר סימון. רבנן אמרי מה השפן הזה יש בו סימני טומאה וסימני טהרה כך היתה מלכות מדי מעמדת צדיק ורשע. א"ר יהודה ב"ר סימון דרוש האחרון בנה של אסתר היה טהור מאמו וטמא מאביו. ואת הארנבת זו יון, אמו של תלמי ארנבת שמה. ואת החזיר זו עמלק (עי' במפרשים שהוא כנוי לאדום).
	משה נתן שלשתן בפסוק א' ולזו בפסוק א'. ולמה. ר' יוחנן ור' שמעון בן לקיש. ר"י אמר שקולה כנגד שלשתן רשב"ל אמר יתירה, מתיב ר"י לר"ש בן אדם הנבא והך כף אל כף. דא מה עביד ליה ר"ל. ותכפל. ר' פנחס ור' חלקיה בשם ר' סימון מכל הנביאים לא פרסמוה אלא שנים. אסף ומשה. אסף אמר (תהילים פ, יד) יכרסמנה חזיר מיער. משה אמר (ויקרא יא, ז)

ואת החזיר כי מפריס פרסה. למה נמשלה לחזיר לומר לך מה חזיר בשעה שהוא רובץ מוציא טלפיו ואומר ראו שאני טהור כך מלכות אדום מתגאה וחומסת וגוזלת ונראה כאילו מצעת בימה. מעשה בשלטון אחד שהיה הורג הגנבים והמנאפים והמכשפים, גחין ואמר לסנקליטיו שלשתן עשיתי בלילה אחד.

XXVI **תהילים, קלז, ח**
בת בבל השדודה, אשרי שישלם לך את גמולך שגמלת לנו.

XXVII **ויקרא, יג, ב**
אדם כי יהיה בעור בשרו שאת או ספחת או בהרת והיה בעור בשרו לנגע צרעת והובא אל אהרן הכהן או אל אחד מבניו הכהנים.

XXVIII **ויקרא רבה, טו, ט**
שאת זו בבל על שום (ישעיה יד, ד) ונשאת המשל הזה על מלך בבל ואמרת איך שבת נוגש שבתה מדהבה, רבי אבא בר כהנא אמר שבתה מדהבה של מלכות שהיא אומרת מדוד והבא, ר"ש בר נחמן אמר מלכות שהיא מדהבת פנים של אדם בשעה שבא אצלה, ורבנן אמרי על שום רישיה דדהב (דניאל ב, לח) אנת הוא ראשה די דהבא, ספחת זו מדי שהעמידה המן הרשע ששף כנחש על שום (בראשית ג, טו) על גחונך תלך, בהרת זו יון שהיתה מבהרת בגזרותיה על ישראל ואומרת להן כתבו על קרן השור שאין לכם חלק באלהי ישראל, נגע צרעת זו אדום שבאתה מכחה של זקן, והיה בעור בשרו לנגע צרעת לפי שבעוה"ז הכהן רואה את הנגעים אבל לעוה"ב אמר הקדוש ברוך הוא אני מטהר אתכם הה"ד וזרקתי עליכם מים טהורים וטהרתם.

XXIX **במדבר, יט ,א-ב**
וידבר ה' אל משה ואל אהרן לאמר. זאת חקת התורה אשר צוה ה' לאמר דבר אל בני ישראל ויקחו אליך פרה אדמה תמימה אשר אין בה מום אשר לא עלה עליה עול.

XXX **ילקוט שמעוני, חקת יט**
פרה זו מצרים שנאמר עגלה יפהפיה מצרים. אדומה זו בבל שנאמר אנת הוא רישא דדהבא. תמימה זו מדי. אמר רבי אבא בר חייא מלכי מדי תמימים היו אין להקב"ה עליהם אלא עבודת אלילים שקבלו מאבותיהם בלבד. אשר אין בה מום זו יון, אלכסנדרוס מוקדון כד חמא לשמעון הצדיק, הוה קאים ליה על רגלוהי...אמרו לו בני פלטין דידיה מן קמי יהודאי את קאים, אמר להון כד אנא נחית לקרב כדמותיה אנא חמי ונצח. אשר לא עלה עליה עול זו מלכות רביעית שלא קבלו עליה עול של הקב"ה, ולא דיה שלא קבלה אלא מחרפת ומגדפת ואומר מי לי בשמים.

XXXI **מהר"ל, נר מצוה הדמיון של המלכיות ושל ישראל לפרה אדומה**
ויש לתמוה מאד, כי מה ענין ד' מלכיות אלו אל פרה אדומה לרמוז בפרה אדומה המלכיות. אבל פירוש ענין, כי פרה אדומה מצותה היא ממדרגה עליונה, עד שאין אדם יכול להשיג את המצוה הזאת. ואף שלמה עם חכמתו אמר (קהלת ז, כג) אמרתי אחכמה והיא רחוקה ממני על מצוה זאת. וכן מה שעמדו ד' מלכיות בעולם, וכן סלוקן מן העולם, הוא בא ממדרגה עליונה מאד. וכאשר תבין דברים אלו, לא היה לך תמיה על אריכת הגלות, ובפרט על מלכות רביעית אל תתמה שכך ארכו לה הימים, כי לפי גודל הכח שיש להם נרמז כח שלהם בפרה אדומה שיש למצוה זאת השגה עליונה במאד מאד. וכן יעקב אבינו כאשר ראה בחלום (בראשית כח, יב) והנה סלם מצב ארצה וגו', (ויקרא רבה ט, ב) ראה מלכות רביעית עולה ולא ראה אותה יורדת, וכל זה, כמו שאין יכול לעמוד על סוד פרה אדומה, וכך אין האדם יכול לעמוד על סוף כח מלכות רביעית. לכך רמז ז"ל (ילקוט חוקת, יט) ענין ארבע מלכיות בפרשת פרה אדומה להודיע לנו כל זה, כי אל יתמה האדם על אריכת הגלות. כי כח אלו ד' מלכיות לה כח עליון מאד, ולכך הוא נמשך ביותר. והנה, בטול אלו ד' מלכיות והחזרת מלכות ישראל נרמז דוקא במצות פרה אדומה, מפני כי בטול ד' מלכיות הוא מדרגה עליונה מאד שיהיה בטל כח מלכיות אלו שהיו מושלים בעולם, ויהיה הפסדם בא ממקום עליון מאד. וכן חזרת מלכות ישראל למקומום הוא בא ממדרגה עליונה מאד. ולא כמו שהוא בעולם הזה, אשר הצלחת ד' מלכיות אינו מן המדרגה העליונה. רק הפסד אלו ד' מלכיות והחזרת מלכות ישראל הוא נרמז

בפרה אדומה, כי המצוה של פרה אדומה מן המדרגה עליונה מאד ומפני עומקה לא נודעה. וכמו שהמצוה הזאת היא פרה אדומה לא נודעה, כך חזרת מלכות ישראל למקומה והפסד ארבע מלכיות לא נודע ולא נגלה הזמן לנביאים. ולפיכך שניהם מן המדרגה העליונה לגמרי למי שיבין הדברים האלו, והם עמוקים וברורים מאד.

SOURCES

PRIMARY SOURCES

- Tanach (Torah, Prophets, Writings), including *Living Torah* by Aryeh Kaplan
- Talmud, Babylonian and *Yerushalmi*
- *Midrash Rabbah*
- *Midrash Tanchuma*
- *Yalkut Shimoni*
- *Yalkut Reuveni*
- *Pirkei d'Rabbi Eliezer*
- *Zohar*

ONLINE PRIMARY SOURCES

- www.aspaklaria.info
- https://www.chabad.org/library/bible_cdo/aid/63255/jewish/The-Bible-with-Rashi.htm
- www.hebrewbooks.org
- www.mechon-mamre.org
- www.sefaria.org.il

OTHER ONLINE SOURCES

- www.aish.com
- www.ancient.eu
- www.arachim.org
- http://blog.webyeshiva.org
- www.britannica.com
- www.chabad.org
- www.etzion.org.il
- http://en.www.wikisource.org
- www.jerusalemlife.com
- www.jewishencyclopedia.com
- www.kby.org
- www.matzav.com
- https://ohr.edu
- www.rgl.org
- www.torahbase.org
- https://tora-forum.co.il
- www.torahlab.org

BIBLICAL COMMENTATORS
LISTED IN CHRONOLOGICAL ORDER; ALL DATES CE UNLESS OTHERWISE INDICATED

Rav Saadia Gaon	882–942
Rashi, Rav Shlomo Yitzchaki	1040–1105
Rabbeinu Avraham Ibn Ezra	1089–1167
Rambam, Rabbeinu Moshe ben Maimon/Maimonides	1135–1204
Radak, Rav David Kimchi	1160–1235
Ramban, Rabbeinu Moshe ben Nachman/Nachmanides	1194–1270
Rabbeinu Bachya ben Asher	1255–1340
Baal HaTurim, Rabbeinu Yaakov ben Asher	1269–1343

Ralbag, Rabbeinu Levi ben Gershon/Gersonides	1288–1344
Akeidat Yitzchak, Rav Yitzchak Arama	1420–1494
Don Isaac Abarbanel	1437–1508
Tzror Hamor, Rav Avraham Saba	1440–1508
Rav Ovadiah Seforno	1475–1550
Imrei Shefer, Rav Natan ben Shimshon Shapira	?–1577
Alshich, Rav Moshe Alshich	1508–1593
Maharal, Gur Aryeh, Rav Yehudah ben Bezalel Loewe	1512–1609
Levush Orah, Rav Mordechai ben Avraham Yafeh	1530–1612
Megalei Amukot, Rav Natan Neta Shapira	1585–1633
Siftei Chachamim, Rav Shabsi ben Yosef Bass	1641–1718
Od Loh Eleh, Rav Eliyahu Itamari	1659–1729
Metzudat David, Rav David Altschuler	1687–1769
Vilna Gaon, Rav Eliyahu ben Shlomo Zalman	1720–1797
Chidah, Maarit Ha'ayin, Rav Chaim Yosef David Azulay	1724–1806
Imrei Shefer, Rav Naftali Tzvi Horwitz	1760–1827
Nachalat Yaakov, Rav Yaakov Lowenbraum, The Gaon from Lisa	1770–1832
Haketav V'hakabbalah, Rav Yaakov Tzvi Mecklenburg	1785–1865
Commentary on Torah, Collected Writings, Rav Samson Raphael Hirsch	1808–1888
Malbim, Rav Meir Leibush ben Yechiel Michel	1809–1879
Ha'emek Davar, Rav Naftali Tzvi Yehudah Berlin (*Netziv*)	1816–1893
Ohr Same'ach, Meshech Chochmah, Rav Meir Simcha HaCohen of Dvinsk	1843–1926
Torah Temimah, Rav Baruch HaLevi Epstein	1860–1940
Oznaim L'Torah, Rav Zalman Sorotzkin	1880–1966
Daat Sofrim, Rav Chaim Rabinowitz	1909–2001
Taam V'daat, Rav Moshe Shternbuch	b. 1928

TALMUDIC COMMENTATORS

Aruch Ha'shalem, Rabbeinu Natan ben Yechiel	11th Century
Yad Ramah, Rav Meir HaLevi Abulafiah	1170–1244
Rabbeinu Yonah	1210–1263
Ein Yaakov, Rav Yaakov ben Shlomo Ibn Haviv	1445–1516
Rav Menachem Azariah da Fano	1548–1620
Beer Sheva, Rav Issaschar Eilenberg	1550–1623
Maharsha, Rav Shmuel Eides	1555–1631
Tosafot Yom Tov, Rav Gershon Shaul Yom-Tov Lipmann-Heller	1579–1654
Iyun Yaakov, Rav Yaakov Reisher	1661–1733
Pnei Yehoshua, Rav Yaakov Yehoshua Falk	1680–1756
Tzelach, Rav Yechezkel Landau	1713–1793
Tiv Gittin, Rav Ephraim Zalman Margulies	1760–1828
Chatam Sofer, Rav Moshe Schreiber	1762–1839
Yad Eliyahu, Rav Eliyahu Rigler	1775–1839
Afikei Yam, Rav Yitzchak Isaac Chaver	1789–1853
Ben Yehoyada, Ben Ish Chai, Rav Yosef Chaim Baghdad	1835–1909
Ranan L'boker, Rav Natan Landau	1840–1907
Siftei Chachamim, Rav Avraham Aba Herzl	1850–1928
She'erit Yaakov, Rav Yitzchak Meir Morgenstern	
Avodah Berurah, Rav Yitzchok Mitnick (chief editor)	

JEWISH HISTORIANS

Sefer Hakabbalah, Avraham ben David	1110–1180
Sefer Yuchsin, Abraham Zacuto	1452–1515

Shalshelet Hakabbalah, Gedaliah ibn Yechya ben Yosef	1515–1587
Tzemach David, Rabbi David Ganz	1541–1613
Seder Hadorot, Rabbi Yechiel Halperin	1660–1746
Dorot Harishonim, Yitzchak Isaac HaLevi (Rabinowitz)	1847–1914
Sefer Toldot Yisroel, Rav Zev Yaavetz	1847–1924
Toldot Tenaim V'Amoraim, Rav Aharon Hayman	1863–1937

RESPONSA

Igrot Moshe, Rav Moshe Feinstein	1895–1986
Minchat Yitzchak, Rav Yitzchak Yaakov Weiss	1902–1989

BIBLIOGRAPHY

Abbott, Jacob. *Alexander the Great*, http://www.gutenberg.org/files/30624/30624-h/30624-h.htm.

Adler, Rav Moshe. עשרה בטבת—תרגום שבעים.

Ariel, Rav Yigal. *Mor V'hadas*, Commentary on *Sefer Daniel*.

Arrian. *Anabasis of Alexander*, https://en.wikisource.org/wiki/The_Anabasis_of_Alexander/Book_II/Chapter_XXIV.

Bevan, Edwyn R. *The House of Ptolemy: A History of Hellenistic Egypt under the Ptolemaic Dynasty*, http://penelope.uchicago.edu/Thayer/E/Gazetteer/Places/Africa/Egypt/_Texts/BEVHOP/2*.html.

Bloch, Rav Yosef Yehudah Leib. *Shiurei Da'at*.

Charles, R.H. (ed.). *Letter of Aristeas*. Oxford: The Clarendon Press, 1913, http://www.ccel.org/c/charles/otpseudepig/aristeas.html.

Chill, Rabbi Abraham. *Abrabanel on Pirke Avot*, compiled and translated.

Clare, John, http://www.johndclare.net/AncientHistory/Alexander_Sources5.html.

Curtius Rufus, http://www.livius.org/sources/content/curtius-rufus/alexander-the-great-enters-babylon/.

Dessler, Rav Eliyahu Eliezer. *Michtav M'Eliyahu*.

Dio Cassius, http://penelope.uchicago.edu/Thayer/E/Roman/Texts/Cassius_Dio/home.html.

Diodorus Siculus, http://penelope.uchicago.edu/Thayer/E/Roman/Texts/Diodorus_Siculus/18A*.html#1.

Dodge, Theodore Ayrault. *Alexander*. New York: Barnes & Noble, 2005 ed.

Fixler, Rav Yoel. דברי תורה פרשת תצוה תשס"ה.

Fox, Robin Lane. *Alexander the Great*. New York: Penguin Group, 2004.

Freeman, Philip. *Alexander the Great*. New York: Simon & Schuster, 2011.

Gergel, Tania (ed.). *Alexander the Great: Selected Texts from Arrian, Curtius and Plutarch*. New York: Penguin Books, 2004.

Gibbon, Edward. *The Decline and Fall of the Roman Empire*, http://oll.libertyfund.org/titles/gibbon-the-history-of-the-decline-and-fall-of-the-roman-empire-vol-1.

Hachimian, Eva. www.hidabroot.com/article/90912/Rabbi-Judah-HaNassi.

HaLevi, Rav Yehudah. *Kuzari*.

Heigh, Rabbi Moshe. "Can The Soul Sin?" *Jewlight*, Vayikra 5757.

Historia Augusta, http://penelope.uchicago.edu/Thayer/E/Roman/Texts/Historia_Augusta/home.html.

Josephus. *Antiquities*. https://www.gutenberg.org/files/2848/2848-h/2848-h.html.

———. *Antiquities*, Book 12, http://penelope.uchicago.edu/josephus/ant-12.html.

———. *Contra Apion*, http://penelope.uchicago.edu/josephus/apion-1.html.

———. *Sefer Yosifun*. Jerusalem: Oraita Aderet, 1999.

Justinus. http://www.attalus.org/info/justinus.html.

Kaplan, Rav Aryeh. *The Infinite Light.*

KiTov, Rav Eliyahu. *Sefer Hatodaah—The Book of Our Heritage.*

Kook, Rav Avraham Yitzchak. *Igrot Harei'ah*, Letters of Rav Kook.

Lichtenstein, HaRav Aharon. "Based on a Sichah, Why Did Rabban Yochanan ben Zakkai Weep?" http://etzion.org.il/en/why-did-rabban-yochanan-ben-zakkai-weep.

Livius. www.livius.org.

Levi, Rav Mordechai. ר' מרדכי לוי/מחוברת אדר תשס"א.

Levovitz, Rav Yerucham. *Da'at Chochmah V'mussar.*

Lewin, Nat. "Protecting Jewish Observance in Secular Courts," *Tradition*, 38:1 2004.

Maharal. Be'er HaGolah.

———. *Netzach Yisrael.*

———. *Tiferet Yisrael.*

———. *Ner Mitzvah.*

Manning, J.G. *The Last Pharaohs: Egypt Under the Ptolemies 305–30 BC.* Princeton University Press, 2012.

Marcus Aurelius. *Meditations.*

McLynn, Frank. *Marcus Aurelius.* Cambridge, MA: De Capo Press, 2010.

Meidan, Rav Yaakov. *Galut V'Hitgalut*, commentary on Sefer Daniel.

Mercer, Charles. *Alexander the Great.* New Word City, 2016.

Miller, Rav Avigdor. *Torah Nation.* New York: Balshon Printing & Offset Co., 1971.

———. *Exalted People.* New York: Balshon Printing & Offset Co., 1984.

Mommsen, Theodore. *The History of Rome* (vol. 1–5) ebook #10706, http://www.gutenberg.org/cache/epub/10706/pg10706.txt.

Philo. http://www.earlyjewishwritings.com/text/philo/book25.html.

Plutarch. http://penelope.uchicago.edu/Thayer/E/Roman/Texts/Plutarch/Lives/Alexander*/html.

Rabinowitz, Rav Tzadok HaKohen. *Poked Ikarim.*

Ramban. *Sefer Geulah.*

Reich, Dr. Aryeh. ד"ר אריה רייך און בר אילן תרגום שבעים—אור או חושך תשס"ד.

Rosensweig, Rabbi Bernard. "If Only My Rabbis," *Tradition* 23(3), Spring 1988.

Sharpe, Samuel. *The History of Egypt under the Ptolemies.* London: Edward Moxon, Leopold Classic Library, 1838.

Siegelbaum, Chana Bracha. http://www.berotbatayin.org/is-antoninus-a-true-convert/.

Spero, Moshe HaLevi. "Remembering and Historical Awareness," *Tradition,* vol. 15, N. 3, Fall 1975, pp. 48–49.

Spetter, Rabbi Moshe. "Translating the Torah into Another Language," 5767.

Stav, Ari. *Techumim* 17 5757.

Suetonius. http://penelope.uchicago.edu/Thayer/E/Roman/Texts/Suetonius/12Caesars/Vespasian*.html.

INDEX

A

Africa 37, 75–77, 80–81, 84, 99, 101, 141, 347

Alexander 5, 7–38, 40–55, 57–64, 66, 68–73, 75–92, 95–105, 108–9, 139, 168, 170–71, 190, 249, 264, 273, 284, 286, 293, 296, 347–49

Alexandria 24, 32, 36, 98–100, 101, 103, 108–11, 113, 126, 131, 133–134, 169–71, 175, 250, 293

Antoninus Pius 96, 167, 169, 201–8, 229, 252

Arc of History 3

Aristotle 11–14, 31, 35, 54, 58–59, 63–64, 95, 100, 107, 262

Athens 8, 14, 17–18, 31, 35

B

Baal HaTanya 162–63

Babylon 8, 10, 17, 22, 25–27, 30, 36, 46, 52, 76, 99, 139, 154, 170, 173, 251, 281–83, 285–86, 288–96, 348

Bucephalus 10–11, 36

C

Cutheans 42–44, 90, 182

D

Dacian Wars 168

Daniel 7, 15–16, 21, 27, 30, 32–34, 46, 49, 52, 79, 97, 99, 104, 202, 249, 280, 283, 285–86, 288, 290–92, 296, 347, 349

Darius 20–21, 25–26, 28, 36, 41, 44–46, 52, 101, 103, 284–86, 294

E

Edom 226, 243, 281–83, 285–89, 291, 293, 296

Egypt 12, 17, 22–24, 33, 36, 40, 44, 52, 76, 84–86, 97–110, 113, 118, 123, 131, 139, 142,

154, 169–71, 175, 214, 220, 250, 259, 270, 272–73, 275, 296, 347, 349–50

Eisav 225–27, 236, 240–43, 245, 247, 252, 278, 280, 287–90, 293

Elders of the South 36, 50–54, 58, 60, 64, 69, 70, 73, 75–76, 80, 249, 256, 264

elephants 29, 106

Esther 7, 27, 128, 281, 287–88, 292, 294

Euclid 108–9

Euphrates 25, 27, 282

F

Flavian Dynasty 143

G

Gan Eden 37, 75, 78–81, 190, 283

Gaugamela 17, 25, 36

Gaza 23, 36

Geviha ben Pesisa 37, 82–85, 87–90, 249, 256

gold 16, 27, 64, 73, 76, 77, 79, 84–87, 89–90, 98, 171, 182, 186–87, 189, 198, 242–44, 282–83, 290, 292–93, 295–96

Granicus 17, 20–21, 36

Great Assembly 13, 38–39, 175

Greece 7–8, 13–14, 16–18, 24–25, 32, 35, 84, 96, 99–100, 139, 249, 251, 281–91, 293, 295–96

Greek city-states 7, 17–18, 46

H

Hadrian 96, 165, 167, 169, 171, 173–78, 184, 186, 189–90, 195, 197, 201–3, 205, 207–8, 229, 249, 251

Hindu Kush 17, 28, 36

homonoia 33

I

India 11, 17, 28–31, 36, 50, 71, 96, 169–70, 206, 286

iron 149, 291

Issus 17, 20–21, 36

J

Jerusalem 22, 41, 46, 82, 89–90, 101–2, 109–10, 113, 133–34, 139, 141, 143, 145–46, 152, 154, 155–57, 160–62, 167, 169, 175, 178, 227, 250

Josephus 9, 40–41, 44–48, 101, 103, 108–9, 113, 128, 133, 139–40, 144, 169, 348

K

Katzia 76, 90–92

Kiddush Hashem 250, 256

L

Lagos 95–96, 102–3, 278

leprosy 194, 295–96

lettuce 225–26, 233, 236, 244

M

Macedonia 7–10, 12, 14, 16–20, 30, 34–35, 98–99, 293

Malchut 221, 240, 256

Marcus Aurelius 96, 167, 174, 201–4, 206, 208–10, 229, 232, 252, 349

Mashiach 220, 270, 281, 284, 293

Meditations 1, 206, 209–10, 252

Memphis 23–24, 98, 108, 169

Mordechai 38, 41, 67, 69, 294

Mountains of Darkness 36, 75–76, 90

N

Nerva 167, 170, 178

Nevuchadnetzar 15, 22, 41, 61, 103, 285–86, 288, 290, 291

Nile 24, 169

O

Olympias 9, 15

Onkelos 149, 179

P

Parthia 168, 189

Pella 9–10, 12, 14, 18, 20, 30, 35, 95

Persia 7–8, 10–11, 17, 19, 21, 25–26, 36, 41, 52, 96, 99, 103, 139, 205–6, 215, 251, 281–91, 294, 296

Pharos Lighthouse 99–100

Philip II 7, 9, 10, 105

Ptolemy II Philadelphus 105–10, 133, 250

Ptolemy I Soter 95, 98–100, 250

Q

Quietus 170

R

Rabban Yochanan ben Zakkai 151–53, 155–56, 158–62, 178–79, 250–51, 256

Rabbi Akiva 52, 62, 130, 157–59, 161, 179, 212–13

Rabbi Meir 52, 141, 214

Rabbi Shimon bar Yochai 213, 220

Rabbi Yehoshua ben Chananya 178–80, 182–93, 195, 197–98, 251, 256

Rabbi Yehudah HaNasi 67, 201, 204, 212–25, 227–31, 233, 235–37, 239–46, 252, 257, 274

radish 233, 235

Rivka Imenu 224–25, 241–42, 287–90

Rome 25, 139, 141–43, 145, 147–49, 155, 157, 162, 167–68, 171, 173, 179–80, 182, 188–89, 191, 194, 201, 204–6, 226, 229, 232, 234–36, 241, 245–47, 251–52, 281–89, 291, 295–97, 349

S

Sacred Band of Thebes 13–14

Shimon HaTzaddik 12–13, 36, 38–40, 43, 45, 47–49, 249, 256, 297

Shushan (Susa) 7, 10, 17, 25, 27–28, 30, 36

silver 27, 77, 79, 84–86, 89, 292–93

soul 55, 58, 183, 202, 207, 217–18, 220, 222–23, 232, 237–38, 348

sun 10, 27, 43, 47, 53–56, 91, 98, 184, 191–92, 198, 212, 239–40, 260, 276, 285–86, 290

T

Titus 71, 141–43, 145–50, 167, 178–79, 205–6, 250–51

Trajan 167–73, 175, 178, 189, 208

Tyre 22–23, 25, 36, 40–41, 44, 76

Tzippori 213–14, 231

V

Vespasian 137, 139, 141–45, 147, 154, 156–59, 162, 178, 249–51, 350

Y

Yaakov Avinu 180, 214, 216–17, 220, 222–23, 225–27, 240–45, 247, 251, 268–69, 272, 278, 280, 284, 287–92, 297

Yedua 44–46

Yefet 84

Yishmael 87, 147, 180

Yitzchak Avinu 86–88, 225, 272–73, 284, 287–89

ABOUT THE AUTHOR

Ari Lieberman holds a B.A. in political science and history from Bar Ilan University and earned an M.B.A. from Temple University. A recent graduate of the Keter HaTorah *Mishnah Berurah semichah* program, he has focused his academic interests on Jewish history, particularly the relationship between famous historic rulers and prominent Jewish advocates. He is already at work on his next project, *The Queens and the Jews*.

ABOUT MOSAICA PRESS

Mosaica Press is an independent publisher of Jewish books. Our authors include some of the most profound, interesting, and entertaining thinkers and writers in the Jewish community today. Our books are available around the world. Please visit us at www.mosaicapress.com or contact us at info@mosaicapress.com. We will be glad to hear from you.